CONTENTS

v

CONTENTS

CONTENTS

CONTENTS

LIST OF ILLUSTRATIONS

EARLY AMERICAN WRITING

THE American story begins in the seventeenth century and can be read in stirring firsthand narratives written at white heat. But to most reading Americans the century remains a murky prologue to the familiar scenes and actors of later days. We appreciate the belles-lettres of the nineteenth century, and we perforce memorize illustrious documents from the eighteenth, and there we stop, indifferent to our roots, although scholars digging about them have uncovered lively genres in the Indian captivity, the colonial treaty, the promotional tract, and other unlikely places.

Just to think of names from the heroic period of settlement we must rack our brains. John Smith kissed Pocahontas, but what else did he do? John Smith has no dimensions, like, say, Ben Franklin, although the one wrote as much about himself as the other. Cotton Mather was a fusty old curmudgeon given to composing splenetic sermons that get courses in American literature off to a sour start. Beyond these misty two, who but antiquarians and quiz kids would know of John Josselyn, Jasper Danckaerts, Henry Norwood, Edward Johnson?

Of course some heckler may ask, who wants to know, but he can, I think, be rapidly silenced. The critics of early American writings say they lack literary value, and in the sense that the colonizers and travelers produced no great verse or drama or reflective essays the criticism can stand, although it quite misses the point. The real point is that the firstcomers to America turned out some graphic and salty and dramatic narrations, doing justice to the epic enterprise that engaged them and produced us; and you may choose or not to call those relations and accounts "literature." I would, on the grounds that factual as well as fictional storytelling can be art. But at any rate and by any name the personal experiences and observations of the new world incidentally set forth by sailors, planters, ministers, soldiers and promoters frequently make fresh and awesome reading.

1

And they should. For grandeur of theme the overseas drive of Europe into virgin North America can scarcely be matched in history. Perhaps because it has a deadened textbook familiarity to us we underrate the feat, but for our time it looms as the outstanding chronicle of mankind. Greek and Roman history stretch across a dozen centuries before their climaxes, and the British, who were nothing when the Romans overran them, have a prehistory of sixteen hundred years before their empire greatness. Starting in a wilderness, the American nation has climbed on top of the world within three and a half hundreds. And for the first hundred of these, when barely a quarter million people had gathered on the Atlantic shore, the permanency of the venture remained in some doubt.

Its supporters had to vanquish formidable hazards, natural, human, and supernatural. The uncertainties of a long sailing voyage, the rigors of winter, the threat of starving, the peril from monsters and vermin, the periodic raids of Indian butchers, all had to be faced. One European group had another to contend with, as the Frenchman, the Spaniard and the Dutchman wrestled with the English for the western world. And besides those dangers created by nature and man lurked others even more dread to the seventeenth century: the divine judgments of God and the diabolic enchantments of Satan. The surmounting of these trials furnishes a majestic motif to the early relations, and adds to their Elizabethan cockiness a note of high seriousness. Our forefathers could not foresee the American destiny, but they sensed a mighty work in the making. The Puritans and the Jesuits were battling infidels and heathen for the glory of God, the planters and traders challenged the wilderness and scrappy rivals for Crown and for Empire, and these powerful drives gave their lives and writings a meaning that we must admire and perhaps envy.

This awareness of epical actions can plainly be seen in the urge to record them, fully and faithfully, that gripped the century's two leading actors. John Smith in his *Generall Historie of Virginia, New England, and the Summer Isles* (1624), which he brought up to date in his autobiography (1630), and Cotton Mather in his *Magnalia Christi Americana* (1702), whose very title indicates an epic, compiled the two richest treasuries we possess of their age. They wrote continuously of what they had seen and heard, gathered and solicited the accounts of their contemporaries, and absorbed their own works into their climactic histories. And if Smith was a swashbuckling Virginian promoter, and Mather a learned minister in Massachusetts Bay, it should be noted that Smith also stresses God's providential handling of human events, and that Mather equally devours the secular records of God's will. Unlike our cold-blooded histories of today, born dead in the library, these are human and personal, filled with the stuff of life and flavored with a sense of righteous purpose.

Such qualities make the *Magnalia* a great book about great things, but unfortunately Cotton Mather seems tagged always as a church historian and ivory tower sermonizer. Actually Mather had an unerring sense for the human-interest story, and some of his yarns read like today's newsstand shockers. If you want sex crimes, war and bloodshed, occult mystery, passionate emotions, hair-raising adventure, the *Magnalia* has them all, told in burning words. When Cotton Mather flayed a heretic, he poured out a stream of clerical abuse that makes a modern truck driver with his meager clichés sound like a pantywaist. Mather put himself body and soul into the issues of his day. He groans with a heartfelt sorrow at the Indian tortures to his people: "I know not, reader, whether you will read this record with dry or tearful eyes; I only know I could not write without tears in mine." He sleuthed the phantasms and prodigies that men observed in his time with relentless curiosity, securing affidavits and testimonies to the wonders, that he might accurately preserve the mysterious ways of God for himself and others to ponder. He even boarded an alleged witch and studied her screechings and bitings before breakfast, in order to penetrate the secrets of diabolism, and save his country and the Church from its dire subversive plot. Cotton had his wry humor too, as when he contrasts the brutal pasting Simon Stone took from the Indians and yet survived, with cream-puff figures in history who die from the tap of a titmouse. In a word, Cotton Mather was a master reporter with an eye for the sensational but with a fiery earnestness in place of the newsman's flippancy.

Nor did the Puritan Protestants monopolize the New World's store of imperishable faith and writing fervor. How the Jesuit Fathers, cultured, aesthetic, France-loving, could plunge into the North American forests to live the punishing life of the savages, with often their ridicule and possibly their tortures for thanks, may well defy our comprehension, but must evoke our awe at the capacities of the human spirit. The Jesuits and other French orders established their missions in the Great Lakes country, in Maine and in Maryland, competing with the Protestant sects for Indian souls in a struggle as fierce as those between man and nature, or God and the Devil, or Frenchman and Englishman. The indomitable Jesuit zeal finds no nobler record than in the martyrdom of Father Isaac Jogues, seized by the Iroquois in present New York State, lacerated over the months into a scarce living skeleton, but writing of his trials with the one thumb and finger left him in a spirit of thankfulness to God for the sweetness of such suffering. Eventually Jogues got back to France, where the Queen kissed his mangled hands, but he must return to Canada, get captured once more, and have an Iroquois split his head open after all. His reports to his Superior were read to bits by Parisian booklovers.

The seventeenth century delighted in wild stories, from the top to the bottom of society. Perhaps that was the last century with so complete a relish, for the eighteenth brought in the cults of Science and Reason, and ever since the educated have scoffed at extraordinary tales as folklore nonsense. When they edit the early narratives, the scholars carefully distinguish fact from romance. But the authors made no such distinctions, and if we would know their minds we must know their folklore. You cannot read far in early Americana without stumbling on fables and marvels. They issued from many directions.

Europeans, as Christians, believed in the direct intervention of God in the universe, to save his people with a providence, perplex them with a prodigy, chastise them with a judgment. They believed in a Devil, who roamed the earth tempting the weak, and in witches, his human mistresses, who spellbound the pious. Puritans seeking strenuously to follow the word of God smelled the forces of Satan all about them, in the bodies of Indians, Quakers, heretics and hags.

In that day of expanding horizons travelers smarted under a reputation for tall tales, and the stout disclaimers each new wanderer made to such fantasy only preceded fresh astonishments. After all, America itself was hard to believe, and the borderline between strange fact and colored fiction could not be neatly staked. The whole tradition of the medieval bestiary with its fabulous zoology, and the natural history of the ancients strewn with the incredible, lay behind the descriptions of the early travelers.

The Indians themselves represented a bizarre phenomenon that could not be disputed, and they added further to the New World's mythology. If the English accepted a personal Devil and his human consorts, they could not very well deny practice in the black art to the red heathen, especially ones so gifted in necromancy. The Eastern tribes boasted famous sorcerers, like Passaconaway, who could make water burn and the trees to dance, and turn a dead snake into a writhing serpent. White men hearing such tales did not scoff; they sniffed brimstone.

The truth itself could amaze, in this heroic grapple with the wilderness. Sagas aplenty lay in the stark tales of boat wrecks off the coastal and island shores, capture and enslavement by the savages, hunting and skirmishing in the deep woods. Warfare never ceased, for if an uneasy peace reigned with the Spaniard and Frenchman, only the briefest truce lasted with the barbarians and none with infidels, and war especially breeds sagas.

Seventeenth-century Americans wrote up this story material with gusto, in long recitals of shipwrecks and captivities, or brief scenes and incidents with which they interlarded their "histories" and "relations." Being men of action they wrote without posturing, in earthy post-Elizabethan English, with its endless sentences and tart phrases. This was a world of the marvelous, and its possessors were attuned to its marvels and afire to give them lasting memorials.

★

If the budding literature of English America begins *de novo,*
in the sense that before 1607 Englishmen had not continuously
lived and written in the New World, a literary tradition can
still be supplied. A vigorous writing of the sea commenced in
the fifteenth century, coincident with England's maritime ex-
pansion, as her mariners and explorers jotted down their itin-
eraries. They in turn emulated chroniclers and voyagers in
foreign tongues who had described remote lands and high
adventures, in the vein initiated by Marco Polo in 1298, while
such histories of discovery as the Spaniard Peter Martyr's *Decades
of the Newe World* needled Elizabethan nationalists to mar-
shal their own achievements. The careful labors of Eden, Hakluyt and Purchas brought together scattered records and manuscripts of English sailings to the ends of the earth in an
inspiring naval library. The sights and deeds of the Cabots,
Hawkins, Frobisher, Magellan, Drake and other famous sea
dogs, written curtly and often crudely, sometimes stirringly,
opened a new genre of English writing, and gave caste to narrative prose. In this tradition, well established by 1600, write the
first sailors to North America, forgotten men like Hariot, Pring,
Rosier, Brereton, picturing the Atlantic coastland for their
fellow Englishmen at home. When the voyages lead to settlement, then the scene of action moves from sea to land, the
viewpoint shifts from England to America, and the "briefe and
true relation" of life in the colonies is born. With John Smith
an American writing begins, in the established form of the
personal record.

In the ensuing century one can of course find colonial writing
in the genres of polite literature. Theology spawned sermons in
number, religious tracts, and such formidable verse as Michael
Wigglesworth's manual for Puritan tots, *The Day of Doom.*
The metaphysical poems Edward Taylor left in manuscript have
won increasing attention since their rediscovery. Satire appears
in the heavy blows at feminine frippery and "polypiety" from
Nathaniel Ward in *The Simple Cobler of Aggawam,* and the
ribald ridicule of Maryland manners by Ebenezer Cook in *The
Sot-Weed Factor.* But the point needs no laboring, that the
transatlantic travelers and wilderness clearers would not excel
in formal letters. Such energy and strength as the colonizers

could spare for writing went chiefly into narration and description of the contemporary scene, that they might attract their countrymen, finance their ventures, and record their fortunes.

The stay-at-homes in Stuart England provided the chief audience for the early Americans, who had to send most of their printing business to the London stationers. Writing largely for the English public, themselves usually born or educated in England, our American authors must be viewed against the general backdrop of Stuart times and, in so far as they were Dutch, French, or German, against that of western Europe between the Reformation and the Enlightenment.

The well-known historical facts bear directly on the character of early American writing. By the seventeenth century's dawn, Europe, and especially England and Holland, had seen the crust of feudalism broken by the rise of middle-class tradesmen and merchants. A new language of economics reflected the values of export goods, cash crops and foreign markets, as English wool manufacturers and merchants-adventurers infiltrated Europe and Asia. From the great religious schism of the previous century had emerged a defiant Protestantism, proclaiming a personal deity and a depraved mankind, but sharing with the Roman Church the medieval view of a God-manipulated universe inscrutable to human minds. Science had yet to render its challenge with Newton's relentless laws, and secular philosophy still lay in shadow, waiting to bring forth the reasonable Locke and the skeptical Hume. Meanwhile the leaven of Renaissance humanism permitted godly men to show a purely human curiosity in the people and events and environment of the earth, since these were, to be sure, all of God's making.

So the tracts and relations of the coastal settlers reveal a middle-class rather than an aristocratic idiom, and a supernatural, not a rationalistic, bias. This makes a happy balance, with the gross concerns of economic interest mated to a healthy regard for the invisible world. Puritan trader and Anglican planter write the record, in a spirit neither emotionally mystical nor slavishly empirical.

We can see the currents of mercantile capitalism and reforming Protestantism running through the early classics. Out of much tedious prose, the journals, logs, diaries, reports that have only documentary interest—and even so touted a writing as William Bradford's *History of Plymouth Plantation* reads like an account book—I would single out a round dozen narrative works as a lively reading list from the first hundred years of the English colonies. These are, besides Smith's *Generall Historie* and Cotton Mather's *Magnalia,* the voyages to New England of John Josselyn and to Virginia of Henry Norwood; Francis Higginson's *New England's Plantation* and William Wood's *New England's Prospect,* both laudatory guidebooks; two providential histories of New England, one set down by Governor John Winthrop as a journal, the other composed by militia captain Edward Johnson; two jaunty, intimate "histories" of other colonies, Robert Beverley's of Virginia and John Lawson's of Carolina; and finally the *Illustrious Providences* compiled by Increase Mather and the *Captivity* of Mary Rowlandson, itself a rare providence.

Consider these our twelve authors. None is of noble blood; at most we have sons of minor gentry. John Winthrop's father was lord of Groton Manor, as he himself became, but his mother had been born to a prosperous tradesman, and both father and son practiced law to supplement their income. Josselyn was the son of a knight. Beverley and Norwood represent the fairly well-to-do Cavalier families which drifted to congenial Virginia, where Beverley through astute politicking and land pyramiding worked his way into the FFV's, marrying a daughter of William Byrd and leaving at his death an estate of thirty-seven thousand acres. Norwood, an active royalist and career soldier, served professionally in France, Africa and New Netherlands, received from Charles II the offices of Treasurer of Virginia and Lieutenant-Governor of Tangier, and eventually retired to an ancestral English estate to live out his years as a country squire. If these four stand for the upper middle, the others fall at best into the middle middle. Three are clergymen and one is a clergyman's wife. Two, Smith and Johnson, served apprenticeships to a merchant and a joiner. Of several we know not even the vocation, so meager are their biographies, but Wood, Josselyn and Lawson must have had means, to depart casually for New World travels. All the men except Smith and Johnson appear to have attended universities, usually Cambridge or Harvard. Lacking funds, Smith had to apprentice out after completing grammar school, but soon took off for a life of soldiering and adventuring. At any rate the writing of all our twelve shows some imprint of intellectual training and tastes.

In this respect, if they belonged only to the swelling Whig middle class of merchants and professional people in England, they rested on top of the American social pyramid. In the plantations, however, even at the top no leisure class existed, no titled nobility living off land income and dabbling in letters when not gambling or at the chase. Our authors wrote under press of heavy duties. John Winthrop governed Massachusetts Bay during many years of political strife between freemen and company, Crown and colony; Increase Mather served a church, presided over Harvard, and acted as special agent for the Bay colony in London, at one time concurrently; a lesser personality like Edward Johnson still handled half a dozen responsibilities, trainband captain, selectman, clerk, proprietor, arms inspector, surveyor, and deputy to the General Court. And so it went; political and clerical duties, the management of land, or the ceaseless round of housewife chores in a frontier parish absorbed our male and female writers.

The middle-class ethic shows up clearly enough in what they wrote. In their loving attention to the lush earth and bountiful forests of New England, Higginson and Wood and John Smith are appealing to economic interest, in the manner of the promotion literature that had begun in their day to coax surplus capital into New World schemes. Their praise does not spring from aesthetic enchantment at natural beauties, but from financial optimism at the profits to be made in fish, furs and crops. They appeal directly to the basic middle-class appetite, land-ownership. "Great pity it is to see so much good ground for corn and for grass as any under the heavens to lie altogether unoccupied," remarked Higginson in closing his sales talk about New England, and sighed to think of the hard shrift grinding down crowded families in old England. Dazzling prospects for trade sprinkle the pages of Josselyn and Beverley and Lawson in their more discursive chronicles: what modern cigarette advertisement packs the punch of Josselyn's hymn to tobacco? *

The new Protestantism equally stamps the age on our authors. We need only look at the titles devised by the Puritans: *Magnalia Christi Americana; The Wonder-Working Providence of Sion's Saviour in New England; The Soveraignty and Goodness of God, Being a Narrative of the Captivity and Restauration of Mrs. Mary Rowlandson.* The New England colonies were born out of Calvin's protests against the medieval Church, much as Virginia grew from the fifteenth century's discovery of Trade. Throughout the Puritan diaries, histories, captivities and military journals the severe hard-won dogmas are sounded: a personal God directs every event, lashes the sinners and warns his saints, helpless and errant as they are, to trust implicitly in his will. Puritans spoke for direct access to the word of God, and blasted the Churches of Rome and England as institutional strait jackets. They denounced as mealymouthed the doctrine of salvation through man's works for all who embraced the Church, and upheld as just and noble the teaching that only an arbitrarily chosen few would by God's grace enter heaven.

So the Mathers and Edward Johnson compiled the records of New England's unfolding history, and Mary Rowlandson set down the events of her captivity and deliverance, to demonstrate that New Englanders were saints, protected by God in the wilderness with innumerable providences and, if sorely tried and tested on occasion, brought through to final triumph. John Winthrop intended his private journal-history for no other eyes, but it too glows with the Puritan's whole-souled acceptance of God's lessons to his people. Indeed, the urge to record privately events of providential import fully matched the desire to make them public. Puritans not only wished to herald abroad the success of their Bible commonwealth, but each individual saint must convince himself that he enjoyed God's grace, and to that end he minutely analyzed his personal history in providential diaries.

The force of dogmatic Christianity blends in our early Americana with a complementary trait, the firm belief of all men

* See Chapter 2, p. 196.

in the supernatural. From the Enlightenment on, Christianity has proved that it can make its peace with rationalism, science and even secularism, but these foes had not arisen in the early days of settlement. Church doctrine, emphasizing the wonderful powers of God and Satan, of saints and witches, slid easily into the realm of fairy lore with which the English peasantry, and gentry too, had long explained the riddles of nature. The presence of Folklore instead of Science (although the empirical method had made some headway in America, and Cotton Mather and John Clayton sent observations on natural history to the Royal Society) among the educated and articulate men of the colonies gives a special flavor of the marvelous to their writings. English folk beliefs found congenial soil in the mysteries of the wilderness and the extravagant myths of the red men.

The extent of this folk belief needs underlining. Rural Englishmen—and England was mostly rural at this time—lived in a world only partly visible. Countrymen glimpsed headless creatures and phantom animals in the night, and heard the rumble of spectral coaches and horses through the village streets. Old wives warned of ill-wishing witches and evil-eyed wizards whose malice could maim, impoverish and kill. In defense, the stricken or fearful employed verbal charms, material amulets and talismans, and magical remedies: creep under a bramblebush to ward away the whooping cough, rub beef on warts and both will decay apace. Or they sought the white magicians, conjurers to put the finger on witches and diviners to spot lost treasures. Animals, birds and plants all brushed the unseen forces of fate; when cows lowed and dogs howled, death would come; the weather on the cuckoo's return forecast the harvest's yield; primroses and snowdrops brought into the home carried disaster. And so on throughout the course of daily life; planting and reaping attended the movements of the heavens, the days of the week and holidays of the year entailed ancient custom, the content of dreams presaged the future. This cargo of belief, transported to the New World with the folk from East Anglia, enters all their literary product, from military history to dusty theology.

Hubbard in his *Indian Wars* tells how the Massachusetts militia halted their march against King Philip when the moon went into eclipse, fearing an evil omen. In his famous diary Samuel Sewall notes dream upon dream and attempts to appraise their meanings. Cotton Mather tacked onto a printed sermon "An Appendix Touching Prodigies in New England," to illustrate how the Lord made known the war to come with blood-red snow and the sound of guns and cannon in the heavens. In his voyage and travel journal, John Josselyn soaks up folk tales like a sponge. From sailors and fishermen he hears of St. Elmo's fire, the spirit that signals a storm, of an enchanted island, a sea serpent, and an aggressive merman. From the Indians he learns of a devil who appears in white man's dress, and himself sees their heavenly flame which announces death. From the English settlers he picks up wondrous tales of half-pig half-lion monsters, and of spectral ships manned by women or bearing a large red horse.

These were no idle fancies, for they governed the actions and molded the concepts of the first Americans. The very discoverers of the continent had been stirred to search by medieval legends of the earthly paradise and the lost Atlantis. Twice in the *Magnalia* Cotton Mather reports the proof of murder by a corpse new-bleeding at the guilty one's touch; thus was the killer of John Sassamon, who had informed the whites of an Indian conspiracy, detected, and the train of events initiated that led to King Philip's War. In Salem court the neighbors of Susanna Martin testified that she had enchanted oxen, cows and puppies, and, in the likeness of a cat, lain on a man in the night, crushing out his breath until in time he remembered the charmed words to drive her off. In olden Scandinavian belief the evil spirit known as Mara had so tormented people in their beds, whence our "nightmare." But the antiquity of folk ideas did not interest the people of Massachusetts, who hanged Goody Martin for sorcery.

The economics of trade, the religion of providences, the folklore of demonism—these seventeenth-century ideas sweep through our early writings with especial vigor. In all our twelve books we can see them shaping the great myth-images of America: a land of boundless riches, a commonwealth personally blessed by God, a fabled frontier alive with marvels.

We can generalize further, and comment on early American

literary conditions, with the yardstick of our dozen authors. None is a professional man of letters. All write wholly or in good part from immediate experience and observation. Beverley and Johnson did not choose, like Sir Walter Raleigh, to write ancient history. Cotton Mather quoted learnedly on spectral evidence—after he had seen witches. Here is no literature or scholarship bred from philosophic musing and library research (although the Mathers and Beverley had and used good private libraries), but culled directly from vigorous living.

Nor could it have been otherwise. Boston alone in English America possessed real publishing facilities; for most of the century Virginia, Pennsylvania, Connecticut and New York printed nothing at all. Americans could not read their own weekly paper until 1704. Even in London the expense of securing stationers' contracts necessarily limited colonial authors to sure-fire portrayals of the New World scene or lobbyist tracts pleading special causes, theological, political and commercial. In Boston nearly half of the first one hundred and fifty printed works concerned theology, and even in this sphere a strict censorship controlled publication. Without a leisure class to patronize literature, or a large literate middle class to be courted, belles-lettres had no chance in the seventeenth century, and not much till the end of the eighteenth. Our early classics therefore were written only on strong urgency, to glorify God and extol the plantations, or, as with Colonel Norwood and Mary Rowlandson, to consecrate a tremendous deliverance. Some of the meatiest writing in those dawning years, like the Indian treaties, the Puritan diaries or the court records of the witchcraft cases, was purely functional and never intended for public reading.

Only the two Mathers, with their swollen bibliographies, come close to being career writers, and their output depended primarily on the sermons they prepared for oral delivery and subsequently published. Still this pressure of pulpit deadlines served its literary turn, for Cotton stands out as the century's most engaging stylist. An encyclopedic commentator on the whole range of human interests, he held his audience whether he expounded on pirates and criminals, fires and earthquakes, Quakerism and Arianism, or commerce and trading. Cotton knew the pulse of his townsmen; fifteen hundred people crowded the

Second Church on an average to hear his sermons, and a loyal reading public enabled him to issue over four hundred and fifty works. He was the news analyst, editorial writer and historical interpreter of his day, although first and last he believed himself only God's servant and shepherd of his Boston flock. Educated wholly in the New World, unlike his father, he writes with an American outlook for fellow-Americans, and heralds the growing independence of colonial culture.

Writings in Dutch, German, French and Latin round out the picture of coastal life, but, save for Father Jogues' captivity, none furnishes a memorable narrative. Valuable sketches of the middle colonies occur in the lengthy journal of Jasper Danckaerts, who traveled from Holland to New York and the neighboring provinces in 1679 and 1680, and in the "Circumstantial Geographical Description" of Francis Daniel Pastorius, civic leader of Germantown. But these books rarely come to life. The Jesuit Relations often burn with zeal and graphic power, but their accounts of inland journeys and Indian conversions fall outside the central literature of American settlement.

★

When the surprise-filled years of the seventeenth century roll away, and the colonies assume economic maturity and political independence in the eighteenth, literature reflects the change. An expert, luminous prose, handling powerful ideas with grace, flows from the founding fathers, Franklin and Jefferson and Hamilton; Tom Paine simplifies those ideas even further for the democratic mass. By the time of independence, society can support belles-lettres. Poetry officially begins with Freneau, the novel with William Hill Brown's *The Power of Sympathy,* the drama with Godfrey's *The Prince of Parthia.* Newspapers and magazines are founded and publish essays, verse, satires, political ballads. The shock of novelty and the thrill of the supernatural have gone from the New World, giving way to rationalism, empiric observation, and constitutional theory. Even in its own realm of Puritan theology, the first century must bow to the metaphysical treatises of Jonathan Edwards. By contrast, the product of our first hundred years appears naïve, primitive, provincial—or, depending on your tastes, vivid, stark and fresh in a way that no later day could ever duplicate.

The early narratives did not, however, totally disappear into antiquarian archives. As the Elizabethan voyages enriched the drama and poetry of their day, describing sea scenes and far-off settings which Shakespeare and his colleagues gladly quarried, so did America's chronicles of settlement fire the minds of her own creative writers, or launch literary forms they would eventually employ. Necessarily the stimulus took time to operate, but by the middle of the nineteenth century we can observe a respectable literary tradition for each of the eight themes represented in this volume. The ocean voyages which open our literary history lead into the sea stories of Cooper and Melville; Melville's *Redburn* and *White-Jacket* and Dana's *Two Years Before the Mast* are in skeleton the same kind of shipboard autobiographies. Our dramatic history may well begin with the Indian treaties that contained the germ of theater, and our first play on a native subject, *Ponteach, or the Savages of America,* dramatizes with brutal realism the frontier diplomacy of red man and white. The Indian captivity becomes early transmuted into fiction by our first consequential novelist, Charles Brockden Brown, in a scene of his *Edgar Huntly,* and ends up titillating the masses as the dime novel and penny-dreadful shocker. In the providential judgments and witchcraft annals which the Puritans particularly contributed to the colonial scene, Hawthorne and Whittier found the romantic antiquities they sought, and turned them into somber sketches and tragic ballads. Hawthorne especially made literary capital of Puritan legends, converting the old theological sin of carnality into the modern social sin of selfishness, with the same sure doom to pay. Native humor starts with the fantastic tales collected by Lawson, Beverley and Josselyn, and the frontier travelers and journalists who follow them pile higher the comic myth, until at last Mark Twain crystallizes it for all time. Warfare with the Indians, and the delineation of Indian traits and customs, have continually attracted our novelists and poets; the frontier tales of Simms and Cooper, and Longfellow's transference of Ojibwa myth into *The Song of Hiawatha,* made the noble savage a household property, and the Wild West movie today keeps him noisily alive. If the seventeenth-century chronicles have unfortunately gone unread, their essence has at any rate been subtly diffused through the imaginative literature that has absorbed their vigor and strength as American root-history.

RICHARD M. DORSON

1
VOYAGES

Where does American literature, or, if you prefer, the literature of American history, begin? We can push it back to the Viking sagas, or at any rate to Columbus's first letter. We can push it forward to the first writings on American soil, although this needs clarification, for they can include many sixteenth-century Spanish papers. We can, and for a long time did, regard factual narratives only as sources for the historian to rewrite, and look for belles-lettres, in which case our literary history would commence with a translation of Ovid made by George Sandys in Jamestown village.

I vote for those writings with literary merit that concern the cluster of plantations on the Atlantic shore and islands from which grew the first thirteen states. These writings initiate a continuous story, and they deal with the American theme, even when they are written by Englishmen in England, or by other Europeans in their homelands and native tongues. Sailors and travelers to North Atlantic waters in the late sixteenth century, then, become the first American authors.

The great collections of voyage tales gathered by Richard Hakluyt and Samuel Purchas have made Englishmen familiar with the feats of their mariners and explorers, and swelled their pride in the English creation of empire and domination of the seas. But by the definition above some of these voyages belong to an American tradition. This historical and literary tradition continues in the overland crossings that opened up and eventually conquered America's vast Western domain, and these later travel narratives show the same qualities of high daring and wonder in an untamed world.

Not every voyage was an adventure, not every adventurous voyage had its scribe, and too often such scribes as there were could scarcely splice a sentence. But the two voyages that follow sufficiently illustrate the hazards confronting English emigrants. For the triple threat of storm, shipwreck and starvation, few

19

fictional stories can match Colonel Norwood's powerful relation. Even when the elements or the dreaded Spanish galleons did not interrupt the crossing, disease and plague could decimate the passengers, as Josselyn casually testifies in his lively logbook. The sense of unknown and overhanging calamities, and a spirit of cocky defiance in their face, pervades these recitals. Men who had such an urge to reach America surely have a place in the American drama.

A VOYAGE TO NEW ENGLAND

John Josselyn

Anno Dom. 1638. April the 26th being Thursday, I came to Gravesend and went aboard the *New Supply,* alias the *Nicholas of London,* a ship of good force, of three hundred tons' burthen, carrying twenty sacre and minion,* manned with forty-eight sailors, the master Robert Taylor, the merchant or undertaker Mr. Edward Ting, with one hundred and sixty-four passengers, men, women, and children.

At Gravesend I began my journal, from whence we departed on the 26th of April, about six of the clock at night, and went down into the Hope.†

The 27th being Friday, we set sail out of the Hope, and about nine of the clock at night we came to an anchor in Margaret Road in three fathom and a half water. By the way we passed a States man-of-war, of five hundred tons, cast away a month before upon the *Goodwin,* nothing remaining visible above water but her mainmast top; sixteen of her men were drowned, the rest saved by fishermen.

The 28th we twined into the Downs, where Captain Clark, one of His Majesty's captains in the Navy, came aboard of us in the afternoon, and pressed two of our trumpeters. Here we had good store of flounders from the fishermen, new taken out of the sea and living, which being readily gutted, were fried while they were warm; methoughts I never tasted of a delicater fish in all my life before.

The third of May being Ascension Day, in the afternoon we weighed out of the Downs. About one of the clock at night the wind took us astays with a gust, rain, thunder, and lightning; and now a servant of one of the passengers sickened of the smallpox.

The eighth day, one Boreman's man, a passenger, was ducked at the main-yardarm (for being drunk with his master's strong

* Kinds of cannon.
† A station for ships in the mouth of the Thames, below Gravesend.

waters, which he stole) thrice, and fire given to two whole sacre at this instant. Two mighty whales we now saw. The one spouted water through two great holes in her head into the air a great height, and making a great noise with puffing and blowing; the seamen called her a souffler. The other was further off, about a league from the ship, fighting with the swordfish and the flailfish, whose strokes upon the back of the whale with a fin that grows upon her back like a flail, we heard with amazement. When presently some more than half as far again we spied a spout from above; it came pouring down like a river of water, and dured a quarter of an hour, making the sea to boil like a pot. If any should light in any ship, she were in danger to presently sink down into the sea, for the spout falleth with an extreme violence all whole together as one drop, or as water out of a vessel, and if any vessel be near, it sucks it in. I saw many of these spouts afterwards at nearer distance.

In the afternoon the mariners struck a porpoise, called also a *marsovius* or sea hog, with an harping iron, and hoisted her aboard. They cut some of it into thin pieces and fried it, when it tastes like rusty bacon or hung beef, if not worse; but the liver boiled and soused some time in vinegar is more grateful to the palate.

About eight of the clock at night a flame settled upon the mainmast; it was about the bigness of a great candle, and is called by our seamen St. Elmo's fire. It comes before a storm, and is commonly thought to be a spirit; if two appear they prognosticate safety. These are known to the learned by the names of Castor and Pollux, to the Italians by St. Nicholas and St. Hermes, by the Spaniards called Corpos Santos.

The ninth day, about two of the clock in the afternoon, we found the head of our mainmast close to the cap twisted and shivered, and we presently after found the fore-topmast cracked a little above the cap. So they wolled them both; and about two of the clock in the morning seven new longboat oars brake away from our starboard quarter with a horrid crack.

The twelfth day being Whitsunday, at prayer time we found the ship's trim a foot by the stern. The party that was sick of the smallpox now died, whom we buried in the sea, tying a bullet (as the manner is) to his neck and another to his legs, and turned him out at a porthole, giving fire to a great gun. In the afternoon one Martin Jay, a stripling, servant to Captain Thomas Cammock, was whipped naked at the capstan, with a cat with nine tails, for filching nine great lemons out of the chirurgeon's cabin, which he ate rinds and all in less than an hour's time.

The thirteenth day we took a shark, a great one, and hoisted him aboard with his two companions—for there is never a shark but hath a mate or two. One is the pilotfish or pilgrim, which lay upon his back close to a long fin; the other fish, somewhat bigger than the pilot (about two foot long) called a remora, hath no scales and sticks close to the shark's belly. So the whale hath the sea gudgeon, a small fish, for his mate, marching before him and guiding him; which I have seen likewise. The seamen divided the shark into quarters, and made more quarter about it than the purser when he makes five quarters of an ox, and after they had cooked him he proved very rough grained, not worthy of wholesome preferment. But in the afternoon we took store of bonitos, or Spanish dolphins, a fish about the size of a large mackerel, beautified with admirable variety of glittering colors in the water, and excellent food.

The fourteenth day we spake with a Plymouth man (about dinner time) bound for Newfoundland, who having gone up westward sprang a leak, and now bore back for Plymouth. Now was Scilly fifty leagues off, and now many of the passengers fell sick of the smallpox and calenture.*

The seventeenth day, the wind at NW about eight of the clock we saw five great ships bound for the [English] Channel, which was to the westward of us, about two leagues off. We thought them to be Flemings; here we expected to have met with pirates, but were happily deceived.

June the first day in the afternoon, very thick foggy weather, we sailed by an enchanted island, saw a great deal of filth and rubbish floating by the ship, heard cawdimawdies, seagulls, and crows (birds that always frequent the shore), but could see nothing by reason of the mist. Towards sunset, when we were past the island, it cleared up.

* A fever.

The fourteenth day of June, very foggy weather, we sailed by an island of ice (which lay on the starboard side) three leagues in length, mountain-high, in form of land, with bays and capes like high cliff land, and a river pouring off it into the sea. We saw likewise two or three foxes or devils skipping upon it. These islands of ice are congealed in the north, and brought down in the springtime with the current to the banks on this side Newfoundland and there stopped, where they dissolve at last to water. By that time we had sailed halfway by it, we met with a French picaroon. Here it was as cold as in the middle of January in England, and so continued till we were some leagues beyond it.

The sixteenth day we sounded, and found thirty-five fathom water upon the bank of Newfoundland. We cast out our hooks for codfish, in thick foggy weather; the cod being taken on a Sunday morning, the sectaries aboard threw those their servants took into the sea again, although they wanted fresh victuals, but the sailors were not so nice. Amongst many that were taken we had some that were wasted fish, and it is observable and very strange that fishes' bodies do grow slender with age, their tails and heads retaining their former bigness. Fish of all creatures have generally the biggest heads, and the first part that begins to taint in a fish is the head.

The nineteenth day, Captain Thomas Cammock (a near kinsman of the Earl of Warwick's) now had another lad, Thomas Jones, that died of the smallpox at eight of the clock at night.

The twentieth day we saw a great number of sea bats or owls, called also flying fish. They are about the bigness of a whiting, with four tinsel wings, with which they fly as long as they are wet, when pursued by other fishes. Here likewise we saw many grandpisces or herring hogs, hunting the schools of herrings. In the afternoon we saw a great fish called the *vehuella* or swordfish, having a long, strong and sharp fin like a sword blade on the top of his head, with which he pierced our ship, and broke it off with striving to get loose. One of our sailors dived and brought it aboard.

The two and twentieth, another passenger died of a consumption. Now we passed by the southern part of Newfoundland,

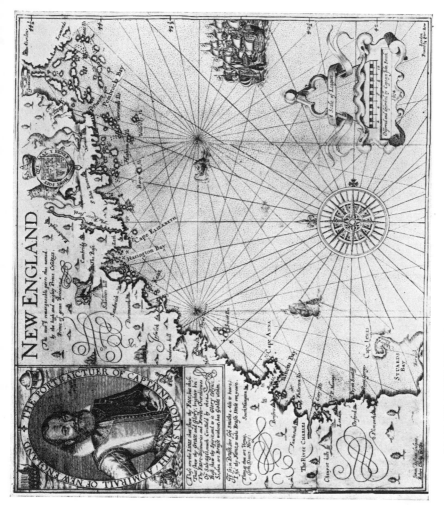

2. MAP OF NEW ENGLAND WITH PORTRAIT OF CAPTAIN JOHN SMITH

Captain John Smith, *The Generall Historie of Virginia, New-England, and the Summer Isles*; London, 1624

within sight of it. The southern part of Newfoundland is said to be not above six hundred leagues from England.

The six and twentieth day, Captain Thomas Cammock went aboard of a bark of three hundred tons, laden with island wine, and but seven men in her and never a gun, bound for Richmond's Island, set out by Mr. Trelaney of Plymouth. Exceeding hot weather now.

The eight and twentieth, one of Mr. Edward Ting's the undertaker's men now died of the phthisic.

The nine and twentieth day, sounded at night, and found one hundred and twenty fathom water; the head of the ship struck against a rock. At four of the clock we descried two sail bound for Newfoundland, and so for the straits; they told us of a general earthquake in New England, of the birth of a monster at Boston, in the Massachusetts Bay a mortality. And now we are two leagues off Cape Ann.

The thirtieth day proved stormy and having lost the sight of the land we saw none until the morning; doubtfully discovering the coast, fearing the lee shore all night we bore out to sea.

July the first day, we sounded at eight of the clock at night, and found ninety-three fathom water, descried land.

The third day, we anchored in the Bay of Massachusetts before Boston. Mr. Ting's other man now died of the smallpox.

The tenth day, I went ashore upon Noddle's Island to Mr. Samuel Maverick (for my passage), the only hospitable man in all the country, giving entertainment to all comers gratis.

Having refreshed myself for a day or two upon Noddle's Island, I crossed the bay in a small boat to Boston, which then was rather a village than a town, there being not above twenty or thirty houses; and presenting my respects to Mr. Winthrop the governor, and to Mr. Cotton the teacher of Boston Church, to whom I delivered from Mr. Francis Quarles the poet the translation of Psalms 16, 25, 51, 88, 113, and 137 into English meter, for his approbation. Being civilly treated by all I had occasion to converse with, I returned in the evening to my lodging.

The twelfth day of July, after I had taken my leave of Mr. Maverick and some other gentlemen, I took boat for the Eastern parts of the country and arrived at Black Point in the province of Maine, which is one hundred and fifty miles from Boston, the fourteenth day, which makes my voyage eleven weeks and odd days.

The country all along as I sailed was no other than a mere wilderness, here and there by the seaside a few scattered plantations, with as few houses.

About the tenth of August, I happened to walk into the woods not far from the seaside, and falling upon a piece of ground overgrown with bushes (called there black currants but differing from our garden currants, they being ripe and hanging in lovely bunches), I set up my piece against a stately oak, with a resolution to fill my belly, being near half a mile from the house. Of a sudden I heard a hollow thumping noise upon the rocks approaching towards me, which made me presently to recover my piece, which I had no sooner cocked than a great and grim overgrown she-wolf appears, at whom I shot, and finding her gorbelly stuffed with flesh newly taken in, I began presently to suspect that she had fallen foul upon our goats, which were then valued (our she-goats) at five pound a goat. Therefore to make further discovery, I descended (it being low water) upon the sea sands, with an intent to walk round about a neck of land where the goats usually kept. I had not gone far before I found the footing of two wolves, and one goat betwixt them, whom they had driven into a hollow betwixt two rocks. Hither I followed their footing, and perceiving by the crows that there was the place of slaughter, I hung my piece upon my back, and upon all fours clambered up to the top of the rock. There I made ready my piece and shot at the dog wolf, who was feeding upon the remainder of the goat, which was only the foreshoulders, head, and horns, the rest being devoured by the she-wolf, even to the very hair of the goat. And it is very observable, that when the wolves have killed a beast or a hog, not a dog wolf amongst them offers to eat any of it till the she-wolves have filled their paunches.

The twenty-fourth of September, being Monday about four of the clock in the afternoon, a fearful storm of wind began to rage, called a hurricane. It is an impetuous wind that goes commonly about the compass in the space of twenty-four hours; it began from the WNW and continued till next morning. The greatest mischief it did us was the wrecking of our shallop and the blowing down of many tall trees, in some places a mile together.

December the tenth happened an eclipse of the moon at eight of the clock at night. It continued till after eleven, as near as we could guess; in old England it began after midnight, and continued till four of the clock in the morning. If seamen would make observation of the time, either of the beginning or ending of the eclipse, or total darkness of sun and moon in all places where they shall happen to be, and confer their observations to some artist, hereby the longitude of all places might be certainly known, which are now very uncertainly reported to us.

1639. May fell out to be extreme hot and foggy. About the middle of May I killed within a stone's throw of our house above fourscore snakes, some of them as big as the small of my leg, black of color and three yards long, with a sharp horn on the tip of their tail two inches in length.

June the six and twentieth day, very stormy, lightning and thunder. I heard now two of the greatest and fearfulest thunderclaps that ever were heard, I am confident. At this time we had some neighboring gentlemen in our house who came to welcome me into the country; where amongst variety of discourse they told me of a young lion (not long before) killed at Piscataway by an Indian; of a sea serpent or snake that lay coiled up like a cable upon a rock at Cape Ann: a boat passing by with English aboard and two Indians, they would have shot the serpent, but the Indians dissuaded them, saying that if he were not killed outright they would be all in danger of their lives.

One Mr. Mittin related of a Triton or merman which he saw in Casco Bay. The gentleman was a great fowler, and used to go out with a small boat or canoe, and fetching a compass about a small island (there being many small islands in the bay) for the advantage of a shot, was encountered with a Triton, who laying his hands upon the side of the canoe, had one of them chopped off with a hatchet by Mr. Mittin, which was in all respects like the hand of a man; the Triton presently sunk, dyeing the water with his purple blood, and was no more seen.

The next story was told by Mr. Foxwell, now living in the province of Maine, who having been to the eastward in a shallop as far as Cape Ann, in his return was overtaken by the night, and fearing to land upon the barbarous shore, he put off a little further to sea. About midnight they were wakened with a loud voice from the shore, calling upon "Foxwell, Foxwell, come ashore," two or three times. Upon the sands they saw a great fire, and men and women hand in hand dancing round about it in a ring. After an hour or two they vanished, and as soon as the day appeared Foxwell puts into a small cove, it being about three quarters flood, and traces along the shore, where he found the footing of men, women, and children shod with shoes; and an infinite number of brands' ends thrown up by the water, but neither Indian nor English could he meet with on the shore nor in the woods.

These with many other stories they told me, the credit whereof I will neither impeach nor inforce, but shall satisfy myself, and I hope the reader hereof, with the saying of a wise, learned, and honorable knight, *that there are many stranger things in the world than are to be seen between London and Stanes.*

September the sixth day, one Mr. John Hickford, the son of Mr. Hickford a linen draper in Cheapside, having been some time in the province of Maine, and now determined to return for England, sold and killed his stock of cattle and hogs. One great sow he had which he made great account of, but being very fat, and not suspecting that she was with pig, he caused her to be killed, and they found twenty-five pigs within her belly—verifying the old proverb, As fruitful as a white sow. And now we were told of a sow in Virginia that brought forth six pigs, their foreparts lions, their hinder parts hogs. I have read that at Brussels, Anno 1564, a sow brought forth six pigs, the first whereof (for the last in generating is always in brute beasts the first brought forth) had the head, face, arms, and legs of a man, but the whole trunk of the body from the neck was of a swine. A sodomitical monster is more like the mother than the father in the organs of the vegetative soul.

The three and twentieth I left Black Point and came to Richmond's Island about three leagues to the eastward, where Mr. Trelaney kept a-fishing. Mr. John Winter, a grave and discreet man, was his agent, and employer of sixty men upon that design.

The four and twentieth day being Monday, I went aboard the *Fellowship* of one hundred and seventy tons, a Flemish bottom, the master George Luxon of Bideford in Devonshire. Several of my friends came to bid me farewell, among the rest Captain Thomas Wannerton, who drank to me a pint of kill-devil, alias rum, at a draught. At six of the clock in the morning we weighed anchor and set sail for the Massachusetts Bay.

The seven and twentieth day being Friday, we anchored in the afternoon in the Massachusetts Bay before Boston. Next day I went aboard of Mr. Hinderson, master of a ship of five hundred tons, and Captain Jackson in the *Queen of Bohemia,* a privateer, and from thence I went ashore to Boston, where I refreshed myself at an ordinary. Next morning I was invited to a fisherman's house somewhat lower within the Bay, and was there presented by his wife with a handful of small pearl, but none of them bored nor orient. From thence I crossed the bay to Charlestown, where at one Long's ordinary I met with Captain Jackson and others. Walking on the back side we spied a rattlesnake a yard and a half long, and as thick in the middle as the small of a man's leg, on the belly yellow, her back spotted with black, russet, yellow, and green, placed like scales. At her tail she had a rattle which is nothing but a hollow shelly business jointed; look how many years old she is, so many rattles she hath in her tail. Her neck seemed to be no bigger than one's thumb; yet she swallowed a live chicken, as big as one they give fourpence for in England, presently as we were looking on.

In the afternoon I returned to our ship. Being no sooner aboard but we had the sight of an Indian pinnace sailing by us made of birch bark, sewed together with the roots of spruce and white cedar (drawn out into threads), with a deck, and trimmed with sails top and topgallant very sumptuously.

The thirtieth day of September, I went ashore upon Noddle's

Island, where when I was come to Mr. Maverick's he would not let me go aboard no more, until the ship was ready to set sail. The next day a grave and sober person described the monster to me that was born at Boston of one Mrs. Dyer, a great sectary, the nine and twentieth of June. It was (it should seem) without a head, but having horns like a beast, and ears, scales on a rough skin like a fish called a thornback, legs and claws like a hawk, and in other respects as a woman-child.

The second of October, about nine of the clock in the morning, Mr. Maverick's Negro woman came to my chamber window, and in her own country's language and tune sang very loud and shrill. Going out to her, she used a great deal of respect towards me, and willingly would have expressed her grief in English; but I apprehended it by her countenance and deportment. Whereupon I repaired to my host to learn of him the cause, and resolved to entreat him in her behalf, for that I understood before, that she had been a Queen in her own country, and observed a very humble and dutiful garb used towards her by another Negro who was her maid. Mr. Maverick was desirous to have a breed of Negroes, and therefore seeing she would not yield by persuasions to company with a Negro young man he had in his house, he commanded him willed–she nilled–she to go to bed to her, which was no sooner done but she kicked him out again. This she took in high disdain beyond her slavery, and this was the cause of her grief.

In the afternoon I walked into the woods on the back side of the house, and happening into a fine broad walk (which was a sledgeway) I wandered till I chanced to spy a fruit as I thought like a pineapple plated with scales. It was as big as the crown of a woman's hat. I made bold to step unto it, with an intent to have gathered it. No sooner had I touched it, but hundreds of wasps were about me. At last I cleared myself from them, being stung only by one upon the upper lip; glad I was that I scaped so well. But by that time I was come into the house my lip was swelled so extremely, that they hardly knew me but by my garments.

The tenth of October, I went aboard and we fell down to Nantasket. Here Mr. Davies (Mr. Hicks the apothecary in

Fleet Street's son-in-law) died of the phthisic aboard on a Sunday in the afternoon. The next day Mr. Luxon our master having been ashore upon the Governor's Island gave me half a score very fair pippins which he brought from thence, there being not one apple tree nor pear planted yet in no part of the country, but upon that island.

The fifteenth day we set sail from Nantasket.

The sixteenth day Mr. Robert Foster, one of our passengers, preached aboard upon the 113th Psalm: *The Lord shall preserve thy going out and thy coming in.* The sectaries began to quarrel with him, especially Mr. Vincent Potter, he who was afterwards questioned for a regicide.

The seventeenth day, towards sunset a lanner settled upon our mainmast top. When it was dark I hired one of the sailors to fetch her down, and I brought her into England with much ado, being fain to feed her with hard eggs. After this day we had very cold weather at sea, our deck in a morning o'erspread with hoary frost, and dangling icicles hung upon the ropes. Some say the sea is hotter in winter than in summer, but I did not find it so.

November the fifth day, about three of the clock in the afternoon, the mariners observed the rising of a little black cloud in the NW, which, increasing apace, made them prepare against a coming storm. The wind in short time grew to boisterous, bringing after us a huge grown sea. At five of the clock it was pitch dark.

The storm augmenting still, the next day about four of the clock afternoon we lost our rudder, and with that our hopes; so necessary a part it is, that a ship without it is like a wild horse without a bridle. Yet Aristotle, that eagle-eyed philosopher, could not give a reason why so small a thing as a helm should rule the ship.

The seventh day at night the wind began to die away; the next day we had leisure to repair our breaches. It continued calm till the thirteenth day, and all the while we saw many dead bodies of men and women floating by us.

The four and twentieth, we arrived before Bideford, having passed before under Lundy Island.

3. THE ARRIVAL OF THE ENGLISH IN VIRGINIA

De Bry, *The Great Voyages*, Part I; Frankfurt, 1590

A VOYAGE TO VIRGINIA

Colonel Henry Norwood *

THE month of August, Anno 1649, being the time I engaged to meet my two comrades, Major Francis Morrison and Major Richard Fox, at London, in order to a full accomplishment of our purpose to seek our fortunes in Virginia (pursuant to our agreement the year before in Holland), all parties very punctually appeared at the time and place assigned, and were all still in the same mind, fully bent to put in practice what we had so solemnly agreed upon. Our inclinations that way being nothing abated, but were rather quickened by the new changes that we saw in the state of things, and that very much for the worse. For if our spirits were somewhat depressed in contemplation of a barbarous restraint upon the person of our King in the Isle of Wight, to what horrors and despairs must our minds be reduced at the bloody and bitter stroke of his assassination, at his palace of Whitehall?

This unparalleled butchery made the rebels cast away the scabbards of their swords with both their hands, in full resolution never to let them meet again, either by submission or capitulation. So that the sad prospect of affairs in this juncture gave such a damp to all the royal party who had resolved to persevere in the principle which engaged them in the war, that a very considerable number of nobility, clergy, and gentry, so circumstanced, did fly from their native country, as from a place infected with the plague, and did betake themselves to travel anywhere to shun so hot a contagion, there being no point on the compass that would not suit with some of our tempers and circumstances, for transportation into foreign lands.

Of the number who chose to steer their course for America,

---

* Norwood was an ardent royalist who supported Charles I during the Civil War, and after his execution (the year of Norwood's voyage) plotted on behalf of his son, for which activity he was imprisoned in the Tower from 1655 to 1659. The restoration of Charles II next year put Norwood on Easy Street for the rest of his life.

such of them as inclined to try their fortunes at Surinam, Barbados, Antigua, and the Leeward Islands were to be men of the first rate, who wanted not money or credit to balance the expense necessary to the carrying on of the sugar works. And this consideration alone was enough to determine our choice for Virginia, had we wanted other arguments to engage us in the voyage. The honor I had of being nearly related to Sir William Berkeley, the governor, was no small incitation to encourage me with a little stock to this adventure. Major Morrison had the King's commission to be captain of the fort, and Mr. Fox was to share in our good or bad success. But my best cargaroon was His Majesty's gracious letter in my favor, which took effect beyond my expectation, because it recommended me (above whatever I had or could deserve) to the governor's particular care.

To proceed then, without any further exordium, to the subject of this narrative. It fell out to be about the first day of September, Anno 1649, that we grew acquainted on the Royal Exchange with Captain John Locker, whose bills upon the posts made us know he was master of a good ship (untruly so called) the *Virginia Merchant,* burden three hundred tons, of force thirty guns or more. We were not long in treaty with the captain, but agreed with him for ourselves and servants at six pounds a head to be transported into James River, our goods to be paid for at the current price.

About the fifteenth day, we were ordered to meet the ship at Gravesend, where the captain was to clear with his merchants and we to make our several payments; which when we had performed, we stayed not for the ship but took post for the Downs, where, with some impatience, we expected her coming there. About the sixteenth ditto, we could see the whole fleet under sail, with a southwest wind; which having brought them to that road, kept them there at anchor, until our money was almost spent at deal.

September 23d the wind veered to the east, and we were summoned by signs and guns to repair on board. We had a fresh large gale three days, which cleared us of the Channel and put us out of soundings. With this propitious beginning we pursued our course for about twenty days, desiring to make the western islands; at which time the cooper began to complain that our water cask was almost empty, alleging that there was not enough in hold for our great family (about three hundred and thirty souls) to serve a month.

Our early want of water gave the master an alarm, and an occasion to consult with his officers for a remedy to so important an evil as that might be, if not timely helped. We were now, by all accounts, very near the western islands. Fayal was that we were likely first to see, and our captain resolved to touch there to supply this defect, as the most commodious port for our purpose; and this was good news to the passengers, who are always glad at sight of land.

The daybreak of October 14th showed us the peak of that island, the highest and most conspicuous land of any I have heard the seamen mention for landmarks, except that of the Tenerife. We stood directly for the harbor, which is also a good road, landlocked by the peak, which stands easterly about a mile distant from the town.

As soon as we had saluted the castle, and returned thanks for being civilly answered, Captain John Tatam, our countryman, did the same from aboard his goodly ship the *John*. He was newly returned from Brazil, in the kingdom of Portugal's service, and now bound for Lisbon with a rich freight and some lady of great note, who with her family took passage with him.

The English merchants from the town came soon on board our ship, and gave us a very civil welcome. Of them, one Mr. Andrews invited me, with my two comrades, to refresh ourselves with fruit and meat such as the island produced. Our captain dined with us at his house, and so did Captain Tatam, who in like courteous manner engaged us all to dine on board his ship the next day. We visited the peach trees for our dessert, of which I took at least a double share, and did not fail to visit and revisit them in the dead of night, to satisfy a ravenous appetite nature has too prodigally given me for that species.

The next morning we surveyed the island, and thought the castle well fortified, especially on the sea-barred parts. The governor very civilly declared he had lately received command from His Majesty the King of Portugal to treat all ships that belonged and were faithful to the King of Great Britain with more than common courtesy—as he, for his part, did in all we could desire.

A little before the time of dinner Captain Tatam had sent his boats to bring us on board his ship; and it was well for us he did so, our ship's longboat having been staved in pieces the night before, by the seamen's neglect, who had all tasted so liberally of new wine that, by the commodiousness of the vintage, they lay up and down dead-drunk in all quarters, in a sad pickle.

The loss of our longboat, as it was likely to make our watering tedious, and chargeable to the owners, so did it expose us to the hazard of many inconveniencies and perils in the whole course of our voyage, wherein frequent occasions occur that render that boat necessary to preserve the whole fabric and lives of the ship and company. But to this breach no other reparation was applicable, but by recourse to that great stock of patience we were to be furnished withal for our support in the mighty straits we must encounter before we come to safe port.

Our captain, disabled hereby to take the best course for our dispatch, made choice of the next best way to effect it, by the island boats; and having ordered his officers to use all diligence, and greater care than before, he led the van into Tatam's boat, which brought us safe on board the *John*.

At our arrival we were welcomed with a whole tier of guns, and with a very kind aspect in the captain. He gave us excellent wines to drink before dinner, and at our meat as good of other sorts for concoction. There was a handsome plenty of fish and fowl, several ways cooked, to relish the Portuguese and the English palates; and, which made our entertainment more complete, he had prevailed with that great lady, with her pretty son of about twelve years old (though contrary to the custom even of the meaner sort at land), to sit at the table with us. She was taller than the ordinary stature of that nation, finely shaped, had a very clear skin, her eyes and hair vying for the blackness and beauty of the jet. Her modesty served, without any other art, to put a tincture of red upon her face; for when she saw herself environed with a company of strange faces, that had or might have had beards upon them, her blushes raised in her face a delicate complexion of red and white.

The captain was our interpreter to tell her how much we esteemed ourselves honored with her presence, which (for her better justification) she was in a manner forced to grant us, the ship affording her no other place fit for her retreat whilst we were there. Her young son sat by her, on whom all our eyes were fixed; and our minds united with one opinion, that the air and lineaments of his face, full of sweetness, made him so like our King when he was of that age, that, everyone whispering his thoughts to his neighbor, we all broke out at length in an open admiration of so great resemblance.

The healths of the two Kings were passing about with thundering peals of cannon; the youth was permitted by his mother to kiss the cup, and drink a small portion to that of our King; and she was in so pleasant an humor at this honor done to her son that, to close our feast, she ordered the table to be covered anew, and a handsome banquet placed upon it, which we must partake of before we parted. To conclude this rare treat, she repeated the health of our King in a sort of choice rich wine that they make in Brazil, and drank the proportion she would take without the allay of water, which till then she drank with little or no wine.

The approaching night made us take leave sooner than our inclinations would have led us ashore, the merchants having told us there was no safe walking the streets in the night, for fear the picaros (a sort of land pirates) should snatch away our hats and looser garments, as they used to treat strangers.

When we had paid our thanks to the captain, we desired his best language to make our compliments to the lady and her son, which she returned with her wishes for our happy voyage.

Whilst we were caressed in this manner on shipboard, the seamen on shore continued in their debauchery, with very little advance of our dispatch. The getting water was so tedious in itself for lack of our boat, and so full of delays by drunken contests of ours with the islanders, and with themselves, that, after some days' stay upon the island, when our captain resolved to sail away, he found the ship in worse condition for liquors than when we came on shore. For if we got a new supply of water, the proportion was hardly enough to balance the expense of beer that was spent in the time we got it.

It was about the 22d of October that we took leave of our landlord and Fayal. We had store of black pigs for 'resh meat, and I carried peaches without number. We parted with an easterly wind a topsail gait, which soon brought us into a trade wind that favored us at fifty or sixty leagues in twenty-four hours, till we came to the height of Bermudas. In that latitude it is the general observation of seamen that the seas are rough and the weather stormy. It was my fortune to have a curiosity to look out, when the officer on the watch showed me a more than ordinary agitation of the sea in one particular place above the rest, which was the effect of what they call a spout, a raging in the bowels of the sea (like a violent birth) striving to break out, and at last springs up like a mine at land, with weight and force enough to have hoisted our ship out of her proper element into the air (had the helm been for it), and to have made her do the somersault. But God's providence secured us from that danger.

The sight of the island was welcome to all. The mariners learned thereby our true distance from Cape Hatteras; and the passengers were relieved with hopes to be soon at shore, from a hungry pestered ship and company.

The gale continued fair till November 8th. Then we observed the water changed, and heaving the lead, we had thirty-five fathom of water which was joyful news; our want of all things necessary for human life made it so.

Towards break of day, weary of my lodging, I visited Mate Putts on the watch and would have treated him with brandy, but he refused that offer unless I could also give him tobacco, which I had not. He said it was near break of day, and he would look out to see what change there was in the water. No sooner were his feet upon the deck, but with stamps and noise he calls up the seamen, crying out, "All hands aloft! Breaches, breaches on both sides! All hands aloft!"

The seamen were soon on deck with this dismal alarm, and saw the cause thereof; but instead of applying their hands for their preservation (through a general despondency) they fell on their knees, commending their souls as at the last gasp. The captain came out at the noise to rectify what was amiss, but seeing how the case stood, his courage failed. Mate Putts (a stout seaman) took heart again, and cried out, "Is there no good fellow that will stand to the helm, and loose a sail?"

But of all the ship's crew there were but two foremastmen that would be persuaded to obey commands, namely Thomas Reasin and John Smith, men of innate courage, who, for their good resolution on that and divers other occasions in the various traverses of this voyage, deserve to have their names kept in lasting remembrance.

One of them got up and loosed the fore-topsail, to put the ship (if possible) in steerage way, and under command; the other stood to the helm, and he shifted it in a nick of time, for the ship was at the point of dashing on the starboard breach. And although in the rest of the voyage she was wont to be blamed for the ill quality of not feeling the helm, she did, in this important instance, redeem her credit, and fell round off for our rescue from that danger. But the sense of this escape lasted but a moment; for no sooner was she fallen from that breach, but another on the larboard bow was ready to receive her. The ship's crew by this time (reproached by the courage of Reasin and Smith) were all at work, and the helm shifting opportunely, she fell off again as before. The light of the day (which now broke forth) did discover our condition to be altogether as perilous as possible, for we now saw ourselves surrounded with breaches; scarce any water like a channel appeared for a way to shun them. In this sad condition the ship struck ground, and raised such a war of water and sand together, which fell on the main-chains, that now all hopes of safety were laid aside. But the ship being still afloat, and the seamen all of them now under command, nothing was omitted for our preservation that was in their power.

Tom Reasin, seeing the ship go ahead in the likeliest water for a channel, and ordering the helm accordingly, heaved the lead. And after a little further advance into that new channel, wholly against his hopes, he had a good deal of water more than the ship drew, which soon mended upon us, the next cast of the lead affording eighteen or twenty foot. We stood to this channel, and the light of the morning enabling the quartermasters to con the ship, we were by this miraculous mercy of

God soon clear of the breaches at Cape Hatteras, and got out to sea.

No sooner was the ship freed of this danger, and gotten a little into the offing, but the seamen (like so many spirits) surveyed each other, as if they doubted the reality of the thing, and shook hands like strangers, or men risen from the other world, and did scarce believe they were what they seemed to be, men of flesh and blood. As they recovered force, they made what sail they could to stand to seaward.

The gale came fresh at northwest, and this fresh gale did soon grow up to a violent storm, which increased to so great a rigor, separating us from the land at the rate of eight leagues a watch, merely with our foreclosures, insomuch that the master thought it necessary to stop that career; and, in order thereunto, he did advise with his officers to bring the ship about, to furl all sails, and to try with the mizzen.

The mountainous towering northwest seas that this storm made were so unruly that the seamen knew not how to work the ship about. We were already at a great distance from land, and something must be done to hinder our running off at that excessive rate. The first thing they did was to lower the main-yard, to give some ease to that mast by laying it on the ship's waist. Our great difficulty was how to deal so with the foresails, that the ship might work about with safety, or at least with as little hazard as possible. All hands were too little to haul the sheet close, in order to bring the ship about. Many great seas were shipped as she came to work through the trough of the sea. Amongst the rest one chanced to break upon the poop (where we were quartered), and that with so sad a weight that we guessed a ton of water at the least did enter the tarpaulin, and set us all on float who were in the roundhouse. The noise it made by discharging itself in that manner was like the report of a great gun, and did put us all into a horrible fright, which we could not soon shake off. This shock being past, the ship about, and our foresail handled, we now lay trying with our mizzen.

I cannot forget the prodigious number of porpoises that did that evening appear about the ship, to the astonishment of the oldest seamen in her. They seemed to cover the surface of the sea as far as our eyes could discern; insomuch that a musket bullet, shot at random, could hardly fail to do execution on some of them. This the seamen would look upon as of bad portent, predicting ill weather; but in our case, who were in present possession of a storm, they appeared too late to gain the credit of foretelling what should come upon us in that kind.

The seas thus enraged and all in foam, the gale still increasing upon us, the officers on the watch made frequent visits to the roundhouse, to prepare the captain for some evil encounter which this mighty tempest must bring forth. And their fears proved reasonable, for, about the hours of ten or eleven, our new disasters did begin with a crash from aloft. All hands were summoned up with loud cries that the fore-topmast was come by the board, not alone but in conjunction with the foremast head broken short off, just under the cap.

This was a sore business, and put all to their wits' end to recover to any competent condition. What could be done was done to prevent further mischiefs; but the whole trim and rigging of a ship depending much upon stays and tackle fixed to that mast, we had reason to expect greater ruins to follow than what had already befallen us. Mate Putts was then on the watch, and did not want his apprehension of what did soon ensue, which in all likelihood was to end in our utter perdition. For about the hours of twelve or one at night, we heard and felt a mighty sea break on our foreship, which made such an inundation on the deck where the mate was walking that he retired back with all diligence up to his knees in water, with short ejaculations of prayers in his mouth, supposing the ship was foundering, and at the last gasp.

This looked like a stroke of death in every seaman's opinion. The ship stood stock-still, with her head under water, seeming to bore her way into the sea. My two comrades and myself lay on our platform, sharing liberally in the general consternation. We took a short leave of each other, men, women, and children. All, assaulted with the fresh terror of death, made a most dolorous outcry throughout the ship, whilst Mate Putts, perceiving the deck almost freed of water, called out aloud for hands to pump. This we thought a lightning before death, but gave me occasion (as having the best sea legs) to look and learn the subject of this astonishing alarm, which proved to arise from no less cause than the loss of our forecastle, with six guns, and our anchors (all but one that was fastened to a cable) together with our two cooks, whereof one was recovered by a strange providence.

This great gap, made by want of our forecastle, did open a passage into the hold for other seas that should break there before a remedy was found out to carry them off, and this made our danger almost insuperable. But it fell out propitiously that there were divers land carpenter passengers who were very helpful in this distress; and in a little time a slight platform of deal was tacked to the timbers, to carry off any ordinary sea in the present strait we were in. Every moment of this growing tempest cut out new work to employ all hands to labor.

The bowsprit, too topheavy in itself, having lost all stays and rigging that should keep it steady, swayed to and fro with such bangs on the bows that at no less rate than the cutting it close off could the ship subsist.

All things were in miserable disorder, and it was evident our danger increased upon us. The stays of all the masts were gone, the shrouds that remained were loose and useless, and it was easy to foretell our main-topmast would soon come by the board. Tom Reasin (who was always ready to expose himself), with an ax in his hand, ran up with speed to prevent that evil, hoping thereby to ease the mainmast and preserve it. But the danger of his person in the enterprise was so manifest that he was called down amain; and no sooner was his foot upon the deck, but what was feared came to pass with a witness; both main and topmast all came down together and, in one shock, fell all to the windward clear into the sea, without hurt to any man's person.

Our mainmast, thus fallen to the broadside, was like to incommode us more in the sea than in her proper station. For the shrouds and rigging not loosing the hold they had of the ship, every surge did so check the mast (whose butt end lay charged to fall perpendicular on the ship's side) that it became a ram to batter and force the plank, and was doing the last execution upon us, if not prevented in time by edge-tools, which freed the ship from that unexpected assault and battery.

Abandoned in this manner to the fury of the raging sea, tossed up and down without any rigging to keep the ship steady, our seamen frequently fell overboard, without any one regarding the loss of another, every man expecting the same fate, though in a different manner. The ceilings of this hulk (for it was no better) were for the same cause so uneasy that, in many tumbles, the deck would touch the sea, and there stand still as if she would never make another. Our mizzenmast only remained, by which we hoped to bring the ship about in proper season, which now lay stemming to the east.

In this posture did we pass the tenth and eleventh days of November. The twelfth in the morning we saw an English merchant, who showed his ensign but would not speak with us, though the storm was abated and the season more fit for communication. We imagined the reason was because he would not be compelled to be civil to us; he thought our condition desperate, and we had more guns than he could resist, which might enable us to take what he would not sell or give. He shot a gun to leeward, stood his course, and turned his poop upon us.

Before we attempted to bring the ship about, it was necessary to refresh the seamen, who were almost worn out with toil and want of rest, having had no leisure of eating set meals for many days. The passengers, overcharged with excessive fears, had no appetite to eat, and (which was worst of all) both seamen and passengers were in a deplorable state as to the remaining victuals, all like to fall under extreme want. For the storm, by taking away the forecastle, having thrown much water into the hold, our stock of bread (the staff of life) was greatly damnified, and there remained no way to dress our meat now that the cookroom was gone; the incessant tumbling of the ship (as has been observed) made all such cookery wholly impracticable. The only expedient to make fire betwixt decks was by sawing a cask in the middle and filling it with ballast, which made a hearth to parch peas and broil salt beef; nor could this be done but with great attendance, which was many times frustrated by being thrown topsy-turvy in spite of all circumspection, to the great defeat of empty stomachs.

The seas were much appeased the seventeenth day, and divers English ships saw and were seen by us, but would not speak with us; only one, who kept the pump always going, for having tasted too liberally of the storm, was so kind as to accost us. He lay by till our wherry (the only surviving boat that was left us) made him a visit. The master showed our men his leaks and proposed that ours would spare him hands to pump, in lieu of anything he could spare for our relief. He promised, however, to keep us company and give us a tow to help to weather the cape, if occasion offered; but that was only a copy of his countenance, for in the night we lost each other and we never heard more of him, though he was bound to our port.

November 13th. The weather now invited us to get the ship about with our mizzen, and having done so, the next consideration was how to make sail. The foremast all this while (as much as was of it) stood its ground; and as it was without dispute that a yard must in the first place be fixed to it, so was it a matter of no small difficulty how to advance to the top of that greasy slippery stump, since he that would attempt it could take no hold himself, nor receive any help for his rise by other hands. This was a case that put all the ship's crew to a nonplus, but Tom Reasin (a constant friend at need, that would not be baffled by any difficulty) showed by his countenance he had a mind to try his skill to bring us out of this unhappy crisis. To encourage him the more, all passengers did promise and subscribe to reward his service, in Virginia, by tobacco, when God should enable us so to do. The proportions being set down, many were the more generous, because they never thought to see the place of payment, but expected to anticipate that by the payment of a greater debt to nature, which was like to be exacted every hour by an arrest of the merciless sea, which made small show of taking bail for our appearance in Virginia.

The manner of Tom Reasin's ascent to this important work was thus. Among the scattered parcels of the ship's stores he had the luck to find about half a dozen iron spikes fit for his purpose. His first onset was to drive one of them into the mast, almost to the head, as high as he could reach; which being done, he took a rope of about ten foot long, and having threaded the same in a block or pulley, so as to divide it in the middle, he made both ends meet in a knot upon the spike, on both sides of the mast; so that the block falling on the contrary side, became a stirrup to mount upon for driving another spike in the same manner. And thus from step to step, observing the best advantage of striking with his hammer in the smoothest sea, he got aloft, drove cleats for shrouds to rest upon, and was soon in a posture of receiving help from his comrades, who got a yard and sails (with other accommodation) such as could be had; and thus we were enabled in few hours' time to make some sail for our port.

The mainyard, that in the storm had been lowered to the waist to lie out of harm's way, was now preferred to the place of a mainmast, and was accordingly fitted and accoutered, and grafted into the stump of what was left in the storm, some eight or ten foot from the deck. It was a hard matter to find out rigging answerable to that new-fashioned mast and yard; topgallant sails and yards were most agreeable to this equipage, and was the best part of our remaining stores. The seas grew every moment smoother, and the weather more comfortable; so that for a while we began to shake off the visage of utter despair, as hoping ere long to see ourselves in some capacity to fetch the cape. We discovered another ship bound to Virginia, who as frankly promised to stand by us, the wind at NNW. We did what could be done by a ship so mangled to get the weather gauge of the Cape Henry, conceiving ourselves to the southward of Cape Hatteras. But by taking an observation on a sunshine day, we found ourselves carried by a current we knew not of to the windward, much beyond all our dead reckonings and allowances for sailing, insomuch that when we thought we had been to the southward of the cape, we found ourselves considerably shot to the north of Achomat, and that in the opinion of Mate Putts, who was as our North Star.

We passed this night with greater alacrity than we had done any other since we had left Fayal; for Mate Putts, our trusty pilot, did confidently affirm that if the gale stood, there would be no question of our dining the next day within the capes. This was seasonable news, our water being long since spent, our meat spoiled or useless, no kind of victuals remaining to sustain life but a biscuit cake a day for a man; at which allowance there was not a quantity to hold out many days.

In the dark time of the night, in tacking about, we lost our new comrade, and with much impatience we expected the approaching day (the wind NW). The morning appeared foggy, as the wind veered to the east, and that did cover and conceal the land from our clearer sight. Howbeit we concluded, by Mate Putts's computation, we were well to the northward of the capes. Many times he would mount the mizzentop for discovery, as the weather seemed to clear up, and would espy and point at certain hummocks of trees that used to be his several landmarks in most of the twenty-two voyages he had made to that plantation. Under this confidence he made more sail, the daylight confirming him in what he thought was right.

All the forenoon we lost the sight of land and marks by trees, by reason of the dark fogs and mists that were not yet dispelled. But as soon as the sun, with a northwest gale, had cleared all the coast (which was about the hours of two or three o'clock) Mate Putts perceived his error from the deck, and was convinced that the hummocks of trees he had seen and relied on for sure landmarks had counter points to the south cape, which had misguided him; and that it was the opening of the bay which made the land at distance out of sight.

This fatal disappointment (which was now past human help) might have met an easy remedy had our sails and rigging been in any tolerable condition to keep the windward gauge (for we had both the capes in our sight), but under our circumstances it was vain to endeavor such a thing, all our equipage, from stem to stern, being no better than that of a western barge, and we could not lie within eleven or twelve points of the wind.

Defeated thus of lively hopes we had the night before entertained to sleep in warm beds with our friends in Virginia, it was a heavy spectacle to see ourselves running at a round rate from it, notwithstanding all that could be done to the contrary. Nothing was now to be heard but sighs and groans through all that wretched family, which must be soon reduced to so short allowance as would just keep life and soul together. Half a biscuit cake a day to each (of which five whole ones made a pound) was all we had to trust to. Of liquors there remained none to quench thirst. Malaga sack was given plentifully to everyone, which served rather to inflame and increase thirst than to extinguish it.

The gale blew fresh (as it used to do) towards night, and made a western sea that carried us off at a great rate. Mate Putts, extremely abashed to see his confidence so miserably deluded, grew sad and contemplative, even to the moving compassion in those whom his unhappy mistake had reduced to this misery. We cherished him the best we could, and would not have him so profoundly sad for what was rather his misfortune than his fault.

The wind continued many days and nights to send us out into the ocean, insomuch that until we thought ourselves at least an hundred leagues from the capes the northwest gale gave us no truce to consider what was best to do. All little helps were used by topgallant sails, and masts placed where they could be fixed, to keep the windward gauge; but, for lack of borolins and other tackle to keep them stiff to draw, every great head sea would check them in the wind, and rend and tear them in pieces. So that it was an ordinary exercise with us to lie tumbling in the sea a watch or two together, driving to leeward, whilst the broken sails were in hand to be repaired.

It would be too great a trial of the reader's patience to be entertained with every circumstance of our sufferings in the remaining part of this voyage, which continued in great extremity for at least forty days from the time we left the land, our miseries increasing every hour. I shall therefore omit the greatest number of our ill encounters, which were frequently repeated on us, and remember only what has in my thoughts been most remarkable, and has made the deepest impression in my memory.

To give us a little breathing, about the nineteenth day the wind shifted to the east, but so little to our avail (the gale so gentle, and the seas made against us like a strong current) that, with the sail we were able to make, we could hardly reckon the ship shortened the way, but that she rather lost ground. In less than two watches the gale faced about; and if we saved our own by the change, it was all we could pretend unto.

Our mortal enemy, the northwest gale, began afresh to send us out to sea, and to raise our terrors to a higher pitch. One of our pumps grew so unfixed that it could not be repaired; the other was kept in perpetual motion; no man was excused to take his turn that had strength to perform it. Amongst the manifold perils that threatened every hour to be our last, we were in mortal apprehension that the guns which were all aloft would show us a slippery trick and some of them break loose, the tackle that held them being grown very rotten. And it was another providence they held so long, considering how immoderately the ship rolled, especially when the sails were mending that should keep them steady, which was very near a third part of our time, whilst we plied to the windward with a contrary gale.

To prevent this danger which must befall when any one gun should get loose, Mate Putts found an expedient by a more than ordinary smooth water, and by placing timber on the hatchway, to supply the place of shrouds, he got them safe in hold. Which tended much to our good, not only in removing the present danger, but by making the ship (as seamen say) more wholesome, by having so great weight removed from her upper works into her center, where ballast was much wanted.

But the intolerable want of all provisions, both of meat and drink, jostled the sense of this happiness soon out of our minds. And to aggravate our misery yet the more, it was now our interest to pray that the contrary gale might stand; for whilst the westerly wind held we had rain water to drink, whereas at east the wind blew dry.

In this miserable posture of ship and provision, we reckoned ourselves driven to the east, in less than a week's time, at least two hundred leagues, which we despaired ever to recover without a miracle of divine mercy. The storm continued so fresh against us, that it confounded the most knowing of our ship's company in advising what course to take. Some reckoned the ship had made her way most southerly, and therefore counseled we should put ourselves in quest of the Bermudas Islands, as to the nearest land we could hope to make. But that motion had great opposition in regard of the winter season, which would daily produce insuperable difficulties, and give greater puzzle in the discovery of it than our circumstances would admit. Others would say, the furthest way about, in our case, would prove the nearest way home; and judged it best to take advantage of the westerly winds and impetuous seas made to our hands, to attempt returning back to the western islands, as a thing more likely to succeed (though at a great distance) than thus to strive against the stream without any hopeful prospect of gaining the capes. But that motion met with a more general aversion, because the run was so long that, though the gale had been in our power to continue it, we could not have subsisted. Backwards we could not go, nor forwards in the course we desired. It followed then of consequence that we must take the middle way; and it was resolved that, without further persisting in endeavoring to gain our port by a close haul, we should raise our tackle and sail tardy for the first American land we could fetch, though we ran to the leeward as far as the coast of New England.

Whilst this determination was agreed and put in practice, the famine grew sharp upon us. Women and children made dismal cries and grievous complaints. The infinite number of rats that all the voyage had been our plague, we now were glad to make our prey to feed on; and as they were ensnared and taken, a well-grown rat was sold for sixteen shillings as a market rate. Nay, before the voyage did end (as I was credibly informed) a woman great with child offered twenty shillings for a rat, which, the proprietor refusing, the woman died.

Many sorrowful days and nights we spun out in this manner, till the blessed feast of Christmas came upon us, which we began with a very melancholy solemnity. And yet, to make some distinction of times, the scrapings of the meal tubs were all amassed together to compose a pudding. Malaga sack, sea water, with fruit and spice, all well fried in oil, were the ingredients of this regale, which raised some envy in the spectators; but allowing some privilege to the captain's mess, we met no obstruction, but did peaceably enjoy our Christmas pudding.

My greatest impatience was of thirst, and my dreams were all of cellars and taps running down my throat, which made my waking much the worse by that tantalizing fancy. Some relief I found very real by the captain's favor in allowing me a share of some butts of small claret he had concealed in a private cellar for a dead lift. It wanted a mixture of water for qualifying it to quench thirst; however, it was a present remedy, and a great refreshment to me.

I cannot forget another instance of the captain's kindness to me, of a like obligation. He singled me out one day to go with him into the hold to seek fresh water in the bottoms of the empty casks. With much ado we got a quantity to satisfy our longing, though for the thickness thereof it was not palatable. We were now each of us astride on a butt of Malaga, which gave the captain occasion to taste of their contents. We tasted and tasted it again; and though the total we drank was not considerable, yet it had an effect on our heads that made us suspend (though we could not forget) our wants of water. The operation this little debauch had upon the captain was very different from what it wrought on me, who felt myself refreshed as with a cordial. But the poor captain fell to contemplate (as it better became him) our sad condition; and being troubled in mind for having brought so many wretched souls into misery, by a false confidence he gave them of his having a good ship, which he now thought would prove their ruin, and being conscious that their loss would lie all at his door, it was no easy matter to appease his troubled thoughts. He made me a particular compliment for having engaged me and my friends in the same bottom, and upon that burst into tears. I comforted him the best I could, and told him we must all submit to the hand of God and rely on His Goodness, hoping that the same providence which had hitherto so miraculously preserved us would still be continued in our favor till we were in safety. We retired obscurely to our friends, who had been wondering at our absence.

The westerly wind continued to shorten our way to the shore, though very distant from our port, but this did not at all incline us to change our resolution of sailing large for the first land; it did rather animate and support us in our present disasters of hunger and thirst, toil and fatigue. The hope of touching land was food and raiment to us.

In this wearisome expectation we passed our time for eight or nine days and nights, and then we saw the water change color, and had soundings. We approached the shore the night of January 3d with little sail, and as the morning of the fourth day gave us light we saw the land, but in what latitude we could not tell, for that the officers whose duty it was to keep the reckoning of the ship had for many days past totally omitted that part; nor had we seen the sun a great while, to take observations, which (though a lame excuse) was all they had to say for that omission.   But in truth it was evident that the desperate estate of the ship and hourly jeopardy of life did make them careless of keeping either log or journal; the thoughts of another account they feared to be at hand did make them neglect that of the ship as inconsiderable.

About the hours of three or four in the afternoon of the twelfth eve, we were shot in fair to the shore.   The evening was clear and calm, the water smooth; the land we saw nearest was some six or seven English miles distant from us, our soundings twenty-five fathoms in good ground for anchor hold.

These invitations were all attractive to encourage the generality (especially the passengers) to execute what we had resolved on for the shore. But one old officer, who was husband for the ship's stores whilst there were any, would not consent on any terms to trust the only anchor that was left us for preservation out of his sight at sea.   His arguments to back his opinion were plausible: as, first, the hazard of losing that only anchor by any sudden storm, bringing with it a necessity to cut or slip, on which every life depended.   Secondly, the shortness of the cable, very unfit for anchorage in the ocean.   And thirdly, the weakness of the ship's crew, many dead and fallen overboard, and the passengers weakened by hunger, dying every day on the decks or at the pump, which with great difficulty was kept going, but must not rest.

Against the old man's reasonings was urged the very small remains of biscuit, at our short allowance, which would hardly hold a week; the assurance of our loss by famine if we should be forced to sea again by a northwest storm; and the great possibility of finding a harbor to save our ship, with our lives and goods, in some creek on the coast.   These last reasons prevailed upon the majority against all negatives, and when the anchor was let loose, Mate Putts was ordered to make the first discovery of what we might expect from the nearest land.   He took with him twelve sickly passengers, who fancied the shore would cure them, and he carried Major Morrison on shore with him in pursuit of such adventures as are next in course to be related. For according to the intelligence that could be got from land, we were to take our measures at sea, either to proceed on in our voyage in that sad condition that has been in some proportion set forth, or to land ourselves and unload the ship, and try our fortunes amongst the Indians.

In four of five hours' time we could discover the boat returning with Mate Putts alone for a setter, which we looked upon as a signal of happy success. When he came on board his mouth was full of good tidings, as, namely, that he discovered a creek that would harbor our ship, and that there was a depth of water on the bar, sufficient for her draught when she was light. That there was excellent fresh water (a taste whereof Major Morrison had sent me in a bottle). That the shore swarmed with fowl, and that Major Morrison stayed behind in expectation of the whole ship's company to follow.

I opened mine ears wide to the motion, and promoted the design of our landing there with all the rhetoric and interest I had. The captain was no less forward for it, hoping thereby to save the lives of the passengers that remained. And that he might not wholly rely on Mate Putts's judgment in a matter wherein he was most concerned, he embarked with me in the wherry, with a kinsman of his and some others; and the seamen were glad of my help to put the boat to shore, my hands having been very well seasoned at the pump by taking my turn for many weeks at the rate of three hours in twenty-four. My passionate desires to be on shore at the fountainhead to drink without stint did not a little quicken me, insomuch that the six or seven miles I rowed on this occasion were no more than the breadth of the Thames at London, at another time, would have been toilsome to me.

In our passage to the shore, the darkness of the evening made us glad to see the fires of our friends at land, which were not only our beacons to direct us to their company, but were also a comfortable relief to our chill bodies when we came near them, the weather being very cold (as it ever is), the wind northwest on that coast.

As soon as I had set my foot on land, and had rendered thanks to Almighty God for opening this door of deliverance to us, after so many rescues even from the jaws of death at sea, Major Morrison was pleased to oblige me beyond all requital in conducting me to the running stream of water, where, without any limitation of short allowance, I might drink my fill. I was glad of so great liberty, and made use of it accordingly by prostrating myself on my belly and setting my mouth against the stream, that it might run into my thirsty stomach without stop. The rest of the company were at liberty to use their own methods to quench their thirst, but this I thought the greatest pleasure I ever enjoyed on earth.

After this sweet refreshment, the captain, myself, and his kinsman crossed the creek in our wherry, invited thither by the cackling of wild fowl. The captain had a gun charged, and the moon shining bright in his favor, he killed one duck of the flock that flew over us, which was roasted on a stick out of hand by the seamen, whilst we walked on the shore of the creek for further discovery.

In passing a small gullet we trod on an oyster bank that did happily furnish us with a good addition to our duck. When the cooks had done their parts, we were not long about ours, but fell on without using the ceremony of calling the rest of our company, which would have been no entertainment to so many, the proverb telling us, *The fewer the better cheer.* The bones, head, legs and inwards were agreed to be the cook's fees; so we gave God thanks, and returned to our friends without making boast of our good fortunes.

Fortified with this repast, we informed ourselves of the depth of water at the bar of the creek, in which the captain seemed satisfied, and made shows in all his deportment of his resolution to discharge the ship there in order to our safety. Towards break of day he asked me in my ear, if I would go back with him on board the ship. I told him, No, because it would be labor lost in case he would persist in his resolution to do what he pretended, which he ratified again by protestations, and so went off with his kinsman, who had a large coarse gown I borrowed of him to shelter me from the sharpest cold I ever felt.

That which had sometimes been a paradox to me was by this experience made demonstrable, viz., that the land on the continent is much colder than that of islands, though in the same latitude. And the reason is evident to any who shall consider the many accidents on the continent that cool the air by winds that come from the land; as in those parts of America, the mighty towering mountains to the northwest, covered all the year with snow, which does refrigerate the air even in the heat of summer, whereas winds coming from the sea are generally warm. And this hath proved a fatal truth to the inhabitants of Virginia, who in the southeast winds have gone to bed in sultry heat and sweat, without any covering, and have awaked in the night stiff and benumbed with cold, without the use of their limbs, occasioned by a shifting of the wind in the night from sea to land.

No sooner had the captain cleared himself of the shore but the daybreak made me see my error in not closing with his motion in my ear. The first object we saw at sea was the ship under sail, standing for the capes with what canvas could be made to serve the turn. It was a very heavy prospect to us who remained (we knew not where) on shore, to see ourselves thus abandoned by the ship, and more, to be forsaken by the boat, so contrary to our mutual agreement. Many hours of hard labor and toil were spent before the boat could fetch the ship; and the seamen (whose act it was to set sail without the captain's order, as we were told after) cared not for the boat whilst the wind was large to carry them to the capes. But Mate Putts, who was more sober and better natured, discovering the boat from the mizzentop, lay by till she came with the captain on board.

In this amazement and confusion of mind that no words can express, did our miserable distressed party condole with each other our being so cruelly abandoned and left to the last despairs of human help, or indeed of ever seeing more the face of man. We entered into a sad consultation what course to take; and having, in the first place, by united prayers, implored the protection of Almighty God, and recommended our miserable estate to the same providence which, in so many instances of mercy, had been propitious to us at sea, the whole party desired me to be as it were the father of this distressed family, to advise and conduct them in all things I thought might most tend to our preservation. This way of government we agreed must necessarily reside in one, to avoid disputes and variety of contradictory humors, which would render our deliverance the more impracticable; and it was thought most reasonable to be placed in me, for the health and strength it had pleased God to preserve unto me above my fellows, more than for any other qualification.

At the time I quitted the ship my servants Thomas Harman, a Dutchman, did at parting advertise me (for I left him on board to look to my goods) that, in the bundle I ordered to be carried with me on shore, I should find about thirty biscuit cakes which he, by unparalleled frugality, had saved out of his own belly in the great dearth and scarcity we lived in. The thoughts of these biscuits entering upon me at the time I was pressed to accept this charge, I thought myself obliged, in Christian equity, to let everyone partake of what I had; and so dividing the bread into nineteen parts (which was our number) perhaps I added the fraction to my own share.

It was, to the best of my remembrance, upon the fifth day of January that we entered into this method of life, or rather into an orderly way unto our graves, since nothing but the image of death was represented to us. But that we might use our utmost endeavors to extract all the good we could out of those evil symptoms that did every way seem to confound us, I made a muster of the most able bodies for arms and labor; and, in the first place, I put a fowling piece into every man's hand that could tell how to use it.

Amongst the rest a young gentleman, Mr. Francis Cary by name, was very helpful to me in the fatigue and active part of this undertaking. He was strong and healthy, and was ready for any employment I could put upon him. He came recommended to me by Sir Edward Thurlan, his genius leading him rather to a planter's life abroad than to any course his friends could propose to him in England; and this rough entrance was like to let him know the worst at first.

All our woodmen and fowlers had powder and shot given them, and some geese were killed for supper. Evening came on apace, and our resolution being taken to stay one night more in these quarters, I sent my cousin Cary to head the creek, and make what discovery he could as he passed along the shore, whether of Indians or any other living creatures that were likely to relieve our wants or end our days. To prepare like men for the latter, we resolved to die fighting, if that should be the case; or if, on the contrary, the Indians should accost us in a mien of amity, then to meet them with all imaginable courtesy, and please them with such trivial presents as they love to deal in, and so engage them into a friendship with us.

My cousin Cary was not absent much above an hour when we saw him return in a contrary point to that he sallied out upon. His face was clouded with ill news he had to tell us, namely, that we were now residing on an island without any inhabitant, and that he had seen its whole extent, surrounded (as he believed) with water deeper than his head; that he had not seen any native, or anything in human shape, in all his round, nor any other creature besides the fowls of the air, which he would, but could not, bring unto us.

This dismal success of so unexpected a nature did startle us more than any single misfortune that had befallen us, and was like to plunge us into utter despair. We beheld each other as miserable wretches sentenced to a lingering death, no man knowing what to propose for prolonging life any longer than he was able to fast. My cousin Cary was gone from us without notice, and we had reason (for what followed) to believe he was under the conduct of an angel; for we soon saw him return with a cheerful look, his hands carrying something we could not distinguish by any name at a distance. But by nearer approach we were able to descry they were a parcel of oysters, which, in crossing the island, as he stepped over a small current of water, he trod upon to his hurt; but laying hands on what he felt with his feet, and pulling it with all his force, he found himself possessed of this booty of oysters, which grew in clusters, and were contiguous to a large bank of the same species. That was our staple subsistence whilst we remained there.

Whilst this very cold season continued, great flights of fowl frequented the island, geese, ducks, curlews, and some of every sort we killed and roasted on sticks, eating all but the feathers. It was the only perquisite belonging to my place of preference to the rest that the right of carving was annexed to it, wherein, if I was partial to my own interest, it was in cutting the wing as large and full of meat as possible; whereas the rest was measured out as it were with scale and compass.

But as the wind veered to the southward, we had greater warmth and fewer fowl, for they would then be gone to colder climates. In their absence we were confined to the oyster bank, and a sort of weed some four inches long, as thick as houseleek, and the only green (except pines) that the island afforded. It was very insipid on the palate; but being boiled with a little pepper (of which one had brought a pound on shore) and helped with five or six oysters, it became a regale for everyone in turn.

In quartering our family we did observe the decency of distinguishing sexes. We made a small hut for the poor weak women to be by themselves; our cabin for men was of the same fashion but much more spacious, as our numbers were.

One morning, in walking on the shore by the seaside, with a long gun in my hand loaded with small shot, I fired at a great flight of small birds called oxeyes and made great slaughter among them, which gave refreshment to all our company. But this harvest had a short end; and as the weather by its warmth chased the fowl to the north, our hunger grew sharper upon us. And in fine, all the strength that remained unto us was employed in a heartless struggling to spin out life a little longer; for we still deemed ourselves doomed to die by famine, from whose sharpest and most immediate darts though we seemed to be rescued for a small time, by meeting these contingent helps on shore, yet still we apprehended (and that on too great probability) they only served to reprieve us for a little longer day of execution, with all the dreadful circumstances of a lingering death.

For the southwest winds that had carried away the fowl brought store of rain, which meeting with a spring tide, our chief magazine, the oyster bank, was overflowed; and as they became more accessible, our bodies also decayed so sensibly that we could hardly pull them out of their muddy beds they grew on. And from this time forward we rarely saw the fowl; they now grew shy and kept aloof when they saw us contriving against their lives.

Add to this, our guns most of them unfixed and out of order, and our powder much decayed, insomuch that nothing did now remain to prolong life but what is counted rather sauce to whet than substance to satisfy the appetite. I mean the oysters, which were not easily gotten by our crazy bodies after the quantity was spent that lay most commodious to be reached, and which had fed us for the first six days we had been on the island. And thus we wished every day to be the last of our lives (if God had so pleased), so hopeless and desperate was our condition, all expectation of human succor being vanished and gone.

Of the three weak women before-mentioned, one had the envied happiness to die about this time; and it was my advice to the survivors, who were following her apace, to endeavor their own preservation by converting her dead carcass into food, as they did to good effect. The same counsel was embraced by those of our sex: the living fed upon the dead, four of our company having the happiness to end their miserable lives on Sunday night the . . . day of January. Their chief distemper, 'tis true, was hunger; but it pleased God to hasten their exit by an immoderate access of cold, caused by a most terrible storm of hail and snow at northwest, on the Sunday aforesaid, which did not only dispatch those four to their long homes, but did sorely threaten all that remained alive, to perish by the same fate.

Great was the toil that lay on my hands (as the strongest to labor) to get fuel together sufficient for our preservation. In the first place I divested myself of my great gown, which I spread at large, and extended against the wind in nature of a screen, having first shifted our quarters to the most calm commodious place that could be found to keep us, as much as possible, from the inclemency of that prodigious storm.

Under the shelter of this traverse I took as many of my comrades as could be comprehended in so small a space; whereas those who could not partake of that accommodation, and were enabled to make provision for themselves, were forced to suffer for it. And it was remarkable that, notwithstanding all the provision that could possibly be made against the sharpness of this cold, either by a well-burning fire consisting of two or three loads of wood, or shelter of this great gown to the windward, we could not be warm. That side of our wearing clothes was singed and burnt which lay towards the flames, whilst the other side that was from the fire became frozen and congealed. Those who lay to the leeward of the flame could not stay long to enjoy the warmth so necessary to life, but were forced to quit and be gone to avoid suffocation by the smoke and flame.

When the day appeared and the sun got up to dissipate the clouds, with downcast looks and dejected the survivors of us entered into a final deliberation of what remained to be done on our parts (besides our prayers to Almighty God) to spin out a little longer time of life, and wait a further providence from heaven for our better relief. There were still some hands that retained vigor, though not in proportion to those difficulties we were to encounter, which humanly did seem insuperable. The unhappy circumstance of our being cooped up on an island was that which took from us all probable hopes of escaping this terrible death that did threaten us every hour. Major Morrison, on whose counsel I had reason to rely most, was extremely decayed in his strength, his legs not being able to support him. It was a wonderful mercy that mine remained in competent strength, for our common good, which I resolved, by God's help, to employ for that end to the last gasp.

In this last resolution we had to make, I could not think on anything worthy my proposal, but by an attempt to cross the creek, and swim to the main (which was not above an hundred yards over) and being there to coast along the woods to the southwest (which was the bearing of Virginia) until I should meet Indians, who would either relieve or destroy us. I fancied the former would be our lot when they should see our conditions, and that no hurt was intended to them; or if they should prove inhuman and of a bloody nature, and would not give us quarter, why even in that case it would be worth this labor of mine to procure a sudden period to all our miseries.

I opened my thoughts to this purpose to the company, who were sadly surprised at the motion; but being fully convinced in their judgment that this was the only course that could be depended on (humanly speaking) for our relief, they all agreed it must be done.

To fortify me for this expedition, it was necessary that some provision should be made for a daily support to me in this my peregrination. Our choice was small; our only friend the oyster bank was all we had to rely on, which being well stewed in their own liquor, and put up into bottles, I made no doubt, by God's blessing, but that two of them well filled would suffice to prolong my life in moderate strength until I had obtained my end. To accomplish this design, my cousin Cary labored hard for oysters, hoping to make one in the adventure.

About the ninth day of our being on the island I fell to my oyster-cookery and made a good progress that very day, when in the heat of my labor my cousin Cary brought me word that he had just in that instant seen Indians walking on the main. I suspended my cookery out of hand, and hastened with all possible speed to be an eyewitness of that happy intelligence; but with all the haste I could make I could see no such thing, but judged it a chimera that proceeded from some operation in my cousin's fancy, who was more than ordinary of a sanguine nature, which made him see (as it were by enchantment) things that were not, having many times been deluded (as I judged) by the same deception.

Defeated in this manner of my hopes to see Indians without the pains of seeking them, I returned to my work, and continued at it till one bottle was full and myself tired. Wherefore, that I might be a little recreated, I took a gun in my hand, and hearing the noise of geese on our shore I approached them privately, and had the good hap to be the death of one. This goose, now in my possession without witnesses, I resolved to eat alone (deducting the head, bones, guts, et cetera, which were the cook's fees), hoping thereby to be much the better enabled to swim the creek, and perform the work I had upon my hand. I hung my goose upon the twist of a tree in a shrubby part of the wood, whilst I went to call aside our cook with his broach, and a coal of fire to begin the roast. But when we came to the place of execution, my goose was gone all but the head, the body stolen by wolves, which the Indians told us after do abound greatly in that island.

The loss of this goose, which my empty stomach looked for with no small hopes of satisfaction, did vex me heartily. I wished I could have taken the thief of my goose to have served him in the same kind, and to have taken my revenge in the law of retaliation. But that which troubled me more was an apprehension that came into my mind, that this loss had been the effect of divine justice on me, for designing to deal unequally with the rest of my fellow sufferers; which I thought, at first blush, looked like a breach of trust. But then again when I considered the equity of the thing, that I did it merely to enable myself to attain their preservation, and which otherwise I could not have done, I found I could absolve myself from any guilt of that kind. Whatever I suffered in this disappointment, the cook lost not all his fees; the head and neck remained for him on the tree.

Being thus overreached by the wolf, it was time to return to my cookery, in order to my sally out of the island; for I had little confidence in the notice frequently brought me of more and more Indians seen on the other side, since my own eyes could never bear witness of their being there.

The next morning, being the ninth or tenth of our being there, I fell to work afresh, hoping to be ready to begin my journey that day; and being very busy, intelligence was brought that a canoe was seen to lie on the broken ground to the south of our island, which was not discovered till now, since our being there. But this I thought might be a mistake cast in the same mold of many others that had deceived those discoverers, who fancied all things real according to their own wishes. But when it was told me that Indians had been at the poor women's cabin in the night, and had given them shellfish to eat, that was a demonstration of reality beyond all suspicion. I went immediately to be informed from themselves, and they both avowed it for truth, showing the shells (the like whereof I never had seen), and this I took for proof of what they said.

The further account these women gave of the Indians was that they pointed to the southeast with their hands, which they knew not how to interpret, but did imagine by their several gestures they would be with them again tomorrow. Their pointing to the southeast was like to be the time they would come, meaning nine o'clock to be their hour, where the sun will be at that time. Had the women understood their language, they could not have learned the time of the day by any other computation than pointing at the sun. It is all the clock they have for the day, as the coming and going of the cabuncks (the geese) is their almanac or prognostic for the winter and summer seasons.

This news gave us all new life, almost working miracles amongst us, by making those who desponded and totally yielded themselves up to the weight of despair and lay down with an intent never more to rise again, to take up their beds and walk. This friendly charitable visit of the Indians did also put a stop to my preparations to seek them, who had so humanely prevented by their seeking ways to preserve and save our lives.

Instead of those preparations for my march which had cost me so much pains, I passed my time now in contriving the fittest posture our present condition would allow us to put on when these angels of light should appear again with the glad tidings of our relief. And the result was, that every able man should have his gun lying by his side, laden with shot, and as fit for use as possible, but not to be handled unless the Indians came to us like enemies (which was very unlikely, the premises considered), and then to sell our lives at as dear a rate as we could; but if they came in an amicable posture, then would we meet them unarmed, cheerfully, which the Indians like, and hate to see a melancholy face.

In these joyful hopes of unexpected deliverance by these Indians did we pass the interval of their absence. Every eye looked sharply out when the sun was at southeast, to peep through the avenues of the wood to discover the approaches of our new friends. When the sun came to the south we thought ourselves forgotten by them and began to doubt the worst, as losing gamesters, at play for their last estate, suspect some stab cast to defeat the hopes of the fairest game. We feared some miscarriage, either from their inconstancy by change of their mind, or that some unlooked-for misfortune that our evil fates reserved for us had interposed for our ruin.

Scouts were sent out to the right and left hands, without discovery of anybody all the forenoon; and then, considering our case admitted no delay, I began to resume my former resolution of swimming to them that would not come to us. But how wholesome soever this counsel might seem in itself, it was most difficult to be put in practice, in regard of the cold time.

The northerly wind that in these climates does blow very cold in the heat of summer does much more distemper the air in the winter season (as our poor comrades felt that Sunday night to their cost) and did send so cold a gale upon the surface of the water in the creek I was to pass that, in the general opinion of all the concerned, it was not a thing to be attempted; and that if I did, I must surely perish in the act. I was easily persuaded to forbear an action so dangerous, and the rather, because I verily believed the Indians would bring us off, if our patience would hold out.

About the hours of two or three o'clock it pleased God to change the face of our condition for the best. For whilst I was busy at the fire in preparations to wait on them, the Indians, who had placed themselves behind a very great tree, discovered their faces with most cheerful smiles, without any kind of arms, or appearance of evil design; the whole number of them (perhaps twenty or thirty in all) consisting of men, women, and children; all that could speak accosting us with joyful countenances, shaking hands with everyone they met. The words *Ny Top*, often repeated by them, made us believe they bore a friendly signification, as they were soon interpreted to signify "My friend."

After many salutations and *Ny Tops* interchanged, the night approaching, we fell to parley with each other, but performed it in signs more confounded and unintelligible than any other conversation I ever met withal; as hard to be interpreted as if they had expressed their thoughts in the Hebrew or Chaldean tongues.

They did me the honor to make all applications to me, as being of largest dimensions, and equipped in a camlet coat glittering with galloon lace of gold and silver—it being generally true that where knowledge informs not, the habit qualifies.

The ears of Indian corn they gave us for present sustenance needed no other interpreter to let them know how much more acceptable it was to us than the sight of dead and living corpses, which raised great compassion in them, especially in the women, who are observed to be of a more soft, tender nature.

One of them made me a present of the leg of a swan, which I ate as privately as it was given me, and thought it so much the more excellent by how much it was larger than the greatest limb of any fowl I ever saw.

The Indians stayed with us about two hours, and parted not

4. INDIANS KILLING WATER FOWL

Du Creux, *Historiae Canadensis Libri Decem;* Paris, 1664

without a new appointment to see us again the next day; and the hour we were to expect them by their pointing to the sun was to be at two o'clock in the afternoon. I made the chief of them presents of ribbon and other slight trade, which they loved, designing, by mutual endearment, to let them see it would gratify their interest as well as their charity to treat us well. *Ha-na Haw* was their parting word, which is "Farewell," pointing again at the place where the sun would be at our next meeting. We took leave in their own words, *Ha-na Haw*.

2

NATURAL WONDERS

In the preface to his historical and descriptive account of Virginia, published in 1705, Robert Beverley beat his potential critics to the punch. " 'Tis agreed," he wrote, "that travelers are of all men the most suspected of insincerity. This does not only hold in their private conversations, but likewise in their grand tours and travels, with which they pester the public and break the bookseller. There are no books (the legends of saints always excepted) so stuffed with poetical stories as voyages; and the more distant the countries lie, which they pretend to describe, the greater license those privileged authors take in imposing upon the world."

Then, after announcing that he would write only gospel truth, Beverley went on to relate extravagant fables of the New World.

Some of the travelers' tales about North America well merited suspicion. While told with solemn assurances and precise details, they strained the credibilities even of seventeenth-century men, and thereby established the tradition of the American tall tale. Never had such luxuriance, size, fecundity, prodigiousness in all the aspects of nature been observed. The voyager from the cramped, pinched English island rubbed his eyes. "Herds of deer are as numerous in this province of Maryland as cuckolds can be in London, only their horns are not so well dressed and tipped with silver," wrote George Alsop, an indentured servant, in 1659. Tract after tract chants the glories of the new land in a sweet paean to a lush earthly paradise.

And in reverse, never had such frights and terrors for human habitation been reported. The fierceness of the creatures, the rigors of climate, the abundance of insects, the flintiness of the soil, all ensured a rapid end by starving, freezing, disease or wild animals. Prosperous merchants had sailed for America, lost all they had in a few months, and died miserably of hunger. In the Jamestown colony one desperate soul had been reduced to eating his wife, powdered and salted.

So the fertility and the sterility of the American earth come

69

in for equally outrageous description; the New World did nothing in a small way. By the first third of the nineteenth century these twin themes appear in endless tall tales, deliberately concocted. As the frontiers receded westward, the same wonders and terrors which Europeans had imputed to the Atlantic coastland move to the new fabulous domain, the Far West. Even today immigrants believe America flows with milk and honey, for the myth has now hardened beyond all cracking.

This myth of American prodigiousness admits of some rational explanations. The New World scale of things was enormous to begin with. Fowl and game did cover the land. And nature offered puzzles and rarities, for here was a zoology and a botany Europeans had never seen. John Lawson spoke aghast of the possum, "the wonder of all the land animals," in whom "the male's pizzle is placed retrograde," so that in the act of coition the mates turned tail to tail. "If a cat has nine lives, this creature surely has nineteen; for if you break every bone in their skin and mash their skull, leaving them for dead, you may come an hour after and they will be gone quite away, or perhaps you meet them creeping away." Besides, it served the self-interest of the colonizers and promoters of the shoestring plantations to color the attractions of the promised land. They had capital invested in very risky enterprises, and they needed swarms of settlers, smiles and grants from the Crown, additional capital from merchants. This so-called "promotion literature" survives in the booster tourist propaganda of the present. The promotion writer painted the virtues of New World living with a poet's fervor, and smote the malicious tales of New World horrors with a businessman's indignation.

FERTILITY

NEW ENGLAND'S PLANTATION

Francis Higginson

LETTING pass our voyage by sea, we will now begin our discourse on the shore of New England. And because the life and welfare of every creature here below doth by the most wide ordering of God's providence depend, next unto himself, upon the temperature and disposition of the four elements, earth, water, air, and fire, therefore I will endeavor to show you what New England is by the consideration of each of these apart, and truly endeavor by God's help to report nothing but the naked truth, and both to tell you of the discommodities as well as of the commodities, though as the idle proverb is, "Travelers may live by authority, and so may take too much sinful liberty that way." Yet I may say of myself as once Nehemiah did in another case: "Shall such a man as I live?" No verily; it becometh not a preacher of truth to be a writer of falsehood in any degree; and therefore I have been careful to report nothing of New England but what I have partly seen with mine own eyes, and partly heard and inquired from the mouths of very honest and religious persons, who by living in the country a good space of time have had experience and knowledge of the state thereof, and whose testimonies I do believe as myself.

First therefore of the earth of New England and all the appurtenances thereof. It is a land of divers and sundry sorts all about Massachusetts Bay, and at Charles River is as fat black earth as can be seen anywhere, and in other places you have a clay soil, in other gravel, in other sandy, as it is all about our plantation at Salem, for so our town is now named.

The form of the earth here in the superficies of it is neither too flat in the plains nor too high in hills, but partakes of both in a mediocrity, and is fit for pasture or for plow or meadow

71

ground as men please to employ it. Though all the country be
as it were a thick wood for the general, yet in divers places there
is much ground cleared by the Indians, and especially about
the plantation; and I am told that about three miles from us a
man may stand on a little hilly place and see divers thousands of
acres of ground as good as need to be, and not a tree in the same.
It is thought here is good clay to make brick and tiles and earthen
pot as need to be. At this instant we are setting a brick kiln
on work to make bricks and tiles for the building of our houses.
For stone, here is plenty of slates at the Isle of Slate in Massachusetts Bay, and limestone, freestone, smoothstone, ironstone,
and marblestone also in such store, that we have great rocks
of it, and a harbor hard by. Our plantation is from thence
called Marble Harbor.

Of minerals there hath yet been but little trial made, yet we are
not without great hope of being furnished in that soil.

The fertility of the soil is to be admired at, as appeareth in
the abundance of grass that groweth everywhere both very thick,
very long and very high in divers places; but it groweth very
wildly with a great stalk and a broad and ranker blade, because
it never had been eaten with cattle, nor mowed with a scythe,
and seldom trampled on by foot. It is scarce to be believed how
our kine and goats, horses and hogs, do thrive and prosper here
and like well of this country. In our plantation we have already
a quart of milk for a penny.

But the abundant increase of corn proves this country to be a
wonderment. Thirty, forty, fifty, sixty are ordinary here; yea
Joseph's increase in Egypt is outstripped here with us. Our
planters hope to have more than a hundredfold this year, and
all this while I am within compass; what will you say of two
hundredfold and upwards? It is almost incredible what great
gain some of our English planters have had by our Indian corn.
Credible persons have assured me, and the party himself
avouched the truth of it to me, that of the setting of thirteen
gallons of corn he hath had increase of it fifty-two hogsheads,
every hogshead holding seven bushels of London measure. And
every bushel was by him sold and trusted to the Indians for so
much beaver as was worth eighteen shillings, so of this thirteen

gallons of corn which was worth six shillings eight pence, he made about three hundred and twenty-seven pounds of it the year following, as by reckoning will appear; where you may see how God blessed husbandry in this land. There is not such great and plentiful ears of corn I suppose anywhere else to be found but in this country, also of variety of colors, as red, blue, and yellow, et cetera; and of one corn there springeth four or five hundred. Little children here by setting of corn may earn much more than their own maintenance.

This country aboundeth naturally with store of roots of great variety and good to eat. Our turnips, parsnips, and carrots are here both bigger and sweeter than is ordinarily to be found in England. Here are store of pumpions [pumpkins], cucumbers, and other things of that nature which I know not. Also divers excellent potherbs grow abundantly among the grass, as strawberry leaves in all places of the country, and plenty of strawberries in their time, and pennyroyal, winter savory, sorrel, brooklime, liverwort, carvel, and watercresses; also leeks and onions are ordinary, and divers physical herbs. Here are also abundance of other sweet herbs delightful to the smell, whose names we know not, and plenty of single damask roses very sweet; and two kinds of herbs that bear two kinds of flowers very sweet, which they say are as good to make cordage or cloth as any hemp or flax we have.

Excellent vines are here up and down in the woods. Our governor hath already planted a vineyard with great hope of increase.

Also, mulberries, plums, raspberries, currants, chestnuts, filberts, walnuts, small nuts, wortleberries, and haws of whitethorn near as good as our cherries in England, they grow in plenty here.

For wood there is not better in the world, I think, here being four sorts of oak differing both in the leaf, timber, and color, all excellent good. There is also good ash, elm, willow, birch, beech, sassafras, juniper, cypress, cedar, spruce, pine, and fir that will yield abundance of turpentine, pitch, tar, masts, and other materials for building both of ships and houses. Also here are store of sumac trees, good for dyeing and tanning of

leather; likewise such trees yield a precious gum called wine benjamin, that they say is excellent for perfumes. Also here be divers
roots and berries wherewith the Indians dye excellent holding
colors that no rain nor washing can alter.   Also we have materials
to make soap ashes and saltpeter in abundance.

For beasts there are some bears, and they say some lions also,
for they have been seen at Cape Ann. Also here are several sorts
of deer, some whereof bring three or four young ones at once,
which is not ordinary in England.   Also wolves, foxes, beavers,
otters, martins, great wildcats, and a great beast called a moose
as big as an ox.   I have seen the skins of all these beasts since I
came to this plantation, excepting lions.   Also here are great
store of squirrels, some greater and some smaller and lesser;
there are some of the lesser sort, they tell me, that by a certain
skill will fly from tree to tree though they stand far distant.

Of the Waters of New England With the Things Belonging to the Same

NEW ENGLAND hath water enough both salt and fresh.   The
greatest sea in the world, the Atlantic Sea, runs all along the
coast thereof.   There are abundance of islands along the shore,
some full of wood and mast to feed swine, and others clear of
wood and fruitful to bear corn. Also we have store of excellent
harbors for ships, as at Cape Ann at Massachusetts Bay, at Salem,
and at many other places; and they are the better because for
strangers there is a very difficult and dangerous passage into
them, but unto such as are well acquainted with them they
are easy and safe enough.

The abundance of seafish are almost beyond believing, and
sure I should scarce have believed it except I had seen it with
mine own eyes.   I saw great store of whales and grampuses, and
such abundance of mackerel that it would astonish one to
behold; likewise codfish abound on the coast, and in their season
are plentifully taken.   There is a fish called a bass, a most sweet
and wholesome fish as ever I did eat.   It is altogether as good
as our fresh salmon, and the season of their coming was begun
when we came first to New England in June, and so continued

about three months' space. Of this fish our fishers take many hundreds together, which I have seen lying on the shore to my admiration; yea their nets ordinarily take more than they are able to haul to land, and for want of boats and men they are constrained to let many go after they have taken them, and yet sometimes they fill two boats at a time with them. And besides bass we take plenty of skate and thornbacks and abundance of lobsters, and the least boy in the plantation may both catch and eat what he will of them. For my own part I was soon cloyed with them, they were so great and fat and luscious. I have seen some myself that have weighed sixteen pounds, but others have had divers times so great lobsters as have weighed twenty-five pounds, as they assure me. Also here is abundance of herring, turbot, sturgeon, cusks, haddock, mullet, eels, crabs, mussels, and oysters.

Besides there is probability that the country is of an excellent temper for the making of salt, for since our coming our fishermen have brought home very good salt which they found candied by the standing of the sea water and the heat of the sun, upon a rock by the seashore. And in divers salt marshes that some have gone through they have found some salt in some places crushing under their feet and cleaving to their shoes.

And as for fresh water the country is full of dainty springs, and some great rivers, and some lesser brooks. At Massachusetts Bay they digged wells and found water at three foot deep in most places, and near Salem they have as fine clear water as we can desire, and we may dig wells and find water where we list.

Thus we see both land and sea abound with store of blessings for the comfortable sustenance of man's life in New England.

Of the Air of New England With the Temper and Creatures in It

THE TEMPER of the air of New England is one special thing that commends this place. Experience doth manifest that there is hardly a more healthful place to be found in the world that agreeth better with our English bodies. Many that have been weak and sickly in old England by coming hither have been thoroughly healed and grown healthful strong. For here is an extraordinary clear and dry air that is of a most healing nature to all such as are of a cold, melancholy, phlegmatic, rheumatic temper of body. None can more truly speak hereof by their own experience than myself. My friends that knew me can well tell how very sickly I have been and continually in physic, being much troubled with a tormenting pain through an extraordinary weakness of my stomach and abundance of melancholic humors. But since I came hither on this voyage, I thank God I have had perfect health, and been free from pain and vomiting, having a stomach to digest the hardest and coarsest fare, who before could not eat finest meat. And whereas my stomach could only digest and did require such drink as was both strong and stale, now I can and do oftentimes drink New England water very well; and I that have not gone without a cap for many years together, neither durst leave off the same, have now cast away my cap and do wear none at all in the daytime. Whereas beforetime I clothed myself with double clothes and thick waistcoats to keep me warm, even in the summertime, I do now go as thin-clad as any, only wearing a light stuff cassock upon my shirt, and stuff breeches of one thickness without linings.*

Besides I have one of my children that was formerly most lamentably handled with sore breaking out of both his hands and feet of the king's evil,† but since he came hither he is very well over what he was, and there is hope of perfect recovery shortly even by the very wholesomeness of the air altering, digesting, and drying up the cold and crude humors of the body. And therefore I think it is a wise course for all cold complexions to come to take physic in New England; for a sup of New England's air is better than a whole draught of old England's ale.

* Higginson died the following August.

† Scrofula was so called from the popular belief in England and France that only the touch of the King or Queen could remove the unsightly swellings. The practice lasted through the reign of Queen Anne (d. 1714), who is supposed to have touched Samuel Johnson when his mother brought the scrofulous babe to London in 1712. In his case this remedy did no good.

Fowls of the air are plentiful here, and of all sorts as we have in England as far as I can learn, and a great many of strange fowls which we know not. Whilst I was writing these things, one of our men brought home an eagle which he had killed in the wood; they say they are good meat. Also here are many kinds of excellent hawks, both sea hawks and land hawks. Myself walking in the woods with another in company, sprung a partridge so big that through the heaviness of his body it could fly but a little way; they that have killed them say they are as big as our hens. Here are likewise abundance of turkey often killed in the woods, far greater than our English turkey, and exceeding fat, sweet, and fleshy, for here they have abundance of feeding all the year long, as strawberries (in summer all places are full of them) and all manner of other berries and fruits. In the wintertime I have seen flocks of pigeons, and have eaten of them; they do fly from tree to tree as other birds do, which our pigeons will not do in England. They are of all colors as ours are, but their wings and tails are far longer and therefore it is likely they fly swifter to escape the terrible hawks in this country. In wintertime this country doth abound with wild geese, wild ducks, and other sea fowl, that a great part of winter the planters have eaten nothing but roast meat of divers fowls which they have killed.

Thus you have heard of the earth, water, and air of New England, now it may be you expect something to be said of the fire proportionable to the rest of the elements.

Indeed I think New England may boast of this element more than of all the rest. For though it be here somewhat cold in the winter, yet here we have plenty of fire to warm us, and that a great deal cheaper than they sell billets and faggots in London; nay, all Europe is not able to afford to make so great fires as New England. A poor servant here that is to possess but fifty acres of land may afford to give more wood for timber and fire, as good as the world yields, than many noblemen in England can afford to do. Here is good living for those that love good fires. And although New England have no tallow to make candles of, yet by the abundance of the fish thereof it can afford oil for lamps. Yea, pine trees that are the most plentiful of all wood doth allow us plenty of candles which are very useful in a house. They are such candles as the Indians commonly use, having no other, and they are nothing else but the wood of the pine tree cloven into two little slices something thin, which are so full of the moisture of turpentine and pitch that they burn as clear as a torch.

Thus of New England's commodities; now I will tell you of some discommodities that are here to be found.

First, in the summer season for these three months, June, July, and August, we are troubled much with little flies called mosquitoes, being the same they are troubled with in Lincolnshire and the Fens, and they are nothing but gnats, which except they be smoked out of their houses are troublesome in the night season.

Secondly, in the winter season for two months space the earth is commonly covered with snow, which is accompanied with sharp biting frosts, something more sharp than is in old England, and therefore are forced to make great fires.

Thirdly, the country, being very full of woods and wilderness, doth also much abound with snakes and serpents of strange colors and huge greatness. Yea, there are some serpents called rattlesnakes, that have rattles in their tails, that will not fly from a man as others will, but will fly upon him and sting him so mortally that he will die within a quarter of an hour after, except the party stung have about him some of the root of an herb called snakeweed to bite on, and then he shall receive no harm; but yet seldom falls it out that any hurt is done by these. About three years since an Indian was stung to death by one of them, but we heard of none since that time.

Fourthly and lastly, here wants as it were good company of honest Christians to bring with them horses, kine, and sheep to make use of this fruitful land. Great pity it is to see so much good ground for corn and for grass as any under the heavens to lie altogether unoccupied, when so many honest men and their families in old England, through the populousness thereof, do make very hard shift to one by the other.

SEA FISH

John Pory

PLYMOUTH town is seated on the ascent of a hill, which besides the pleasure of variable objects entertaining the unsatisfied eye, such is the wholesomeness of the place (as Governor Bradford told me) that for the space of one whole year died not one man, woman, or child. This healthfulness is accompanied with much plenty both of fish and fowl every day in the year, as I know no place in the world that can match it.

In March the eels come forth out of places where they lie bedded all winter, into the fresh streams, and thence into the sea, and in their passages are taken in pots. In September they run out of the sea into the fresh streams, to bed themselves in the ground all winter, and are taken again in pots as they return homewards. In winter the inhabitants dig them up, being bedded in gravel not above two or three foot deep, and all the rest of the year they may take them in pots in the salt water of the bay. They are passing sweet, fat, and wholesome, having no taste at all of the mud, and are as great as ever I saw any.

In April and May come up another kind of fish which they call herring, or alewives, in infinite schools into a small river running under the town, and so into a great pond or lake of a mile broad where they cast their spawn, the water of the said river being in many places not above half a foot deep. Yea, when a heap of stones is reared up against them a foot high above the water, they leap and tumble over and will not be beaten back with cudgels. Which confirmeth what was thought a fable of Friar Beatus Odericus, namely, that in some parts where he had traveled, the fish in the springtime did cast themselves out of the sea upon the dry land. The inhabitants during the said two months take them up every day in hogsheads, and with those they eat not they manure the ground, burying two or three in each hill of corn, and may, when they are able, if they see cause, lade whole ships with them.

Into another river some two miles to the northeast of Plymouth

all the month of May the great smelts pass up to spawn likewise in troops innumerable, which with a scoop or a bowl or a
piece of bark a man may cast up upon the bank.   About midway
come into the harbor the many schools of bass and bluefish,
which they take with seines—some fishes of a foot and a half, some
of two foot, and some of three foot long, and with hooks those of
four and five foot long.   They enter also at flowing water
[flood tide] up into the small creeks, at the mouths whereof the
inhabitants, spreading their nets, have caught five and seven
hundred at a time.   These continue good May, June, July,
and August.

Now as concerning the bluefish, in delicacy it excelleth all
kind of fish that ever I tasted; I except not the salmon of the
Thames in his prime season, nor any other fish.   We called it by
a compound name of black, white, blue, sweet, fat; the skin and
scales blue; the flesh next under the scale for an inch deep black,
and as sweet as the marrow of an ox; the residue of the flesh
underneath pure white, fat, and of a taste requiring no addition
of sauce. By which alluring qualities it may seem dangerously
tending to a surfeit, but we found by experience that having
satisfied and in a manner glutted ourselves therewith, it proved
wholesome unto us and most easy of digestion.

In the same bay lobsters are in season during the four months,
so large, so full of meat, and so plentiful in number, as no man
will believe that hath not seen. For a knife of three halfpence I
bought ten lobsters that would well have dined forty laboring
men; and the least boy in the ship, with an hour's labor, was able
to feed the whole company with them for two days: which if
those of the ship that come home do not affirm upon their oaths,
let me forever lose my credit.

Without the bay in the ocean sea, they have all the year long
in a manner goodly fishing of cod and hake as in other parts
of Canada. Within two miles southward from their plantation
do begin goodly ponds and lakes of fresh water, continuing well
nigh twenty miles into the land, some with islands in them, the
water being as clear as crystal, yielding great variety of fish.
Mussels and clams they have all the year long, which being the
meanest of God's blessings here, and such as these people fat
their hogs with at a low water, if ours upon any extremity did

enjoy in the South Colony they would never complain of famine or want, although they wanted bread. Not but that by God's blessing the South Colony using their industry may in few years attain to that plenty, pleasure, and strength as that they shall not need much to envy or fear the proudest nations in Europe.

Oysters there are none, but at Massachusetts some twenty miles to the north of this place there are such huge ones by savages' report as I am loath to tell. For ordinary ones, of which there be many, they make to be as broad as a bushel, but one among the rest they compared to the great cabin in the *Discovery,* and being sober and well-advised persons, grew very angry when they were laughed at or not believed! I would have had Captain Jones to have tried out the truth of this report; and what was the reason?

"If," said I, "the oysters be so great and have any pearls in them, then must the pearls be answerable in greatness to the oysters, and proving round and orient also, would far exceed all other jewels in the world! Yea, what strange and precious things might be found in so rare a creature!"

But his employing his pinnace in discovery, his graving* of the ship, his haste away about other occasions and business, would not permit Captain Jones to do that which often since he wished he could have done.

DOVES HIDE THE SUN

John Clayton

THEIR turtledoves are of a duskish blue color, much less than our common pigeon; the whole train is longer much than the tails of our pigeons, the middle feather being the longest. There is the strangest story of a vast number of these pigeons that come in a flock a few years before I came thither. They say they came through New England, New York, and Virginia, and were so prodigious in number as to darken the sky for several hours in the place over which they flew, and brake massive boughs

---

* Cleaning a ship's bottom and sides and surfacing it with pitch.

where they light; and many like things which I have had asserted to me by many eyewitnesses of credit, so that to me it was without doubt, the relators being very sober persons, and all agreeing in a story. Nothing of the like ever happened since, nor did I ever see past ten in a flock together that I remember. I am not fond of such stories, and had suppressed the relating of it but that I have heard the same from very many.

FLORA AND FAUNA

WONDERFUL ANTIPATHIES *

Increase Mather

THERE are wonders in the works of creation as well as providence, the reason whereof the most knowing amongst mortals are not able to comprehend. "Dost thou know the balancings of the clouds, the wondrous works of him who is perfect in knowledge?" I have not yet seen any who give a satisfactory reason of those strange fountains in New Spain which ebb and flow with the sea, though far from it, and which fall in rainy weather and rise in dry; or concerning that pit near St. Bartholomew's, into which if one cast a stone, though ever so small, it makes a noise as great and terrible as a clap of thunder. It is no difficult thing to produce a world of instances concerning which the usual answer is, an occult quality is the cause of this strange operation, which is only a fig leaf whereby our common philosophers seek to hide their own ignorance.

Nor may we (with Erastus) deny that there are marvelous sympathies and antipathies in the nature of things. We know that the horse does abominate the camel; the mighty elephant is afraid of a mouse; and they say that the lion, who scorneth to turn his back upon the stoutest animal, will tremble at the crowing of the cock. Some men also have strange antipathies in their natures against that sort of food which others love and live upon. I have read of one that could not endure to eat either bread or flesh; of another that fell into a swooning fit at the

---

* The concept of "remarkables in nature" dating back to Genesis, as distinct from the remarkable providences currently produced by God, is here illustrated. It helps explain the readiness of the settlers to credit zoological and botanical marvels in the New World.

smell of a rose; others would do the like at the smell of vinegar, or at the sight of an eel or a frog. There was a man that if he did hear the sound of a bell, he would immediately die away; another if he did happen to hear anyone sweeping a room, an inexpressible horror would seize upon him; another if he heard one whetting a knife, his gums would fall a-bleeding; another was not able to behold a knife that had a sharp point without being in a strange agony. Quercetus speaketh of one that died as he was sitting at the table, only because an apple was brought into his sight. There are some who, if a cat accidentally comes into the room, though they neither see it nor are told of it, will presently be in a sweat, and ready to die away. There was lately one living in Stow Market that, whenever it thundered, would fall into a violent vomiting, and so continue until the thunderstorm was over. A woman had such an antipathy against cheese that if she did but eat a piece of bread cut with a knife which a little before had cut cheese, it would cause a delirium; yet the same woman when she was with child delighted in no meat so much as in cheese. There was lately (I know not but that he may be living still) a man that, if pork or anything made of swine's flesh were brought into the room, would fall into a convulsive Sardonian laughter, nor can he for his heart leave as long as that object is before him, so that if it should not be removed, he would certainly laugh himself to death.

It is evident that the peculiar antipathies of some persons are caused by the imaginations of their parents. There was one that would fall into a syncope if either a calf's head or a cabbage were brought near him. There were *naevi materni* upon the hypochondria of this person; on his right side there was the form of a calf's head, on his left side a cabbage imprinted there by the imagination of his loving mother. Most wonderful is that which Libavius and others report, concerning a man that would be surprised with a lipothymy [fainting] at the sight of his own son—nay, upon his approaching near unto him, though he saw him not. For which some assigned this reason, that the mother when she was with child used to feed upon such meats as were abominable to the father; but others said that the midwife who brought him into the world was a witch.

BEARS

William Wood

FOR bears they be common, being a great black kind of bear, which be most fierce in strawberry time, when they have young ones. At this time likewise they will go upright like a man and climb trees, and swim to the islands; which, if the Indians see, there will be more sportful bearbaiting than Paris Garden can afford. For seeing the bears take water, an Indian will leap after him, where they go to water cuffs for bloody noses and scratched sides; in the end the man gets the victory, riding the bear over the watery plain till he can bear him no longer.

In the winter they take themselves to the clefts of rocks and thick swamps, to shelter them from the cold; and food being scant in those cold and hard times, they live only by sleeping and sucking their paws, which keepeth them as fat as they are in summer. There would be more of them if it were not for the wolves, which devour them; a kennel of those ravening renegadoes, setting on a poor single bear, will tear him as a dog will tear a kid. It would be a good change if the country had for every wolf a bear, upon the condition all the wolves were banished; so should the inhabitants be not only rid of their greatest annoyance but furnished with more store of provisions, bears being accounted very good meat, esteemed of all men above venison. Again they never prey upon the English cattle, or offer to assault the person of any man, unless being vexed with a shot and a man run upon them before they be dead, in which case they will stand in their own defense, as may appear by this instance.

Two men going a-fowling appointed at evening to meet at a certain pond side, to share equally and to return home. One of these gunners having killed a seal or sea calf brought it to the side of the pond where he was to meet his comrade, afterwards returning to the seaside for more gain; and having loaded himself with more geese and ducks he repaired to the pond, where he saw a great bear feeding on his seal. This caused him to throw down his load and give the bear a salute, which though it was but with goose shot, yet tumbled him over and over. Thereupon the man, supposing him to be in a manner dead, ran and beat him with the hand of his gun. The bear, perceiving him to be such a coward to strike him when he was down, scrambled up, standing at defiance with him, scratching his legs, tearing his clothes and face. He stood it out till his six-foot gun was broken in the middle, then being deprived of his weapon he ran up to the shoulders into the pond, where he remained till the bear was gone and his mate come in, who accompanied him home.

WOLVES

John Josselyn

THE wolf seeketh his mate and goes a-clicketing at the same season with foxes, and bring forth their whelps as they do, but their kennels are under thick bushes by great trees in remote places by the swamps. He is to be hunted as the fox from Holy-Rood Day till the Annunciation. They commonly go in routs—a rout of wolves is twelve or more—sometimes by couples.

In 1664 we found a wolf asleep in a small dry swamp under an oak. A great mastiff which we had with us seized upon him and held him till we had put a rope about his neck, by which we brought him home, and tying of him to a stake we baited him with smaller dogs, and had excellent sport; but his hinder leg being broken, they knocked out his brains.

Some time before this we had an excellent course after a single wolf upon the hard sands by the seaside at low water for a mile or two. At last we lost our dogs, it being (as the Lancashire people phrase it) twilight, that is, almost dark, and went beyond them, for a mastiff bitch had seized upon the wolf being gotten into the sea, and there held him till one went in and led him out, the bitch keeping her hold till they had tied his legs, and so carried him home like a calf upon a staff between two men.

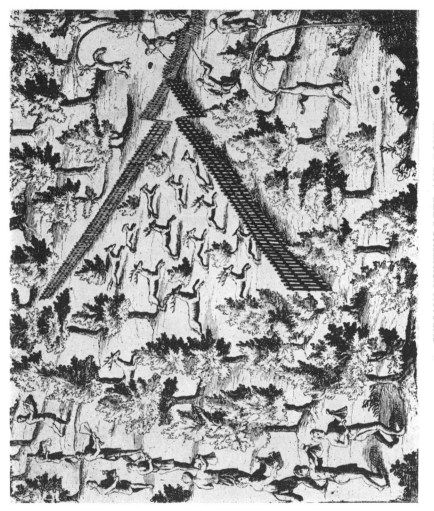

5. INDIANS HUNTING DEER AND FOXES

Sieur de Champlain, *Voyages et Descouvertes faites en La Nouvelle France;* Paris, 1619

Being brought into the house, they unbound him and set him upon his legs, he not offering in the least to bite or so much as to show his teeth, but clapping his stern betwixt his legs and leering towards the door would willingly have had his liberty. But they served him as they did the other, knocked his brains out, for our dogs were not then in a condition to bait him.

Their eyes shine by night as a lantern. The fangs of a wolf hung about children's necks keep them from frightening, and are very good to rub their gums with when they are breeding of teeth. The gall of a wolf is sovereign for swelling of the sinews. The fiants or dung of a wolf drunk with white wine helpeth the colic.

THE SKUNK

John Josselyn

THE skunk is almost as big as a raccoon, perfect black and white or piebald, with a bush-tail like a fox, an offensive carrion. The urine of this creature is of so strong a scent that if it light upon anything, there is no abiding of it; it will make a man smell, though he were of Alexander's complexion; and so sharp, if he do but whisk his bush which he pisseth upon in the face of a dog hunting of him, and that any of it light in his eyes, it will make him almost mad with the smart thereof.

THE PORCUPINE

John Josselyn

THE porcupine, in some parts of the country eastward towards the French, are as big as an ordinary mongrel cur; a very angry creature, and dangerous, shooting a whole shower of quills when aroused at their enemies: which are of that nature that, wherever they stick in the flesh, they will work through in a short time, if not prevented by pulling of them out. The Indians make use of their quills, which are hardly a handful long, to adorn the edges of their birchen dishes, and weave curious bags or pouches (dyeing some of them red, others yellow and blue) in works like Turkish work.

TURTLES

Thomas Ashe

THE tortoise, more commonly called by our West Indians the turtle, are of three sorts: the hawksbill, whose shell is that which we call the turtle or tortoise shell; the green turtle, whose shell being thin is little regarded, but its flesh is more esteemed than the hawksbill tortoise; the loggerhead turtle or tortoise, which has neither good shell or flesh, so is little minded or regarded. They are a sort of creature which live both on land and water, in the day usually keeping the sea, swimming on the surface of the water, in fair weather delighting to expose themselves to the sun, oftentimes falling asleep, lying, as I have seen several times, without any motion on the waters, till disturbed by the approach of some ship or boat, when being quick of hearing they dive away. In the night they often come ashore to feed and lay their eggs in the sand, which once covered they leave to the influence of the sun. In due time the sun produces her young ones, which dig their passage out of the sand and immediately make their way towards the water.

At the season when they most usually come ashore, which is in April, May, and June, the seamen or turtlers at some convenient distance watch their opportunity, getting between them and the sea, and turn them on their backs, from whence they are unable ever to rise, by which means the seamen or turtlers sometimes turn forty or fifty in a night, some of two, three, four hundred weight. If they are far distant from the harbor or market to which they design to bring them, they kill the turtles, cutting them to pieces, which salted they barrel. This is the way of killing at the Cayman's, an island lying to the leeward of Jamaica.

Turtle barreled and salted, if well conditioned, is worth from eighteen to twenty-five shillings the barrel. If near their market or harbor they bring them in sloops alive, and afterwards keep them in crawls, which is a particular place of salt water of depth and room for them to swim in, pallisadoed or staked in round above the water's surface, where upon occasion they take them out and kill them, and cutting them to pieces sell their flesh for twopence or threepence the pound.

The belly, which they call the callope of the turtle, peppered and salted, or roasted and baked, is an excellent dish, much esteemed by our nation in the West Indies. The rest of the flesh boiled makes as good and nourishing broth as the best capon in England, especially if some of the eggs are mixed with it. These are some white and others of a yellow or golden color, in largeness not exceeding a walnut, wrapped in a thin skin or membrane, sweet in taste, nourishing and wholesome, and of this property, that they never grow hard by boiling. The liver is black; it freely opens and purges the body; if little of it be eaten, it dyes the excrement a deep black color. The fat in color inclines to a sea green; in taste it is sweet and luscious, equaling if not surpassing the best marrow; if freely eaten it deeply stains the urine of its color; it is of a very penetrating, piercing quality, highly commended in strains and aches. Of it the turtlers oftentimes make an oil, which in lamps burns much brighter and sweeter than common lamp or train oil. In general, the flesh is commended for a good antiscorbutis and an anti-venereal diet; many in the former, and some that have been far gone in consumptions, with the constant use alone of this diet have been thoroughly recovered and cured in three or four months.

The turtle hath three hearts, by thin pellicles only separated, which has caused some to philosophize on its amphibious nature, alluding to those participating and assimulating qualities which it has to the rest of the universe, it swimming like a fish, laying eggs like a fowl, and feeding on grass like an ox. This I am assured of, that after it is cut to pieces, it retains a sensation of life three times longer than any known creature in the creation. Before they kill them they are laid on their backs, where hopeless of relief, as if sensible of their future condition, for some hours they mourn out their funerals, the tears plenti-fully flowing from their eyes, accompanied with passionate sobs and sighs, in my judgment nothing more like than such who are surrounded and overwhelmed with troubles, cares, and griefs, which raises in strangers both pity and compassion.

Completely six hours after the butcher has cut them into pieces and mangled their bodies, I have seen the callope when going to be seasoned, with pieces of their flesh ready to be cut into steaks, vehemently contract with great reluctancy and rise against the knife, with sometimes the whole mass of flesh in a visible tremulation and concussion. To him who first sees it, it seems strange and admirable.

THE ALLIGATOR

John Lawson

THE alligator is the same as the crocodile, and differs only in name. They frequent the sides of rivers, in the banks of which they make their dwellings a great way underground, the hole or mouth of their dens lying commonly two feet under water, after which it rises till it be considerably above the surface thereof. Here it is that this amphibious monster dwells all the winter, sleeping away his time till the spring appears, when he comes from his cave and daily swims up and down the streams. He always breeds in some fresh stream or clear fountain of water, yet seeks his prey in the broad salt waters that are brackish, not on the seaside, where I never met with any. He never devours men in Carolina, but uses all ways to avoid them, yet he kills swine and dogs, the former as they come to feed in the marshes, the others as they swim over the creeks and waters. They are very mischievous to the weirs made for taking fish, into which they come to prey on the fish that are caught in the weir, from whence they cannot readily extricate themselves, and so break the weir in pieces, being a very strong creature. This animal in these parts sometimes exceeds seventeen foot long. It is impossible to kill them with a gun, unless you chance to hit them about the eyes, which is a much softer place than the rest of their impenetrable armor. They roar and make a hideous noise against bad weather, and before they come out of their dens in the spring.

I was pretty much frightened with one of these once, which happened thus. I had built a house about half a mile from an

Indian town on the fork of Neuse River, where I dwelt by myself, excepting a young Indian fellow and a bulldog that I had along with me. I had not then been so long a sojourner in America as to be thoroughly acquainted with this creature. One of them had got his nest directly under my house, which stood on pretty high land and by a creekside, in whose banks his entering place was, his den reaching the ground directly on which my house stood. I was sitting alone by the fireside (about nine o'clock at night, sometime in March), the Indian fellow being gone to the town to see his relations, so that there was nobody in the house but myself and my dog; when all of a sudden, this ill-favored neighbor of mine set up such a roaring that he made the house shake about my ears, and so continued like a bittern (but a hundred times louder if possible) for four or five times. The dog stared as if he was frightened out of his senses; nor indeed could I imagine what it was, having never heard one of them before. Immediately again I had another lesson; and so a third. Being at that time amongst none but savages, I began to suspect they were working some piece of conjuration under my house, to get away my goods; not but that at another time I have as little faith in their, or any others, working miracles by diabolical means as any person living. At last my man came in, to whom when I had told the story, he laughed at me and presently undeceived me, by telling me what it was that made that noise.

THE RATTLESNAKE

John Clayton

THE rattlesnake is so called from certain rattles at the end of the tail. These rattles seem like so many perished joints, being a dry husk over certain joints, and the common opinion is that there are as many rattles or joints as the snake is years old. I killed four or five, and they had each eleven, twelve, or thirteen joints, but the young ones have no rattles of a year or two; they may be known notwithstanding, being very regular diced or checkered, black and gray on the backs. The old shake and shiver these rattles with wonderful nimbleness when they are any ways disturbed; their bite is very deadly, yet not always of the same force but more or less mortal accordingly as the snake is in force or vigor, and therefore in June or July much worse and more mortal than in March and April. This snake is a very majestic sort of creature, and will scarce meddle with anything unless provoked; but if anything offend it, it makes directly at them.

I was told a pleasant story of an old gentleman, Colonel Clayborn as I remember was his name, the same that sent the rattlesnakes to the Royal Society some years since. He had an odd fancy of keeping some of these snakes always in barrels in the house, and one time an Indian, pretending he could charm them so as to take them by the neck in his hand without biting of him, the old gentleman caused a rattlesnake to be brought forth. The Indian began his charm with a little wand, whisking it round and round the rattlesnake's head, bringing it by degrees nigher and nigher, and at length flung the switch away and whisked his hand about in like manner, bringing his hand nigher still and nigher, by taking less circles; when the old gentleman immediately hit the snake with his crutch, and the snake snapped the Indian by the hand and bit him very sharply betwixt the fingers, which put his charm to an end, and he roared out. But he stretched his arm out as high as he could, calling for a string, wherewith he bound his arm as hard as possibly he could and clapped a hot burning coal thereon and singed it stoutly, whereby he was cured, but looked pale a long while after. And I believe this truly one of the best ways in the world of curing the bite either of viper or mad dog.

THE HORN SNAKE

John Lawson

OF THE horn snakes, I never saw but two that I remember. They are like the rattlesnake in color, but rather lighter. They hiss exactly like a goose when anything approaches them. They strike at their enemy with their tail (and kill whatsoever they wound with it), which is armed at the end with a horny substance, like a cock's spur. This is their weapon. I have heard it credibly reported, by those who said they were eyewitnesses, that a small locust tree, about the thickness of a man's arm, being struck by one of these snakes at ten o'clock in the morning, then verdant and flourishing, at four in the afternoon was dead, and the leaves red and withered.

THE BAT

John Lawson

THE bat or reremouse is the same as in England. The Indian children are much addicted to eat dirt, and so are some of the Christians. But roast a bat on a skewer, then pull the skin off, and make the child that eats dirt eat the roasted reremouse and he will never eat dirt again. This is held as an infallible remedy. I have put this amongst the beasts as partaking of both natures, of the bird and mouse kind.

EAGLES

Arnoldus Montanus

THE air of New Netherlands abounds with all sorts of birds. Besides falcon, sparrow hawks, fish hawks, and other birds of prey, there are here numbers of eagles differing from each other; for some are grayish, others browner, except the head, neck, tail, and striking feathers, which are of a snow-white color. All have a strong body, bones without marrow, claws as long as a man's finger, the bill strong and crooked, the brains dry, the eyes small and hollow, the feathers hard, the right foot bigger than the left (both ill-looking), the blood gross, the excrements highly offensive.

They build their nests in old groves where the ground is clear of underwood; also beside water, as they feed on fish and devour all sorts of fowls, and even rabbits, hares, tortoises, and other four-footed game that sleep in the open air. Yea, when

6. FLORA AND FAUNA

John Lawson, *A New Voyage to Carolina*; London, 1709

ahungered they attack each other. Some eagles strike their prey at midday, others at the rising of the sun. They fall like lightning on the game they pursue, as the blood of animals serves them for drink. They are exceedingly lascivious, so that they go together more than thirty times a day, not only with their own kind, but even with the female hawks and she-wolves.

They hatch out the large eggs in thirty and the small in twenty days. They usually breed two to three young, whose eyes they turn toward the sun's rays. If these regard the light of heaven without blinking they bring them up, otherwise those that cannot stand such a test are driven from the nest. The young as soon as they begin to fly are taken up into the air, and, left there to themselves, are sustained by the old birds, who drive them away whenever they are fit to strike at game.

Their sharp-sightedness is most remarkable, for lifted up in the clouds far beyond the eye of man, they perceive the smallest fish in the river and a skulking hare in the stubble. Their breath stinks badly, wherefore the carcasses on which they feed rot rapidly. Though lascivious, they are long-lived; they die mostly of hunger, as the bill becomes by age so crooked that they cannot open anything. Whereupon they finally fly to the highest regions towards the sun, tumble down into the coldest stream, pluck out their feathers, clammy with sweat, and thus breathe their last.

TOBACCO

John Josselyn

TOBACCO or tabacca is so called from Tabaco or Tabago, one of the Caribbean Islands about fifty English miles from Trinidad. The right name, according to Monardus, is picielte, but others will petum, or nicotian from Nicot, a Portingal, to whom it was presented for a rarity in 1559 by one that brought it from Florida. Great contest there is about the time when it was first brought into England. Some will have Sir John Hawkins the first, others Sir Francis Drake's mariners. Others again say that one Mr. Lane, employed by Sir Walter Raleigh, brought it first into England; all conclude that Sir Walter Raleigh brought it first in use.

It is observed that no one kind of foreign commodity yieldeth greater advantage to the public than tobacco. It is generally made the compliment of our entertainments, and hath made more slaves than Mahomet. There is three sorts of it merchantable: the first horse tobacco, having a broad long leaf piked at the end; the second, round-pointed tobacco; third, sweet-scented tobacco. These are made up into cane, leaf, or ball. There is little of it planted in New England, neither have they learned the right way of curing of it. It is sown in April upon a bed of rich mold sifted. They make a bed about three yards long or more according to the ground they intend to plant, and a yard and a half over; this they tread down hard, then they sow their seed upon it as thick as may be, and sift fine earth upon it, then tread it down again as hard as possible they can. When it hath gotten four or six leaves, they remove it into the planting ground; when it begins to bud towards flowering, they crop off the top, for the flower draws away the strength of the leaf. For the rest I refer you to the planter, being not willing to discover their mysteries. The Indians in New England use a small round-leafed tobacco, called, by them or the fishermen, poke. It is odious to the English.

The virtues of tobacco are these. It helps digestion, the gout, the toothache, prevents infection by scents; it heats the cold, and cools them that sweat, feedeth the hungry, spent spirits restoreth, purgeth the stomach, killeth nits and lice; the juice of the green leaf healeth green wounds, although poisoned; the syrup for many diseases, the smoke for the phthisic, cough of the lungs, distillations of rheum, and all diseases of a cold and moist cause; good for all bodies cold and moist taken upon an empty stomach; taken upon a full stomach it precipitates digestion. Immoderately taken it drieth the body, inflameth the blood, hurteth the brain, weakens the eyes and the sinews.

THE JAMESTOWN WEED

Robert Beverley

THE Jamestown Weed (which resembles the thorny apple of Peru, and I take to be the plant so called) is supposed to be one of the greatest coolers in the world. This being an early plant was gathered very young for a boiled salad by some of the soldiers sent thither to pacify the troubles of Bacon, and some of them eat plentifully of it, the effect of which was a very pleasant comedy, for they turned natural fools upon it for several days. One would blow up a feather in the air; another would dart straws at it with much fury; and another stark naked was sitting up in a corner like a monkey grinning and making mows at them; a fourth would fondly kiss and paw his companions and sneer in their faces, with a countenance more antic than any in a Dutch droll.

In this frantic condition they were confined, lest they should in their folly destroy themselves, though it was observed that all their actions were full of innocence and good nature. Indeed, they were not very cleanly, for they would have wallowed in their own excrements, if they had not been prevented. A thousand such simple tricks they played, and after eleven days returned to themselves again, not remembering anything that had passed.

LOVE FLOWERS

Robert Beverley

OF spontaneous flowers they have an unknown variety: the finest crown imperial in the world; the cardinal flower, so much extolled for its scarlet color, which is almost in every branch; the moccasin flower, and a thousand others not yet known to English herbalists. Almost all the year round the levels and vales are beautified with flowers of one kind or other, which make their woods as fragrant as a garden. From these materials their wild bees make vast quantities of honey, but their magazines are very often rifled by bears, raccoons, and suchlike liquorish vermin.

About two years ago, walking out to take the air, I found a little without my pasture fence a flower as big as a tulip, and upon a stalk resembling the stalk of a tulip. The flower was of a flesh color, having a down upon one end while the other was plain. The form of it resembled the pudenda of a man and woman lovingly joined in one. Not long after I had discovered this rarity, and while it was still in bloom, I drew a grave gentleman about an hundred yards out of his way to see this curiosity, not telling him anything more than that it was a rarity, and such, perhaps, as he had never seen nor heard of. When we arrived at the place I gathered one of them and put it into his hand, which he had no sooner cast his eye upon but he threw it away with indignation, as being ashamed of this waggery of nature. It was impossible to persuade him to touch it again, or so much as to squint towards so immodest a representation. Neither would I presume to mention such an indecency, but that I thought it unpardonable to omit a production so extraordinary.

THE TULIP TREE

John Lawson

THE tulip trees, which are by the planters called poplars, as nearest approaching that wood in grain, grow to a prodigious bigness, some of them having been found one and twenty foot in circumference. I have been informed of a tulip tree that was ten foot in diameter, and another wherein a lusty man had his bed and household furniture, and lived in it till his labor got him a more fashionable mansion. He afterwards became a noted man in his country for wealth and conduct.

THE CYPRESS

John Lawson

CYPRESS is not an evergreen with us, and is therefore called the bald cypress, because the leaves during the winter season turn red, not recovering their verdure till the spring. These trees are the largest for height and thickness that we have in this part of the world, some of them holding thirty-six foot in circumference. Upon incision they yield a sweet-smelling grain, though not in great quantities; and the nuts which these trees bear plentifully yield a most odoriferous balsam that infallibly cures all new and green wounds, which the inhabitants are well acquainted withal. Of these great trees the periaugers and canoes are scooped and made, which sort of vessel are chiefly to pass over the rivers, creeks, and bays, and to transport goods and lumber from one river to another. Some are so large as to carry thirty barrels, though of one entire piece of timber. Others that are split down the bottom and a piece added thereto will carry eighty or a hundred. Several have gone out of our inlets on the ocean to Virginia, laden with pork and other produce of the country.

Of these trees curious boats for pleasure may be made, and other necessary craft. Some years ago a foolish man in Albemarle and his son had got one of these canoes decked. She held, as I take it, sixteen barrels. He brought her to the collectors to be cleared for Barbados, but the officer took him for a man that had lost his senses, and argued the danger and impossibility of performing such a voyage in a hollow tree. The fellow would hearken to no advice of that kind, till the gentleman told him if he did not value his own life, he valued his reputation and honesty, and so flatly refused clearing him. Upon which the canoe was sold and, I think, remains in being still.

THE ANCIENT
NEW ENGLAND STANDING DISH

John Josselyn

POMPIONS [pumpkins] there be of several kinds, some proper to the country. They are drier than our English pompions, and better tasted. You may eat them green. But the housewives' manner is to slice them when ripe and cut them into dice, and so fill a pot with them of two or three gallons, and stew them upon a gentle fire a whole day; as they sink they fill again with fresh pompions, not putting any liquor to them, and when it is stewed enough, it will look like baked apples. This they dish, putting butter to it and a little vinegar (with some spice, as ginger, et cetera), which makes it tart, like an apple, and so sew it up, to be eaten with fish or flesh. It provokes urine extremely, and is very windy.

THE POWER OF RUM

John Josselyn

I SHALL conclude this section with a strange cure effected upon a drummer's wife, much afflicted with a wolf in her breast. The poor woman lived with her husband at a town called by the Indians Casco, but by the English Falmouth, where for some time she assuaged the pain of her sore by bathing it with strong malt beer, which it would suck in greedily, as if some living creature. When she could come by no more beer (for it was brought from Boston, along the coasts, by merchants), she made use of rum—a strong water drawn from sugar canes—with which it was lulled asleep. At last, to be rid of it altogether, she put a quantity of arsenic to the rum, and, bathing of it as formerly, she utterly destroyed it and cured herself. But her kind husband, who sucked out the poison as the sore was healing, lost all his teeth, but without further danger or inconvenience.

UGLY RUMORS

Christopher Levett

THEY say the country is good for nothing but to starve so many people as come in it.

It is granted that some have been starved to death, and others have hardly escaped, but where was the fault, in the country or in themselves? That the country is as I have said, I can bring one hundred men to justify it; but if men be neither industrious nor provident, they may starve in the best place of the world.

About two years since one Mr. Weston sent over about fifty persons to plant, with little provision. When they came there, they neither applied themselves to planting of corn nor taking of fish more than for their present use, but went about to build castles in the air and making forts, neglecting the plentiful time of fishing. When winter came their forts would not keep out hunger, and they, having no provision beforehand and wanting both powder and shot to kill deer and fowl, many were starved to death, and the rest hardly escaped. There are four of his men which escaped now at my plantation, who have related unto me the whole business.

Again, this last year there went over divers at one time and to one place with too little provision; some of them are dead, yet I cannot hear of any that were merely starved, except one whose name was Chapman, a Londoner, and whether he was starved or no is uncertain; but if he were, God's just judgment did appear.

For this man brought at the least eighty pounds' worth of provision, and no more but himself and two servants, which was sufficient for at the least eighteen months, if it had been well used. And yet in five months after his arrival in New England he died miserably.

Let me tell you a strange thing of this man. (I have it but by relation from one of his companions.) He paid for his passage, and his men's, and provision, so that he needed not to have spent anything until his arrival in New England, yet would he at Plymouth (where the ship stayed too long for him and others) spend seven or eight pound a week in wine, tobacco, and whores, and for the maintaining of this expense he daily fetched his provision from aboard and sold it at a low rate. And when they were at sea, his tobacco being spent, he gave usually sixpence for a pipe; he gave also a suit of clothes, valued to be worth fifty shillings, for so much tobacco as was not worth half a crown. Nay, at last, as his comrade told me, he was glad to become servant to one of his servants. Then his master told him that if he would work he would allow him one biscuit cake a day, if not he should have but half a cake. He made choice of half a cake, without work; and so a base, lazy fellow made a lamentable end.

Where was the fault now, in the man or in the country?

Council for Virginia

UNTO idleness you may join treasons, wrought by those un-hallowed creatures that forsook the colony and exposed their desolate brethren to extreme misery. You shall know that twenty-eight or thirty of the company were appointed (in the ship called the *Swallow*) to truck for corn with the Indians, and having obtained a great quantity by trading, the most seditious of them conspired together, persuaded some and enforced others, to this barbarous project. They stole away the ship, they made a league amongst themselves to be professed pirates, with dreams of mountains of gold and happy robberies. Thus at one instant they wronged the hopes and subverted the cares of the colony, who, depending upon their return, foreslowed to look out for further provision. They created the Indians our implacable enemies by some violence they had offered; they carried away the best ship (which should have been a refuge in extremities); they weakened our forces by subtraction of their arms and succors.

These are that scum of men that, failing in their piracy, that being pinched with famine and penury, after their wild roving upon the sea, when all their lawless hopes failed, some decided to remain with other pirates they met upon the sea, the others resolved to return for England, and bound themselves by mutual oath to agree all in one report, to discredit the land, to deplore the famine, and to protest that this their coming away proceeded from desperate necessity. These are they that roared out the tragical history of the man eating of his dead wife in Virginia, when the master of this ship willingly confessed before forty witnesses that at their coming away, they left three months victuals and all the cattle living in the fort. Sometimes they reported that they saw this horrible action, sometimes that Captain Davies said so, sometimes that one Beadle the lieutenant of Captain Davies did relate it, varying this report into diversity of false colors, which hold no likeness and proportion. But to clear all doubts, Sir Thomas Gates thus relateth the tragedy.

"There was one of the company who mortally hated his wife and therefore secretly killed her, then cut her in pieces and hid her in divers parts of his house. When the woman was missing, the man was suspected, his house searched, and parts of her mangled body were discovered. To excuse himself he said that his wife died, that he hid her to satisfy his hunger, and that he fed daily upon her. Upon this, his house was again searched, where they found a good quantity of meal, oatmeal, beans, and peas. He thereupon was arraigned, confessed the murder, and was burned for his horrible villainy."

Robert Beverley

THAT which makes this country most unfortunate is that it must submit to receive its character from the mouths not only of unfit but very unequal judges, for all its reproaches happen after this manner.

Many of the merchants and others that go thither from England make no distinction between a cold and a hot country, but wisely go sweltering about in their thick clothes all the summer, because they used to do so in their northern climate, and then unfairly complain of the heat of the country. They greedily surfeit with their delicious fruits, and are guilty of great intemperance through the exceeding generosity of the inhabitants, by which means they fall sick, and then unjustly complain of the unhealthiness of the country. In the next place, the sailors for want of towns there are put to the hardship of rolling most of the tobacco a mile or more to the waterside; this splinters their hands sometimes, and provokes them to curse the country. Such exercise, and a bright sun, makes them hot, and then they imprudently fall to drinking cold water, or perhaps new cider, which in its season they find at every planter's house. Or else they greedily devour all the green fruit and unripe trash they can meet with, and so fall into fluxes, fevers, and the bellyache; and then, to spare their own indiscretion, they in their tarpaulin language cry, "God d . . . the country."

This is the true state of the case, as to the complaints of its being sickly, for by the most impartial observation I can make, if people will be persuaded to be temperate and take due care of themselves, I believe it is as healthy a country as any under heaven. But the extraordinary pleasantness of the weather, and the goodness of the fruit, lead people into many temptations. The clearness and brightness of the sky add new vigor to their spirits, and perfectly remove all splenetic and sullen thoughts. Here they enjoy all the benefits of a warm sun, and by their shady groves are protected from its inconvenience. Here all their senses are entertained with an endless succession of native pleasures. Their eyes are ravished with the beauties of naked nature. Their ears are serenaded with the perpetual murmur of brooks, and the thorough bass which the wind plays when it wantons through the trees; the merry birds too join their pleasing notes to this rural concert, especially the mock-birds, who love society so well that whenever they see mankind they will perch upon a twig very near them and sing the sweetest wild airs in the world. (But what is most remarkable in these melodious animals, they will frequently fly at small distances before a traveler, warbling out their notes several miles on end, and by their music make a man forget the fatigues of his journey.) Their taste is regaled with the most delicious fruits, which without art they have in great variety and perfection. And then their smell is refreshed with an eternal fragrancy of flowers and sweets, with which nature perfumes and adorns the woods almost the whole year round.

Have you pleasure in a garden? All things thrive in it most

surprisingly; you can't walk by a bed of flowers but, besides the entertainment of their beauty, your eyes will be saluted with the charming colors of the hummingbird, which revels among the flowers and licks off the dew and honey from their tender leaves, on which it only feeds. Its size is not half so large as an English wren, and its color is a glorious shining mixture of scarlet, green, and gold. Colonel Byrd, in his garden, which is the finest in that country, has a summerhouse set round with the Indian honeysuckle, which all the summer is continually full of sweet flowers, in which these birds delight exceedingly. Upon these flowers I have seen ten or a dozen of these beautiful creatures together, which sported about me so familiarly that with their little wings they often fanned my face.

On the other side, all the annoyances and inconveniences of the country may fairly be summed up under these three heads, thunder, heat, and troublesome vermin.

I confess, in the hottest part of summer they have sometimes very loud and surprising thunder, but rarely any damage happens by it. On the contrary, it is of such advantage to the cooling and refining of the air that it is oftener wished for than feared. But they have no earthquakes, which the Caribbean Islands are so much troubled with.

Their heat is very seldom troublesome, and then only by the accident of a perfect calm, which happens perhaps two or three times in a year and lasts but a few hours at a time; and even that inconvenience is made easy by cool shades, by open airy rooms, summerhouses, arbors, and grottoes. But the spring and fall afford as pleasant weather as Mahomet promised in his paradise.

All the troublesome vermin that ever I heard anybody complain of are either frogs, snakes, mosquitoes, chinches, seedticks, or redworms, by some called potato lice. Of all which I shall give an account of in their order.

Some people have been so ill informed as to say that Virginia is full of toads, though there never yet was seen one toad in it. The marshes, fens, and watery grounds are indeed full of harmless frogs, which do no hurt except by the noise of their croaking notes, but in the upper parts of the country, where the land is high and dry, they are very scarce. In the swamps and running streams they have frogs of an incredible bigness, which are called bullfrogs, from the roaring they make. Last year I found one of these near a stream of fresh water, of so prodigious a magnitude that when I extended its legs I found the distance betwixt them to be seventeen inches and a half. I am confident six Frenchmen might have made a comfortable meal of its carcass.

Some people in England are startled at the very name of the rattlesnake, and fancy every corner of that province so much pestered with them that a man goes in constant danger of his life that walks abroad in the woods. But this is as gross a mistake as most of the other ill reports of this country. For in the first place this snake is very rarely seen, and when that happens, it never does the least mischief, unless you offer to disturb it and thereby provoke it to bite in its own defense. But it never fails to give you fair warning by making a noise with its rattle, which may be heard at a convenient distance. For my own part, I have traveled the country as much as any man in it of my age, by night and by day, above the inhabitants as well as among them; and yet I never did see a rattlesnake alive and at liberty in all my life. I have seen them indeed after they have been killed, or pent up in boxes to be sent to England. The bite of this viper, without some immediate application, is certainly death; but remedies are so well known that none of their servants are ignorant of them. I never knew any that had been hurt by these, or any other of their snakes, although I have a general knowledge all over the country, and have been in every part of it.

They have several other snakes which are seen more frequently and have very little or no hurt in them, viz., such as they call black snakes, water snakes, and corn snakes. The black viper snake and the copper-bellied snake are said to be as venomous as the rattlesnakes, but they also are as seldom seen. These three poisonous snakes bring forth their young alive, whereas the other three sorts lay eggs, which are hatched afterwards; and that is the distinction they make, esteeming only those to be venomous which are viviparous. They have likewise the horn snake, so called from a sharp horn it carries in its tail, with which it assaults anything that offends it, with that force, that it will strike its tail into the butt end of a musket, from whence it is not able to disengage itself.

All sorts of snakes will charm both birds and squirrels, and the Indians pretend to charm them. Several persons have seen squirrels run down a tree directly into a snake's mouth; they have likewise seen birds fluttering up and down and chattering at these snakes, till at last they have dropped down just before them.

Some few years ago, I was bear hunting in the woods above the inhabitants, and having straggled from my companions, I was entertained at my return with the relation of a pleasant rencounter between a dog and rattlesnake about a squirrel. The snake had got the head and shoulders of the squirrel into his mouth, which being something too large for his throat, it took him up some time to moisten the fur of the squirrel with his spawl, to make it slip down. The dog took this advantage, seized the hinder parts of the squirrel, and tugged with all his might. The snake on the other side would not let go his hold for a long time, till at last, fearing he might be bruised by the dog's running away with him, he gave up his prey to the enemy, which he ate, and we ate the snake, which was dainty food.

Louis Hennepin

SOME days after, Nikanape, brother to Chessagouasse, the most considerable chief of the Illinois, who was then absent, invited us to a great feast; and before we sat down to eat made a long speech, very different from what the other captains had told us upon our arrival. He said that he had invited us not so much to give us a treat as to endeavor to dissuade us from the resolution we had taken, to go down to the sea by the great river Mississippi. He added that several had perished, having ventured upon the same enterprise, the banks of that river being inhabited by barbarous and bloody nations whom we should be unable to resist, notwithstanding our valor and the goodness of our arms; that that river was full of dangerous monsters, as crocodiles, tritons (meaning a sea monster), and serpents; that supposing

Ætatis suæ 21. Aº. 1616.

Matoaks als Rebecka daughter to the mighty Prince
Powhatan Emperour of Attanoughkomouck als Virginia
converted and baptized in the Christian faith, and
Wife to the wor.ll M.r Tho: Rolff.

7. POCAHONTAS
Attributed to British School, 1616

the bark we designed to build was big enough to protect us against the dangers he had mentioned, yet it would avail us nothing against another which was inevitable.

"For," said he, "the river Mississippi is so full of rocks and falls towards its mouth, that the rapidity of the current cannot be mastered, which will carry your bark into a horrid whirlpool that swallows up everything that comes near it, and even the river itself, which appears no more, losing itself in that hideous and bottomless gulf."

3

REMARKABLE PROVIDENCES

"The Lord teaches us what such sad providences speak unto us all," wrote John Hull in his diary one day in 1657. *That diary, which he titled* Some Observable Passages of Providence Toward the Country, *reads like a catalogue of horrors. Two women go raving mad and refuse to eat; another walks naked to church; a man dreams of fighting with devils. The heavens are continually perturbed, with great storms of hail as big as duck eggs, flaming comets and stars, the blare of guns and drums. Violent deaths occur all over the place; a boy shoots his father in the bowels, an Indian slays a pregnant housewife, a tailor is found dead on the Lord's day morning after a night in a wine cellar — "a tippling fellow, profanely malignant against the ways of people and God." Burning homes, epidemics of smallpox, and lightning bolts carry off the settlers with swift and sudden blows. The Pequot Indians, made arrowproof by Satan, roast white captives alive, taunting them: "Where is your God and Christ's help now?" In answer the whites rise up and smite the Pequots with swords and bullets.*

John Hull's diary can be matched with other Puritan journals which talk of "dark and dreadful" and "solemn and awful" providences. Increase Mather gathered together the outstanding providences in New England's history into one of the most remarkable books in American literature. Members of other Protestant sects, and the Roman Catholics, were not far behind in noting acts of providence. Indeed, the seventeenth century can produce few words as highly charged as "providence."

What was a providence? To the seventeenth-century Christian, every event on earth and movement in the heavens could be directly caused by God, if he so willed. Or, if he preferred, God could work his will through ordinary means. Any unusual or untoward happening, therefore, required close scrutiny and analysis, to determine what God had in mind. The remarkable happening—the providence—must have a message for man. Of course the broad outlines of the divine will were well enough known, and some providences needed no interpretation. God's wrath struck the idolatrous, the blasphemers, the heathen, the transgressors of his law and the followers of Satan with sure and obvious judgments. On the reverse side, his goodness saved the faithful from the most perilous plight, by holy deliverances and preservations.

But some providences could not be immediately appraised. The blazing star in the sky, the spectral army besieging the Gloucester garrison, the sudden plague of rats and their as sudden removal on the Bermuda Isles—what did these prodigies portend? John Smith's scribe admits that wild cats or extreme cold might have killed off the rats, but points out that God can work with or against nature, so these hypotheses still explain nothing. Clearly in such a rarity "there was joined with and besides the ordinary and manifest means, a more immediate and secret work of God."

So Christians looked for secret works in all kinds of melancholy accidents which upset the normal flow of events. A minor matter like the plugging of a waterspout agitated Samuel Sewall, who eventually read its providential meaning as a joyous deliverance from drenching by a thundershower that came two days later. Lightning blasts, delivered from God's very citadel, should be closely observed in all their effects. Accidental or premature death was surely a grim and puzzling providence. Was this outward saint an inner heretic? Were the people being warned of more devastating wrath to come? Only a fool would disregard an accidental turn of events, and legal contracts today still defer to "acts of God."

For us the providences possess an entirely unintended interest. Since there were no American newspapers in the seventeenth century, they become our meatiest source for the news of that day. The providences were carefully recorded by erudite ministers and educated laymen, who double-checked them for accuracy with eyewitness testimonies and supporting affidavits. Basically they represent on-the-spot reporting of sensational events.

JUDGMENTS

A RAT PLAGUE

John Smith

BUT the great God of heaven being angry at somewhat happened in those proceedings [1617], caused such an increase of silly rats in the space of two years so to abound, before they regarded them, that they filled not only those places where the people were first landed but, swimming from place to place, spread themselves into all parts of the country, insomuch that there was no island but it was pestered with them.* And some fishes have been taken with rats in their bellies, which they caught in swimming from isle to isle. Their nests they had almost in every tree, and in most places their burrows in the ground like conies. They spared not the fruits of the plants, or trees, nor the very plants themselves, but ate them up. When they had set their corn, the rats would come by troops in the night and scratch it out of the ground. If by diligent watch any escaped till it came to earing, it should then very hardly escape them. And they became noisome even to the very persons of men.

They used all the diligence they could for the destroying of them, nourishing cats both wild and tame for that purpose. They used ratsbane, and many times set fire on the woods, that oft ran half a mile before it was extinct. Every man was enjoined to set twelve traps, and some of their own accord have set near an hundred, which they ever visited twice or thrice in a night. They also trained up their dogs to hunt them, wherein they became so expert that a good dog in two or three hours would kill forty of fifty. Many other devices they used to destroy them, but could not prevail, finding them still increasing against them. Nay, the rats so devoured the fruits of the earth that they were destitute of bread for a year or two; so that when they had it afterwards,

* This occurred on the Summer Isles, i.e., the Bermudas, which the English had colonized together with the mainland.

they were so weaned from it, they easily neglected to eat it with their meat. Besides, they endeavored so much for the planting of tobacco for present gain, that they neglected many things that might more have prevailed for their good; which caused amongst them much weakness and mortality, since the beginning of this vermin.

At last it pleased God, but by what means it is not well known, to take the rats away; insomuch that the wild cats and many dogs which lived on them were famished, and many of them leaving the woods came down to their houses and to such places where they used to garbage their fish, and became tame. Some have attributed the destruction of them to the increase of wild cats, but that is not likely they should be so suddenly increased rather at that time than four years before; and the chief occasion of this supposition was because they saw some companies of them leave the woods, and show themselves for want of food. Others say, to the coldness of winter, which notwithstanding is never so great there as with us in March, except it be in the wind; besides, the rats wanted not the feathers of young birds and chickens, which they daily killed, and palmetto moss to build themselves warm nests out of the wind, as usually they did. Neither doth it appear that the cold was so mortal to them, seeing they would ordinarily swim from place to place and be very fat even in the midst of winter.

It remaineth, then, that as God doth sometimes effect his will without subordinate and secondary causes, so we need not doubt but that in the speedy increase of this vermin, as also by the preservation of so many of them by such weak means as they then enjoyed, and especially in the so sudden removal of this great annoyance, there was joined with and besides the ordinary and manifest means, a more mediate and secret work of God.

A PLAGUE OF WEEVILS

Jasper Danckaerts

THE lives of the planters in Maryland and Virginia are very godless and profane. They listen neither to God nor his commandments, and have neither church nor cloister. Sometimes there is someone who is called a minister, who does not as elsewhere serve in one place—for in all Virginia and Maryland there is not a city or a village—but travels for profit, and for that purpose visits the plantations through the country and there addresses the people. But I know of no public assemblages being held in these places. You hear often that these ministers are worse than anybody else, yea, are an abomination.

When the ships arrive with goods, and especially with liquors such as wine and brandy, they attract everybody (that is, masters) to them, who then indulge so abominably together that they keep nothing for the rest of the year, yea, do not go away as long as there is any left, or bring anything home with them which might be useful to them in their subsequent necessities. It must, therefore, go hard with the household, and it is a wonder if there be a single drop left for the future. They squander so much in this way that they keep no tobacco to buy a shoe or a stocking for their children, which sometimes causes great misery.

While they take so little care for provisions, and are otherwise so reckless, the Lord sometimes punishes them with insects, flies and worms, or with intemperate seasons, causing great famine. As happened a few years ago in the time of the last Dutch war with the English, when the Lord sent so many weevils (*eenkorentjes*) that all their grain was eaten up as well as most all the other productions of the field, by reason of which such a great famine was caused that many persons died of starvation, and a mother killed her own child and ate it, and then went to her neighbors, calling upon them to come and see what she had done, and showing them the remains of her child, whereupon she was arrested and condemned to be hung.

When she sat or stood on the scaffold, she cried out to the people, in the presence of the governor, that she was now going to God, where she would render an account and would declare before him that what she had done she did in the mere delirium of hunger, for which the governor alone should bear the guilt; inasmuch as this famine was caused by the *eenkorentjes,* a visitation from God, because he, the governor, undertook in the preceding summer an expedition against the Dutch, residing on the South River, who maintained themselves in such a good posture of defense that he could accomplish but little. When he went to the *Hoere-kil* on the west side of that river, not far from the sea, also he was not able to do much; but as the people subsisted there only by cultivating wheat, and had at this time a fine and abundant harvest in the fields—and from such harvests the people of Maryland generally and under such circumstances as these particularly, were fed—he set fire to it, and all their other fruits, whether of the trees or the field. Whereby he committed two great sins at the same time, namely, against God and his goodness, and against his neighbors, the Dutch, who lost it, and the English who needed it; and had caused more misery to the English in his own country than to the Dutch in the enemy's country.

This wretched woman, protesting these words substantially against the governor, before heaven and in the hearing of everyone, was then swung up.

A WHOREDOM UNMASKED

Cotton Mather

About the year 1646, here was one Mary Martin whose father going from hence to England left her in the house of a married man, who yet became so enamored on her that he attempted her chastity.

Such was her weakness and folly that she yielded unto the temptations of that miserable man; but yet with such horrible regret of mind, that begging of God for deliverance from her temptations, her plea was, "That if ever she were overtaken again, she would leave herself unto his justice, to be made a public example."

Heaven will convince the sinful children of men that the vows which they make, relying on the stability and resolution of their own hearts, are of no significancy. A chain of hell was upon her, and the forfeited grace of heaven was withheld from her; she fell a *third* time into the sin against which her vows had been uttered.

Afterwards going to service in Boston, she found herself to have conceived; but she lived with a favorable mistress, who would admit and allow no suspicion of her dishonesty.

A question (like that convincing one of our Saviour's unto the woman of Samaria) was once oddly put unto her: "Mary, where is thy husband?" And one said also, "Did I not think thou wert an honest and sincere creature, I should verily think thou wert with child!" These passages, which were warnings from God unto her guilty soul, did serve only to strike her with amazement—not with any true repentance.

She concealed her crime till the time of her delivery; and then being delivered alone by herself in a dark room, she murdered the harmless and helpless infant, hiding it in a chest from the eyes of all but the jealous God.

The blood of the child cried, when the cry of the child itself was thus cruelly stifled. Some circumstance quickly occurred which obliged her friends to charge her with an unlawful birth. She denied it impudently. A further search confuted her denial. She then said, the child was dead-born, and she had burned it to ashes. With an hypocritical tear, she added, "Oh, that it were true, that the poor babe were anywhere to be seen!" At last it was found in her chest; and when she touched the face of it before the jury, the blood came fresh into it. So she confessed the whole truth concerning it.

Great endeavors were used that she might be brought unto a true faith in the blood of the Lord Jesus Christ for the pardon of her blood-guiltiness; and, it may be, none endeavored it more than that reverend man, old Mr. Wilson, who wrote several sheets of pathetical instructions to her while she was in prison. That renowned man, old Mr. Cotton also, did his part in endeavoring that she might be renewed by repentance, and preached a sermon on Ezekiel 16: 20, 21. "Is this of thy whoredoms a small matter, that thou hast slain my children?" Whereof great notice was taken.

It was hoped that these endeavors were not lost; her carriage in her imprisonment and at her execution was very penitent. But there was this remarkable at her execution. She acknowledged her *twice* essaying to kill her child before she could make an end of it; and now, through the unskillfulness of the executioner, she was turned off the ladder twice before she died.

OF BUGGERY

Cotton Mather

On June 6, 1662, at New Haven, there was a most unparalleled wretch (one Potter, by name, about sixty years of age) executed for damnable bestialities, although this wretch had been for now twenty years a member of the church in that place, and kept up among the holy people of God there a reputation for serious Christianity. It seems that the unclean devil which had the possession of this monster had carried all his lusts with so much fury into this one channel of wickedness that there was no notice taken of his being wicked in any other. Hence 'twas that he was devout in worship, gifted in prayer, forward in edifying discourse among the religious, and zealous in reproving the sins of the other people. Everyone counted him a saint, and he enjoyed such a peace in his own mind that in several fits of sickness wherein he seemed "nigh unto death," he seemed "willing to die"; yea, "death," he said, "smiled on him."

Nevertheless, this diabolical creature had lived in most infandous buggeries for no less than fifty years together; and now at the gallows there were killed before his eyes a cow, two heifers, three sheep, and two sows, with all of which he had committed his brutalities. His wife had seen him confounding himself with a bitch ten years before; and he then excused his filthiness as well as he could unto her, but conjured her to keep it secret. He afterwards hanged that bitch himself, and then returned unto his former villainies, until at last his son saw him hideously conversing with a sow. By these means the burning jealousy of the Lord Jesus Christ at length made the churches to know that he had all this while seen the covered filthiness of this hellish hypocrite, and exposed him also to the just judgment of death from the civil court of judicature.

Very remarkable had been the warnings which this hellhound had received from heaven to repent of his impieties. Many years before this he had a daughter who dreamt a dream which caused her in her sleep to cry out most bitterly. And her father then, with much ado, obtaining of her to tell her dream, she told him she dreamt that she was among a great multitude of people to see an execution, and it proved her own father that was to be hanged, at whose turning over she thus cried out. This happened before the time that any of his cursed practices were known unto her.

A HERETIC BEARS A MONSTER

John Winthrop

THE wife of one William Dyer, a milliner in the New Exchange, a very proper and fair woman, and both of them notoriously infected with Mrs. Hutchinson's errors* and very censorious and troublesome (she being of a very proud spirit, and much addicted to revelations), had been delivered of child some few months before, October 17, 1638, and the child buried (being stillborn) and viewed of none but Mrs. Hutchinson and the midwife, one Hawkins's wife, a rank Familist ** also. And another woman had a glimpse of it, who, not being able to keep counsel as the other two did, some rumor began to spread that the child was a monster. One of the elders, hearing of it, asked Mrs. Hutchinson when she was ready to depart; whereupon she told him how it was, and said she meant to have it chronicled,† but excused her concealing of it till then (by advice, as she said, of Mr. Cotton). Which coming to the governor's knowledge, he called another of the magistrates and that elder, and sent for the midwife, and examined her about it.

* Boston boiled over after the arrival of Anne Hutchinson in 1634, for this spirited woman held weekly meetings of Puritan housewives in her home to spread the so-called antinomian heresy. She argued that the Christian should determine his state of grace through his own inner sense of faith, and not by kowtowing to the scriptural and civil law. The ministers hated this attack on their source of power, and were able to get her banished by Governor Winthrop in 1637.

** The Familist (Family of Love) sect, popular in England during the sixteenth and seventeenth centuries, followed the antinomian principle in emphasizing the religious emotions, at the expense of creed and dogma.

† Public registration of births, marriages, and deaths was maintained in the Bay Colony with great care.

At first she confessed only that the head was defective and misplaced, but being told that Mrs. Hutchinson had revealed all, and that he intended to have it taken up and viewed, she made this report of it, viz.: It was a woman child, stillborn, about two months before the just time, having life a few hours before; it came hiplings till she turned it; it was of ordinary bigness; it had a face but no head, and the ears stood upon the shoulders and were like an ape's; it had no forehead, but over the eyes four horns, hard and sharp (two of them were above one inch long, the other two shorter), the eyes standing out, and the mouth also; the nose hooked upward; all over the breast and back full of sharp pricks and scales, like a thornback; the navel and all the belly, with the distinction of the sex, were where the back should be, and the back and hips before, where the belly should have been; behind, between the shoulders, it had two mouths, and in each of them a piece of red flesh sticking out; it had arms and legs as other children, but instead of toes it had on each foot three claws, like a young fowl, with sharp talons.

The governor speaking with Mr. Cotton about it, he told him the reason why he advised them to conceal it: 1. Because he saw a providence of God in it, that the rest of the women which were coming and going in the time of her travail should then be absent. 2. He considered that if it had been his own case, he should have desired to have had it concealed. 3. He had known other monstrous births, which had been concealed, and that he thought God might intend only the instruction of the parents, and such other to whom it was known. The like apology he made for himself in public, which was well accepted.

OF RAILING QUAKERS

Increase Mather

MANY remarkable examples to our present purpose have happened in New England, and more than I shall at present take notice of. All wise men that are acquainted therewith observe the blasting rebukes of Providence upon the late singing and dancing Quakers in signal instances, two or three of which may be here recorded, that so others may hear and fear, and do no more so wickedly.

The first instance shall be that which concerns the unhappy man that was murdered in Long Island, of which a good hand in those parts, in a letter bearing date December 12, 1681, writes as follows:

"There went down about a month since three mad Quakers, called Thomas Case's crew, one man named Denham, belonging to Newer-snicks, and two women with him belonging to Oyster Bay; these went down to Southold, where they meet with Samuel Banks of Fairfield, the most blasphemous villain that ever was known in these parts. These joining together with some other inhabitants of Southold of the same spirit, there went into their company a young merchant named Thomas Harris, who was somewhat inclining to the Quakers before (he belonged to Boston). They all go about him, and fell a-dancing and singing, according to their diabolical manner. After some time the said Harris began to act like them, and to dance and sing, and to speak of extraordinary raptures of joy, and to cry out upon all others as devils that were not of their religion; which also they do frequently.

"When the said Harris manifested these signs of conversion, as they accounted it, they solemnly accepted of him as one of their company, and Banks or Denham (for I have forgotten which of the two) gave him this promise, 'that henceforth his tongue should be as the pen of a ready writer, to declare the praises of their Lord.' After this, the young man, who was sober and composed before, ran up and down, singing joy, and calling such devils as should say anything in way of opposition, and said his father was a devil that begat him. Quickly after he went from the town of Southold to a farm belonging to that town, to the house of a Quaker of the same spirit, and went to bed before the rest of the family; and when a young man of the same house went to go to bed to him, he told him that he must get up and go to Southold that night, where he had left Banks and the rest. The young man endeavored to persuade him to lie still till day, but he would not, but got up and went away. After some time he was missed, and inquiry made for him, but he could not be heard of; only his hat and gloves and neckcloth were found in the road from the farm to the town. And two days after, Banks, looking into a Bible, suddenly shut it again, crying out his friend Harris was dead.

"The next day he was found by the seaside, about a quarter of a mile from the place where his hat and other things were found, but out of the road, with three holes like stabs in his throat, and no tongue in his head, nor the least sign thereof, but all was clear to his neck bone within, his mouth close shut, one of his eyes hanging down upon his cheek out of his head, the other sunk so deep in his head that at first it seemed quite out, but was whole there. And Mr. Joshua Hobart, who was one of them to view his dead body, told me that there was no sign of any tongue left in his mouth. 'Such was the end of that tongue which had the promise of being as the pen of a ready writer.'

"Further, the night after he was buried, Captain Young (who is high sheriff, and chiefly concerned in looking after the business), as he told me himself, being in bed in the dead of the night, was awakened by the voice of this Harris calling to his window very loud, requiring him to see that justice was done him. This voice came three times in that night. The next night when he was asleep it came into his house, close to his bedside, and called very loud, asking him if he heard him and awaked him." Thus concerning that tragical story.

BLASPHEMERS, DRUNKARDS, AND HEATHEN

Increase Mather

THE hand of God was very remarkable in that which came to pass in the Narragansett country in New England, not many weeks since. For I have good information that on August 28, 1683, a man there (viz., Samuel Wilson), having caused his dog to mischief his neighbor's cattle, was blamed for his so doing. He denied the fact with imprecations, wishing that he might never stir from that place if he had so done. His neighbor, being troubled at his denying the truth, reproved

8. INCREASE MATHER

Jan van der Spriett, 1688

him, and told him he did very ill to deny what his conscience knew to be truth. The atheist thereupon used the name of God in his imprecations, saying, "He wished to God he might never stir out of that place, if he had done that which he was charged with." The words were scarce out of his mouth before he sunk down dead and never stirred more, a son-in-law of his standing by and catching him as he fell to the ground.

A thing not unlike to this happened (though not in New England) yet in America, about a year ago. For in September, 1682, a man at the isle of Providence, belonging to a vessel whereof one Wollery was master, being charged with some deceit in a matter that had been committed to him, in order to his own vindication horribly wished "that the Devil might put out his eyes if he had done as was suspected concerning him." That very night a rheum fell into his eyes, so as that within a few days he became stark blind. His company, being astonished at the divine hand which thus conspicuously and signally appeared, put him ashore at Providence and left him there. A physician being desired to undertake his cure, hearing how he came to lose his sight refused to meddle with him. This account I lately received from credible persons, who knew and have often seen the man whom the Devil (according to his own wicked wish) made blind, through the dreadful and righteous judgment of God.

Moreover, that worse than brutish sin of drunkenness hath been witnessed against from heaven by severe and signal judgments. It was a sign of the fearful wrath of God upon that notorious drunkard at a place called Seatucket in Long Island, who, as he was in drink, fell into the fire (the people in the house then being in bed and asleep), and so continued for some considerable time, until he received his death wound. At his first awakening he roared out, "Fire! Fire!," as if it had been one in hell, to the great astonishment of all that heard him. One in the house flung a pail of water on him to quench his clothes, but that added to his torment; so he continued yelling after an hideous manner, "Fire! Fire!," and within a day or two he died in great misery. And though this drunkard died by fire, it is remarkable that many of those who have loved drink have died by water, and that at the very time when their under-

standings have been drowned by drink. It is an awful consideration that there have been at several times above forty persons
in this land whom death hath found in that woeful plight, so
that their immortal souls have gone out of drunken bodies
to appear before God the judge of all.

That remarkable judgment hath first or last fallen upon
those who have sought the hurt of the people of God in New
England is so notorious as that it is become the observation of
every man. This Israel in the wilderness hath eat up the
nations his enemies; he hath broke their bones, and pierced them
through with his arrows. Some adversaries have escaped longer
unpunished than others; but then their ends have been of all
the most woeful and tragical at last. I shall instance only in
what hath lately come to pass with respect unto the heathen
who rose up against us, thinking to swallow us up quick when
their wrath was kindled against us. Blessed be the Lord, who
hath not given us a prey to their teeth! The chieftains amongst
them were all cut off, either by sword or sickness, in the war
time, excepting those in the Eastern parts, whose ringleaders
outlived their fellows; but now God hath met with them.

There were in special two of those Indians who shed much
innocent blood, viz., Simon and Squando. As for bloody Simon,
who was wont to boast of the mischiefs he had done, and how
he had treacherously shot and killed such and such Englishmen,
he died miserably the last winter. Another Indian discharging
a gun happened to shoot Simon so as to break his arm. After
which he lived two years, but in extremity of pain, so as that
the Indians when inquired of how Simon did, their usual
answer was, "Worse than dead." He used all means that earth
and hell (for he betook himself to powaws [medicine men])
could afford him for his recovery, but in vain. Thus was the
wickedness of that murderer at last returned upon his own head.

Concerning Squando, the sachem* of the Indians at Saco, the
story of him is upon sundry accounts remarkable. Many years

---

* Among the Algonkian tribes of the Northeast "sachem" meant
the tribal chieftain. A "sagamore" might be a lesser chief, or a
synonym for sachem. Among the Virginia Indians encountered by
John Smith the tribal head was called a "werowance."

ago he was sick and near unto death, after which he said that one pretending to be the Englishman's God appeared to him in the form of an English minister and discoursed with him, requiring him to leave off his drinking of rum, and religiously to observe the Sabbath day and to deal justly amongst men, withal promising him that if he did so, then at death his soul should go upwards to an happy place; but if he did not obey these commandments, at death his soul should go downwards and to be forever miserable. But this pretended God said nothing to him about Jesus Christ. However, this apparition so wrought upon Squando as that he left his drunkenness, and became a strict observer of the Sabbath day; yea, so that he always kept it as a day of fast, and would hear the English ministers preach, and was very just in his dealing. But in the time of the late Indian war he was the principal actor in the bloody tragedies in that part of the country. The last year the pretended Englishman's God appeared to him again, as afore, in the form of a minister, requiring him to kill himself, and promising him that if he did obey he should live again the next day and never die more. Squando acquainted his wife and some other Indians with this new apparition; they most earnestly advised him not to follow the murderous counsel which the specter had given. Nevertheless he since hath hanged himself, and so is gone to his own place. This was the end of the man that disturbed the peace of New England.

GOD STRIKES THE FOULMOUTHED

A Jesuit Missionary

VARIOUS things happen worthy of recital, in one of which the divine mercy was manifest, in the other the divine justice.

On the day upon which a certain man was about to abjure heresy and expiate the sins of his past life by confession, a flame, having caught in the interior part of his house during his absence, running up the doorpost, had burst out at the top. When he had perceived the thing, for he was not far distant, he suddenly called to a neighbor, but finds no assistance; he runs then to another, when he finds only two who will go with him; and although all this time the fire was burning, and the house was built of dry logs, nevertheless relief arrived before any great injury had happened. Some feared lest by this unexpected occurrence he might be deterred from conversion. It happened far otherwise, however; for his house being almost uninjured, he thence drew the conclusion that God was propitious to him and approved his design by a manifest token. Wherefore, uniting a great reformation in morals with the faith he professed, he now sheds abroad the very sweet savor of a good example upon all who are acquainted with him.

The other man, though he had felt some internal drawings of God, and had for some time made use of means which seemed to lead toward conversion, yet on a certain day determined to cast aside all such thoughts and go back to the customary paths of his earlier life. In the time when he meditated better thoughts he had obtained prayer beads for himself; but afterwards, having changed his mind, he was accustomed to smoke them in his pipe with tobacco, after grinding them to powder, often boasting that he was eating up his "Ave Marias"; for so he called the beads by telling of which the salutation of the angel is recited.

But the divine vengeance did not let the wicked crime go long unpunished. For scarcely a year having passed, on the returning vigil of the day on which he had abandoned his purpose of embracing the Catholic faith, a more sacrilegious playfulness possessed him, as was noticed by his companions. Therefore, in the afternoon, when he had betaken himself to the river for the purpose of swimming, scarcely had he touched the water when a huge fish, having suddenly seized the wicked man before he could retreat to the bank, tore away, at a bite, a large portion of his thigh, by the pain of which most merited laceration the unhappy wretch was in a short time hurried away from the living—the divine justice bringing it about that he, who a little while before boasted that he had eaten up his "Ave Maria beads," should see his own flesh devoured, even while he was yet living.

John Winthrop

ONE Abraham Shurd of Pemaquid and one Captain Wright and others coming to Piscataqua, being bound for this bay in a shallop with £200 worth of commodities, one of the seamen, going to light a pipe of tobacco, set fire on a barrel of powder, which tore the boat in pieces. That man was never seen; the rest were all saved, but the goods lost.

The man that was blown away with the powder in the boat at Piscataqua was after found with his hands and feet torn off. This fellow, being wished by another to forbear to take any tobacco till they came to the shore, which was hard by, answered that if the Devil should carry him away quick, he would take one pipe. Some in the boat were so drunk and fast asleep, as they did not awake with the noise.

UNGODLY SERVANTS

John Eliot

JOHN MOODY came to the land in the year 1633. He had no children; he had two menservants that were ungodly, especially one of them who in his passion would wish himself in hell and use desperate words, yet had a good measure of knowledge. These two servants would go to the oyster bank in a boat, and did, against the counsel of their governor, where they lay all night. And in the morning early when the tide was out, they gathering oysters did unskillfully leave their boat afloat in the verges of the channel, and quickly the tide carried it away so far into the channel that they could not come near it, which made them cry out and hollo, but being very early and remote were not heard till the water had risen very high upon them, to the armholes as it's thought. And then a man from Rockbrough meetinghouse hill heard them cry and call, and he cried and ran with all speed, and seeing their boat swam to it and hasted to them, but they were both so drowned before any help could possibly come. A dreadful example of God's displeasure against obstinate servants.

A TALKY BARBER

Edward Johnson

To END this year 1639 the Lord was pleased to send a very sharp winter, and more especially in strong storms of weekly snows, with very bitter blasts. And here the reader may take notice of the sad hand of the Lord against two persons who were taken in a storm of snow as they were passing from Boston to Roxbury, it being much about a mile distant, and a very plain way. One of Roxbury sending to Boston his servant maid for a barber-chirurgeon to draw his tooth, they lost their way in their passage between, and were not found till many days after, and then the maid was found in one place and the man in another, both of them frozen to death.

In which sad accident this was taken into consideration by divers people, that this barber* was more than ordinary laborious to draw men to those sinful errors that were formerly so frequent and now newly overthrown by the blessing of the Lord upon the endeavor of his faithful servants with the word of truth—he having a fit opportunity, by reason of his trade. So soon as any were set down in his chair, he would commonly be cutting off their hair and the truth together. Notwithstanding some report better of the man, the example is for the living; the dead is judged of the Lord alone.

TROUBLE WITH JADES

Rev. Joseph Green

1710. November 6. Preparing for winter. Benjamin Hutchinson in my orchard.

---

* "He was William Dyneby, and his son, then unborn, was from this occurrence baptized *Fathergone*. Very strange is it, that this storm was on *15 October*." (Handwritten note in margin of Michigan State Library copy.)

7. Storm at night. Captain Eastes' brother here. I went to Benjamin Hutchinson and prayed him to keep his horses out of my orchard. He told me if my feed was not eaten quickly the snow would cover it, et cetera.

8. Benjamin Hutchinson's horses in every night this week.

11. I at study. Sent for Benjamin Hutchinson and prayed him to mend up his fence, which he did and kept them out this one night.

17. Benjamin Hutchinson's three jades, having been here in my orchard every night this week, had got such a hankering that they would not easily be drove out, so that J. H. tried last night at nine o'clock to get them out till he was cold and tired, and forced to leave them in. And as we were trying to get them out this morning, the two jades trying to jump out at once by the well, one pressed another so he jumped into my well, and although we got him out with Mr. Hutchinson's help, yet he soon died. Snow.

18. Snow. I went to Mr. H. He said I might pay for one-half of his colt, and that he could by the law force me to pay all. I told him I was no ways to blame about his colt being killed; but I looked at it as a providential rebuke unto him for suffering his jades to afflict me. I told him he only was to blame, because I had spake and sent to him ten times to look to his horses. He told me nobody desired him to fetter his horses in the winter, and that folks' fields was mostly common.

27. I told Benjamin Hutchinson I would give his boys twenty shillings for his colt that fell into my well, and also the damage his horses had done me this month, which I valued twenty shillings more. And he said that would satisfy him and all his family. I told him I gave it to him to make him easy and if that end was not obtained I should account my money thrown away. For I knew no law did oblige me to pay for his colt, that came over a lawful fence into my well.

January 22. I was called up at four o'clock to pray with Benjamin Hutchinson's child; it died at six o'clock.

OF NEW ENGLAND'S ENEMIES

John Winthrop

JULY 27, 1640. Being the second day of the week, the *Mary Rose*, a ship of Bristol, of about two hundred tons, lying before Charlestown, was blown in pieces with her own powder, being twenty-one barrels; wherein the judgment of God appeared. For the master and company were many of them profane scoffers at us, and at the ordinances of religion here; so as our churches keeping a fast for our native country they kept aboard at their common service, when all the rest of the masters came to our assemblies; likewise the Lord's day following. And a friend of his going aboard next day and asking him why he came not on shore to our meetings, his answer was that he had a family of his own, and they had as good service aboard as we had on shore. Within two hours after this (being about dinner time) the powder took fire (no man knows how) and blew all up, viz., the captain and nine or ten of his men, and some four or five strangers.

There was a special providence that there were no more, for many principal men were going aboard at that time, and some were in a boat near the ship, and others were diverted by a sudden shower of rain, and others by other occasions. There was one man saved, being carried up in the scuttle, and so let fall in the same into the water, and being taken up by the ferryboat near dead, he came to himself the next morning, but could not tell anything of the blowing up of the ship, or how he came there. The rest of the dead bodies were after found, much bruised and broken. Some goods were saved, but the whole loss was estimated at £2,000. A twenty-shilling piece was found sticking in a chip, for there was about £300 in money in her, and fifteen tons of lead, and ten pieces of ordnance, which a year after were taken up, and the hull of the ship drawn ashore.

This judgment of God upon these scorners of his ordinances and the ways of his servants (for they spake very evil of us, because they found not so good a market for their commodities as they expected) gives occasion to mention other examples of

like kind which fell out at this and other times, by which it
will appear how the Lord hath owned this work, and preserved and prospered his people here beyond ordinary ways of
providence.

One Captain Mason of London, a man in favor at court, and
a professed enemy to us, had a plantation at Piscataqua, which
he was at great charge about, and set up a sawmill, but nothing
prospered. He provided a ship, which would have been employed to have brought a general governor, or in some other design to our prejudice, but in launching of it her back was broken.
He also employed Gardiner, and Morton, and others, to prosecute
against us at council table, and by a quo warranto, so as Morton
wrote divers letters to his friends here, insulting against us, and
assuring them of our speedy ruin. But the Lord still disap-
pointed them, and frustrated all their designs. As for this
Mason, he fell sick and died soon after, and in his sickness he
sent for the minister and bewailed his enmity against us, and
promised, if he recovered, to be as great a friend to New England
as he had formerly been an enemy.

Sir Ferdinand Gorges also had sided with our adversaries
against us, but underhand, pretending by his letters and speeches
to seek our welfare; but he never prospered. He attempted
great matters and was at large expenses about his province here,
but he lost all.

One Austin (a man of good estate) came with his family in
the year 1638 to Quinipiack, and not finding the country as he
expected he grew discontented, saying that he could not subsist here, and thereupon made off his estate, and with his family
and £1000 in his purse he returned for England in a ship bound
for Spain, against the advice of the godly there who told him
he would be taken by the Turks. And it so fell out, for in
Spain he embarked himself in a great ship bound for England
which carried £200,000 in money, but the ship was taken by
the Turks, and Austin and his wife and family were carried to
Algiers, and sold there for slaves.

The Lord showed his displeasure against others, though godly,
who have spoken ill of this country and so discouraged the hearts
of his people, even the lords and others of Providence having
spoken too much in that kind, thinking thereby to further their

9. JOHN WINTHROP
Artist and date unknown.

own plantation.* They set out a ship the last year with passengers and goods for Providence, but it was taken by the Turks. Captain Newman, the same year, having taken good prizes in their service, returning home, when he was near Dover was taken by a Dunkirker and all lost. Mr. Humfrey, who was now for Providence with his company, raised an ill report of this country, but were here kept, in spite of all their endeavors and means to have been gone this winter, and his corn and all his hay to the value of £160 were burnt by his own servants, who made a fire in his barn, and gunpowder which accidentally took fire consumed all. Himself having at the court before petitioned for some supply of his want, whereupon the court gave him £250. Soon after also Providence was taken by the Spaniards, and the lords lost all their care and cost to the value of above £60,000.

The sudden fall of land and cattle, and the scarcity of foreign commodities and money, with the thin access of people from England, put many into an unsettled frame of spirit, so as they concluded there would be no subsisting here, and accordingly they began to hasten away, some to the West Indies, others to the Dutch at Long Island, et cetera (for the governor there invited them by fair offers), and others back for England. Among others who returned thither there was one of the magistrates, Mr. Humfrey, and four ministers and a schoolmaster. These would needs go against all advice, and had a fair and speedy voyage till they came near England, all which time three of the ministers, with the schoolmaster, spake reproachfully of the people and of the country.

But the wind coming up against them they were tossed up and down, being in December, so long till their provisions and other necessaries were near spent and they were forced to strait allowance. Yet at length the wind coming fair again, they got into the Sleeve,† but then there arose so great a tempest at SE as they could bear no sail, and so were out of hope of being saved (being in the night also). Then they humbled themselves before the Lord and acknowledged God's hand to be justly out against

* The Providence referred to is the island Providence, or Catalina, off the Nicaraguan coast.

† The English Channel, French *La Manche*.

them for speaking evil of this good land and the Lord's people here. Only one of them, Mr. Phillips of Wrentham, in England, had not joined with the rest but spake well of the people and of the country; upon this it pleased the Lord to spare their lives. And when they expected every moment to have been dashed upon the rocks (for they were hard by the Needles) he turned the wind so as they were carried safe to the Isle of Wight by St. Helen's.

Yet the Lord followed them on shore. Some were exposed to great straits and found no entertainment, their friends forsaking them. One had a daughter that presently ran mad, and two other of his daughters, being under ten years of age, were discovered to have been often abused by divers lewd persons and filthiness in his family. The schoolmaster had no sooner hired a house and gotten in some scholars, but the plague set in, and took away two of his own children.

DELIVERANCES

THE STARVING TIME IN VIRGINIA
AND THE PRESERVATION THROUGH SIR THOMAS GATES

John Smith

(The lowest point in the affairs of Jamestown came in the winter of 1609-1610, the "Starving Time," when it seemed the colony would go under. An English fleet setting out with help for Jamestown in June, 1609, had been badly battered by the storm that gave Shakespeare his *Tempest,* and the ship of the new lieutenant-governor, Sir Thomas Gates, foundered off the Bermudas. Gates and his people survived the winter, built two pinnaces, and reached Jamestown on May 23, 1610, finding a colony of skeletons living on mushrooms and herbs. Actually it was not Gates but Lord De La Warr who saved the colony by arriving with fresh men and supplies a fortnight later, to meet Gates sailing down the James River with all the colonists in a final departure.)

Now we all found the loss of Captain Smith, yea, his greatest maligners could now curse his loss. As for corn, provision, and contribution from the savages, we had nothing but mortal wounds with clubs and arrows. As for our hogs, hens, goats, sheep, horses, or what lived, our commanders, officers, and savages daily consumed them; some small proportions sometimes we tasted, till all was devoured. Then swords, arms, pieces, or anything we traded with the savages, whose cruel fingers were so oft imbrued in our blood that what by their cruelty, our governor's indiscretion, and the loss of our ships, of five hundred within six months after Captain Smith's departure (October, 1609–March, 1610), there remained not past sixty men, women, and children, most miserable and poor creatures; and those were preserved for the most part by roots, herbs, acorns, walnuts, berries, and now and then a little fish. They that had starch in these extremities made no small use of it; yea, even the very skins of our horses.

138

Nay, so great was our famine that a savage we slew and buried, the poorer sort took him up again and ate him; and so did divers one another boiled and stewed with roots and herbs. And one amongst the rest did kill his wife, powdered [salted] her, and had eaten part of her before it was known. For which he was executed, as he well deserved. Now whether she was better roasted, boiled, or carbonadoed, I know not; but of such a dish as powdered wife I never heard of.

This was that time which still to this day we called the Starving Time. It were too vile to say, and scarce to be believed, what we endured. But the occasion was our own, for want of providence, industry, and government, and not the barrenness and defect of the country, as is generally supposed. For till then in three years, for the numbers were landed us, we had never from England provision sufficient for six months, though it seemed by the bills of lading sufficient was sent us, such a glutton is the sea and such good fellows the mariners. We as little tasted of the great proportion sent us as they of our want and miseries, yet notwithstanding they ever overswayed and ruled the business, though we endured all that is said and chiefly lived on what this good country naturally afforded. Yet had we been even in Paradise itself with those governors, it would not have been much better with us; yet there was amongst us, who had they had the government as Captain Smith appointed, but that they could not maintain it, would surely have kept us from those extremities of miseries. This in ten days more would have supplanted us all with death.

But God, that would not this country should be unplanted, sent Sir Thomas Gates and Sir George Somers with one hundred and fifty people most happily preserved by the Bermudas to preserve us [May 21, 1610]. Strange it is to say how miraculously they were preserved in a leaking ship, as at large you may read in the ensuing history of those islands.

Council for Virginia

To RETURN therefore unto the main channel of this discourse, and to dispel the clouds of fear that threaten shipwrecks and sea dangers. For we are not to extenuate the sea's tempestuous violence, nor yet therefore to despair of God's assisting providence. For true it is that when Sir Thomas Gates, Sir George Somers, and Captain Newport were in the height of 27 on the 24th of July, 1609, there arose such a storm as if Jonah had been flying unto Tarsus; the heavens were obscured, and made an Egyptian night of three days' perpetual horror; the women lamented; the hearts of the passengers failed; the experience of the sea captains was amazed; the skill of the mariners was confounded. The ship most violently leaked, and though two thousand tons of water by pumping from Tuesday noon till Friday noon was discharged, notwithstanding the ship was half filled with water, and those which labored to keep others from drowning were half drowned themselves in laboring.

But God that heard Jonah crying out of the belly of hell, he pitied the distresses of his servants. For behold, in the last period of necessity, Sir George Somers descried land, which was by so much the more joyful, by how much their danger was despairful. The islands on which they fell were the Bermudas, a place hardly accessible, through the environing rocks and dangers; notwithstanding they were forced to run their ship on shore, which through God's providence fell betwixt two rocks that caused her to stand firm and not immediately to be broken, God continuing his mercy unto them, that with their longboats they transported to land before night all their company, men, women, and children, to the number of one hundred and fifty. They carried to shore all the provision of unspent and unspoiled victuals, all their furniture and tackling of the ship, leaving nothing but bared ribs as a prey unto the ocean.

These islands of the Bermudas have ever been accounted as an enchanted pile of rocks, and a desert inhabitation for devils. But all the fairies of the rocks were but flocks of birds, and all the devils that haunted the woods were but herds of swine. Yea, and when Acosta in his first book of the histories of the Indies averreth that though in the continent there were divers beasts and cattle, yet in the islands of Hispaniola, Jamaica, Margarita, and Dominica there was not one hoof, it increaseth the wonder how our people in the Bermudas found such abundance of hogs that for nine months' space they plentifully sufficed, and yet the number seemed not much diminished. Again, as in the great famine of Israel God commanded Elias to flee to the brook Cedron, and there fed him by ravens, so God provided for our disconsolate people in the midst of the sea by fowls, but with an admirable difference: unto Elias the ravens brought meat, unto our men the fowls brought themselves for meat. For when they whistled or made any strange noise, the fowls would come and sit on their shoulders; they would suffer themselves to be taken and weighed by our men, who would make choice of the fattest and fairest, and let fly the lean and lightest. An accident, I take it, that cannot be paralleled by any history, except when God sent abundance of quail to feed his Israel in the barren wilderness. Lastly they found the berries of cedar, the palmetto tree, the prickly pear, sufficient fish, plenty of tortoises, and divers other kinds, which sufficed to sustain nature. They found diversity of woods, which ministered materials for the building of two pinnaces, according to the direction of the three provident governors.

Consider all these things together. At the instant of need they descried land; half an hour more had buried their memorial in the sea. If they had fell by night, what expectation of light from an uninhabited desert? They fell betwixt a labyrinth of rocks, which they conceived are moldered into the sea by thunder and lightning. This was not Ariadne's thread, but the direct line of God's providence. If it had not been so near land, their company or provision had perished by water. If they had not found hogs and fowl and fish, they had perished by want of fire. If there had not been timber they could not have transported themselves to Virginia, but must have been forgotten forever. *Nimium timet qui Deo non credit;* he is too impiously fearful that will not trust in God so powerful.

What is there in all this tragical comedy that should discourage us with impossibility of the enterprise when of all the fleet one only ship by a secret leak was endangered, and yet in the gulf of despair was so graciously preserved? *Quae videtur paena, est medicina;* that which we account a punishment of evil is but a medicine against evil.

MORTAL WOUNDS THAT DO NOT KILL

Cotton Mather

AT THIS time there happened a remarkable thing. I know not whether the story told by Plato be true, that one Herus Armenius (whom Clemens will have to be Zoroaster), being slain in war, lay ten days among the dead, and then, being brought away and on the twelfth day laid on a funeral pile, he came to life again. But it is true that one Simon Stone, being here wounded with shot in nine several places, lay for dead (as it was time!) among the dead. The Indians coming to strip him attempted with two several blows of an hatchet at his neck to cut off his head, which blows added, you may be sure, more enormous wounds unto those portholes of death, at which the life of the poor man was already running out as fast as it could. Being charged hard by Lieutenant Bancroft, they left the man without scalping him; and the English now coming to bury the dead, one of the soldiers perceived this poor man to fetch a gasp, whereupon an Irish fellow then present advised them to give him another dab with an hatchet, and so bury him with the rest. The English, detesting this barbarous advice, lifted up the wounded man and poured a little fair water into his mouth, at which he coughed; then they poured a little strong water after it, at which he opened his eyes. The Irish fellow was ordered now to hail a canoe ashore to carry the wounded men up the river unto a chirurgeon; and as Teague was foolishly pulling the canoe ashore with the cock of his gun, while he held the muzzle in his hand, his gun went off and broke his arm, whereof he remains a cripple to this day. But Simon Stone was thoroughly cured, and is at this day a very lusty man; and as he was born with two thumbs on one hand, his neighbors have thought him to have at least as many hearts as thumbs!

Reader, let us leave it now unto the sons of Aesculapius to

dispute out the problem, "What wounds are to be judged mortal?" The sovereign arbiter of life and death seems to have determined it, "That no wounds are mortal, but such as he shall in his holy providence actually make so." On the one side, let it be remembered that a scratch of a comb has proved mortal; that the incomparable anatomist Spigelius, at the wedding of his daughter, gathering up the relics of a broken glass, a fragment of it scratched one of his fingers, and all his exquisite skill in anatomy could not prevent its producing an empyema that killed him; that Colonel Rossiter, cracking a plum stone with his teeth, broke his tooth, and lost his life; that the Lord Fairfax, cutting a corn in his foot, cut asunder the thread of his life; that Mr. Fowler, a vintner, playing with his child, received a little scratch of a pin, which turned unto a gangrene that cost him his life. And, reader, let the remembrance of such things cause thee to live preparing for death continually.

But then, on the other side, that nothing may be despaired of, remember Simon Stone. And, besides him, I call to remembrance that the Indians, making an assault upon Deerfield, in this present war, they struck an hatchet some inches into the skull of a boy there, even so deep that the boy felt the force of a wrench used by 'em to get it out. There he lay a long while weltering in his blood; they found him, they dressed him, considerable quantities of his brain came out from time to time when they opened the wound; yet the lad recovered and is now a living monument of the power and goodness of God. And in our former war there was one Jabez Musgrove who, though he were shot by the Indians with a bullet that went in at his ear and went out at his eye on the other side of his head, and a brace of bullets that went into his right side, a little above his hip, and passing through his body within the backbone went out at his left side, yet he recovered and lived many years after it.

Certainly this fellow was worthy to have been at least a lackey to the Hungarian nobleman whose portraiture Dr. Patin saw in a gallery at Innsbruck, representing a wound made in his eye with a lance, which penetrated into the substance of the brain, even to the hinder part of the head, and yet proved not a mortal wound.

A Jesuit Missionary

IT HAS also pleased the Divine Goodness, by the virtue of his holy cross, to effect something beyond mere human power. The circumstances are these. A certain Indian, called an Anacostian from his country but now a Christian, whilst he was making his way with others through a wood fell behind his companions a little, when some savages of the tribe of the Susquesehanni, which I have mentioned before, attacked him suddenly from an ambuscade, and with a strong and light spear of locust wood (from which they make their bows), with an oblong iron point, pierced him through from the right side to the left at a hand's breadth below the armpit near the heart itself with a wound two fingers broad at each side. From the effect of this when the man had suddenly fallen, his enemies fly with the utmost precipitation. But his friends who had gone on before, recalled by the sudden noise and shout, return and carry the man from the land to the boat, which was not far distant, and thence to his home at Piscataway, and leave him speechless and out of his senses.

The occurrence being reported to Father White, who by chance was but a short distance away, he hastened to him the following morning and found the man before the doors, lying on a mat before the fire and enclosed by a circle of his tribe—not indeed altogether speechless, or out of his senses, as the day before, but expecting the most certain death almost every moment, and with a mournful voice joining in the song with his friends that stood around, as is the custom in the case of the more distinguished of these men when they are thought to be certainly about to die. But some of his friends were Christians, and their song, which, musically indeed but with plaintive inflection of tone they modulated, was "May he live, O God! if it so please thee!" And they repeated it again and again, until the Father attempted to address the dying man, who immediately knew the Father and showed him his wounds.

The Father pitied him exceedingly; but since he saw the danger to be most imminent, omitting other things he briefly runs over the principal articles of faith, and repentance of his sins being excited, he received his confession. Then elevating his soul with hope and confidence in God, he recited the gospel which is appointed to be read for the sick, as also the Lauretan litanies of the Blessed Virgin, and told him to commend himself to her most holy intercessions, and to call unceasingly upon the most sacred name of Jesus. Then the Father, applying the sacred relics of the most holy cross which he carried in a casket hung to his neck but had now taken off, to the wound on each side, before his departure (for it was necessary to depart, for the purpose of administering baptism to an aged Indian, who was considered about to die before the morrow) directed the by-standers, when he should breathe his last, to carry him to the chapel for the purpose of burial.

It was now noon when the Father departed. And the following day, at the same hour, when by chance he was borne along in his boat, he saw two Indians propelling a boat with oars towards him; and when they had come alongside one of them put his foot into the boat in which the Father was sitting. Whilst he gazed on the man with fixed eyes, being in doubt, for in a measure he recognized by his features who he was, but in part recollected in what state he had left him the day before, the man, on a sudden having thrown open his cloak and having disclosed the cicatrices of the wounds, or rather a red spot on each side as a trace of the wound, immediately removed all doubt from him. Moreover, in language of great exultation he exclaims that he is entirely well, nor from the hour at which the Father had left yesterday had he ceased to invoke the most holy name of Jesus, to whom he attributed his recovered health. All who were in the boat with the Father, taking cognizance of the thing both by seeing and hearing, breaking forth into praise of God and thanksgiving, were greatly rejoiced and confirmed in the faith at this miracle.

But the Father, advising the man that, always mindful of so great and manifest a blessing, he should return thanks, and persevere to treat that holy name and most holy cross with love and reverence, dismisses the same from him. Then the man, returning to his own boat together with the other, boldly propelled it with the oar, which he could not have done, unless he had been of sound and entire strength.

ESCAPES FROM THE DEEP

John Smith

IN THE interim happened to a certain number of private persons as miserable and lamentable an accident as ever was read or heard of, and thus it was.

In the month of March [1615], a time most subject of all others to such tempests, on a Friday there went seven men in a boat of two or three tons to fish. The morning being fair, so eager they were of their journey, some went fasting; neither carried they either meat or drink with them, but a few palmetto berries. But being at their fishing place some four leagues from the shore, such a tempest arose, they were quickly driven from sight of land in an overgrown sea, despairing of all hope, only committing themselves to God's mercy, let the boat drive which way she would.

On Sunday, the storm being somewhat abated, they hoisted sail as they thought towards the island. In the evening it grew stark calm; so that being too weak to use their oars, they lay adrift that night.

The next morning Andrew Hilliard (for now all his companions were past strength either to help him or themselves) before a small gale of wind spread his sail again.

On Tuesday one died, whom they threw overboard. On Wednesday three. And on Thursday at night the sixth.

All these but the last were buried by Hilliard in the sea, for so weak he was grown he could not turn him over as the rest, whereupon he stripped him, ripping his belly with his knife; throwing his bowels into the water, he spread his body abroad tilted open with a stick, and so lets it lie as a cistern to receive some lucky rainwater. And this God sent him presently after, so that in one small shower he recovered about four spoonfuls of rainwater, to his unspeakable refreshment. He also preserved near half a pint of blood in a shoe, which he did sparingly drink of to moist his mouth. Two several days he fed on his flesh, to the quantity of a pound.

On the eleventh day from his losing the sight of land, two

flying fishes fall in his boat, whose warm juicy blood he sucked to his great comfort. But within an hour after, to his greater comfort you will not doubt, he once again descried the land, and within four hours after was cast upon a rock near to Port Royal, where his boat was presently split in pieces. But himself, though extremely weak, made shift to clamber up so steep and high a rock as would have troubled the ablest man in the isle to have done that by day which he did by night.

Being thus astride on a rock, the tumbling sea had gotten such possession in his brains that a good while it was before his giddy head would suffer him to venture upon the forsaking it. Towards the morning he crawls ashore, and then to his accomplished joy discerns where he is, and travels half a day without any refreshment than water, whereof wisely and temperately he stinted himself, otherwise certainly he had drunk his last.

In which case he attains a friend's house, where at the first they took him for a ghost, but at last acknowledged and received him with joy. His story, after some hours of recovery of strength to tell it, they heard out with admiration. He was not long after conveyed to the town, where he received his former health and was living in the year 1622.

Father Edward Knott

ANOTHER man, who was of noble birth, had been reduced to such poverty by his own unrestrained licentiousness that he sold himself into this colony [Maryland]. Here, when he had been recalled by one of ours to the right faith and the fruit of good living, he always anxiously doubted whether he had entered upon the safe road. And on one occasion, when he had entrusted himself to the sea in a small skiff and a frightful storm arose such as he had never seen, although he had often met with storms at sea, and certain shipwreck seemed already at hand, he earnestly prayed to God that in confirmation of the faith he had lately received—if it was really true—he would ward off the impending danger. God heard his prayer and, turning the storm in another direction, confirmed his wavering mind with tranquil peace.

Not long afterwards this man was brought to the last extremity by a severe disease, and after taking all the sacraments, about an hour before his death asked his Catholic attendant to pray for him. It is probable that an evil angel presented himself to his sight; for almost at the very point of death he called the same attendant and said, with a cheerful voice: "Don't you see my good angel? Behold him standing near to carry me away; I must depart." And thus happily (as we are permitted to hope) he breathed his last. Since his burial, a very bright light has often been seen at night around his tomb, even by Protestants.

P R O D I G I E S

HERALDS OF WAR

Cotton Mather

IN the year 1674 one John Sausaman, an Indian that had been sent forth from the English to preach the gospel unto his countrymen, addressed the Governor of Plymouth with information that King Philip,* with several nations of the Indians besides his own, were plotting the destruction of the English throughout the country. This John Sausaman was the son of Christian Indians; but he, apostatizing from the profession of Christianity, lived like a heathen in the quality of a secretary to King Philip; for he could write, though the King his master could not so much as read. But after this, the grace of our Lord Jesus Christ recovered him from his apostasy, and he gave such notable evidences and expressions of his repentance that he was not only admitted unto the communion of the Lord's Table in one of the Indian churches, but he was also employed every Lord's day as an instructor among them.

But before the truth of the matter could be inquired into, poor John was barbarously murdered by certain Indians, who, that the murder might not be discovered, cut a hole through the ice of the pond where they met with him and put in the dead body, leaving his hat and his gun upon the ice, that so others might suppose him to have there drowned himself. It being rumored that Sausaman was missing, the neighbors did seek, and find, and bury his dead body. But upon the jealousies on the spirits of men that he might have met with some foul play for his discovering on the Indian plot, a jury was empaneled, unto whom it appeared that his neck was broken, which is one Indian way of murdering, and that his head was extremely swollen, and that he had several other wounds upon him, and that when he was taken out of the pond no water issued out of him.

It was remarkable that one Tobias, a counselor of King Philip's whom they suspected as the author of this murder, approaching to the dead body, it would still *fall a-bleeding afresh*, as if it had newly been slain; yea, that upon the repetition of the experiment, it still happened so, albeit he had been deceased and interred for a considerable while before. Afterwards an Indian called Patuckson gave in his testimony that he saw this Tobias, with certain other Indians, killing of John Sausaman; and it was further testified that John Sausaman, before he died, had expressed his fears that those very Indians would be his death. Hereupon Tobias with two other Indians being apprehended, they were after a fair trial for their lives by a jury consisting half of English and half of Indians, convicted, and so condemned. And though they were all successively turned off the ladder at the gallows, utterly denying the fact, yet the last of them happening to break or slip the rope, did, before his going off the ladder again, confess that the other Indians did really murder John Sausaman, and that he was himself, though no actor in it, yet a looker on.

Things began by this time to have an ominous aspect. Yea, and now we speak of things ominous, we may add, some time before this, in a clear, still, sunshiny morning, there were divers persons in Malden who heard in the air, on the southeast of them, a great gun go off, and presently thereupon the report of small guns like musket shot, very thick discharging, as if there had been a battle. This was at a time when there was nothing visible done in any part of the colony to occasion such noises. But that which most of all astonished them was the flying of bullets, which came singing over their heads and seemed very near to them; after which, the sound of drums passing along westward was very audible. And on the same day in Plymouth Colony in several places invisible troops of horses were heard riding to and fro.

Now, reader, prepare for the event of these prodigies, but count me not struck with a Livian superstition in reporting prodigies for which I have such incontestible assurance.*

---

* King Philip's War in New England occurred the following year.

Bacon's Rebellion in Virginia

ABOUT the year 1675 appeared three prodigies in that country, which from the attending disasters were looked upon as ominous presages.

The one was a large comet every evening for a week or more at southwest thirty-five degrees high, streaming like a horse tail westwards until it reached almost the horizon, and setting towards the northwest.

Another was flights of pigeons in breadth nigh a quarter of the midhemisphere, and of their length was no visible end; whose weights brake down the limbs of large trees whereon these rested at nights, of which the fowlers shot abundance and eat them. This sight put the old planters under the more portentous apprehensions, because the like was seen (as they said) in the year 1640 when the Indians committed the last massacre, but not after until that present year 1675.

The third strange appearance was swarms of flies about an inch long, and big as the top of a man's little finger, rising out of the spigot holes in the earth, which eat the new-sprouted leaves from the tops of the trees without other harm, and in a month left us.*

OMENS AND SIGNS IN DIARIES

Samuel Sewall

MONDAY, April 29, 1695. The morning is very warm and sunshiny; in the afternoon there is thunder and lightning, and about two P.M. a very extraordinary storm of hail, so that the ground was made white with it, as with the blossoms when fallen; 'twas as big as pistol and musket bullets. It broke of the glass of the new house about four hundred and eighty squares of the front; of Mr. Sergeant's about as much; Colonel Shrimpton, Major General, Governor Bradstreet, New Meetinghouse, Mr. Willard, et cetera.

* Bacon's Rebellion began in 1675.

Mr. Cotton Mather dined with us, and was with me in the new kitchen when this was. He had just been mentioning that more ministers' houses than others proportionably had been smitten with lightning, inquiring what the meaning of God should be in it. Many hailstones broke through the glass and flew to the middle of the room or farther. People afterward gazed upon the house to see its ruins. I got Mr. Mather to pray with us after this awful providence. He told God he had broken the brittle part of our house, and prayed that we might be ready for the time when our clay tabernacles should be broken. 'Twas a sorrowful thing to me to see the house so far undone again before 'twas finished. It seems at Milton on the one hand, and at Lewis's on the other, there was no hail.

I mentioned to Mr. Mather that Monmouth made his descent into England about the time of the hail in '85, summer, that much cracked our southwest windows.

Increase Mather

FEBRUARY 4TH, 1675. 'Tis reported that at Nosset an Indian squaw being with child, the child was heard crying three days before it was born. [There had been some difficulty in the church there a little before.—Jeremy Belknap.]

12th. This week one that was taken captive at Groton made an escape out of the enemy's hands. His name is Blood, a troublesome man in that place! I wish that the return of such a man to us may not be ominous of a return of blood!

May 15, 1676. At Lieutenant Howland's garrison in Plymouth was seen in the air an Indian bow pointing from east to west.

1681. This year begins awfully. The latter end of last year was attended with a fearful blazing star whereby the whole earth hath been alarmed. Now we hear rumors as of some prodigies observed in Connecticut Colony. 'Tis reported that at Wallingford an Indian appeared in the star. Guns and drums heard at Middletown and Guilford. (The report occasioned by a drum which somebody did really beat but was supposed to be an invisible hand.) Rumors and great fears lest New England should be involved in another war with the Indians.

10. SAMUEL SEWALL

Attributed to Nathaniel Emmons, *ca.* 1720-1730

BEFORE AND AFTER DEATH

Cotton Mather

STRANGE premonitions of death approaching are matters of such a frequent occurrence in history that one is ready now to look upon them as no more than matters of common occurrence. The learned know that Suetonius hardly lets one of his twelve Caesars die without them; and the vulgar talk of them as things happening every day amongst their smaller neighbors.

Even within a fortnight of my writing this, there was a physician who sojourned within a furlong of my own house. This physician, for three nights together, was miserably distressed with dreams of his being drowned. On the third of these nights his dreams were so troublesome that he was cast into extreme sweats, by struggling under the imaginary water. With the sweats yet upon him, he came down from his chamber, telling the people of the family what it was that so discomposed him. Immediately there came in two friends that asked him to go a little way with them in a boat upon the water. He was at first afraid of gratifying the desire of his friends, because of his late presages. But it being a very calm time, he recollected himself. "Why should I mind my dreams, or distrust the divine providence?" He went with them, and before night, by a thunderstorm suddenly coming up, they were all three of them drowned. I have just now inquired into the truth of what I have thus related; and I can assert it.

But apparitions after death are things which, when they occur, have more of strangeness in them. And yet they have been often seen in this land; particularly, persons that have died abroad at sea have, within a day after their death, been seen by their friends in their houses at home. The sights have occasioned much notice and much discourse at the very time of them; and records have been kept of the time (reader, I write but what hath fallen within my own personal observation), and it hath been afterwards found that very time when they thus appeared.

I will, from several instances which I have known of this thing, single out one that shall have in it much of demonstration as well as of particularity.

It was on the second of May, in the year 1687, that a most ingenious, accomplished, and well-disposed young gentleman, Mr. Joseph Beacon by name, about five o'clock in the morning as he lay, whether sleeping or waking he could not say (but he judged the latter of them), had a view of his brother, then at London, although he was now himself at our Boston, distanced from him a thousand leagues. This his brother appeared to him in the morning (I say) about five o'clock, at Boston, having on him a Bengal gown which he usually wore, with a napkin tied about his head. His countenance was very pale, ghastly, deadly, and he had a bloody wound on one side of his forehead.

"Brother!" says the affrighted Joseph.

"Brother!" answered the apparition.

Said Joseph, "What's the matter, brother? How came you here?"

The apparition replied, "Brother! I have been most barbarously and inhumanely murdered by a debauched fellow, to whom I never did any wrong in my life." Whereupon he gave a particular description of the murderer, adding, "Brother, this fellow, changing his name, is attempting to come over unto New England, as Foy or Wild. I would pray you, on the first arrival of either of these, to get an order from the governor to seize the person whom I have now described; and then do you indict him for the murder of me your brother. I'll stand by you and prove the indictment." And so he vanished.

Mr. Beacon was extremely astonished at what he had seen and heard; and the people of the family not only observed an extraordinary alteration upon him for the week following, but have also given me under their hands a full testimony that he then gave them an account of this apparition. All this while, Mr. Beacon had no advice of anything amiss attending his brother then in England. But about the latter end of June following he understood, by the common ways of communication, that the April before his brother, going in haste by night to call a coach for a lady, met a fellow then in drink with his doxy in his hand. Some way or other the fellow thought himself affronted in the hasty passage of this Beacon, and immediately ran into the fireside of a neighboring tavern, from whence he fetched out a fire-fork, wherewith he grievously wounded Beacon on the skull, even in that very part where the apparition showed his wound. Of this wound he languished until he died, on the second of May, about five of the clock in the morning, at London. The murderer, it seems, was endeavoring an escape, as the apparition affirmed; but the friends of the deceased Beacon seized him and, prosecuting him at law, he found the help of such friends as brought him off without the loss of his life; since which, there has no more been heard of the business.

The history I received of Mr. Joseph Beacon himself, who, a little before his own pious and hopeful death, which followed not long after, gave me the story written and signed with his own hand, and attested with the circumstances I have already mentioned.

I know not how far the reader will judge it agreeable unto the matters related in this article, if I do insert—but I *will* here insert a passage which I find thus entered among my own adversaria.

"14 day 2 mo. 1684. Mr. J. C., deacon of the church in Charlestown, told me that his wife having been sick for divers months, was on the 31st of August last seized with the pangs of death; in which being delirious, and asking divers times 'who would go with her, whither she was going?,' at length she said, 'Well, my son Robert will go.' And addressing her speech thereupon as unto him, she expressed her satisfaction that they should go together. This son of hers was at that time in Barbados; and his friends here have since learned that he also died there, and this at the very hour when his mother here gave up the ghost; and (which is further odd) not without the like expressions concerning his mother, that his mother had concerning him."

ACTIONS OF A DUNGHILL COCK

John Smith

THEN began the general assize (June, 1622), where not fewer than fifty civil, or rather uncivil, actions were handled and twenty criminal prisoners brought to the bar. Such a multitude of such vile people were sent to this plantation [Virginia] that Butler thought himself happy his time was so near expired. Three of the foulest acts were these: the first for the rape of a married woman, which was acquitted by a senseless jury; the second for buggering a sow; and the third for sodomy with a boy, for which they were hanged.

During the time of the imprisonment of this buggerer of the sow, a dunghill cock belonging to the same man did continually haunt a pig of his also, and to the wonder of all them that saw it, who were many, did so frequently tread the pig as if it had been one of his hens, that the pig languished and died within a while after. And then the cock resorted to the very same sow (that this fellow was accused for) in the very same manner. And as an addition to all this, about the same time two chickens were hatched, the one whereof had two heads; the other crowed very loud and lustily within twelve hours after it was out of the shell.

NECROMANCY WITH A PINNACE

John Winthrop

(JANUARY 2, 1644.) Captain Chaddock having bought from the French a pinnace of about thirty tons, he had manned and fitted her to go in her to Trinidad, and riding before Boston ready to depart, and eight men aboard her, one striking fire with a pistol, two barrels of powder took fire and blew her up. Five of the men being in the cabin were destroyed, and the other three being in the other part were much scorched and hurt, but got into their boat and were saved. The captain himself was then on shore at Boston. It is observable that these men making no use of the sudden loss of three of their company, but falling to drinking, et cetera, that very evening this judgment came thus upon them. It is also to be observed that two vessels have thus been blown up in our harbor, and both belonging to such as despised us and the ordinance of God amongst us.

The 18th of this month two lights were seen near Boston, and a week after the like was seen again. A light like the moon arose about the NE point in Boston, and met the former at

Noddle's Island, and there they closed in one, and then parted, and closed and parted divers times, and so went over the hill in the island and vanished. Sometimes they shot out flames and sometimes sparkles. This was about eight of the clock in the evening, and was seen by many.

About the same time a voice was heard upon the water between Boston and Dorchester, calling out in a most dreadful manner, "Boy, boy, come away, come away." And it suddenly shifted from one place to another a great distance, about twenty times. It was heard by divers godly persons. About fourteen days after, the same voice in the same dreadful manner was heard by others on the other side of the town towards Noddle's Island.

These prodigies having some reference to the place where Captain Chaddock's pinnace was blown up a little before, gave occasion of speech of that man who was the cause of it, who professed himself to have skill in necromancy, and to have done some strange things in his way from Virginia hither, and was suspected to have murdered his master there; but the magistrates here had not notice of him till after he was blown up. This is to be observed: that his fellows were all found, and others who were blown up in the former ship were also found, and others also who have miscarried by drowning, et cetera, have usually been found, but this man was never found.

SPECTER SHIPS

Noahdiah Russell

January 26th [1682]. It being Sabbath day, the morning was very cold. At noon very warm. At night between four and five of the clock there was a thundershower which came from the southwest wherein was a great storm of hail. The hailstones were nearly the bigness of a bullet; they broke several squares of glass at college, for they came with a strong wind. They broke glass at Roxbury, and at Lynn it shattered many windows. Moreover at Lynn after sundown as it began to be darkish an honest old man, Mr. Handford, went out to look for a new moon, thinking the moon had changed, when in the west he espied a strange black cloud in which, after some space, he saw a man in arms complete standing with his legs straddling and having a pike in his hands which he held across his breast—which sight the man with his wife saw and many others.

After a while the man vanished, in whose room appeared a spacious ship seeming under sail though she kept the same station. They saw it, they said, as apparently as ever they saw a ship in the harbor, which was to their imagination the handsomest of ever they saw—with a lofty stem, the head to the south, the hull black, the sails bright. A long and resplendent streamer came from the top of the mast. This was seen for a great space both by these and others of the same town. After this they went in, where tarrying but a while and looking out again all was gone and the sky as clear as ever.

This news was sent in a letter to Mrs. Margaret Mitchell of Cambridge, dated February 3rd, 1682, from Mr. Jeremiah Shephard, minister at Lynn.

John Lawson

I cannot forbear inserting here a pleasant story that passes for an uncontested truth amongst the inhabitants of this place: which is, that the ship which brought the first colonies does often appear among them, under sail, in a gallant posture, which they call Sir Walter Raleigh's ship. And the truth of this has been affirmed to me by men of the best credit in the country.

John Winthrop

THERE appeared over the harbor at New Haven, in the evening, the form of the keel of a ship with three masts, to which were suddenly added all the tackling and sails, and presently after, upon the top of the poop, a man standing with one hand akimbo under his left side, and in his right hand a sword stretched out toward the sea. Then from the side of the ship which was from the town arose a great smoke, which covered all the ship, and in that smoke she vanished away; but some saw her keel sink into the water. This was seen by many, men and women, and it continued about a quarter of an hour.

Cotton Mather *

BEING Londoners, or merchants and men of traffic and business, their design was in a manner wholly to apply themselves unto trade. But the design failing, they found their great estates sink so fast that they must quickly do something. Whereupon in the year 1646, gathering together almost all the strength which was left them, they built one ship more, which they freighted for England with the best part of their tradable estates; and sundry of their eminent persons embarked themselves in her for the voyage. But, alas! The ship was never heard of; she foundered in the sea, and in her were lost not only the hopes of their future trade but also the lives of several excellent persons, as well as divers manuscripts of some great men in the country, sent over for the service of the Church, which were now buried in the ocean. The fuller story of that grievous matter, let the reader with a just astonishment accept from the pen of the reverend person who is now the pastor of New Haven. I wrote unto him for it, and was thus answered.

"REVEREND AND DEAR SIR: In compliance with your desires, I now give you the relation of that APPARITION OF A SHIP IN THE AIR, which I have received from the most credible, judicious, and curious surviving observers of it.

"In the year 1647, besides much other lading, a far more rich treasure of passengers (five or six of which were persons of chief note and worth in New Haven) put themselves on board a new ship, built at Rhode Island, of about one hundred and fifty tons; but so walty that the master (Lamberton) often said she would prove their grave. In the month of January, cutting their way through much ice, on which they were accompanied with the Reverend Mr. Davenport, besides many other friends, with many fears, as well as prayers and tears, they set sail. Mr. Davenport in prayer, with an observable emphasis, used these words: 'Lord, if it be thy pleasure to bury these our friends in the bottom of the sea, they are thine; save them.'

* Mather made further inquiry into the New Haven specter ship mentioned by Winthrop.

"The spring following, no tidings of these friends arrived with the ships from England. New Haven's heart began to fail her. This put the godly people on much prayer, both public and private, 'that the Lord would (if it was his pleasure) let them hear what he had done with their dear friends, and prepare them with a suitable submission to his Holy Will.' In June next ensuing, a great thunderstorm arose out of the northwest, after which (the hemisphere being serene) about an hour before sunset a ship of like dimensions with the aforesaid, with her canvas and colors abroad (though the wind northerly), appeared in the air coming up from our harbor's mouth, which lies southward from the town, seemingly with her sails filled under a fresh gale, holding her course north, and continuing under observation, sailing against the wind for the space of half an hour.

"Many were drawn to behold this great work of God; yea, the very children cried out, 'There's a brave ship!' At length, crowding up as far as there is usually water sufficient for such a vessel, and so near some of the spectators as that they imagined a man might hurl a stone on board her, her maintop seemed to be blown off, but left hanging in the shrouds; then her mizzentop; then all her masting seemed blown away by the board. Quickly after the hulk brought unto a career, she overset, and so vanished into a smoky cloud, which in some time dissipated, leaving, as everywhere else, a clear air. The admiring spectators could distinguish the several colors of each part, the principal rigging, and such proportions, as caused not only the generality of persons to say, 'This was the mold of their ship, and thus was her tragic end,' but Mr. Davenport also in public declared to this effect, 'That God had condescended, for the quieting of their afflicted spirits, this extraordinary account of his sovereign disposal of those for whom so many fervent prayers were made continually. Thus I am, Sir,

"Your humble servant,
"JAMES PIERPONT."

Reader, there being yet living so many credible gentlemen that were eyewitnesses of this wonderful thing, I venture to publish it for a thing as undoubted as 'tis wonderful.

ACCIDENTS

AN INJURY

Increase Mather

REMARKABLE was the preservation and restoration which the gracious providence of God vouchsafed to Abigail Eliot, the daughter of elder Eliot, of Boston in New England. Concerning whom a near and precious relation of hers informs me that when she was a child about five years old, playing with other children under a cart, an iron hinge, being sharp at the lower end, happened to strike her head between the right ear and the crown of her head, and pierced into the skull and brain. The child making an outcry, the mother came and immediately drew out the iron, and thereupon some of the brains of her child, which stuck to the iron, and other bits were scattered on her forehead.

Able chirurgeons were sent for—in special Mr. Oliver and Mr. Prat. The head being uncovered, there appeared just upon the place where the iron pierced the skull a bunch as big as a small egg. A question arose, whether the skin should not be cut and dilated from the orifice of the wound to the swelling, and so take it away. This Mr. Prat inclined unto, but Mr. Oliver opposed, pleading that then the air would get to the brain, and the child would presently die. Mr. Oliver was desired to undertake the cure; and thus was his operation. He gently drove the soft matter of the bunch into the wound, and pressed so much out as well as he could; there came forth about a spoonful; the matter which came forth was brains and blood (some curdles of brain were white and not stained with blood); so did he apply a plaster.

The skull wasted where it was pierced to the bigness of a half-crown piece of silver or more. The skin was exceeding tender, so that a silver plate, like the skull, was always kept in the place to defend it from any touch or injury. The brains of the child did swell and swage according to the tides. When it was spring tide her brain would heave up the tender skin, and fill the place sometimes; when it was neap tide, they would be sunk and fallen within the skull. This child lived to be the mother of two children; and (which is marvelous) she was not by this wound made defective in her memory or understanding.

LIGHTNING

Increase Mather

ANOTHER sad disaster happened January 24th, 1665/6, when one Mr. Brooks of Hampshire, going from Winchester towards his house near Andover in very bad weather, was himself slain by lightning, and the horse he rode on under him. For about a mile from Winchester he was found with his face beaten into the ground, one leg in the stirrup, the other in the horse's mane; his clothes all burned off his back, not a piece as big as an handkerchief left entire, and his hair and all his body singed. With the force that struck him down, his nose was beaten into his face and his chin into his breast, where was a wound cut almost as low as to his navel; and his clothes being as aforesaid torn, the pieces were so scattered and consumed that not enough to fill the crown of a hat could be found. His gloves were whole, but his hands in them singed to the bone. The hipbone and shoulder of his horse burnt and bruised, and his saddle torn in little pieces.

There is another remarkable passage about lightning which happened at Duxbury, in New England, concerning which I have lately received this following account.

September 11, 1653 (being the Lord's day), there were small drizzling showers, attended with some seldom and scarce perceivable rumbling thunders, until towards the evening. At that time, Mr. Constant Southworth of Duxbury, returning home after evening exercise in company with some neighbors, discoursing of some extraordinary thunderclaps with lightning, and the awful effects and consequents thereof, being come into his own house (there were present in one room himself, his wife, two children, viz., Thomas, he was afterwards drowned, and

Benjamin, he was long after this killed by the Indians, with Philip Delano, a servant), there broke perpendicularly over the said house and room a most awful and amazing clap of thunder, attended with a violent flash or rather flame of lightning, which brake and shivered one of the needles of the katted or wooden chimney, carrying divers splinters seven or eight rods' distance from the house.

It filled the room with smoke and flame, and set fire in the thatch of a lean-to which was on the back side of a room adjoining to the former, in which the five persons above-mentioned were. It melted some pewter, so that it ran into drops on the outside, as is often seen on tinware; melted round holes in the top of a fire-shovel proportionable in quantity to a small goose shot; struck Mrs. Southworth's arm so that it was for a time benumbed; smote the young child Benjamin in his mother's arms, deprived it of breath for a space, and to the mother's apprehension squeezed it as flat as a plank; smote a dog stone dead which lay within two foot of Philip Delano. The dog never moved out of his place or posture in which he was when smitten, but giving a small yelp and quivering with his toes, lay still, blood issuing from his nose or mouth. It smote the said Philip, made his right arm senseless for a time, together with the middle finger in special of his right hand, which was benumbed and turned as white as chalk or lime, yet attended with little pain. After some few hours, that finger began to recover its proper color at the knuckle, and so did gradually whiten unto its extremity; and although the said Delano felt a most violent heat upon his body, as if he had been scorched in the midst of a violent burning fire, yet his clothes were not singed, neither had the smell of fire passed thereon.

Samuel Danforth

FEBRUARY 5, 1666. It pleased God this summer to arm the caterpillars against us, which did much damage in our orchards, and to exercise the Bay with a severe drought. The churches in the Bay sought the Lord by fasting and prayer. Our church of Roxbury began, the 19th of April. The Lord gave rain the

11. MAP OF VIRGINIA WITH PICTURE OF POWHATAN

Captain John Smith, *The Generall Historie of Virginia, New-England, and the Summer Isles*; London, 1624

next day. The rest of the churches in like manner besought the Lord, 21st of April. And it pleased God to send rain more plentifully on the 23rd day following.

At which time happened a sad accident at Marshfield, for in that town a certain woman, sitting in her house (some neighbors being present) and hearing dreadful thunder cracks, spake to her son and said, "Boy, shut the door, for I remember this time four years we had like to have been killed by thunder and lightning." The boy answered, "Mother, it's all one with God whether the door be shut or open." The woman said again, "Boy, shut the door." At her command the boy shut the door. But immediately there came a ball of fire from heaven down the chimney and slew the old woman (whose name was Goodwife Phillips), and the boy, and an old man, a neighbor that was present, and a dog that was in the house, but a little child that was in the arms of the old man escaped. And a woman with child being present was sore amazed.

FALLING INTO THINGS

Samuel Sewall

JANUARY 20, 1701/2, between 11 and 12 forenoon, the father was pecking ice off the mill wheel, slipped in, and was carried and crushed and killed with the wheel.

Saturday, January 24, 4 *post meridiem*. Mary Bowtel of Cambridge was burned to death in her own fire, being in a fit as is supposed. Her right arm and left hand were burnt quite off; her bowels burnt out, et cetera. Coroner Green told us this at Charlestown, January 27. 'Tis very remarkable that two such awfully violent deaths should fall out in one and the same week at Boston and Cambridge.

A man drowned in the cellar of the Queenshead Tavern; went to take out the plug and dropped in. It seems he had the falling sickness.

September 28, 1708. A very pretty boy of four years old, son of Sam Rand, grandson of Wm. Pain, was flourishing at training this day; fell into a scurvy open privy before night; of which loathsome entertainment he died in a day or two.

4

INDIAN CAPTIVITIES

As the concentration camp stands in our time for the ultimate in human horror and degradation, so in colonial days did the Indian captivity. When the Indians raided a white man's village they usually sought to secure prisoners, to be used for slaves, sold to the French, or ransomed by the English. These captives, after seeing their kinfolk murdered, must hike all day through the forests carrying burdens on the long foodless marches back to the Indian country. Laggards, the sick, complaining children, and bedridden mothers had only the tomahawk as alternative. At the journey's end, if they survived, they faced the prospect of gauntlet-runnings and sadistic brutalities. All the time they were at the caprice of any savage who might in a whim crack their skulls with his hatchet. After months or years might come escape or release.

This is the general pattern of the captivity experience, which combines heartbreak, terror, exhaustion, starvation, and excruciating tortures. Clothed in personal details, it becomes a harrowing experience just to read. Some of the examples of Indian tortures will upset weak stomachs, and the ones here given by no means cover all the variations; as putting hot coals into the mouths of suckling babies, until their lips get too scorched to suck and they must die in their mothers' arms; or burying a captive vertically in the ground with only his head above, scalping him, and lighting a fire close by until his brains boil and his eyes gush out of their sockets.

Autobiographical accounts of captivity and escape, which extend over two centuries, enjoyed wide vogue and ran through many editions. They were written as testimonials to God's providence, as hate tracts against the Indians, as sensational adventure yarns for the dime-novel audience. Recently the literary historians have given them serious attention, recognizing their naturally dramatic structure of seizure, detention, and return. Phillips Carleton likens them to the Icelandic sagas, being pristine records of the first violent struggles of settlement, and speaks earnestly for their literary values. "Our Indian captiv-

*ities are known mostly to historians and anthropologists and col-
lectors of Americana. At most they have the faint immortality of
preserved folklore. It is my contention that these captivities
deserve better treatment as literature; they are, I believe, unique,
vigorously written narratives containing in their painful realism,
their simple unaffected prose, their revelation of a pioneer
people, the virtues of true literature."*

The captivity stories have historical values too. They become
remarkable records of fortitude and faith, notably those of the
Jesuit missionary Father Jogues and the minister's wife Mary
Rowlandson. They illustrate Indian behavior in ways apparent
only to the day-by-day and inside observer. Carved pure out of
the American scene, they make real indeed a frightful and ever-
present danger to which the pioneer settlers were exposed.

THE CAPTURE OF JOHN SMITH

John Smith

(On December 10, 1607, when Jamestown had been settled only a few months, John Smith left the village for an exploring expedition up the Chickahominy River. Reaching the Indian town of Apocant, he there left seven of his men in the barge, and went ahead with the other two in a canoe. Contrary to orders, George Cassen went ashore from the barge, and was picked up by a large band of deer-hunting Indians, who were infuriated to discover the white men in their hunting area. They learned from Cassen of Smith's whereabouts, and then flayed their prisoner alive with mussel shells. The rest of the men in the barge escaped back to Jamestown, while the Pamunkey Indians followed Smith, slew his comrades, and surrounded him, with his one Indian guide, to initiate one of the most famous adventures in American history.)

BUT our comedies never endured long without a tragedy, some idle exceptions being muttered against Captain Smith for not discovering the head of Chickahominy River, and being taxed by the Council to be too slow in so worthy an attempt. The next voyage he proceeded so far that with much labor by cutting of trees in sunder he made his passage; but when his barge could pass no farther he left her in a broad bay out of danger of shot, commanding none should go ashore till his return. Himself with two English and two savages went up higher in a canoe; but he was not long absent, but his men went ashore, whose want of government gave both occasion and opportunity to the savages to surprise one George Cassen, whom they slew, and much failed not to have cut off the boat and all the rest.

Smith, little dreaming of that accident, being got to the marshes at the river's head, twenty miles in the desert, had his two men slain (as is supposed) sleeping by the canoe, whilst himself by fowling sought them victual. Finding he was beset with two hundred savages, two of them he slew, still defending himself with the aid of a savage his guide, whom he bound to his arm with his garters and used him as a buckler, yet he was shot in his thigh a little and had many arrows that stuck in his clothes but no great hurt, till at last they took him prisoner.

When this news came to Jamestown, much was their sorrow for his loss, few expecting what ensued.

Six or seven weeks* those barbarians kept him prisoner. Many strange triumphs and conjurations they made of him, yet he so demeaned himself amongst them, as he not only diverted them from surprising the fort, but procured his own liberty and got himself and his company such estimation amongst them that those savages admired him more than their own *quiyouckosucks*.†

The manner how they used and delivered him is as followeth:

The savages having drawn from George Cassen whither Captain Smith was gone, prosecuting that opportunity they followed him with three hundred bowmen conducted by the King of Pamunkey, who in divisions searching the turnings of the river found Robinson and Emry by the fireside; those they shot full of arrows and slew. Then finding the captain, as is said, that used the savage that was his guide as his shield (three of them being slain and divers other so galled), all the rest would not come near him. Thinking thus to have returned to his boat, regarding them, as he marched, more than his way, he slipped up to the middle in an oasis creek and his savage with him; yet durst they not come to him till being near dead with cold he threw away his arms. Then according to their composition they drew him forth and led him to the fire, where his men were slain. Diligently they chafed his benumbed limbs.

He demanding for their captain, they showed him Opechankanough, King of Pamunkey, to whom he gave a round ivory double compass dial. Much they marveled at the playing of the fly and needle, which they could see so plainly and yet not touch it, because of the glass that covered them. But when he demonstrated by that globelike jewel the roundness of the earth and skies, the sphere of the sun, moon, and stars, and how the sun did chase the night round about the world continually, the greatness of the land and sea, the diversity of nations, variety of

* Rather about three weeks, December 16, 1607–January 8, 1608.
† Medicine men.

complexions, and how we were to them antipodes, and many other suchlike matters, they all stood as amazed with admiration.

Notwithstanding, within an hour after they tied him to a tree, and as many as could stand about him prepared to shoot him. But the King holding up the compass in his hand, they all laid down their bows and arrows, and in a triumphant manner led him to Orapaks, where he was after their manner feasted and well used.

Their order in conducting him was thus. Drawing themselves all in file, the King in the midst had all their pieces and swords borne before him. Captain Smith was led after him by three great savages holding him fast by each arm; and on each side six went in file with their arrows nocked. But arriving at the town of Orapaks (which was but only thirty or forty hunting houses made of mats, which they remove as they please, as we our tents), all the women and children staring to behold him, the soldiers first all in file performed the form of a *Bissome* so well as could be; and on each flank, officers as sergeants to see them keep their orders. A good time they continued this exercise, and then cast themselves in a ring, dancing in such several postures, and singing and yelling out such hellish notes and screeches: being strangely painted everyone his quiver of arrows, and at his back a club; on his arm a fox or an otter's skin, or some such matter for his vambrace *; their heads and shoulders painted red, with oil and pocono [sand] mingled together, which scarletlike color made an exceeding handsome show; his bow in his hand, and the skin of a bird with her wings abroad dried, tied on his head; a piece of copper, a white shell, a long feather, with a small rattle growing at the tails of their snakes tied to it, or some suchlike toy.

All this while Smith and the King stood in the midst guarded, as before is said; and after three dances they all departed. Smith they conducted to a long house, where thirty or forty tall fellows did guard him; and ere long more bread and venison was brought him than would have served twenty men. I think his stomach at that time was not very good; what he left they put in baskets and tied over his head. About midnight they set the

---

* In medieval armor, the piece designed to protect the forearm.

meat again before him. All this time not one of them would eat a bit with him, till the next morning they brought him as much more; and then did they eat all the old, and reserved the new as they had done the other, which made him think they would fat him to eat him. Yet in this desperate estate, to defend him from the cold one Maocassater brought him his gown, in requital of some beads and toys Smith had given him at his first arrival in Virginia.

Two days after a man would have slain him (but that the guard prevented it) for the death of his son, to whom they conducted him to recover the poor man, then breathing his last. Smith told them that at Jamestown he had a water would do it, if they would let him fetch it. But they would not permit that, but made all the preparations they could to assault Jamestown, craving his advice; and for recompense he should have life, liberty, land, and women. In part of a tablet book he writ his mind to them at the fort, what was intended, how they should follow that direction to affright the messengers, and without fail send him such things as he writ for, and an inventory with them. The difficulty and danger he told the savages of the mines, great guns, and other engines exceedingly affrighted them, yet according to his request they went to Jamestown, in as bitter weather as could be of frost and snow, and within three days returned with an answer.

But when they came to Jamestown, seeing men sally out as he had told them they would, they fled. Yet in the night they came again to the same place where he had told them they should receive an answer, and such things as he had promised them; which they found accordingly, and with which they returned with no small expedition, to the wonder of them all that heard it, that he could either divine, or the paper could speak.

Smith Entertained with "Most Strange and Fearful Conjurations"

Not long after, early in a morning a great fire was made in a long house, and a mat spread on the one side, as on the other. On the one they caused him to sit, and all the guard went out

12. THE INDIANS' CONJURATION ABOUT SMITH

Captain John Smith, *The Generall Historie of Virginia, New-England, and the Summer Isles;* London, 1624

12ᵃ. KING POWHATAN COMMANDS SMITH TO BE SLAIN

of the house, and presently came skipping in a great grim fellow, all painted over with coal mingled with oil; and many snakes and weasel skins stuffed with moss, and all their tails tied together so as they met on the crown of his head in a tassel. And round about the tassel was as a coronet of feathers, the skins hanging round about his head, back, and shoulders, and in a manner covered his face. With a hellish voice and a rattle in his hand, with most strange gestures and passions, he began his invocation, and environed the fire with a circle of meal; which done, three more suchlike devils came rushing in with the like antic tricks, painted half black, half red; but all their eyes were painted white, and some red strokes like muchachos along their cheeks.

Round about him those friends danced a pretty while, and then came in three more as ugly as the rest, with red eyes and white strokes over their black faces. At last they all sat down right against him, three of them on the one hand of the chief priest and three on the other. Then all with their rattles began a song, which ended, the chief priest laid down five wheat corns. Then straining his arms and hands with such violence that he sweat, and his veins swelled, he began a short oration. At the conclusion they all gave a short groan, and then laid down three grains more. After that, began their song again, and then another oration, ever laying down so many corns as before, till they had twice encircled the fire. That done, they took a bunch of little sticks prepared for that purpose, continuing still their devotion, and at the end of every song and oration they laid down a stick betwixt the divisions of corn. Till night neither he nor they did either eat or drink; and then they feasted merrily, with the best provisions they could make. Three days they used this ceremony, the meaning whereof they told him was to know if he intended them well or no. The circle of meal signified their country, the circles of corn the bounds of the sea, and the sticks his country. They imagined the world to be flat and round, like a trencher, and they in the midst.

After this they brought him a bag of gunpowder, which they carefully preserved till the next spring to plant as they did their corn, because they would be acquainted with the nature of that seed.

In the Presence of Powhatan

At last they brought him to Werowacomoco [chief's town], where was Powhatan their Emperor. Here more than two hundred of those grim courtiers stood wondering at him, as he had been a monster, till Powhatan and his train had put themselves in their greatest braveries. Before a fire upon a seat like a bedstead he sat covered with a great robe, made of raccoon skins, and all the tails hanging by. On either hand did sit a young wench of sixteen or eighteen years, and along on each side the house, two rows of men, and behind them as many women with all their heads and shoulders painted red—many of their heads bedecked with the white down of birds, but everyone with something, and a great chain of white beads about their necks.

At his entrance before the King, all the people gave a great shout. The Queen of Appamatuck was appointed to bring him water to wash his hands, and another brought him a bunch of feathers (instead of a towel) to dry them. Having feasted him after their best barbarous manner they could, a long consultation was held. But the conclusion was, two great stones were brought before Powhatan; then as many as could laid hands on him, dragged him to them, and thereon laid his head. And being ready with their clubs to beat out his brains, Pocahontas, the King's dearest daughter, when no entreaty could prevail, got his head in her arms, and laid her own upon his to save him from death.

Whereat the Emperor was contented he should live to make him hatchets and her bells, beads, and copper; for they thought him as well of all occupations as themselves. For the King himself will make his own robes, shoes, bows, arrows, pots; plant, hunt, or do anything so well as the rest.

> *They say he bore a pleasant show,*
> *But sure his heart was sad.*
> *For who can pleasant be, and rest,*
> *That lives in fear and dread:*
> *And having life suspected, doth*
> *It still suspected lead.*

Two days after [January 7, 1608], Powhatan having disguised himself in the most fearful manner he could, caused Captain Smith to be brought forth to a great house in the woods, and there upon a mat by the fire to be left alone. Not long after, from behind a mat that divided the house was made the most dolefulest noise he ever heard. Then Powhatan, more like a devil than a man, with some two hundred more as black as himself, came unto him and told him now they were friends, and presently he should go to Jamestown to send him two great guns and a grindstone, for which he would give him the country of Capahowasic, and for ever esteem him as his son Nantaquoud.

So to Jamestown with twelve guides Powhatan sent him. That night they quartered in the woods, he still expecting (as he had done all this long time of his imprisonment) every hour to be put to one death or other, for all their feasting. But Almighty God (by his divine providence) had mollified the hearts of those stern barbarians with compassion. The next morning betimes they came to the fort, where Smith, having used the savages with what kindness he could, he showed Rawhunt, Powhatan's trusty servant, two demiculverings and a millstone to carry Powhatan. They found them somewhat too heavy; but when they did see him discharge them, being loaded with stones, among the boughs of a great tree loaded with icicles, the ice and branches came so tumbling down that the poor savages ran away half dead with fear. But at last we regained some conference with them, and gave them such toys and sent to Powhatan, his women, and children such presents as gave them in general full content.

THE CONDITION OF THE CAPTIVES
THAT FROM TIME TO TIME FELL INTO THE HANDS OF THE INDIANS: WITH SOME VERY REMARKABLE ACCIDENTS

Cotton Mather

WE have had some occasion, and shall have more, to mention captives falling into the hands of the Indians. We will here, without anything worthy to be called a digression, come to a little standstill, and with mournful hearts look upon the condition of the captives in those cruel hands. Their condition truly might be expressed in the terms of the ancient Lamentations (thus by some translated) Lamentations 4:3: "The daughter of my people is in the hands of the cruel, that are like the ostrich in the wilderness."

Truly the "dark places" of New England, where the Indians had their unapproachable kennels, were "habitations of cruelty"; and no words can sufficiently describe the cruelty undergone by our captives in those habitations. The cold, and heat, and hunger, and weariness, and mockings, and scourgings, and insolencies endured by the captives would enough deserve the name of cruelty; but there was this also added unto the rest, that they must ever now and then have their friends made a "sacrifice of devils" before their eyes, but be afraid of dropping a tear from those eyes, lest it should upon that provocation be next their own turn to be so barbarously sacrificed. Indeed, some few of the captives did very happily escape from their barbarous oppressors by a flight wisely managed; and many more of them were bought by the French, who treated them with a civility ever to be acknowledged, until care was taken to fetch 'em home. Nevertheless, many scores of 'em died among the Indians; and what usage they had may be gathered from the following relations, which I have obtained from credible witnesses.

RELATION I. James Key, son to John Key, of Quochecho, was a child of about five years of age, taken captive by the Indians at Salmon Falls; and that hellish fellow, Hope Hood, once a servant of a Christian master in Boston, was become the master of this little Christian. This child lamenting with tears the want of parents, his master threatened him with death if he did not refrain his tears; but these threatenings could not extinguish the natural affections of a child. Wherefore, upon his next lamentations, this monster stripped him stark naked and lashed both his hands round a tree, and scourged him so that from the crown of his head unto the sole of his foot he was all over bloody and swollen. And when he was tired with laying on his blows on the forlorn infant he would lay him on the ground, with taunts remembering him of his parents. In this misery the poor creature lay horribly roaring for divers days together, while his master, gratified with the music, lay contriving of new torments where-with to martyr him. It was not long before the child had a sore eye, which his master said proceeded from his weeping on the forbidden accounts; whereupon, laying hold on the head of the child with his left hand, with the thumb of his right he forced the ball of his eye quite out, therewithal telling him "that when he heard him cry again he would serve t'other so too and leave him never an eye to weep withal."

About nine or ten days after, this wretch had occasion to remove with his family about thirty miles further; and when they had gone about six miles of the thirty, the child being tired and faint sat him down to rest, at which this horrid fellow being pro-voked, he buried the blade of his hatchet in the brains of the child, and then chopped the breathless body to pieces before the rest of the company and threw it into the river. But for the sake of these and other such truculent things done by Hope Hood, I am resolved that in the course of our story I will watch to see what becomes of that hideous *loup-garou*, if he come to his end, as I am apt to think he will, before the story.

RELATION II. Mehitabel Goodwin, being a captive among the Indians, had with her a child about five months old which, through hunger and hardship (she being unable to nourish it) often made most grievous ejaculations. Her Indian master told her that if the child were not quiet he would soon dispose of it; which caused her to use all possible means that his Netopship might not be offended, and sometimes carry it from the fire out of his hearing, where she sat up to the waist in snow and frost for several hours until it was lulled asleep. She thus for several days preserved the life of her babe, until he saw cause to travel with his own cubs farther afield; and then, lest he should be retarded in his travel, he violently snatched the babe out of its mother's arms and before her face knocked out its brains, and stripped it of the few rags it had hitherto enjoyed, and ordered her the task to go wash the bloody clothes. Returning from this melancholy task, she found the infant hanging by the neck in a forked bough of a tree. She desired leave to lay it in the earth; but he said it was better as it was, for now the wild beasts would not come at it (I am sure they had been at it!) and she might have the comfort of seeing it again if ever they came that way.

The journey now before them was like to be very long, even as far as Canada, where his purpose was to make merchandise of his captive, and glad was the captive of such happy tidings. But the desperate length of the way, and want of food, and grief of mind wherewith she now encountered, caused her within a few days to faint under her difficulties. When at length she sat down for some repose, with many prayers and tears unto God for the salvation of her soul, she found herself unable to rise, until she espied her furious executioner coming towards her with fire in his eyes, the Devil in his heart, and his hatchet in his hand, ready to bestow a mercy stroke of death upon her. But then this miserable creature got on her knees, and with weeping and wailing and all expressions of agony and entreaty, prevailed on him to spare her life a little, and she did not question but God would enable her to "walk a little faster." The merciless tyrant was prevailed withal to spare her this time. Nevertheless, her former weakness quickly returning upon her, he was just going to murder her, but a couple of Indians just at that instant coming in suddenly called upon him to "hold his hand"; whereat such an horror surprised his guilty soul that he ran away. But hearing them call his name he returned, and then permitted these his friends to ransom his prisoner from him.

RELATION III. Mary Plaisted, the wife of Mr. James Plaisted, was made a captive by the Indians about three weeks after her delivery of a male child. They then took her, with her infant, off her bed, and forced her to travel in this her weakness the best part of a day, without any respect of pity. At night the cold ground in the open air was her lodging, and for many a day she had no nourishment but a little water with a little bear's flesh; which rendered her so feeble that she with her infant were not far from totally starved. Upon her cries to God, there was at length some supply sent in by her master's taking a moose, the broth whereof recovered her. But she must now travel many days through woods and swamps and rocks, and over mountains and frost and snow, until she could stir no farther. Sitting down to rest, she was not able to rise until her diabolical master helped her up; which, when he did, he took her child from her, and carried it unto a river, where, stripping it of the few rags it had, he took it by the heels and against a tree dashed out his brains, and then flung it into the river. So he returned unto the miserable mother, telling her "she was now eased of her burden, and must walk faster than she did before!"

RELATION IV. Mary Ferguson, taken captive by the Indians at Salmon Falls, declares that another maid, of about fifteen or sixteen years of age, taken at the same time, had a great burden imposed on her. Being overborne with her burden, she burst out into tears, telling her Indian master "that she could go no further." Whereupon he immediately took off her burden, and leading her aside into the bushes, he cut off her head, and scalping it, he ran about laughing and bragging what an act he had now done; and showing the scalp unto the rest, he told them "they should all be served so if they were not patient."

In fine, when the children of the English captives cried at any time, so that they were not presently quieted, the manner of the Indians was to dash out their brains against a tree. And very often, when the Indians were on or near the water, they took the small children and held them under water till they had near drowned them, and then gave them unto their distressed mothers to quiet 'em. And the Indians in their frolics would whip and beat the small children, until they set them into grievous outcries, and then throw them to their amazed mothers for them to quiet them again as well as they could.

This was Indian captivity! Reader, a modern traveler assures us that at the Villa Ludovisia, not far from Rome, there is to be seen the body of a petrified man; and that he himself saw by a piece of the man's leg, broken for satisfaction, both the bone and the stone crusted over it. All that I will say is that if thou canst read these passages without relenting bowels, thou thyself art as really petrified as the man at Villa Ludovisia.

A NOTABLE EXPLOIT
PERFORMED BY A WOMAN

Cotton Mather

ON MARCH 15, 1697, the savages made a descent upon the skirts of Haverhill, murdering and captivating about thirty-nine persons and burning about half a dozen houses. In this broil one Hannah Dustan, having lain in bed about a week, attended with her nurse, Mary Neff, a body of terrible Indians drew near unto the house where she lay, with designs to carry on their bloody devastations. Her husband hastened from his employments abroad unto the relief of his distressed family; and first bidding seven of his eight children (which were from two to seventeen years of age) to get away as fast as they could unto some garrison in the town, he went in to inform his wife of the horrible distress come upon them.

Ere she could get up, the fierce Indians were got so near that, utterly despairing to do her any service, he ran out after his children, resolving that on the horse which he had with him, he would ride away with that which he should in this extremity find his affections to pitch most upon, and leave the rest unto the care of the Divine Providence. He overtook his children about forty rod from his door, but then such was the agony of his parental affections that he found it impossible for him to distinguish any one of them from the rest; wherefore he took up a courageous resolution to live and die with them all. A party of Indians came up with him; and now, though they fired at him, and he fired at them, yet he manfully kept at the rear of his little army of unarmed children, while they marched off with the pace of a child of five years old until, by the singular providence of God, he arrived safe with them all unto a place of safety about a mile or two from his house.

But his house must in the meantime have more dismal tragedies acted at it. The nurse, trying to escape with the newborn infant, fell into the hands of the formidable savages; and those furious tawnies coming into the house bid poor Dustan to rise immediately. Full of astonishment, she did so; and sitting down in the chimney with an heart full of most fearful expectation, she saw the raging dragons rifle all that they could carry away, and set the house on fire.

About nineteen or twenty Indians now led these away, with about half a score other English captives, but ere they had gone many steps they dashed out the brains of the infant against a tree. And several of the other captives, as they began to tire in the sad journey, were soon sent unto their long home; the savages would presently bury their hatchets in their brains, and leave their carcasses on the ground for birds and beasts to feed upon. However, Dustan (with her nurse), notwithstanding her present condition, traveled that night about a dozen miles, and then kept up with their new masters in a long travel of an hundred and fifty miles, more or less, within a few days ensuing, without any sensible damage in their health from the hardships of their travel, their lodging, their diet, and their many other difficulties.

These two poor women were now in the hands of those whose "tender mercies are cruelties"; but the good God, who hath all "hearts in his own hands," heard the sighs of these prisoners, and gave them to find unexpected favor from the master who had laid claim unto them. That Indian family consisted of twelve persons—two stout men, three women, and seven children—and for the shame of many an English family that has the character of prayerless upon it, I must now publish what these poor women assure me. 'Tis this. In obedience to the instructions which the French have given them, they would have prayers in their family no less than thrice every day—in the morning, at noon, and in the evening; nor would they ordinarily let their children eat or sleep without first saying their prayers. Indeed, these idolaters were, like the rest of their whiter brethren, persecutors, and would not endure that these poor women should retire to their English prayers, if they could hinder them. Nevertheless, the poor women had nothing but fervent prayers to make their lives comfortable or tolerable; and by being daily sent out upon business they had opportunities, together and asunder, to do like another Hannah, in "pouring out their souls before the

Lord." Nor did their praying friends among ourselves forbear to "pour out" supplications for them.

Now, they could not observe it without some wonder that their Indian master sometimes when he saw them dejected would say unto them, "What need you trouble yourself? If your God will have you delivered, you shall be so!" And it seems our God would have it so to be. This Indian family was now traveling with these two captive women (and an English youth taken from Worcester, a year and a half before) unto a rendezvous of savages which they call a town, somewhere beyond Penacook; and they still told these poor women that when they came to this town they must be stripped, and scourged, and run the gauntlet through the whole army of Indians. They said this was the fashion when the captives first came to a town, and they derided some of the fainthearted English, which, they said, fainted and swooned away under the torments of this discipline. But on April 30, while they were yet, it may be, about an hundred and fifty miles from the Indian town, a little before break of day, when the whole crew was in a dead sleep (reader, see if it prove not so!), one of these women took up a resolution to imitate the action of Jael upon Sisera. And being where she had not her own life secured by any law unto her, she thought she was not forbidden by any law to take away the life of the murderers by whom her child had been butchered.

She heartened the nurse and the youth to assist her in this enterprise. All furnishing themselves with hatchets for the purpose, they struck such home blows upon the heads of their sleeping oppressors, that ere they could any of them struggle into any effectual resistance, "at the feet of these poor prisoners, they bowed, they fell, they lay down; at their feet they bowed, they fell; where they bowed, there they fell down dead." Only one squaw escaped, sorely wounded, from them in the dark; and one boy, whom they reserved asleep, intending to bring him away with them, suddenly waked, and scuttled away from this desolation.

But cutting off the scalps of the ten wretches they came off, and received fifty pounds from the General Assembly of the province as a recompense of their action; besides which they received many presents of congratulation from their more private friends. But none gave them a greater taste of bounty than Colonel Nicholson, the Governor of Maryland, who, hearing of their action, sent them a very generous token of his favor.

CAPTIVITY OF FATHER ISAAC JOGUES AMONG THE MOHAWKS

By Himself

(Father Isaac Jogues, the writer of the following narrative, was born at Orléans, in France, in 1607 and, embracing the rule of St. Ignatius, became a member of the Society of Jesus in 1624. Although a poet and scholar, he sought a foreign mission, and was sent to Canada soon after his ordination in 1636. After a short stay at Miscou, he proceeded to the country of the Wyandots or Hurons, in Upper Canada, and remained there amid every privation till 1642, when he was sent to Quebec by his Superior for necessaries of various kinds. On his return voyage he was taken prisoner, and he thus relates his sufferings in a letter written from Rensselaerswyck, now Albany, to the Provincial in France. The letter, which is in a pure and classic Latin, was first published by Alegambe in his *Mortes Illustres,* and subsequently by Tanner in his *Societas Militans,* both rare works. A sworn copy of the original letter is preserved at Montreal in manuscript.—John Gilmary Shea.)

Reverend Father in Christ,
  The Peace of Christ:

We sailed from the Huron territory on the 13th of June, 1642, in four small boats, here called canoes; we were twenty-three souls in all, five of us being French. This line of travel is, in itself, most difficult for many reasons, and especially because, in no less than forty places, both canoes and baggage had to be carried by land on the shoulders. It was now too full of danger from fear of the enemy, who, every year, by lying in wait on the roads to the French settlements, carry off many as prisoners; and, indeed, Father John Brebeuf was all but taken the year before. Besides this, not long before they carried off two

Frenchmen, but afterwards brought them back to their countrymen unharmed, demanding peace on most unjust terms, and then conducted themselves in a very hostile manner, so that they were driven off by the cannons of the fort. On this they declared that, if they took another Frenchman prisoner, they would torture him cruelly, like their other captives, and burn him alive by a slow fire.

The Superior, conscious of the dangers I was exposed to on this journey, which was, however, absolutely necessary for God's glory, so assigned the task to me that I might decline it if I chose. "I did not, however, resist; I did not go back" (Isaiah 1:5), but willingly and cheerfully accepted this mission imposed upon me by obedience and charity. Had I declined it, it would have fallen to another far more worthy than myself.

Having, therefore, loosed from St. Mary's of the Hurons, amid ever-varying fears of the enemy, dangers of every kind, losses by land and water, we at last, on the thirtieth day after our departure, reached in safety the Conception of the Blessed Virgin. This is a French settlement or colony, called Three Rivers, from a most charming stream near it, which discharges itself into the great river St. Lawrence by three mouths. We returned hearty thanks to God, and remained here and at Quebec about two weeks.

The business which had brought us having been concluded, we celebrated the feast of our holy Father Ignatius and, on the second of August, were once more on our way for Huronia. The second day after our departure had just dawned when, by the early light, some of our party discovered fresh footprints on the shore. While some were maintaining that they were the trail of the enemy, others that of a friendly party, Eustace Ahatsistari, to whom for his gallant feats of arms all yielded the first rank, explained: "Brothers! Be they the bravest of the foe, for such I judge them by their trail, they are no more than three canoes, and we number enough not to dread such a handful of the enemy." We were, in fact, forty, for some other had joined us.

We consequently urged on our way, but had scarcely advanced a mile when we fell into an ambush of the enemy, who lay in two divisions on the opposite banks of the river, to the number of seventy in twelve canoes.

As soon as we reached the spot where they lay in ambush, they poured in a volley of musketry from the reeds and tall grass where they lurked. Our canoes were riddled but, though well supplied with firearms, they killed none, one Huron only being shot through the hand. At the first report of the firearms the Hurons almost to a man abandoned the canoes which, to avoid the more rapid current of the center of the river, were advancing close by the bank, and in headlong flight plunged into the thickest of the woods. We four Frenchmen, left with a few, either already Christians or at least catechumens, offering up a prayer to Christ, faced the enemy. We were, however, outnumbered, being scarcely twelve or fourteen against thirty; yet we fought on, till our comrades, seeing fresh canoes shoot out from the opposite bank of the river, lost heart and fled.

Then a Frenchman named René Goupil, who was fighting with the bravest, was taken with some of the Hurons. When I saw this, I neither could nor cared to fly. Where, indeed, could I escape, barefooted as I was? Conceal myself amid the reeds and tall grass I could indeed, and thus escape; but could I leave a countryman, and the unchristened Hurons already taken or soon to be? As the enemy, in hot pursuit of the fugitives, had passed on, leaving me standing on the battlefield, I called out to one of those who remained to guard the prisoners, and bade him make me a fellow captive to his French captive, that, as I had been his companion on the way, so would I be in his dangers and death. Scarce giving credit to what he heard, and fearful for himself, he advanced and led me to the other prisoners.

"Dearest brother," I then exclaimed, "wonderfully hath God dealt with us! 'But He is the Lord, let Him do what is good in His sight,' I Kings 3:18. As it hath pleased Him, so hath it come to pass, blessed be His name." Then hearing his confession, I gave him absolution. I now turned to the Huron prisoners and, instructing them one by one, baptized them; as new prisoners were constantly taken in their flight, my labor was constantly renewed. At length Eustace Ahatsistari, that famous Christian chief, was brought in; when he saw me he exclaimed, "Solemnly did I swear, brother, that I would live or die by thee." What I answered, I know not, so had grief overcome me.

Last of all, William Couture was dragged in; he too had set

out from Huronia with me. When he saw all in confusion he had with the rest taken to the woods, and being a young man endowed with great gifts in body as well as in mind had by his great agility left the enemy far behind. When he looked around and could see nothing of me, "Shall I," he said to himself, "abandon my dear Father, a prisoner in the hands of savages, and fly without him? Not I." Then returning by the path which he had taken in flight, he gave himself up to the enemy. Would that he had fled, nor swelled our mournful band! for, in such a case, it is no comfort to have companions, especially those whom you love as yourself. Yet such are the souls who though but laymen (with no views of earthly reward) serve God and the Society among the Hurons.

It is painful to think, even, of all his terrible sufferings. Their hate was enkindled against all the French, but especially against him, as they knew that one of their bravest had fallen by his hand in the fight. He was accordingly first stripped naked, all his nails torn out, his very fingers gnawed, and a broadsword driven through his right hand. Mindful of the wounds of our Lord Jesus Christ, he bore, as he afterwards told me, this pain, though most acute, with great joy.

When I beheld him, thus bound and naked, I could not contain myself, but, leaving my keepers, I rushed through the midst of the savages who had brought him, embraced him most tenderly, exhorted him to offer all this to God for himself, and those at whose hands he suffered. They at first looked on in wonder at my proceedings; then, as if recollecting themselves, and gathering all their rage, they fell upon me, and, with their fists, thongs, and a club, beat me till I fell senseless. Two of them then dragged me back to where I had been before, and scarcely had I begun to breathe when some others, attacking me, tore out, by biting, almost all my nails, and crunched my two forefingers with their teeth, giving me intense pain. The same was done to René Goupil, the Huron captives being left untouched.

When all had come in from the pursuit, in which two Hurons were killed, they carried us across the river, and there shared the plunder of the twelve canoes (for eight had joined us). This was very great for, independent of what each Frenchman had with him, we had twenty packages containing church plate and vestments, books and other articles of the kind—a rich cargo indeed, considering the poverty of our Huron mission. While they were dividing the plunder, I completed the instruction of such as were unchristened, and baptized them. Among the rest was one sere, octogenarian chief who, when ordered to enter the canoe to be borne off with the rest, exclaimed, "How shall I, a hoary old man, go to a strange and foreign land? Never! Here will I die." As he absolutely refused to go, they slew him on the very spot where he had just been baptized.

Raising then a joyful shout which made the forest ring, "as conquerors who rejoice after taking a prey" (Isaiah 9:3), they bore us off, twenty-two captives, towards their own land; three had been killed. By the favor of God our sufferings on that march, which lasted thirteen days, were indeed great—hunger and heat and menaces, the savage fury of the Indians, the intense pain of our untended and now putrefying wounds, swarming even with worms. But no trial came harder upon me than when, five or six days after, they would come up to us, weary with the march, and in cold blood, with minds in no wise aroused by passion, pluck out our hair and beard, and drive their nails, which are always very sharp, deep into parts most tender and sensitive to the slightest impression. But this was outward; my internal sufferings affected me still more when I beheld that funeral procession of doomed Christians pass before my eyes, among them five old converts, the main pillars of the infant Huron church.

Indeed, I ingenuously admit that I was again and again unable to withhold my tears, mourning over their lot and that of my other companions, and full of anxious solicitude for the future. For I beheld the way to the Christian faith closed by these Iroquois on the Hurons and countless other nations, unless they were checked by some seasonable dispensation of Divine Providence.

On the eighth day we fell in with a troop of two hundred Indians going out to fight. And as it is the custom for the savages, when out on war parties, to initiate themselves as it were by cruelty, under the belief that their success will be greater as they shall have been more cruel, they thus received us. First rendering thanks to the sun, which they imagine presides over war, they congratulated their countrymen by a joyful volley of musketry. Each then cut off some stout clubs in the neighboring wood in order to receive us. When, therefore, we landed from the canoes, they fell upon us from both sides with their clubs with such fury that I, who was the last, and therefore most exposed to their blows, sank, overcome by their number and severity, before I had accomplished half the rocky way that led to the hill on which a stage had been erected for us. I thought I should soon die there; and so, partly because I could not, partly because I cared not, I did not arise. How long they spent their fury on me, He knows for whose love and sake I suffered all, and for whom it is delightful and glorious to suffer.

Moved at length by a cruel mercy, and wishing to carry me into their country alive, they refrained from beating me. And thus half dead and drenched in blood, they bore me to the stage. I had scarce begun to breathe when they ordered me to come down, to load me with scoffs and insults, and countless blows on my head and shoulders, and indeed on my whole body. I should be tedious were I to attempt to tell all that the French prisoners suffered. They burnt one of my fingers, and crunched another with their teeth; others already thus mangled, they so wrenched by the tattered nerve that, even now, though healed, they are frightfully deformed. Nor indeed was the lot of my fellow sufferers much better.

But one thing showed that God watched over us, and was trying us rather than casting us off. One of these savages, breathing nought but blood and cruelty, came up to me, scarce able to stand on my feet, and, seizing my nose with one hand, prepared to cut it off with a large knife which he held in the other. What could I do? Believing that I was soon to be burnt at the stake, unmoved I awaited the stroke, groaning to my God in heart; when, stayed as if by a supernatural power, he drew back his hand in the very act of cutting. About a quarter of an hour after he returned, and as if condemning his cowardice and faintheartedness, again prepared to do it; when again held back by some unseen hand, he departed. Had he carried out his design my fate was sealed, for it is not their custom to grant life to captives thus mutilated. At length, late at night and last of all, I was taken to my captors, without receiving a morsel of food, which I had scarcely touched for several days. The rest of the night I spent in great pain.

My sufferings, great in themselves, were heightened by the sight of what a like cruelty had wreaked on the Christian Hurons, fiercer than all in the case of Eustace; for they had cut off both his thumbs, and, through the stump of his left, with savage cruelty, they drove a sharp stake to his very elbow. This frightful pain he bore most nobly and piously.

The following day we fell in with some other war canoes, who cut off some of our companions' fingers, amid our great dread.

At last, on the tenth day about noon we left our canoes and performed on foot the rest of the journey, which lasted four days. Besides the usual hardships of the march, now came that of carrying the baggage. (Although my share of this was done quite remissly, both because I was unable and because I disdained to do it, for my spirit was haughty, even in fetters and death; so that only a small package was given me to bear.) We were now racked by hunger, from the ever-increasing want of food. Thus, three days in succession (until on the fourth we were met by a party from the village) we tasted nothing but some berries, once gathered on the way. For my part, I had in the beginning of the march neglected to avail myself of the food which our canoes had supplied abundantly, that I might not offer to their fire and torture a strong and vigorous frame, for I ingenuously confess my weakness. And when my body, worn down by fasting, called for food, it found nothing but water; for, on the second day, when we halted, weary with our march, they set a large kettle on the fire as if to prepare food, but it was merely to enable us to drink as much as each chose of the water thus slightly warmed.

At last on the eve of the Assumption of the Blessed Virgin we reached the first village of the Iroquois. I thank our Lord Jesus Christ that, on the day when the whole Christian world exults in the glory of his Mother's Assumption into heaven, he called us to some small share and fellowship of his sufferings and cross. Indeed, we had during the journey always foreseen that it would be a sad and bitter day for us. It would have been easy for René and myself to escape that day and the flames, for, being unbound and often at a distance from our guards, we might in the darkness of night have struck off from the road, and even though we should never reach our countrymen, we would at least meet a less cruel death in the woods. He constantly refused to do this, and I was resolved to suffer all that could befall me, rather than forsake in death Frenchmen and Christian Hurons, depriving them of the consolation which a priest can afford.

On the eve of the Assumption then, about three o'clock we reached a river which flows by their village. Both banks were filled with Iroquois and Hurons formerly captured, now coming forth to meet us, the latter to salute us by a warning that we were to be burnt alive; the former received us with clubs, fists and stones.

And as baldness or thin hair, a shaved or lightly covered head, is an object of their aversion, this tempest burst in its fury on my bare head. Two of my nails had hitherto escaped; these they tore out with their teeth, and with their keen nails stripped off the flesh beneath to the very bones. When satisfied with the cruelties and mockeries which we thus received by the riverside, they led us to their village on the top of the hill.

At its entrance we met the youth of all that district awaiting us with clubs, in a line on each side of the road.

Conscious that if we withdrew ourselves from the ranks of those chastised, we no less withdrew ourselves from that of the children, we cheerfully offered ourselves to our God, thus like a father chastising us, that in us he might be well pleased. Our order was as follows. In the front of the line they placed a Frenchman, alas entirely naked, not having even his drawers. René Goupil was in the center, and I last of all closed the line. (We were more fortunate, as they had left us our shirts and drawers.) The Iroquois scattered themselves through our lines between us and the Hurons, both to check our speed and to afford more time and ease to our torturers to strike us thus separately as we passed. Long and cruelly indeed did the "wicked work upon my back" (Psalm 127:3), not with clubs merely but even with iron rods, which they have in abundance from their proximity to the Europeans. One of the first, armed with a ball of iron of the size of a fist slung to a thong, dealt me so violent a blow that I should have fallen senseless, had not fear of a second given me strength and courage. Running then our long race amid this fearful hail of blows, we with difficulty reached the stage erected in the center of the village.

If each here presented a face to excite compassion, that of René was certainly the most pitiable. Being by no means quick or active, he had received so many blows all over his body, but especially on his face, that nothing could be distinguished there but the white of his eyes: more beautiful truly as he more resembled Him whom we have beheld "as a leper, and smitten by God for us, in whom there was no comeliness or beauty" (Isaiah 53:2).

We had but just time to gain breath on this stage when one with a huge club gave us Frenchmen three terrible blows on the bare back. The savages now took out their knives and began to mount the stage and cut off the fingers of many of the prisoners; and, as a captive undergoes their cruelty in proportion to his dignity, they began with me, seeing by my conduct, as well as by their words, that I was in authority among the French and Hurons. Accordingly, an old man and a woman approached the spot where I stood; he commanded his companion to cut off my thumb; she at first drew back, but at last, when ordered to do so three or four times by the old wretch, as if by compulsion she cut off my left thumb where it joins the hand. (She was an Algonquin, that is, one of that nation which dwells near the French, in New France; she had been captured a few months before, and was a Christian. Her name was Jane. Surely it is pleasing to suffer at the hands of those for whom you would die, and for whom you chose to suffer the greatest torment, rather than leave them exposed to the cruelty of visible and invisible enemies.)

Then, taking in my other hand the amputated thumb, I offered it to Thee, my true and living God, calling to mind the sacrifice which I had for seven years constantly offered Thee in Thy Church. At last, warned by one of my comrades to desist, since they might otherwise force it into my mouth and compel me to eat it as it was, I flung it from me on the scaffold and left it I know not where.

René had his right thumb cut off at the first joint. I must thank the Almighty that it was His will that my right should be untouched, thus enabling me to write this letter to beg my dear fathers and brothers to offer up their masses, prayers, supplications, and entreaties in the Holy Church of God, to which we know that we are now entitled by a new claim, for she often prays for the afflicted and the captive.

On the following day, the Assumption of the Blessed Virgin, after spending the morning on the stage, we were taken about midday to another village some two miles distant from the first. As I was on the point of marching, the Indian who had brought me, loath to lose my shirt, sent me off naked, except an old and wretched pair of drawers. When I beheld myself thus stripped, "Surely, brother," said I, "thou wilt not send me off thus naked; thou hast taken enough of our property to enrich thee." This touched him, and he gave me enough of the hempen bagging in which our packages had been put up to cover my shoulders and part of my body. But my shoulders, mangled by their blows and stripes, could not bear this rough and coarse cloth. On the way, while scarcely and at last not at all covered by it, the heat of the sun was so intense that my skin was dried as though in an oven, and peeled off from my back and arms.

As we entered the second village, blows were not spared, though this is contrary to their usual custom, which is to be content with once bastinadoing the prisoners. The Almighty surely wished us to be somewhat likened in this point to his apostle, who glories that he was thrice beaten with rods; and although they received us with fewer blows than the last, their blows were the more cruel since, being less embarrassed by the crowd, they were better aimed, some striking constantly on the shins to our exquisite pain.

The rest of the day we spent on the stage, and the night in a hut tied down half naked to the bare ground, at the mercy of all ages and sexes. For we had been handed over to the sport of the children and youth, who threw hot coals on our naked bodies, which, bound as we were, it was no easy matter to throw off. In this manner they make their apprenticeship in cruelty, and from less, grow accustomed to greater. We spent there two days and nights with scarcely any food or sleep, in great anguish of mind as far as I was concerned. For from time to time they mounted the stage, cutting off the fingers of my Huron companions, binding hard cords around their fists with such violence that they fainted, and while each of them suffered but his own pain, I suffered that of all. I was afflicted with as intense grief as you can imagine a father's heart to feel at the sight of his children's misery; for, with the exception of a few old Christians, I had begotten them all recently in Christ by baptism.

Yet amid all this the Lord gave me such strength that, suffering myself, I was able to console the suffering Hurons and French. So that, both on the road and on the stage, when the tormenting crowd of "saluters" (for so they call those who wreak their cruelty on the captives as they arrive) had dropped away, I exhorted them, at one time generally, at another individually, to preserve their patience, nor lose confidence which would have a great reward; to remember "that, by many tribulations, it behooves us to enter the kingdom of heaven"; that the time was come indeed, foretold to us by God, when he said: "Ye shall lament and weep, but the world shall rejoice, but your sorrow shall be turned into joy"; that we were like to a "woman in travail, who, when she brings forth, hath sorrow, because her hour is come; but, when she has brought forth, no longer remembers her anguish for joy that a man is born into the world" (John 16:21). So should they feel assured that in a few days these momentary pains would give place to never-ending joys. And surely I had reason to rejoice when I beheld them so well disposed, especially the older Christians, Joseph, Eustace, and the other two, for on the very day that we reached the first village, Theodore had freed himself from his bonds; but as during the battle he had had his shoulder blade broken by the butt end of a musket, he died on his way to the French.

Never till now had the Indian scaffold beheld French or other Christians captives. So that, contrary to usual custom, we were led around through all their villages to gratify the general curiosity. The third, indeed, we entered scatheless, but on the scaffold a scene met my eyes more heart-rending than any torment; it was a group of four Hurons, taken elsewhere by some other party, and dragged here to swell our wretched company. Among other cruelties every one of these had lost some fingers, and the eldest of the band his two thumbs. Joining these, I at once began to instruct them, separately, on the articles of faith; then on the very stage itself I baptized two, with raindrops gathered from the leaves of a stalk of Indian corn given us to chew. The other two I christened as we were led by a stream on our way to another village.

At this place, cold setting in after the rain, we suffered extremely from it, as we were entirely uncovered. Often shivering with cold on the stage, I would without orders come down and enter some hut, but I had scarcely begun to warm myself when I was commanded to return to the scaffold.

William Couture had thus far lost none of his fingers. This exciting the displeasure of an Indian in this village, he sawed off the forefinger of his right hand in the middle; the pain was most excruciating, as for this amputation he employed not a knife but in its stead a kind of shell, there very abundant. As it could not cut the sinews which were hard and slippery, he wrenched the finger so violently that, when the sinews gave way, the poor fellow's arm swelled fearfully up to the very elbow. An Indian, touched by mercy, took him to his hut and kept him there two days which we spent in that village, leaving me in ignorance and great anxiety as to his fate.

At nightfall we were taken to a hut where the youth awaited us. They ordered us to sing as other captives are wont to do; we at last complied, for alas, what else could we do? But we sang the "Canticles of the Lord in a strange land." Torture followed the chanting, and its fury burst especially on René and myself, for the good savage still kept William in his hut. Accordingly, on me and especially on René, they threw hot ashes and live coals, burning him terribly in the breast.

They next hung me up between two poles in the hut, tied by the arms above the elbow with coarse rope woven of the bark of trees. Then I thought I was to be burnt, for this is one of their usual preliminaries. And that I might know that if I had thus far borne anything with fortitude or even with patience, these came not from myself but from him who gives strength to the weary—now, as though left to myself in this torture, I groaned aloud, for "I will glory in my infirmities that the power of Christ may dwell in me" (2 Corinthians 12:9), and from my intense pain I begged my torturers to ease me some little from those hard, rough ropes. But God justly ordained that the more I pleaded, the more tightly they drew my chains.

At last when I had been hanging thus about a quarter of an hour, they unloosed me as I was on the point of fainting. I render these thanks, O Lord Jesus, that I have been allowed to learn, by some slight experience, how much thou didst deign to suffer on the cross for me, when the whole weight of thy most sacred body hung not by ropes, but by thy hands and feet pierced by hardest nails! Other chains followed these, for we were tied to the ground to pass the rest of the night. What did they not then do to my poor Huron companions thus tied hand and foot? What did they not attempt on me? But once more I thank thee, Lord, that thou didst save me, thy priest, ever unsullied from the impure hands of the savages. When we had thus spent two days in that village we were led back to the second which we had entered, that our fate might be finally determined.

We had now been for seven days led from village to village, from scaffold to scaffold, become a spectacle to God and to His angels (as we may hope from His divine goodness), a scoff and jeer to the vilest savages—when we were at last told that that day should end our lives amid the flames. Though, in sooth, this last act was not without its horrors, yet the good pleasure of God and the hope of a better life subject to no sin rendered it more one of joy. Then, addressing my French and Huron companions as it were for the last time, I bid them be of good heart, amid their mental and bodily sufferings to think "diligently upon him that had endured such opposition of sinners against himself, not to be weary, fainting in their minds" (Hebrews 12:3), but to hope that the morrow would unite us to our God to reign forever.

Fearing lest we might be torn from one another, I especially advised Eustace to look towards me when we could not be together, and by placing his hands on his breast and raising his eyes to heaven to show his contrition for his sins, so that I could absolve him, as I had already frequently done after hearing his confession on the way and after our arrival. As advised, he several times made the signal.

The sachems, however, on further deliberation resolved that no precipitate step was to be taken with regard to the French, and when they had summoned us before the council, they declared that our lives were spared. To almost all the Hurons likewise they granted their lives. Three were excepted, Paul, Eustace, and Stephen, who were put to death in the three villages which make up the tribe: Stephen in the village where we were, known as Andagoron, Paul in Ossernenon, and Eustace in Teonontogen. The last was burned in almost every part of his body and then beheaded; he bore all most piously, and while it is usual for dying captives to cry out

> *"Exoriatur nostris ex ossibus ultor"*
> *"May an avenger arise from our ashes"*

he, on the contrary, in the Christian spirit which he had so deeply imbibed in baptism, implored his countrymen standing around not to let any feeling for his fate prevent the concluding of a peace with the Iroquois.

Paul Ononhoratoon, who after going through the usual fiery ordeal was tomahawked in the village·of Ossernenon, was a young man of about twenty-five, full of life and courage; for such they generally put to death, to sap as it were the lifeblood of the hostile tribe. With a noble contempt of death arising, as he openly professed on the way, from his hope of a better life, this generous man had repeatedly, when the Iroquois came up to me to tear out my nails or inflict some other injury, offered himself to them, begging them to leave me and turn their rage on him. May the Lord return him a hundredfold with usury for that heroic charity which led him to give his life for his friends, and for those who had begotten him in Christ in bondage!

Towards evening of that day they carried off William Couture, whom they regarded as a young man of unparalleled courage, to Teonontogen, the farthest village of their territory, and gave him to an Indian family. It is the custom of these savages, when they spare a prisoner's life, to adopt him into some family to supply the place of a deceased member, to whose rights he in a manner succeeds; he is subject thenceforward to no man's orders except those of the head of the family, who, to acquire this right, offers some presents. But seeing that René and I were less vigorous, they led us to the first village, the residence of the party that had captured us, and left us there till some new resolution should be taken.

After so many a long day spent fasting, after so many sleepless nights, after so many wounds and stripes, and especially after such heart-rending anguish of mind, when at last time was, so to speak, given us to feel our sufferings, we sank into a state of helplessness, scarce able to walk or even stand erect; neither night nor day brought a moment of repose. This resulted from many causes, but chiefly from our still untended wounds; this state was rendered more trying by the myriads of lice, fleas, and bedbugs, of which the maimed and mutilated state of our fingers did not permit us to clear our persons. Besides this we suffered from hunger; more truly here than elsewhere is the saying

"Cibus   non   utilis   aegro."
"Food is hurtful to the sick."

So that, with nothing to add to their American corn (which in Europe we call Turkish), carelessly bruised between two stones, but unripe squashes, we were brought to the brink of the grave—and René especially, whose stomach refused this food, and who from his many wounds had almost lost his sight.

The Indians then, seeing us fail day by day, hunted up in the village some small fishes and some bits of meat dried by the fire and sun, and pounding these, mixed them with our sagamité.

After three weeks, we were just recovering from our illness when they sought to put us to death.

The two hundred Indians who had maltreated us so on the way advanced into New France, to the point where the river Iroquois, so called from them, empties into the great river St. Lawrence. Here, seeing a party of the French engaged in laying the foundations of Fort Richelieu, they thought they could easily kill some and carry off the rest as prisoners. Accordingly, to the number of two hundred, in a single column and almost all armed with muskets, they rushed almost unexpected upon the whites engaged in the various works. At the first onset of the foe the French, though but a handful compared to the number of the savages, flew to arms, and so bravely and successfully repulsed their fierce assailants that, after killing two and wounding many more, they put the rest to flight. The war party returned furious, and, as though they had been greatly wronged who had gone forth to do wrong, demanded the death of those of us who were yet alive. They asserted it to be a shame that three Frenchmen should live quietly among them when they had so lately slain three Iroquois. By these complaints, René's safety especially and my own were in great jeopardy. He alone who, as He gave, protecteth life, warded off the blow.

On the eve of the Nativity of the Blessed Virgin, one of the principal Hollanders, who have a settlement not more than twenty leagues from these Indians, came with two others, to endeavor to effect our liberation. He remained there several days, offered much, promised more, obtained nothing. But, as they are a wily and cunning race of savages, in order not to appear to refuse all that a friend asked, but to concede something to his desires, they lyingly asserted that they would in a few days restore us to our countrymen. This was perhaps the wish of some of them, but in the latter part of September (for constant rain had put the matter off till that time) a final council was held on our fate, although provisions had been prepared and men appointed to take us back. Here the opinion of the few well inclined was rejected. Confusion carried the day, and some clamorous chiefs declared that they would never suffer a Frenchman to be taken back alive. The council broke up in alarm, and each as if in flight returned home, even those who came from other villages. Left thus to the cruelty of bloodthirsty men, attempts were constantly made on our lives. Some, tomahawk in hand, prowled around the cabins to find and dispatch us. However, towards the close of the council, God had inspired me with some thought that induced me to draw my companions together without the village in a field belonging to the house where I was. Here, ignorant of what had transpired, we lay hid as it were in safety until the storm, beneath which we should all have fallen had we remained in the village, was somewhat calmed.

William was after this taken back by his master to his own

village. René and I, perceiving that there was now no hope of our return, withdrew to a neighboring hill which commands the village, in order to pray. Here, remote from every witness and from all officious intrusion, we resigned ourselves entirely to God and to his holy will. On our road back to the village we were reciting our beads, and had already completed four decades of the rosary, when we met two young men who commanded us to return to the village. "Dear brother," said I, "we know not what may be, in this period of general excitement, the design of these men. Let us commend ourselves earnestly to God, and to the most Blessed Virgin, our good Mother." We had reached the village in prayer when, at its very entrance, one of the two whom we had met, plucking forth his tomahawk which was concealed in his dress, dealt René so deadly a blow on the head that he fell lifeless, invoking the most holy name of Jesus as he fell. We had happily, mindful of the indulgence thereby gained, often reminded each other to close our life by uttering, with our dying voice, that most holy name.

At the sight of the reeking hatchet, I knelt down on the spot and, uncovering my head, awaited a like blow. But, when I had been there a moment or two, they bade me rise, as they had no right to kill me, for I was the slave of another family. Rising then in haste, I ran to my still-breathing companion and conferred absolution, which I was in the habit of giving him after his confession every other day. Then two other blows, dealt before my very face, added him to the number of the blessed.

He was thirty-five years of age, eminent for his simplicity of manners, his innocence of life, his patience in adversity, entirely submissive to God, whom he in all things regarded as present before his eyes, and resigned to His most holy will in love. As he was very pious, and accustomed to be with the Christians, or such as were most intimate with our Christians, he daily spent a long time in prayer, to the wonder and even suspicion of the savages, so novel did it seem to them. These suspicions were confirmed in their minds when one day, taking off the cap of a child in the hut where he lived, he made him make a sign of the cross on his breast and forehead; for a superstitious old

Indian, the grandfather of the boy, seeing this, ordered him to be killed. This I afterwards learned from the boy's mother, who told me that he had been killed by the old man for that reason.

And now the middle of October was come, when the Indians leave their villages to go and hunt deer, which they take by traps or kill with their guns, in the use of which they are very skillful. This season, to the Indians one of relaxation and enjoyment, brought its new burden of sorrows for me; for I was given to a party, who were first amazed at me, then ridiculed, and at last began to hate me.

Mindful of the character imposed upon me by God, I began with modesty to discourse with them of the adoration of one only God, of the observance of His commandments, of heaven, hell, and the other mysteries of our Faith, as fully as I was able. At first, indeed, they listened, but when they saw me constantly recur to these things, and especially when the chase did not meet with the desired success, then they declared that I was an Otkon [demon], who caused them to take so little game. But what turned their ill will into perfect rage and fury, so to speak, was this.

It is a custom with all these nations to have recourse, in their hunting, fishing, war, sickness, and the like, to a certain demon whom they call Aireskoi. Whoever desires his fishing, hunting, or other expeditions to be successful takes meat and other of the better articles of food, and begs the oldest of the house or village to "bless" them for him, if I may use the term; and there are some to whose blessings they attach more value than to others. The old man, standing opposite the one that holds the meat, in a loud and distinct voice speaks thus: "O demon Aireskoi, behold, we offer this meat to thee, and from it we prepare thee a banquet, that thou mayest eat thereof, and show us where the deer are lurking, mayest lead them into our traps;" (if not during the chase) "that by thee we may again behold the spring, taste the new harvest, and again engage in the chase in the fall;" (if in illness) "that by these we may recover health."

The very first time I heard a formula couched in such words I was filled with a deep detestation of this savage superstition, and firmly resolved to abstain forever from meats thus offered. They interpreted this abstinence on my part, and this contempt of their demon, as the cause of their taking so little game ("the wicked have hated me without cause"—John 15:25). As under the influence of this hate they would neither listen to my instructions nor help me to acquire their language, in which I refuted their fables, I resolved to devote my time entirely to spiritual exercises.

Accordingly, I went forth every morning from the midst of this Babylon, that is, our hut where constant worship was paid to the Devil and to dreams, and "saved myself in the mountain" (Genesis 19:17), a neighboring hill. Here I had formed a large cross on a majestic tree by stripping off the bark, and at its foot I spent the whole day with my God, whom almost alone in those vast regions I worshiped and loved—sometimes in meditation or in prayer, at other times reading an "Imitation of Christ" which I had just before recovered. This for some time was unperceived; but on one occasion, finding me as was my wont in prayer before my cross, they attacked me most violently, saying that they hated the cross; that it was a sign that they and their friends the neighbors (Europeans) knew not, alluding to the Dutch Protestants.

Upon this I changed my conduct, and whereas I had before carefully avoided praying or kneeling in their hut, that I might not give them the slightest reason to complain (for we should, especially among savages, but little accustomed to such things, act in all prudence), I now conceived that I should not longer refrain from those pious exercises which make up a spiritual life, a life I far preferred to my temporal one. This I believed would be serviceable to them when the moment of their conversion should come, "which the Father hath put in His own power" (Acts 1:7).

While thus an object of their enmity, I certainly suffered much from hunger and cold, the contempt of the lowest of the men, the bitter hatred of their women.

The latter, who are the greatest gainers by the hunting season, regarded me as the cause of their want and poverty. I suffered most from hunger, for as almost all the venison on which they chiefly lived had been offered to the Devil in these oblations, I spent many days fasting; and almost every night when I came in fasting, I would see our Egyptians sitting over their fleshpots, which my severe, though self-imposed, law prevented my touching. And although reasons occurred to me, at times dissuading me from this course, yet by God's grace I never suffered myself to break my resolution.

I suffered also greatly from cold, amid the deep snows under my scanty, worn-out cloak, especially at night when ordered to sleep uncovered on the bare ground on some rough bark. For though they had plenty of deerskins, perfectly useless to them, not one was given to me; now, when sometimes on a very bitter night I would, overcome by the cold, secretly take one, they rose at once and pulled it from me, so great was their enmity against me. My skin was now in such a state that I could with David say, "It had withered with the filth of dust" (Job 7:5). It burst with cold, and gave me great pain all over my body.

My unhealed fingers were another source of misery, for the wounds were hardly closed by the middle of January. In the village, however, a thin skin was added to my worn-out cloak; in this wretched guise I traversed the streets of our village, begging that the Lord would one day join me with his saints who formerly served him in "sheepskins and goatskins, distressed, afflicted, of whom the world was not worthy" (Hebrews 11:37). And I daily saw the Indians well dressed in the cloth and garments which our baggage had plentifully supplied, while I was shivering night and day with cold. But this was little; more was I moved to see these heathen men unworthily profane things dedicated to the service of God. One of them had made himself leggings of two of the veils used at mass.

About the middle of March, when the snow had melted away, they took me with them to their fishing ground. The party consisted of the old man and woman, a little boy and myself. Four days' travel brought us to a lake where we caught nothing but a few little fishes. The intestines of these generally served as a seasoning for our sagamité, the fish being laid by to carry back to the village. Such food as this, with the intestines of deer full of blood and half-putrefied excrement, and mushrooms boiled, and rotten oysters, and frogs, which they eat whole, head and feet, not even skinned or cleaned—such food had hunger, custom, and want of better made, I will not say tolerable, but even pleasing.

A war party came in bringing twenty-two prisoners, but belonging to a nation with whom they had as yet never been at war. Still, in violation of all right and justice, they were beaten with clubs and stripes, and mutilated by the usual cutting off of fingers. Five of them were to be put to death, for all the rest, being boys and girls or women, were kept as slaves. Their instruction was now an object of my solicitude, for I was ignorant of their language; yet by God's grace I was able, by a few words that I picked up, but chiefly by the kindness of one who knew both languages, to instruct and baptize them. This happened at Easter. At Whitsuntide they brought in new prisoners, three women with their little children, the men having been killed near the French settlements. They were led into the village entirely naked, not even with any kind of petticoat on, and after being severely beaten on the way, had their thumbs cut off. One of them, a thing not hitherto done, was burnt all over her body, and afterwards thrown into a huge pyre. And worthy of note is a strange rite I then beheld, when this woman was burnt.

At each wound which they inflicted, by holding lighted torches to her body, an old man in a loud voice exclaimed, "Demon Aireskoi, we offer thee this victim, whom we burn for thee, that thou mayest be filled with her flesh, and render us ever anew victorious over our enemies." Her body was cut up, sent to the various villages, and devoured. For about midwinter, grieving as it were that they had refrained from eating the flesh of some prisoners, they had, in a solemn sacrifice of two bears which they offered to their demon, uttered the words, "Justly dost thou punish us, O Demon Aireskoi. Lo, this long time we have taken no captives; during the summer and fall, we have taken none of the Algonquins. (These they consider properly their enemies.) We have sinned against thee, in that we ate not the last captives thrown into our hands; but, if we shall ever again capture any, we promise thee to devour them as we now consume these two bears." And they kept their word.

13. MARTYRDOM OF FATHER JOGUES AND OTHER JESUIT MISSIONARIES

Du Creux, *Historiae Canadensis Libri Decem;* Paris, 1664

This poor woman I baptized in the midst of the flames, unable to do so before, and then only while raising a drink to her parched lips.

But I am now weary of so long and so prolix a letter. I therefore earnestly beg Your Reverence ever to recognize me, though unworthy, as one of yours; for, though a savage in dress and manner, and almost without God in so tossed a life, yet as I have ever lived a son of the most holy Church of Rome and of the Society, so do I wish to die. Obtain for me from God, Reverend Father, by your holy sacrifices, that although I have hitherto but ill employed the means he gave me to attain the highest sanctity, I may at least employ well this last occasion which he offers me. Your bounty owes this surely to your son who has recourse to you, for I lead a truly wretched life, where every virtue is in danger. Faith in the dense darkness of paganism; hope in so long and hard trials; charity amid so much corruption, deprived of all the sacraments. Purity is not indeed here endangered by delights; yet it is in danger amid this promiscuous and intimate intercourse of both sexes, in the perfect liberty of each to hear and do what he pleases, and most of all in their constant nakedness. For here, willing or not, you must often see what elsewhere is shut out not only from wandering but even from curious eyes.

Hence I daily groan to my God, begging him not to leave me without help amid the dead; begging him, I say, that amid so much impurity and such superstitious worship of the Devil to which he has exposed me, naked as it were, and unarmed, "my heart may be undefiled in his justifications" (Psalm 118:80) so that, when that good Shepherd shall come, "who will gather together the dispersed of Israel" (Psalm 146:2), He may gather us from among the nations to bless His holy name. Amen! Amen!

Your Reverence's
Most humble servant and son in Christ,
ISAAC JOGUES

Rensselaerswyck in New Netherland,
August 5, 1643

MEMOIRS OF ODD ADVENTURES
AND SIGNAL DELIVERANCES IN THE CAPTIVITY
OF JOHN GYLES, ESQ.

By Himself

Containing the Occurrences of the First Year

ON the second day of August, 1689, in the morning, my honored father, Thomas Gyles, Esq., went with some laborers, my two elder brothers, and myself to one of his farms which lay on the river about three miles above Fort Charles, adjoining Pemaquid Falls, there to gather in his English harvest, and labored securely till noon. After we had dined our people went to their labor, some in one field to their English hay, the others to another field of English corn, except my father, the youngest of my two brothers, and myself, who tarried near to the farmhouse in which we had dined, till about one of the clock, when we heard the report of several great guns from the fort. Upon the hearing of them my father said that he hoped it was a signal of good news, and that the Great Council had sent back the soldiers to cover the inhabitants (for on report of the revolution they had deserted). But to our great surprise, about thirty or forty Indians at that moment discharged a volley of shot at us, from behind a rising ground near our barn.

The yelling of the Indians, the whistling of their shot, and the voice of my father, whom I heard cry out "What now! What now!," so terrified me (though he seemed to be handling a gun), that I endeavored to make my escape. My brother ran one way and I another, and looking over my shoulder I saw a stout fellow, painted, pursuing me with a gun and a cutlass glittering in his hand which I expected every moment in my brains. I presently fell down, and the Indian took me by the left hand, offered me no abuse, but seized my arms, lifted me up, and pointed to the place where the people were at work about the hay, and led me that way. As we passed we crossed my father, who looked very pale and bloody, and walked very slowly. When we came to the place, I saw two men shot down on the flats, and one or two more knocked on their heads with hatchets, crying out, "O Lord," et cetera.

There the Indians brought two captives, one a man, and my brother James, he that endeavored to escape by running from the house when I did. He was about fourteen years of age. The eldest brother, whose name was Thomas, wonderfully escaped by land to the Barbican, a point of land on the west side of the river opposite to the fort, where several fishing vessels lay. He got on board one of them and came to sail that night.

After they had done what mischief they could, they sat down, making us sit with them, and after some time arose, pointing to us to go eastward. They marched about a quarter of a mile and then made a halt, and brought my father to us and made proposals to him by old Moxus, who told him that those were strange Indians who shot him, and that he was sorry for it. My father replied that he was a dying man, and wanted no favor of them but to pray with his children; which being granted, he recommended us to the protection and blessing of God Almighty, then gave us the best advice, and took his leave for this life, hoping in God that we should meet in a better world. He parted with a cheerful voice, but looked very pale by reason of his great loss of blood, which boiled out of his shoes. The Indians led him aside. I heard the blows of the hatchet, but neither shriek nor groan. I afterwards heard that he had five or seven shot-holes through his waistcoat or jacket, and that the Indians covered him with some boughs.

The Indians led us, their captives, on the east side of the river towards the fort, and when we came within a mile and a half of the fort and town, and could see the fort, we saw firing and smoke on all sides. Here we made a short stop, and then moved within or near the distance of three-quarters of a mile from the fort, into a thick swamp. There I saw my mother and my two little sisters, and many other captives taken from the town. My mother asked me of my father. I told her that he was killed, but could say no more for grief. She burst into tears, and the Indians moved me a little further off, and seized me to a tree.

The Indians came to New Harbor, and sent spies several days to observe how and where the people were employed, et cetera, who found that the men were generally at work at noon, and left about their houses only women and children. Therefore the Indians divided themselves into several parties, some ambushing the way between the fort and the houses, as likewise between them and the distant fields; and then alarming the farthest off first, they killed and took the people as they moved toward the town and fort, at their pleasure, so that very few escaped to the fort. Mr. Pateshall was taken and killed as he lay with his sloop near the Barbican.

On the first stir about the fort, my youngest brother was at play near the same and ran in, and so by God's goodness was preserved. Captain Weems with great courage and resolution defended the weak old fort two days, till that he was much wounded and the best of his men killed, and then beat for a parley. And the conditions were:

1. That they, the Indians, should give him Mr. Pateshall's sloop.

2. That they should not molest him in carrying off the few people that had got into the fort, and three captives that they had taken.

3. That the English should carry off in their hands what they could from the fort.

On these conditions the fort was surrendered, and Captain Weems went off. And soon after the Indians set on fire the fort and houses, which made a terrible blast and was a melancholy sight to us poor captives, who were sad spectators.

After the Indians had thus laid waste Pemaquid, they moved us all to New Harbor, about two miles east of Pemaquid, a small harbor much used by fishermen. Before the war there were about twelve houses, but the rumor of war disposed them to secure themselves by forsaking their habitations. And when we turned our backs on the town, my heart was ready to break! I saw my mother; she spake to me, but I could not answer her. That night we tarried at New Harbor, and the next day went in their canoes for Penobscot. About noon, the canoe which my mother and that which I was in, came side by side, whether accidentally or by my mother's desire, I cannot say. She asked me how I did. I think I said "Pretty well," though my heart was full of grief.

Then she said, "Oh, my child! How joyful and pleasant would it be if we were going to old England, to see your uncle Chalker and other friends there! Poor babe, we are going into the wilderness, the Lord knows where!" She burst into tears, and the canoes parted.

That night following the Indians with their captives lodged on an island.

A few days after, we arrived at Penobscot Fort, where I again saw my mother, my brother and sisters, and many other captives. I think we tarried here eight days, and in that time the Jesuit of the place had a great mind to buy me. My Indian master made a visit to the Jesuit, and carried me with him. (The Indian that takes and will keep a captive is accounted his master, the captive his property till he give or sell him to another). I saw the Jesuit show him pieces of gold, and understood afterward that he tendered them for me. The Jesuit gave me a biscuit, which I put into my pocket and dare not eat but buried it under a log, fearing that he had put something in it to make me love him. For I was very young, and had heard much of the Papists torturing the Protestants, so that I hated the sight of a Jesuit.

When my mother heard the talk of my being sold to a Jesuit, she said to me, "Oh, my dear child, if it were God's will, I had rather follow you to your grave, or never see you more in this world, than you should be sold to a Jesuit; for a Jesuit will ruin you, body and soul!" And it pleased God to grant her request, for she never saw me more! (Though she and my two little sisters were, after several years' captivity, redeemed, but she died before I returned. And my brother who was taken with me was after several years' captivity most barbarously tortured to death by the Indians.)

My Indian master carried me up Penobscot River to a village called Madawamkee, which stands on a point of land between the main river and a branch which heads to the east of it. At home I had ever seen strangers treated with the utmost civility, and being a stranger, I expected some kind treatment here, but I soon found myself deceived. For I presently saw a number of squaws got together in a circle dancing and yelling, and an old grimace squaw took me by the hand and led me to the ring, where the other squaws seized me by the hair of my head and by my hands and feet, like so many furies. But my master presently laying down a pledge, they released me.

A captive among the Indians is exposed to all manner of abuses, and to the utmost tortures, unless his master, or some of his master's relations, lay down a ransom, such as a bag of corn or a blanket or suchlike, by which they may redeem them from their cruelties for that dance, so that he shall not be touched by any.

The next day we went up that eastern branch of Penobscot River many leagues, carried overland to a large pond, and from one pond to another, till in a few days we went down a river which vents itself into St. John's River. But before we came to the mouth of this river, we carried over a long carrying place* to Medoctec Fort, which stands on a bank of St. John's River. My Indian master went before, and left me with an old Indian and two or three squaws. The old man often said (which was all the English he could speak), "By and by come to a great town and fort." So that I comforted myself in thinking how finely I should be refreshed when I came to this great town.

After some miles' travel we came in sight of a large cornfield, and soon after of the fort. To my great surprise, two or three squaws met us, took off my pack, and led me to a large hut or wigwam, where thirty or forty Indians were dancing and yelling round five or six poor captives, who had been taken some months before from Quochecho, at the time Major Waldron was so barbarously butchered by them.

★

* A carrying place is a path or track in which they pass from one river or part of a river or pond to another; 'tis so called, because the Indians are obliged to carry their baggage over them.—John Gyles.

Major Waldron's* garrison was taken in the beginning of
April after a Sabbath. I have heard the Indians say at a feast
that there being a truce for some days, they contrived to send in
two squaws to take notice of the numbers, lodgings, and other
circumstances of the people in his garrison, and if they could
obtain leave to lodge there, to open the gates and whistle.
(They said the gates had no locks, but were fastened with pins,
and that they kept no watch.) The squaws had a favorable
season to prosecute their projection, for it was dull weather
when they came and begged leave to lodge in the garrison. They
told the major that a great number of Indians were not far
from them, with a considerable quantity of beaver, who would
trade with him the next day. Some of the people were very much
against their lodging in the garrison, but the major said, "Let
the poor creatures lodge by the fire."

The squaws went into every apartment and observed the
numbers in each, and when all the people were asleep arose and
opened the gates and gave the signal. The other Indians came
to them, and having received account of the state of the
garrison, they divided according to the number of people in
each apartment, and soon took and killed them all. The major
lodged within an inner room, and when the Indians broke in
upon him he cried out "What now! What now!," jumped out of
bed in only his shirt, and drove them out with his sword through
two or three doors. And as he was returning to his apartment,
an Indian came behind him and knocked him on the head with
his hatchet, stunned him, and hauled him out and set him upon
a long table in his hall, and bid him "judge Indians again."
Then they cut and stabbed him, and he cried out "O Lord! O
Lord!" They bid him order his book of accounts to be brought,
and cross out all the Indian debts (for he had traded much

---

* The Major (Richard) Waldron here referred to was a prominent
figure in New Hampshire affairs from his arrival in 1645 until his
murder in his own house, June 28, 1689. Thirteen years earlier, during
King Philip's War, Waldron had invited the hostile Indians to treat
with him, and when they appeared he seized, killed and enslaved
some two hundred. At the commencement of King William's War
the Indians secured their revenge on the seventy-four-year-old pioneer
in the manner described above.

with the Indians). And after they had tortured him to death, they burned the garrison and drew off.

This narration I heard from their mouths at a general meeting, and have reason to think it true. And it should be a warning to all persons who have the care of garrisons, for the greatest losses we meet with are for want of due caution and circumspection.

I was whirled in among the circle of Indians, and we prisoners looked on each other with a sorrowful countenance. Presently one of them was seized by each hand and foot by four Indians who swung him up, and let his back with force fall on the hard ground, till they had danced (as they call it) round the whole wigwam, which was thirty or forty feet in length. But when they torture a boy they take him up between two. This is one of their customs of torturing captives. Another is to take up a person by the middle with his head downward, and jolt him till one would think his bowels would shake out of his mouth. Sometimes they will take a captive by the hair of the head, stoop him forward, and strike him on the back and shoulder, till the blood gush out of his mouth and nose. Sometimes an old shriveled squaw will take up a shovel of hot embers and throw them into a captive's bosom. If he cry out, the other Indians will laugh and shout and say, "What a brave action our old grandmother has done." Sometimes they torture them with whips, et cetera.

The Indians looked on me with a fierce countenance, signifying that it would be my turn next. They champed cornstalks and threw them into my hat, which was in my hand. I smiled on them, though my heart ached. I looked on one and another, but could not perceive that any eye pitied me. Presently came a squaw and a little girl, and laid down a bag of corn in the ring. The little girl took me by the hand, making signs for me to go out of the circle with them, but not knowing their custom I supposed that they designed to kill me, and would not go out with them. Then a grave Indian came and gave me a short pipe, and said in English, "Smoke it," then took me by the hand and led me out. My heart ached, thinking myself near my end. But he carried me to a French hut, about a mile from the Indian fort. The Frenchman was not at home, but his wife, who was a squaw, had some discourse with my Indian friend, which I did not understand. We tarried about two hours, and returned to the village, where they gave me some victuals. Not long after I saw one of my fellow captives, who gave me a melancholy account of their sufferings after I left them.

After some weeks had passed we left the village and went up St. John's River about ten miles, to a branch called Medouk-scenecasis, where there was one wigwam. At our arrival an old squaw saluted me with a yell, taking me by the hair and one hand, but I was so rude as to break her hold and quit myself. She gave me a filthy grin, and the Indians set up a laugh; so it passed over. Here we lived upon fish, wild grapes, roots, et cetera, which was hard living to me.

When the winter came on we went up the river till the ice came down and run thick in the river, and then, according to the Indian custom, laid up our canoes till the spring. Then we traveled sometimes on the ice and sometimes on the land, till we came to a river that was open and not fordable, where we made a raft and passed over, bag and baggage. I met with no abuse from them in this winter's hunting, though I was put to great hardships in carrying burdens and for want of food. But they underwent the same difficulty, and would often encourage me, saying in broken English, "By by great deal moose." But they could not answer any question I asked them. So that, knowing little of their customs and way of life, I thought it tedious to be constantly moving from place to place; yet it might be in some respects an advantage, for it ran still in my mind that we were traveling to some settlement. And when my burden was overheavy, and the Indians left me behind, and the still evening came on, I fancied I could see through the bushes and hear the people of some great town; which hope might be some support to me in the day, though I found not the town at night.

Thus we were hunting three hundred miles from the sea, and knew no man within fifty or sixty miles of us. We were eight or ten in number, and had but two Indian men with guns, on whom we wholly depended for food, and if any disaster had happened, we must all have perished. Sometimes we had no manner of sustenance for three or four days; but God wonderfully provides for all creatures. In one of these fasts, God's providence was remarkable. Our two Indian men, in hunting, startled a moose, when there was a shallow crusted snow on the ground. The moose discovered them and ran with great force into a swamp. The Indians went round the swamp, and finding no track, returned at night to the wigwam and told what had happened. The next morning they followed him on the track and soon found the moose lying on the snow, for, crossing the roots of a large tree that had been blown up, the roots having ice underneath, the moose, in his furious flight broke through and hitched one of his hind legs in among the roots so fast that, by striving to get it out, he pulled his thighbone out of the socket at the hip. Thus extraordinarily were we provided for in our great strait.

Sometimes they would take a bear, which go into dens in the fall of the year without any sort of food, and lie there without any four or five months, never going out till spring of the year, in which time they neither lose or gain in flesh. If they went into their dens fat they came out so, or if they went in lean they will come out lean. I have seen some that have come out with four whelps,* and both old and young very fat; and then we feasted. An old squaw and a captive, if any present, must stand without the wigwam, shaking their hands and bodies as in a dance and singing, *"Wegage oh nelo woh,"* which if Englished would be "Fat is my eating." This is to signify their thankfulness in feasting times. And when this was spent, we fasted till further success.

The way of their preserving meat is by stripping off the flesh from the bones and drying them over a smoke, by which 'tis kept sound months or years without salt.

We moved still further up the country after moose when our store was out, so that by the spring we had got to the northward of the Lady mountains. And when the spring came on and the rivers broke up, we moved back to the head of St. John's River,

---

* Guillim in his heraldry mentions it as the opinion of some naturalists that they bring forth an unformed embryo, and lick their litter into shape—a gross mistake! I have seen their foetus of all sizes taken out of the matrix by the Indians, and they are as much and as well shaped as the young of any animal.—John Gyles.

and there made canoes of moose hides, sewing three or four together and pitching the seams with charcoal beaten and mixed with balsam. Then we went down the river to a place called Madawescook. There an old man lived and kept a sort of trading house, where we tarried several days; then went further down the river till we came to the greatest falls in these parts, called Checanekepeag, where we carried a little way over the land, and putting off our canoes, we went downstream still. And as we passed down by the mouths of any large branches we saw Indians; but when any dance was proposed, I was bought off. At length we arrived at the place where we left our birch canoes in the fall, and put our baggage into them, and went in them down to the fort.

There we planted corn, and after planting went a-fishing, and to look for and dig roots till the corn was fit to weed. After weeding we took a second tour on the same errand, and returned to hill our corn, and after hilling we went some distance from the fort and field up the river to take salmon and other fish, and dry them for food, till the corn was filled with milk. Some of it we dried then, the other as it ripened. When the corn is in the milk, they gather it in a large kettle and boil it on the ears till it is pretty hard, and then take it up and shell it off the cob with clamshells, and dry it on bark in the sun. When it is thoroughly dried, a kernel is no bigger than a pea, and would keep years, and when it is boiled again it swells as large, and tastes incomparably sweeter than other corn. When we had so gathered our corn and dried it, we put some into Indian barns; that is, into holes in the ground lined and covered with bark and then with dirt. The rest we carried up the river upon our next winter hunting.

Thus God wonderfully favored me and carried me through the first year of my captivity.

Of the Abusive and Barbarous Treatment Which Several Captives Met With from the Indians

WHEN any great number of Indians meet, or when any captives have been lately taken, or when any captives desert and are retaken, the Indians have a dance, and at these dances torture the unhappy people who fall into their hands. My unfortunate brother, who was taken with me, after about three years' captivity deserted with an Englishman who was taken from Casco Bay, and was retaken by the Indians at New Harbor and carried back to Penobscot Fort. Here they were both tortured at a stake by fire for some time; then their noses and ears were cut off, and they made to eat them. After this they were burned to death at the stake, the Indians at the same time declaring they would serve all deserters in the same manner. Thus they divert themselves in their dances!

On the second spring of my captivity, my Indian master and his squaw went to Canada, but sent me down the river with several Indians to the fort, in order to plant corn. The day before we came to the planting ground we met two young Indian men who seemed to be in great haste. After they had passed us, I understood that they were going with an express to Canada, and that there was an English vessel at the mouth of the river. I not being perfect in their language, nor knowing that English vessels traded with them in time of war, supposed a peace was concluded on, and that the captives would be released, and was so transported with this fancy that I slept but little if any that night.

Early the next morning we came to the village, where my ecstasy ended; for I had no sooner landed but three or four Indians dragged me to the great wigwam, where they were yelling and dancing round James Alexander, a Jersey man, who was taken from Falmouth, in Casco Bay. This was occasioned by two families of Cape Sable Indians who, having lost some friends by a number of English fishermen, came some hundreds of miles to revenge themselves on the poor captives. They soon came to me and tossed me about till I was almost breathless, and then threw me into the ring to my fellow captive, and took him out again and repeated their barbarities on him. Then I was hauled out again by three Indians, by the hair of my head, and held down by it till one beat me on the back and shoulders so long that my breath was almost beat out of my body. Then others put a tomahawk into my hands, and ordered me to get up and dance and sing Indian, which I performed with the greatest reluctance, and in the act seemed determined to purchase my death by killing two or three of those monsters of cruelty, thinking it impossible to survive their bloody treatment. But it was impressed on my mind that it was not in their power to take away your life, so I desisted.

Then those Cape Sable Indians came to me again like bears bereaved of their whelps, saying, "Shall we who have lost relations by the English suffer an English voice to be heard among us?" et cetera. Then they beat me again with the ax. Then I repented that I had not sent two or three of them out of the world before me, for I thought that I had much rather die than suffer any longer. They left me the second time, and the other Indians put the tomahawk into my hands again and compelled me to sing. Then I seemed more resolute than before to destroy some of them; but a strange and strong impulse that I should return to my own place and people suppressed it as often as such a notion rose in my breast. Not one of the Indians showed the least compassion, but I saw the tears run down plentifully on the cheeks of a Frenchman that sat behind—which did not relieve the tortures that poor James and I were forced to endure of the most part of this tedious day, for they were continued till the evening, and were the most severe that ever I met with in the whole six years that I was a captive with the Indians.

After they had thus inhumanly abused us, two Indians took us up and threw us out of the wigwam, and we crawled away on our hands and feet, and were scarce able to walk for several days.

Some time after they again concluded on a merry dance when I was at some distance from the wigwam dressing leather, and an Indian was so kind as to tell me that they had got James Alexander, and were in search for me. My Indian master and his squaw bid me run as for my life into a swamp and hide, and not to discover myself unless they both came to me, for then I might be assured the dance was over. I was now master of their language, and a word or a wink was enough to excite me to take care of one. I ran to the swamp and hid in the thickest place I could find. I heard hallooing and whooping all around me; sometimes they passed very near, and I could hear some threaten and others flatter me, but I was not disposed to dance, and if they had come upon me I had resolved to show them a pair of heels, and they must have had good luck to have catched me. I heard no more of them till about evening (for I think I slept), when they came again, calling, "Chon! Chon!," but John would not trust them.

After they were gone, my master and his squaw came where they told me to hide, but could not find me; and when I heard them say with some concern that they believed the other Indians had frightened me into the woods and that I was lost, I came out, and they seemed well pleased. They told me James had a bad day of it; that as soon as he was released he ran into the woods, and they believed he was gone to the Mohawks. James soon returned and gave a melancholy account of his sufferings; and the Indians' fright concerning the Mohawks passed over. (They often had terrible apprehensions of the incursions of those Indians, who are called also Maquas, a most ambitious, haughty, and bloodthirsty people, from whom the other Indians take their measures and manners, their modes and changes of dress, et cetera.)

One very hot season, a great number gathered together at the village, and being a very droughty people, they kept James and myself night and day fetching water from a cold spring that ran out of a rock hill about three-quarters of a mile from the fort. In going thither we crossed a large interval cornfield, and then a descent to a lower interval before we ascended the hill to the spring. James being almost dead, as well as I, with this continual fatigue, contrived to fright the Indians. He told me of his plan but conjured me to secrecy, yet said he knew that I could keep counsel. The next dark night James, going for water, set his kettle on the descent to the lowest interval, and ran back to the fort, puffing and blowing as in the utmost surprise, and told his master that he saw something near the spring that looked like Mohawks (which were only stumps). His master, being a most courageous warrior, went with him to make discovery. When they came to the brow of the hill, James pointed to the stumps, and withal touched his kettle with his toe, which gave it motion downhill, and at every turn of the kettle the bail clattered; upon which James and his master could see a Mohawk in every stump on motion and turned tail to, and he was the best man that could run fastest. This alarmed all the Indians in the village. They, though about thirty or forty in number, packed off, bag and baggage, some up the river and others down, and did not return under fifteen days, when the heat of the weather being finally over, our hard service was abated for this season. I never heard that the Indians understood the occasion of the fright; but James and I had many a private laugh about it.

But my most intimate and dear companion was one John Evans, a young man taken from Quochecho. We, as often as we could, met together and made known our grievances to each other, which seemed to ease our minds. But when it was known by the Indians, we were strictly examined apart, and falsely accused that we were contriving to desert. We were too far from the sea to have any thought of that, and when they found our stories agreed we received no punishment. An English girl captive about this time would often falsely accuse us of plotting to desert, but we made the truth so plainly appear, that she was checked and we released. But the third winter of my captivity, John Evans went into the country, and the Indians imposed a heavy burden on him while he was extremely weak from long fasting; and as he was going off the upland over a place of ice which was very hollow, he broke through, fell down, and cut his knee very much. Notwithstanding he traveled for some time, but the wind and cold were so forcible that they soon overcame him, and he sat or fell down, and all the Indians passed by him. Some of them went back the next day after him or his pack, and found him, with a dog in his arms, both frozen as stiff as a stake.

Thus all of my fellow captives were dispersed and dead, but through infinite and unmerited goodness I was supported under and carried through all difficulties.

Of Further Difficulties and Deliverances

ONE winter as we were moving from place to place our hunters killed some moose, and one lying some miles from our wigwams, a young Indian and myself were ordered to fetch part of it. We set out in the morning when the weather was promising, but it proved a very cold, cloudy day. It was late in the evening when we arrived at the place where the moose lay, so that we had no time to provide materials for fire or shelter. At the same time a storm of snow came on very thick, and continued till the next morning. We made a small fire with what little rubbish we could find around us, which, with the heat of our bodies, melted the snow upon us as fast as it fell, and filled our clothes with water. Nevertheless, early in the morning we took our loads of moose flesh, and set out in order to return to our wigwams. We had not traveled far before my moose-skin coat (which was the only garment that I had on my back, and the hair was in most places worn off) was froze stiff round my knees like a hoop, as likewise my snowshoes and shoe-clouts to my feet. Thus I marched the whole day without fire or food. At first I was in great pain, then my flesh numbed, and I felt at times extremely sick and thought I could not travel one foot further, but wonderfully revived again.

After long traveling I felt very drowsy and had thoughts of sitting down, which, had I done, without doubt I had fallen on my final sleep, as my dear companion Evans had done before. For my Indian companion, being better clothed, had left me long before. But again my spirits revived as much as if I had received the richest cordial. Some hours after sunset I recovered the wigwam, and crawled in with my snowshoes on. The Indians cried out, "The captive is froze to death!" They took off my pack, and where that lay against my back was the only place that was not frozen. The Indians cut off my snowshoes and stripped the clouts from my feet, which were as void of feeling as any frozen flesh could be.

I had not sat long by the fire before the blood began to circulate, and my feet to my ankles turned black and swelled with bloody blisters, and were inexpressibly painful. The Indians said one to another, "His feet will rot and he'll die." Nevertheless I slept well at night. Soon after, the skin came off my feet from my ankles, whole like a shoe, and left my toes naked without a nail, and the ends of my great toe bones bare, which in a little time turned black, so that I was obliged to cut the first joint off with my knife. The Indians gave me rags to bind up my feet, and advised me to apply fir balsam, but withal said that they believed it was not worth while to use means, for I should certainly die. But by the use of my elbows and a stick in each hand, I shoved myself on my bottom over the snow from one tree to another, till I got some fir balsam, then burned it in a clamshell till it was of a consistence like salve, and applied it to my feet and ankles. And by the divine blessing, within a week I could go about upon my heels with my staff. Also through God's goodness, we had provisions enough, so that we did not remove under ten or fifteen days. Then the Indians made two little hoops, something in the form as a snowshoe, and seized them to my feet, and I followed them in their tracks on my heels from place to place; sometimes half leg-deep in snow and water, which gave me the most acute pain imaginable; but I was forced to walk or die. But within a year my feet were entirely well, and the nails came on my great toes, so that a very critical eye could scarcely perceive any part missing, or that they had been frozen at all.

I was once fishing with an Indian for sturgeon, and the Indian darting one, his feet slipped and turned the canoe bottom upwards, with me under it, I holding fast the crossbar (for I could not swim) with my face to the bottom of the canoe. But I turned myself, and brought my breast to bear on the crossbar, expecting every minute that the Indian would have towed me to the bank. But "he had other fish to fry." Thus I continued a quarter of an hour without want of breath, till the current drove me on a rocky point where I could reach bottom. There I stopped and turned up my canoe. I looked about for the Indian, and he was half a mile distant up the river. I went to him and asked why he did not tow me to the bank, seeing he knew that I could not swim. He said he knew that I was under the canoe, for there were not bubbles anywhere to be seen, and that I should drive on the point. Therefore he took care of his fine sturgeon, which was eight or ten feet long.

While at the Indian village, I had been cutting wood and was binding it up with an Indian rope in order to carry it to the wigwam, when a stout, ill-natured young fellow, about twenty years of age, threw me backward, sat on my breast, and pulling out his knife said that he would kill me, for he had never yet killed an English person. I told him that he might go to war, and that would be more manly than to kill a poor captive who was doing their drudgery for them. Notwithstanding all that I could

14. SOUTHERN INDIAN WARRIOR

De Bry, *The Great Voyages*, Part I; Frankfurt, 1590

say, he began to cut and stab me on my breast. I seized him by
the hair, and tumbled him off me onto his back, and followed him
with my fist and knee so that he presently said he had enough.
But when I saw the blood run and felt the smart, I at him again,
and bid him get up and not lie there like a dog; told him of his
former abuses offered to me and other poor captives, and that
if ever he offered the like to me again, I would pay him double.
I sent him before me, took up my burden of wood, and came to
the Indians and told them the whole truth; and they commended
me. And I don't remember that he offered me the least abuse
afterwards, though he was big enough to have dispatched two of
me.

Of Remarkable Events of Providence in the Deaths of Several Barbarous Indians

THE priest of this river was of the order of St. Francis, a gentleman of a humane, generous disposition. In his sermons he most
severely reprehended the Indians for their barbarities to the
captives. He would often tell them that, excepting their errors
in religion, the English were a better people than themselves, and
that God would remarkably punish such cruel wretches, and had
begun to execute his vengeance upon such! He gave an account of
the retaliations of providence to those murderous Cape Sable
Indians above-mentioned, one of whom got a splinter into his
foot, which festered and rotted his flesh till it killed him. Another run a fishbone into her hand or arm, and she rotted to
death, notwithstanding all means that were used. In some such
manner they all died, so that not one of those two families lived
to return home. Were it not for this remark of the priest, I should
not, perhaps, have made the observation.

There was an old squaw who ever endeavored to outdo all
others in cruelty to captives. Wherever she came into a wigwam,
where any poor, naked, starved captives were sitting near the
fire, if they were grown persons she would privately take up a
shovel of hot coals and throw them into their bosoms. Young
ones she would take by the hand or leg and drag them through
the fire. The Indians according to their custom left their village
in the fall of the year and dispersed themselves for hunting, and

after the first or second removal, they all strangely forgot that old squaw and her grandson, about twelve years of age. They were found dead in the place where they were left, some months afterward, and no further notice was taken of them. This was very much observed by the priest, and seemed strange to all that heard it, for the Indians were generally very careful not to leave their old or young.

In the latter part of summer or beginning of autumn, the Indians were frequently frighted by the appearance of strange Indians passing up and down this river in canoes, and about that time the next year died more than one hundred persons, old and young, all or most of those that saw those strange Indians! The priest said it was a sort of plague. A person seeming in perfect health would bleed at the mouth and nose, turn blue in spots, and die in two or three hours. It was very tedious to me who was forced to move from place to place this cold season. The Indians applied red ocher to my sores which by God's blessing cured me. This sickness being at the worst as winter came on, the Indians all scattered, and the blow was so great to them that they did not settle or plant at their village while I was on the river, and I know not whether they have to this day. Before they thus deserted the village, when they came in from hunting they would be drunk and fight for several days and nights together, till they had spent most of their skins in wine and brandy, which was brought to the village by a Frenchman.

Of My Three Years' Captivity With the French

WHEN about six years of my doleful captivity had passed, my second Indian master died, whose squaw and my first Indian master disputed whose slave I should be, and some malicious persons advised them to end the quarrel by putting a period to my life. But honest Father Simon, the priest of the river, told them that it would be a heinous crime, and advised them to sell me to the French. There came annually one or two men-of-war to supply the fort, which was on the river about thirty-four leagues from the sea. The Indians having advice of the arrival of a man-of-war at the mouth of the river, they (about thirty or forty in number) went aboard. For the gentlemen from France made a present to them every year, and set forth the riches and victories of their monarch, et cetera. At this time they presented a bag or two of flour, with some prunes, as ingredients for a feast.

I, who was dressed up in an old greasy blanket, without cap, hat, or shirt (for I had had no shirt for the six years but that which was on my back when I was taken), was invited into the great cabin, where many well-rigged gentlemen were sitting, who would fain have had a full view of me. I endeavored to hide myself behind the hangings, for I was much ashamed, thinking of my former wearing clothes, and of my living with people who could rig as well as the best of them. My master asked me whether I chose to be sold aboard the man-of-war or to the inhabitants. I replied with tears, I should be glad if he would sell me to the English from whom I was taken; but that if I must be sold to the French, I chose to be sold to the lowest inhabitants on the river, or those nearest to the sea, about twenty-five leagues from the mouth of the river; for I thought if I were sold to the gentlemen aboard the man-of-war, I should never return to the English.

This was the first sight I had of salt water in captivity, and the first time that I had tasted salt or bread.

My master presently went ashore, and after a few days all the Indians went up the river. And when we came to the house which I mentioned to my master, he went ashore with me and tarried all night. The master of the house spoke kindly to me in Indian, for I could not then speak one word of French. Madam also looked pleasant on me, and gave me some bread. The next day I was sent six leagues further up the river to another French house. My master and the friar tarried with Monsieur Dechouffour, the gentleman who had entertained us the night before. Not long after, Father Simon came and said, "Now you are one of us, for you are sold to that gentleman by whom you were entertained the other night."

I replied, "Sold!—to a Frenchman!" I could say no more, went into the woods alone, and wept till I could scarce see or stand! The word *sold,* and that to a people of that persuasion which my dear mother so much detested, and in her last words manifested so great fears of my falling into! The thoughts of these almost broke my heart.

When I had thus given vent to my passions, I rubbed my eyes, endeavoring to hide my grief. But Father Simon, perceiving that my eyes were swollen, called me aside and bid me not to grieve, for the gentleman to whom I was sold was of a good humor; he had formerly bought two captives of the Indians, who both went home to Boston. This in some measure revived me. But, he added, he did not suppose that I would ever incline to go to the English, for the French way of worship was much to be preferred. He said also that he should pass that way in about ten days, and if I did not like to live with the French better than with the Indians, he would buy me again.

On the day following, Father Simon and my Indian master went up the river six and thirty leagues to their chief village, and I went down the river six leagues with two Frenchmen to my new master. He kindly received me, and in a few days madam made me an Osnaburg shirt and French cap, and a coat out of one of my master's old coats. Then I threw away my greasy blanket and Indian flap, and looked as smart as punch. And I never more saw the old friar, the Indian village, or my Indian master, till about fourteen years after I saw my Indian master at Port Royal, whither I was sent by the government with a flag of truce for exchanging prisoners; and again, about twenty-four years since, he came to Fort George to see me, where I made him very welcome.

Some time after, Colonel Hawthorne attempted the taking of the French fort up this river. We heard of him some time before he came up the river, by the guard that Governor Villebon had ordered at the river's mouth. Monsieur the gentleman whom I lived with had gone to France, and madam advised with me. She then desired me to nail a paper on the door of our house, containing as follows:

"I entreat the general of the English not to burn my house or barn, nor destroy my cattle. I don't suppose that such an army comes up this river to destroy a few inhabitants, but for the fort above us. I have shown kindness to the English captives as we were capacitated, and have bought two captives of the Indians and sent them to Boston. We have one now with us, and he shall go also when a convenient opportunity presents, and he desires it."

This done, madam said to me, "Little English, we have shown you kindness, and now it lies in your power to serve or disserve us, as you know where our goods are hid in the woods, and that monsieur is not at home. I could have sent you to the fort and put you under confinement, but my respect to you and assurance of your love to us has disposed me to confide in you, persuaded that you will not hurt us or our affairs. And now, if you will not run away to the English who are coming up the river, but serve our interest, I will acquaint monsieur of it on his return from France, which will be very pleasing to him. And I now give my word that you shall have liberty to go to Boston on the first opportunity, if you desire it; or any other favor in my power shall not be denied you."

I replied, "Madam, it is contrary to the nature of the English to requite evil for good. I shall endeavor to serve you and your interest. I shall not run to the English, but if I am taken by them shall willingly go with them, and yet endeavor not to disserve you, either in your person or goods."

This said, we embarked and went in a large boat and canoe two or three miles up an eastern branch of the river that comes from a large pond, and in the following evening sent down four hands to make discovery. And while they were sitting in the house the English surrounded it and took one of the four. The other three made their escape in the dark, through the English soldiers, and came to us and gave a surprising account of affairs.

Again madam said to me, "Little English, now you can go from us, but I hope you will remember your word."

I said, "Madam, be not concerned. I will not leave you in this strait."

She said, "I know not what to do with my two poor little babes."

I said, "Madam, the sooner we embark and go over the great pond the better."

Accordingly we embarked and went over the pond. The next day we spoke with Indians who were in a canoe, and they gave us an account that Signecto town was taken and burnt. Soon after we heard the great guns at Governor Villebon's fort, which the English engaged several days. They killed one man, then drew off and went down the river, for it was so late in the fall that had they tarried a few days longer in the river, they would have been froze in for the winter.

Hearing no report of the great guns for several days, I with two others went down to our house to make discovery. We found our young lad who was taken by the English when they went up the river, for the general was so honorable that on reading the note on our door, he ordered that the house and barn should not be burnt, nor their cattle and other creatures killed, except one or two and the poultry for their use. And at their return they ordered the young lad to be put ashore. Finding things in this posture, we returned and gave madam an account. She acknowledged the many favors which the English had showed her, with gratitude, and treated me with great civility.

The next spring, monsieur arrived from France in the man-of-war, who thanked me for my care of his affairs, and said he would endeavor to fulfill what madam had promised me.

Accordingly, in the year 1698, peace being proclaimed, a sloop came to the mouth of the river with ransom for one Michael Cooms. I put monsieur in mind of his word, telling him there was now an opportunity for me to go and see the English. He advised me to tarry and told me that he would do for me as for his own, et cetera. I thanked him for his kindness, but chose rather to go to Boston, for I hoped that I had some relations yet alive. Then he advised me to go up to the fort and take my leave of the governor, which I did, and he spake very kindly to me. Some days after I took my leave of madam, and monsieur went down to the mouth of the river with me to see me safe on board. He asked the master, Mr. Starkee, a Scotchman, whether I must pay for my passage; if so, he would pay it himself rather than I should have it to pay at my arrival at Boston, but he gave me not a penny. The master told him that there was nothing to pay, and that if the owner should make any demand he would pay it himself, rather than a poor prisoner should suffer, for he was glad to see any English person come out of captivity.

On the 20th of June I took my leave of monsieur, and the sloop came to sail for Boston, where we arrived on the 28th of the same, at night. In the morning after my arrival a youth came on board and asked many questions relating to my captivity, and at length gave me to understand that he was my little brother, who was at play with some other children at Pemaquid when I was taken captive, and upon hearing the guns and seeing the

Indians run, made their escape into the fort. He told me my elder brother, who made his escape from the farm whence I was taken, and our two little sisters were alive, and that our mother had been dead some years. Then we went ashore and saw our elder brother.

On the 2nd of August, 1689, I was taken, and on the 28th of June, 1698, I arrived at Boston, so that I was absent eight years, ten months, and seventeen days. In all which time, though I underwent extreme difficulties, yet I saw much of the goodness of God. May the most powerful and beneficent Being accept of this public testimony of it, and bless my experiences to excite others to confide in his all-sufficiency, through the infinite merits of JESUS CHRIST.

A NARRATIVE OF THE CAPTIVITY AND RESTORATION OF MRS. MARY ROWLANDSON

By Herself

ON THE tenth of February, 1675, came the Indians with great numbers upon Lancaster. Their first coming was about sunrising. Hearing the noise of some guns, we looked out; several houses were burning, and the smoke ascending to heaven. There were five persons taken in one house; the father and the mother and a sucking child they knocked on the head; the other two they took and carried away alive. There were two others, who being out of their garrison upon some occasion were set upon; one was knocked on the head, the other escaped. Another there was who running along was shot and wounded, and fell down; he begged of them his life, promising them money (as they told me), but they would not hearken to him but knocked him on the head, and stripped him naked, and split open his bowels. Another, seeing many of the Indians about his barn, ventured and went out, but was quickly shot down. There were three others belonging to the same garrison who were killed; the Indians, getting up upon the roof of the barn, had advantage to shoot down upon them over their fortification. Thus these murderous wretches went on, burning and destroying before them.

At length they came and beset our own house, and quickly it was the dolefulest day that ever mine eyes saw. The house stood upon the edge of a hill; some of the Indians got behind the hill, others into the barn, and others behind anything that could shelter them; from all which places they shot against the house, so that the bullets seemed to fly like hail. And quickly they wounded one man among us, then another, and then a third. About two hours (according to my observation, in that amazing time) they had been about the house before they prevailed to fire it, which they did with flax and hemp which they brought out of the barn, and there being no defense about the house, only two flankers* at two opposite corners and one of them not finished. They fired it once and one ventured out and quenched it, but they quickly fired it again, and that took.

Now is the dreadful hour come that I have often heard of (in time of war, as it was the case of others), but now mine eyes see it. Some in our house were fighting for their lives, others wallowing in their blood, the house on fire over our heads, and the bloody heathen ready to knock us on the head if we stirred out. Now might we hear mothers and children crying out for themselves, and one another, "Lord, what shall we do?" Then I took my children (and one of my sisters, hers) to go forth and leave the house; but as soon as we came to the door and appeared, the Indians shot so thick that the bullets rattled against the house as if one had taken an handful of stones and threw them, so that we were fain to give back. We had six stout dogs belonging to our garrison, but none of them would stir, though another time, if any Indian had come to the door, they were ready to fly upon him and tear him down. The Lord hereby would make us the more to acknowledge his hand, and to see that our help is always in him.

But out we must go, the fire increasing and coming along behind us, roaring, and the Indians gaping before us with their guns, spears and hatchets to devour us. No sooner were we out of the house but my brother-in-law (being before wounded, in defending the house, in or near the throat) fell down dead, where-

* Flankers were projections from which blank walls (curtains) could be enfiladed.—C. H. Lincoln.

at the Indians scornfully shouted, and hallooed, and were presently upon him, stripping off his clothes. The bullets flying thick, one went through my side, and the same (as would seem) through the bowels and hand of my dear child in my arms. One of my elder sister's children, named William, had then his leg broken, which the Indians perceiving, they knocked him on the head. Thus were we butchered by those merciless heathen, standing amazed, with the blood running down to our heels.

My eldest sister being yet in the house, and seeing those woeful sights, the infidels hauling mothers one way and children another, and some wallowing in their blood, and her elder son telling her that her son William was dead, and myself was wounded, she said, "And, Lord, let me die with them." Which was no sooner said, but she was struck with a bullet, and fell down dead over the threshold. I hope she is reaping the fruit of her good labors, being faithful to the service of God in her place. In her younger years she lay under much trouble upon spiritual accounts, till it pleased God to make that precious Scripture take hold of her heart, 2 Corinthians 12:9. *And he said unto me, my grace is sufficient for thee.* More than twenty years after I have heard her tell how sweet and comfortable that place was to her.

But to return. The Indians laid hold of us, pulling me one way and the children another, and said, "Come go along with us." I told them they would kill me. They answered, if I were willing to go along with them, they would not hurt me.

Oh, the doleful sight that now was to behold at this house! *Come, behold the works of the Lord, what desolations he hath made in the earth.* Of thirty-seven persons who were in this one house, none escaped either present death or a bitter captivity, save only one, who might say as he, Job 1:15, *And I only am escaped alone to tell the news.* There were twelve killed, some shot, some stabbed with their spears, some knocked down with their hatchets. When we are in prosperity, oh, the little that we think of such dreadful sights, and to see our dead friends and relations lie bleeding out their heart blood upon the ground. There was one who was chopped into the head with a hatchet, and stripped naked, and yet was crawling up and down. It is a solemn sight to see so many Christians lying in their blood, some here and some there, like a company of sheep torn by wolves, all of them stripped naked by a company of hellhounds, roaring, singing, ranting, and insulting, as if they would have torn our very hearts out; yet the Lord by his Almighty power preserved a number of us from death, for there were twenty-four of us taken alive and carried captive.

I had often before this said that if the Indians should come, I should choose rather to be killed by them than taken alive. But when it came to the trial my mind changed; their glittering weapons so daunted my spirit that I chose rather to go along with those (as I may say) ravenous beasts than that moment to end my days. And that I may the better declare what happened to me during that grievous captivity, I shall particularly speak of the several removes we had up and down the wilderness.

The First Remove

Now away we must go with those barbarous creatures, with our bodies wounded and bleeding, and our hearts no less than our bodies. About a mile we went that night, up upon a hill within sight of the town, where they intended to lodge. There was hard by a vacant house (deserted by the English before, for fear of the Indians). I asked them whether I might not lodge in the house that night, to which they answered, "What, will you love Englishmen still?" This was the dolefulest night that ever my eyes saw. Oh, the roaring and singing and dancing and yelling of those black creatures in the night, which made the place a lively resemblance of hell! And as miserable was the waste that was there made, of horses, cattle, sheep, swine, calves, lambs, roasting pigs, and fowl (which they had plundered in the town), some roasting, some lying and burning, and some boiling to feed our merciless enemies; who were joyful enough though we were disconsolate. To add to the dolefulness of the former day and the dismalness of the present night, my thoughts ran upon my losses and sad bereaved condition. All was gone, my husband gone (at least separated from me, he being in the Bay; and to add to my grief, the Indians told me they would kill him as he came homeward), my children gone, my relations and friends gone, our house and home and all our comforts within door and without, all was gone (except my life), and I knew not but the next moment that might go too. There remained nothing to me but one poor wounded babe, and it seemed at present worse than death that it was in such a pitiful condition, bespeaking compassion, and I had no refreshing for it, nor suitable things to revive it. Little do many think what is the savageness and brutishness of this barbarous enemy, ay, even those that seem to profess more than others among them, when the English have fallen into their hands.

The Second Remove

BUT now, the next morning, I must turn my back upon the town, and travel with them into the vast and desolate wilderness, I knew not whither. It is not my tongue or pen can express the sorrows of my heart and bitterness of my spirit that I had at this departure; but God was with me, in a wonderful manner carrying me along and bearing up my spirit, that it did not quite fail. One of the Indians carried my poor wounded babe upon a horse; it went moaning all along, "I shall die, I shall die." I went on foot after it, with sorrow that cannot be expressed. At length I took it off the horse, and carried it in my arms till my strength failed, and I fell down with it. Then they set me upon a horse with my wounded child in my lap, and there being no furniture upon the horse's back, as we were going down a steep hill we both fell over the horse's head, at which they like inhumane creatures laughed and rejoiced to see it, though I thought we should there have ended our days, as overcome with so many difficulties. But the Lord renewed my strength still and carried me along, that I might see more of his power; yea, so much that I could never have thought of, had I not experienced it.

After this it quickly began to snow, and when night came on they stopped. And now down I must sit in the snow, by a little fire, and a few boughs behind me, with my sick child in my lap calling much for water, being now (through the wound) fallen into a violent fever. My own wound also was growing so stiff that I could scarce sit down or rise up; yet so it must be that I must sit all this cold winter night upon the cold snowy ground, with my sick child in my arms, looking that every hour would be the last of its life, and having no Christian friend near me, either to comfort or help me. Oh, I may see the wonderful power of

God, that my spirit did not utterly sink under my affliction. Still the Lord upheld me with his gracious and merciful spirit, and we were both alive to see the light of the next morning.

The Third Remove

THE morning being come, they prepared to go on their way. One of the Indians got up upon a horse, and they set me up behind him, with my poor sick babe in my lap. A very wearisome and tedious day I had of it, what with my own wound, and my child being so exceeding sick and in a lamentable condition with her wound. It may be easily judged what a poor feeble condition we were in, there being not the least crumb of refreshment that came within either of our mouths, from Wednesday night to Saturday night, except only a little cold water.

This day in the afternoon, about an hour by sun, we came to the place where they intended, viz., an Indian town called Menameset, north of Quabaug. When we were come, oh, the number of pagans (now merciless enemies) that there came about me, that I may say as David, Psalm 27:13, *I had fainted, unless I had believed,* etc. The next day was the Sabbath. I then remembered how careless I had been of God's holy time, how many Sabbaths I had lost and misspent, and how evilly I had walked in God's sight; which lay so close unto my spirit, that it was easy for me to see how righteous it was with God to cut off the thread of my life and cast me out of his presence for ever. Yet the Lord still showed mercy to me and upheld me; and as he wounded me with one hand, so he healed me with the other.

This day there came to me one Robert Pepper (a man belonging to Roxbury), who was taken in Captain Beers's fight, and had been now a considerable time with the Indians and up with them almost as far as Albany to see King Philip, as he told me, and was now very lately come into these parts. Hearing, I say, that I was in this Indian town, he obtained leave to come and see me. He told me he himself was wounded in the leg at Captain Beers's fight, and was not able some time to go; but as they carried him, and as he took oaken leaves and laid them to his wound, through the blessing of God he was able to travel again. Then I took oaken leaves and laid to my side, and with the blessing of God it cured me also; yet before the cure was wrought, I may say, as it is in Psalm 38:5,6, *My wounds stink and are corrupt. . . . I am troubled; I am bowed down greatly; I go mourning all the day long.*

I sat much alone with a poor wounded child in my lap, which moaned night and day, having nothing to revive the body or cheer the spirits of her. But instead of that, sometimes one Indian would come and tell me one hour, "Your master will knock your child in the head," and then a second, and then a third, "Your master will quickly knock your child in the head." This was the comfort I had from them, miserable comforters are ye all, as he said. Thus nine days I sat upon my knees, with my babe in my lap, till my flesh was raw again. My child being even ready to depart this sorrowful world, they bade me carry it out to another wigwam (I suppose because they would not be troubled with such spectacles), whither I went with a very heavy heart, and down I sat with the picture of death in my lap. About two hours in the night, my sweet babe like a lamb departed this life, on February 18, 1675, it being about six years and five months old. It was nine days from the first wounding in this miserable condition, without any refreshing of one nature or other except a little cold water.

I cannot but take notice how at another time I could not bear to be in the room where any dead person was, but now the case is changed; I must and could lie down by my dead babe, side by side all the night after. I have thought since of the wonderful goodness of God to me, in preserving me in the use of my reason and senses in that distressed time, that I did not use wicked and violent means to end my own miserable life.

In the morning, when they understood that my child was dead, they sent for me home to my master's wigwam. (By my master in this writing must be understood Quanopin, who was a sagamore, and married King Philip's wife's sister; not that he first took me, but I was sold to him by another Narragansett Indian, who took me when first I came out of the garrison). I went to take up my dead child in my arms to carry it with me, but they bid me let it alone; there was no resisting, but go I must and leave it. When I had been at my master's wigwam, I took the first opportunity I could get to go look after my dead child; when I came

I asked them what they had done with it. They told me it was upon the hill. Then they went and showed me where it was, where I saw the ground was newly digged, and there they told me they had buried it. There I left that child in the wilderness, and must commit it, and myself also, in this wilderness condition to him who is above all.

God having taken away this dear child, I went to see my daughter Mary, who was at this same Indian town, at a wigwam not very far off, though we had little liberty or opportunity to see one another. She was about ten years old, and taken from the door at first by a Praying Indian and afterward sold for a gun. When I came in sight she would fall a-weeping, at which they were provoked, and would not let me come near her, but bade me be gone; which was a heart-cutting word to me. I had one child dead, another in the wilderness I knew not where, the third they would not let me come near to: *Me* (as he said) *have ye bereaved of my children: Joseph is not, and Simeon is not, and ye will take Benjamin also, all these things are against me.*

I could not sit still in this condition, but kept walking from one place to another. And as I was going along, my heart was even overwhelmed with the thoughts of my condition, and that I should have children and a nation which I knew not ruled over them. Whereupon I earnestly entreated the Lord that he would consider my low estate and show me a token for good and, if it were his blessed will, some sign and hope of some relief. And indeed quickly the Lord answered, in some measure, my poor prayers. For as I was going up and down mourning and lamenting my condition, my son came to me and asked me how I did. I had not seen him before since the destruction of the town, and I knew not where he was till I was informed by himself that he was amongst a smaller parcel of Indians, whose place was about six miles off. With tears in his eyes he asked me whether his sister Sarah was dead, and told me he had seen his sister Mary, and prayed me that I would not be troubled in reference to himself. The occasion of his coming to see me at this time was this. There was, as I said, about six miles from us a small plantation of Indians, where it seems he had been during his captivity; and at this time there were some forces of the Indians gathered out of our company and some also from them (among whom was my son's master) to go to assault and burn Medfield. In this time of the absence of his master, his dame brought him to see me. I took this to be some gracious answer to my earnest and unfeigned desire.

The next day, viz., to this, the Indians returned from Medfield, all the company, for those that belonged to the other small company came through the town that now we were at. But before they came to us, oh, the outrageous roaring and whooping that there was. They began their din about a mile before they came to us. By their noise and whooping they signified how many they had destroyed (which was at that time twenty-three). Those that were with us at home were gathered together as soon as they heard the whooping, and every time that the other went over their number, those at home gave a shout, that the very earth rung again. And thus they continued till those that had been upon the expedition were come up to the sagamore's wigwam; and then, oh, the hideous insulting and triumphing that there was over some Englishmen's scalps that they had taken (as their manner is) and brought with them.

I cannot but take notice of the wonderful mercy of God to me in those afflictions, in sending me a Bible. One of the Indians that came from Medfield fight had brought some plunder and came to me and asked me if I would have a Bible, he had got one in his basket. I was glad of it, and asked him whether he thought the Indians would let me read? He answered, yes. So I took the Bible, and in that melancholy time it came into my mind to read first the 28th chapter of Deuteronomy, which I did, and when I had read it, my dark heart wrought on this manner, That there was no mercy for me, that the blessings were gone, and the curses come in their room, and that I had lost my opportunity. But the Lord helped me still to go on reading till I came to Chapter 3 the seven first verses, where I found, There was mercy promised again, if we would return to him by repentance; and though we were scattered from one end of the earth to the other yet the Lord would gather us together, and turn all those curses upon our enemies. I do not desire to live to forget this Scripture, and what comfort it was to me.

Now the Indians began to talk of removing from this place,

some one way and some another. There were now besides myself nine English captives in this place (all of them children, except one woman). I got an opportunity to go and take my leave of them; they being to go one way and I another, I asked them whether they were earnest with God for deliverance. They told me, they did as they were able, and it was some comfort to me that the Lord stirred up children to look to him. The woman, viz., Goodwife Joslin, told me she would never see me again, and that she could find in her heart to run away. I wished her not to run away by any means, for we were near thirty miles from any English town, and she very big with child, and had but one week to reckon, and another child in her arms, two years old, and bad rivers there were to go over, and we were feeble, with our poor and coarse entertainment. I had my Bible with me; I pulled it out and asked her whether she would read; we opened the Bible and lighted on Psalm 27, in which psalm we especially took notice of that, *ver. ult., Wait on the Lord: be of good courage, and he shall strengthen thine heart: wait, I say, on the Lord.*

The Fourth Remove

AND now I must part with that little company I had. Here I parted from my daughter Mary (whom I never saw again till I saw her in Dorchester, returned from captivity), and from four little cousins and neighbors, some of which I never saw afterward; the Lord only knows the end of them. Amongst them also was that poor woman before-mentioned, who came to a sad end, as some of the company told me in my travel. She having much grief upon her spirit, about her miserable condition, being so near her time, she would be often asking the Indians to let her go home. They not being willing to that, and yet vexed with her importunity, gathered a great company together about her, and stripped her naked, and set her in the midst of them; and when they had sung and danced about her (in their hellish manner) as long as they pleased, they knocked her on the head, and the child in her arms with her. When they had done that, they made a fire and put them both into it, and told the other children that were with them that if they attempted to go home they would serve them in like manner. The children said she did not shed one tear, but prayed all the while.

But to return to my own journey. We traveled about half a day or little more, and came to a desolate place in the wilderness, where there were no wigwams or inhabitants before. We came about the middle of the afternoon to this place, cold and wet and snowy and hungry and weary, and no refreshing for man but the cold ground to sit on, and our poor Indian cheer.

Heartaching thoughts here I had about my poor children, who were scattered up and down among the wild beasts of the forest. My head was light and dizzy (either through hunger or hard lodging or trouble, or all together), my knees feeble, my body raw by sitting double night and day, that I cannot express to man the affliction that lay upon my spirit; but the Lord helped me at that time to express it to himself. I opened my Bible to read, and the Lord brought that precious Scripture to me, Jeremiah 31:16. *Thus saith the Lord, Refrain thy voice from weeping, and thine eyes from tears, for thy work shall be rewarded . . . and they shall come again from the land of the enemy.* This was a sweet cordial to me, when I was ready to faint; many and many a time have I sat down and wept sweetly over this Scripture. At this place we continued about four days.

The Fifth Remove

THE occasion (as I thought) of their moving at this time was the English Army, it being near and following them. For they went as if they had gone for their lives, for some considerable way, and then they made a stop, and chose some of their stoutest men and sent them back to hold the English Army in play whilst the rest escaped. And then, like Jehu, they marched on furiously, with their old and with their young; some carried their old decrepit mothers, some carried one and some another. Four of them carried a great Indian upon a bier, but going through a thick wood with him they were hindered and could make no haste, whereupon they took him upon their backs and carried him, one at a time, till they came to Baquaug River. Upon a Friday a little after noon we came to this river. When all the company was come up and were gathered together, I thought to count the number of them, but they were so many, and being somewhat in motion, it was beyond my skill. In this travel, because of my wound, I was somewhat favored in my load; I carried only my knitting work and two quarts of parched meal. Being very faint, I asked my mistress to give me one spoonful of the meal, but she would not give me a taste.

They quickly fell to cutting dry trees, to make rafts to carry them over the river, and soon my turn came to go over. By the advantage of some brush which they had laid upon the raft to sit upon, I did not wet my foot (though many of themselves at the other end were mid-leg deep), which cannot but be acknowledged as a favor of God to my weakened body, it being a very cold time. I was not before acquainted with such kind of doings or dangers. *When thou passest through the waters I will be with thee; and through the rivers, they shall not overflow thee,* Isaiah, 43:2. A certain number of us got over the river that night, but it was the night after the Sabbath before all the company was got over. On the Saturday they boiled an old horse's leg which they had got, and so we drank of the broth, as soon as they thought it was ready, and when it was almost all gone they filled it up again.

The first week of my being among them I hardly ate anything. The second week I found my stomach grow very faint for want of something, and yet it was very hard to get down their filthy trash. But the third week, though I could think how formerly my stomach would turn against this or that, and I could starve and die before I could eat such things, yet they were sweet and savory to my taste.

I was at this time knitting a pair of white cotton stockings for my mistress, and had not yet wrought upon a Sabbath day; when the Sabbath came they bade me go to work. I told them it was the Sabbath day and desired them to let me rest, and told them I would do as much more tomorrow; to which they answered me they would break my face. And here I cannot but take notice of the strange providence of God in preserving the heathen. They were many hundred, old and young, some sick and some lame, many had papooses at their backs, the greatest number at this time with us were squaws, and they traveled with all they had, bag and baggage, and yet they got over this river aforesaid; and on Monday they set their wigwams on fire, and away they went. On that very day came the English Army after them to this river, and saw the smoke of their wigwams, and yet this river put a stop to them. God did not give them courage or activity to go over after us; we were not ready for so great a mercy as victory and deliverance; if we had been, God would have found out a way for the English to have passed this river, as well as for the Indians with the squaws and children and all their luggage. *Oh that my people had hearkened to me, and Israel had walked in my ways! I should soon have subdued their enemies, and turned my hand against their adversaries.* Psalm 81:13, 14.

The Sixth Remove

ON MONDAY (as I said) they set their wigwams on fire and went away. It was a cold morning, and before us there was a great brook with ice on it. Some waded through it, up to the knees and higher, but others went till they came to a beaver dam, and I amongst them, where through the good providence of God I did not wet my foot. I went along that day mourning and lamenting, leaving farther my own country, and traveling into the vast and howling wilderness, and I understood something of Lot's wife's temptation when she looked back. We came that day to a great swamp, by the side of which we took up our lodging that night. When I came to the brow of the hill that looked toward the swamp, I thought we had been come to a great Indian town (though there were none but our own company). The Indians were as thick as the trees: it seemed as if there had been a thousand hatchets going at once; if one looked before one, there was nothing but Indians, and behind one, nothing but Indians, and so on either hand, I myself in the midst, and no Christian soul near me. And yet how hath the Lord preserved me in safety? Oh, the experience that I have had of the goodness of God, to me and mine!

The Seventh Remove

AFTER a restless and hungry night there, we had a wearisome time of it the next day. The swamp by which we lay was, as it were, a deep dungeon, and an exceeding high and steep hill before it. Before I got to the top of the hill I thought my heart and legs and all would have broken and failed me. What through faintness and soreness of body, it was a grievous day of travel to me. As we went along I saw a place where English cattle had been; that was comfort to me, such as it was. Quickly after that we came to an English path, which so took with me that I thought I could have freely lain down and died. That day, a little after noon, we came to Squakeag, where the Indians quickly spread themselves over the deserted English fields, gleaning what they could find; some picked up ears of wheat that were trickled down, some found ears of Indian corn, some found groundnuts, and others sheaves of wheat that were frozen together in the shock, and went to threshing of them out. Myself got two ears of Indian corn, and whilst I did but turn my back one of them was stolen from me, which much troubled me.

There came an Indian to them at that time with a basket of horse liver. I asked him to give me a piece. "What," says he, "can you eat horse liver?" I told him I would try, if he would give a piece, which he did, and I laid it on the coals to roast. But before it was half ready they got half of it away from me, so that I was fain to take the rest and eat it as it was, with the blood about my mouth, and yet a savory bit it was to me. For to the hungry soul every bitter thing is sweet. A solemn sight methought it was, to see fields of wheat and Indian corn forsaken and spoiled, and the remainders of them to be food for our merciless enemies. That night we had a mess of wheat for our supper.

The Eighth Remove

ON THE morrow morning we must go over the river, i.e., Connecticut, to meet with King Philip. Two canoes full they had carried over; the next turn I myself was to go, but as my foot was upon the canoe to step in there was a sudden outcry among them, and I must step back; and instead of going over the river, I must go four or five miles up the river farther northward. Some of the Indians ran one way and some another. The cause of this rout was, as I thought, their espying some English scouts who were thereabout. In this travel up the river, about noon the company made a stop and sat down, some to eat and others to rest them.

As I sat amongst them, musing of things past, my son Joseph unexpectedly came to me. We asked of each other's welfare, bemoaning our doleful condition and the change that had come upon us. We had husband and father and children and sisters and friends and relations and house and home and many comforts of this life; but now we may say, as Job, *Naked came I out of my mother's womb, and naked shall I return thither: The Lord gave, and the Lord hath taken away; blessed be the name of the Lord.* I asked him whether he would read; he told me he earnestly desired it. I gave him my Bible, and he lighted upon that comfortable Scripture, Psalm 118:17, 18. *I shall not die, but live, and declare the works of the Lord. The Lord hath chastened me sore, yet he hath not given me over to death.* "Look here, Mother," says he, "did you read this?" And here I may take occasion to mention one principal ground of my setting forth these lines: even as the Psalmist says, to declare the works of the Lord and his wonderful power in carrying us along, preserving us in the wilderness, while under the enemy's hand, and returning of us in safety again, and his goodness in bringing to my hand so many comfortable and suitable Scriptures in my distress.

But to return, we traveled on till night, and in the morning we must go over the river to Philip's crew. When I was in the canoe I could not but be amazed at the numerous crew of pagans that were on the bank on the other side. When I came ashore they gathered all about me, I sitting alone in the midst. I observed they asked one another questions, and laughed and rejoiced over their gains and victories. Then my heart began to fail, and I fell a-weeping, which was the first time to my remembrance that I wept before them. Although I had met with so much affliction, and my heart was many times ready to break, yet could I not shed one tear in their sight, but rather had been all this while in a maze, and like one astonished; but now I may say, as Psalm 137:1, *By the rivers of Babylon, there we sat down, yea, we wept when we remembered Zion.*

There one of them asked me why I wept. I could hardly tell what to say, yet I answered, they would kill me. "No," said he, "none will hurt you." Then came one of them and gave me two spoonfuls of meal to comfort me, and another gave me half a pint of peas; which was more worth than many bushels at another time.

Then I went to see King Philip. He bade me come in and sit down, and asked me whether I would smoke it (a usual compliment nowadays amongst saints and sinners), but this no way suited me. For though I had formerly used tobacco, yet I had left it ever since I was first taken. It seems to be a bait the Devil lays to make men lose their precious time. I remember with shame how formerly when I had taken two or three pipes I was presently ready for another, such a bewitching thing it is. But I thank God, he has now given me power over it; surely there are many who may be better employed than to lie sucking a stinking tobacco pipe.

Now the Indians gather their forces to go against Northampton. Overnight one went about yelling and hooting to give notice of the design. Whereupon they fell to boiling of ground-nuts and parching of corn (as many as had it) for their provision; and in the morning away they went.

During my abode in this place, Philip spake to me to make a shirt for his boy, which I did, for which he gave me a shilling. I offered the money to my master, but he bade me keep it, and with it I bought a piece of horseflesh. Afterwards he asked me to make a cap for his boy, for which he invited me to dinner. I went, and he gave me a pancake, about as big as two fingers; it was made of parched wheat, beaten and fried in bear's grease, but I thought I never tasted pleasanter meat in my life. There was a squaw who spake to me to make a shirt for her sannup [husband], for which she gave me a piece of bear. Another asked me to knit a pair of stockings, for which she gave me a quart of peas. I boiled my peas and bear together, and invited my master and mistress to dinner, but the proud gossip, because I served them both in one dish, would eat nothing, except one bit that he gave her upon the point of his knife.

Hearing that my son was come to this place, I went to see him, and found him lying flat upon the ground. I asked him how he could sleep so. He answered me that he was not asleep but at prayer, and lay so, that they might not observe what he was doing.

I pray God he may remember these things now he is returned in safety. At this place (the sun now getting higher), what with the beams and heat of the sun, and the smoke of the wigwams, I thought I should have been blind. I could scarce discern one wigwam from another. There was here one Mary Thurston of Medfield, who seeing how it was with me lent me a hat to wear; but as soon as I was gone, the squaw who owned that Mary Thurston came running after me and got it away again. Here was the squaw that gave me one spoonful of meal. I put it in my pocket to keep it safe; yet notwithstanding somebody stole it, but put five Indian corns in the room of it, which corns were the greatest provisions I had in my travel for one day.

The Indians returning from Northampton brought with them some horses and sheep and other things which they had taken. I desired them that they would carry me to Albany upon one of those horses and sell me for powder, for so they had sometimes discoursed. I was utterly hopeless of getting home on foot, the way that I came. I could hardly bear to think of the many weary steps I had taken to come to this place.

.   .   .   .

The Sixteenth Remove

WE BEGAN this remove with wading over Baquaug River. The water was up to the knees, and the stream very swift, and so cold that I thought it would have cut me in sunder. I was so weak and feeble that I reeled as I went along, and thought there I must end my days at last, after my bearing and getting through so many difficulties. The Indians stood laughing to see me staggering along; but in my distress the Lord gave me experience of the truth and goodness of that promise, Isaiah 43:2: *When thou passest through the waters, I will be with thee; and through the rivers, they shall not overflow thee.* Then I sat down to put on my stockings and shoes, with the tears running down mine eyes, and many sorrowful thoughts in my heart, but I got up to go along with them.

Quickly there came up to us an Indian who informed them that I must go to Wachusett to my master, for there was a letter come from the Council to the sagamores about redeeming the captives, and that there would be another in fourteen days, and that I must be there ready. My heart was so heavy before that I could scarce speak or go in the path; and yet now so light that I could run. My strength seemed to come again and recruit my feeble knees and aching heart; yet it pleased them to go but one mile that night, and there we stayed two days. In that time came a company of Indians to us, near thirty, all on horseback. My heart skipped within me, thinking they had been Englishmen at the first sight of them, for they were dressed in English apparel, with hats, white neckcloths, and sashes about their waists, and ribbons upon their shoulders; but when they came near, there was a vast difference between the lovely faces of Christians and the foul looks of those heathens, which much damped my spirit again.

The Seventeenth Remove

A COMFORTABLE remove it was to me, because of my hopes. They gave me a pack, and along we went cheerfully. But quickly my will proved more than my strength; having little or no refreshing, my strength failed me and my spirit was almost quite gone. Now may I say with David, Psalm 109:22,23,24, *I am poor and needy, and my heart is wounded within me. I am gone like the shadow when it declineth; I am tossed up and down like the locust. My knees are weak through fasting, and my flesh faileth of fatness.*

At night we came to an Indian town, and the Indians sat down by a wigwam discoursing, but I was almost spent and could scarce speak. I laid down my load and went into the wigwam, and there sat an Indian boiling of horses' feet (they being wont to eat the flesh first, and when the feet were old and dried, and they had nothing else, they would cut off the feet and use them). I asked him to give me a little of his broth or water they were boiling in. He took a dish and gave me one spoonful of samp,* and bid me take as much of the broth as I would. Then I put some of the hot water to the samp and drank it up, and my spirit came again. He gave me also a piece of the rough or ridding of the small

* "Coarse meal of Indian corn, or a kind of porridge made from this."— (Dictionary of American English).

guts, and I broiled it on the coals; and now may I say with Jonathan, *See, I pray you, how mine eyes have been enlightened, because I tasted a little of this honey,* 1 Samuel 14:29. Now is my spirit revived again; though means be never so inconsiderable, yet if the Lord bestow his blessing upon them, they shall refresh both soul and body.

The Eighteenth Remove

WE TOOK up our packs and along we went, but a wearisome day I had of it. As we went along I saw an Englishman stripped naked and lying dead on the ground, but knew not who it was. Then we came to another Indian town, where we stayed all night. In this town there were four English children, captives, and one of them my own sister's. I went to see how she did, and she was well, considering her captive condition. I would have tarried that night with her, but they that owned her would not suffer it. Then I went into another wigwam, where they were boiling corn and peas, which was a lovely sight to see, but I could not get a taste thereof. Then I went to another wigwam, where there were two of the English children; the squaw was boiling horses' feet. Then she cut me off a little piece, and gave one of the English children a piece also. Being very hungry, I had quickly eat up mine, but the child could not bite it, it was so tough and sinewy, but lay sucking, gnawing, chewing, and slobbering of it in the mouth and hand. Then I took it of the child and eat it myself, and savory it was to my taste. Then may I say as Job, Chapter 6:7, *The things that my soul refused to touch are as my sorrowful meat.* Thus the Lord made that pleasant refreshing, which another time would have been an abomination. Then I went home to my mistress's wigwam, and they told me I disgraced my master with begging, and if I did so any more they would knock me in the head. I told them they had as good knock me in the head as starve me to death.

The Nineteenth Remove

THEY said, when we went out, that we must travel to Wachusett this day. But a bitter weary day I had of it, traveling now three days together, without resting any day between. At last, after many weary steps, I saw Wachusett Hills, but many miles off. Then we came to a great swamp, through which we traveled up to the knees in mud and water, which was heavy going to one tired before. Being almost spent, I thought I should have sunk down at last and never got out; but I may say, as in Psalm 94:18, *When my foot slipped, thy mercy, O Lord, held me up.*

Going along, having indeed my life but little spirit, Philip, who was in the company, came up and took me by the hand and said, "Two weeks more and you shall be mistress again." I asked him if he spake true. He answered, "Yes, and quickly you shall come to your master again" (who had been gone from us three weeks).

After many weary steps we came to Wachusett, where he was, and glad I was to see him. He asked me when I washed me. I told him not this month. Then he fetched me some water himself, and bid me wash, and gave me the glass to see how I looked, and bid his squaw give me something to eat. So she gave me a mess of beans and meat, and a little groundnut cake. I was wonderfully revived with this favor showed me, Psalm 106:46, *He made them also to be pitied of all those that carried them captives.*

My master had three squaws, living sometimes with one and sometimes with another one. One was this old squaw at whose wigwam I was, and with whom my master had been those three weeks. Another was Wettimore, with whom I had lived and served all this while. A severe and proud dame she was, bestowing every day in dressing herself neat as much time as any of the gentry of the land; powdering her hair and painting her face, going with necklaces, with jewels in her ears and bracelets upon her hands. When she had dressed herself, her work was to make girdles of wampum and beads. The third squaw was a younger one, by whom he had two papooses. By that time I was refreshed by the old squaw, with whom my master was, Wettimore's maid came to call me home, at which I fell a-weeping. Then the old squaw told me, to encourage me, that if I wanted victuals I should come to her, and that I should lie there in her wigwam. Then I went with the maid, and quickly came again and lodged there. The squaw laid a mat under me and a good rug over me—the first time I had any such kindness showed me. I understood that Wettimore thought that if she should let me go and serve with the old squaw, she would be in danger to lose not only my service but the redemption pay also. And I was not a little glad to hear this, being by it raised in my hopes that in God's due time there would be an end of this sorrowful hour.

Then came an Indian and asked me to knit him three pair of stockings, for which I had a hat and a silk handkerchief. Then another asked me to make her a shift, for which she gave me an apron. Then came Tom and Peter with the second letter from the Council about the captives. Though they were Indians, I gat them by the hand and burst out into tears; my heart was so full that I could not speak to them.

But recovering myself, I asked them how my husband did, and all my friends and acquaintances. They said, "They are all very well but melancholy." They brought me two biscuits and a pound of tobacco. The tobacco I quickly gave away. When it was all gone, one asked me to give him a pipe of tobacco. I told him it was all gone. Then began he to rant and threaten. I told him when my husband came I would give him some. "Hang him rogue," says he, "I will knock out his brains if he comes here." And then again in the same breath they would say that if there should come an hundred without guns they would do them no hurt: so unstable and like mad men they were. So that fearing the worst, I durst not send to my husband, though there were some thoughts of his coming to redeem and fetch me, not knowing what might follow. For there was little more trust to them than to the master they served.

When the letter was come, the sagamores met to consult about the captives, and called me to them to inquire how much my husband would give to redeem me. When I came I sat down among them, as I was wont to do, as their manner is. Then they bade me stand up, and said they were the "General Court." * They bid me speak what I thought he would give. Now knowing that all we had was destroyed by the Indians, I was in a great strait; I thought if I should speak of but a little, it would be

---

* General Court was the official style of the colonial assembly of Massachusetts.—C. H. Lincoln.

slighted, and hinder the matter, if of a great sum, I knew not where it would be procured. At a venture, I said "Twenty pounds," yet desired them to take less. But they would not hear of that, but sent that message to Boston, that for twenty pounds I should be redeemed. It was a Praying Indian that wrote their letter for them.

There was another Praying Indian who told me that he had a brother that would not eat horse, his conscience was so tender and scrupulous (though as large as hell for the destruction of poor Christians). Then, he said, he read that Scripture to him, 2 Kings 6:25, *There was a great famine in Samaria; and, behold, they besieged it, until an ass's head was sold for fourscore pieces of silver, and the fourth part of a cab of dove's dung for five pieces of silver.* He expounded this place to his brother and showed him that it was lawful to eat that in a famine which is not at another time. "And now," says he, "he will eat horse with any Indian of them all."

There was another Praying Indian who, when he had done all the mischief that he could, betrayed his own father into the English hands, thereby to purchase his own life. Another Praying Indian was at Sudbury fight, though, as he deserved, he was afterward hanged for it. There was another Praying Indian so wicked and cruel as to wear a string about his neck, strung with Christians' fingers. Another Praying Indian, when they went to Sudbury fight, went with them, and his squaw also with him, with her papoose at her back.

Before they went to that fight, they got a company together to powaw; the manner was as followeth. There was one that kneeled upon a deerskin, with the company round him in a ring, who all kneeled, striking upon the ground with their hands and with sticks, and muttering or humming with their mouths. Besides him who kneeled in the ring, there also stood one with a gun in his hand. Then he on the deerskin made a speech, and all manifested assent to it; and so they did many times together. Then they bade him with the gun go out of the ring, which he did, but when he was out, they called him in again; but he seemed to make a stand. Then they called the more earnestly, till he returned again. Then they all sang. Then they gave him two guns, in either hand one. And so he on the deerskin began again; and at the end of every sentence in his speaking they all assented, humming or muttering with their mouths, and striking upon the ground with their hands. Then they bade him with the two guns go out of the ring again; which he did, a little way. Then they called him in again, but he made a stand, so they called him with greater earnestness; but he stood reeling and wavering, as if he knew not whether he should stand or fall, or which way to go. Then they called him with exceeding great vehemency, all of them, one and another. After a little while he turned in, staggering as he went, with his arms stretched out, in either hand a gun. As soon as he came in, they all sang and rejoiced exceedingly awhile. And then he upon the deerskin made another speech, unto which they all assented in a rejoicing manner; and so they ended their business, and forthwith went to Sudbury fight.

To my thinking they went without any scruple but that they should prosper and gain the victory. And they went out not so rejoicing, but they came home with as great a victory. For they said they had killed two captains and almost an hundred men. One Englishman they brought along with them; and he said it was too true, for they had made sad work at Sudbury, as indeed it proved. Yet they came home without that rejoicing and triumphing over their victory which they were wont to show at other times, but rather like dogs (as they say) which have lost their ears. Yet I could not perceive that it was for their own loss of men. They said they had not lost above five or six, and I missed none, except in one wigwam. When they went, they acted as if the Devil had told them that they should gain the victory; and now they acted as if the Devil had told them they should have a fall. Whether it were so or no I cannot tell, but so it proved, for quickly they began to fall, and so it held on that summer, till they came to utter ruin. They came home on a Sabbath day, and the powaw that kneeled upon the deerskin came home (I may say, without abuse) as black as the Devil.

When my master came home, he came to me and bid me make a shirt for his papoose, of a Holland-laced pillowbere. About that time there came an Indian to me and bid me come to his wigwam at night and he would give me some pork and groundnuts. Which I did, and as I was eating, another Indian said to me, "He seems to be your good friend, but he killed two Englishmen at Sudbury, and there lie their clothes behind you." I looked behind me, and there I saw bloody clothes, with bullet holes in them; yet the Lord suffered not this wretch to do me any hurt. Yea, instead of that, he many times refreshed me; five or six times did he and his squaw refresh my feeble carcass. If I went to their wigwam at any time, they would always give me something, and yet they were strangers that I never saw before. Another squaw gave me a piece of fresh pork, and a little salt with it, and lent me her pan to fry it in; and I cannot but remember what a sweet, pleasant, and delightful relish that bit had to me, to this day. So little do we prize common mercies when we have them to the full.

The Twentieth Remove

IT WAS their usual manner to remove, when they had done any mischief, lest they should be found out; and so they did at this time. We went about three or four miles, and there they built a great wigwam, big enough to hold a hundred Indians, which they did in preparation to a great day of dancing. They would say now amongst themselves that the governor would be so angry for his loss at Sudbury that he would send no more about the captives, which made me grieve and tremble. My sister being not far from the place where we now were, and hearing that I was here, desired her master to let her come and see me, and he was willing to it and would go with her; but she, being ready before him, told him she would go before, and was come within a mile or two of the place. Then he overtook her, and began to rant as if he had been mad, and made her go back again in the rain; so that I never saw her till I saw her in Charlestown. But the Lord required many of their ill doings, for this Indian her master was hanged afterwards at Boston.

The Indians now began to come from all quarters, against their merry dancing day. Among some of them came one Goodwife Kettle. I told her my heart was so heavy that it was ready to break. "So is mine too," said she, but yet said, "I hope we shall hear some good news shortly." I could hear now how earnestly my sister desired to see me, and I as earnestly desired to see her; and yet neither of us could get an opportunity. My daughter was also now about a mile off, and I had not seen her in nine or ten weeks, as I had not seen my sister since our first taking. I earnestly desired them to let me go and see them; yea, I entreated, begged, and persuaded them but to let me see my daughter, and yet so hardhearted were they that they would not suffer it. They made use of their tyrannical power whilst they had it, but through the Lord's wonderful mercy their time was now but short.

On a Sabbath day, the sun being about an hour high in the afternoon, came Mr. John Hoar (the Council permitting him, and his own forward spirit inclining him) together with the two forementioned Indians, Tom and Peter, with their third letter from the Council. When they came near, I was abroad; though I saw them not, they presently called me in and bade me sit down and not stir. Then they catched up their guns and away they ran, as if an enemy had been at hand, and the guns went off apace. I manifested some great trouble, and they asked me what was the matter. I told them I thought they had killed the Englishman (for they had in the meantime informed me that an Englishman was come). They said no, they shot over his horse and under, and before his horse, and they pushed him this way and that way, at their pleasure, showing what they could do. Then they let him come to their wigwams. I begged of them to let me see the Englishman, but they would not. But there was I fain to sit their pleasure. When they had talked their fill with him, they suffered me to go to him. We asked each other of our welfare, and I asked him how my husband did, and all my friends. He told me they were all well, and would be glad to see me. Amongst other things which my husband sent me there came a pound of tobacco, which I sold for nine shillings in money; for many of the Indians for want of tobacco smoked hemlock and ground ivy. It was a great mistake in any who thought I sent for tobacco for myself, for through the favor of God that desire was overcome.

I now asked them whether I should go home with Mr. Hoar. They answered "No," one and another of them, and, it being night, we lay down with that answer. In the morning Mr. Hoar invited the sagamores to dinner; but when we went to get it ready, we found that they had stolen the greatest part of the provision Mr. Hoar had brought, out of his bags in the night. And we may see the wonderful power of God in that one passage, in that when there was such a great number of the Indians together, and so greedy of a little good food, and no English there but Mr. Hoar and myself, that there they did not knock us in the head and take what we had; there being not only some provision but also trading cloth, a part of the twenty pounds agreed upon. But instead of doing us any mischief, they seemed to be ashamed of the fact, and said it were some "matchit" [bad] Indian that did it. Oh, that we could believe that there is no thing too hard for God! God showed his power over the heathen in this, as he did over the hungry lions when Daniel was cast into the den.

Mr. Hoar called them betimes to dinner, but they ate very little, they being so busy in dressing themselves and getting ready for their dance, which was carried on by eight of them, four men and four squaws, my master and mistress being two. He was dressed in his Holland shirt, with great laces sewed at the tail of it; he had his silver buttons, his white stockings, his garters were hung round with shillings, and he had girdles of wampum upon his head and shoulders. She had a kersey coat, and covered with girdles of wampum from the loins upward; her arms from her elbows to her hands were covered with bracelets, there were handfuls of necklaces about her neck, and several sorts of jewels in her ears. She had fine red stockings and white shoes, her hair powdered and face painted red that was always before black. And all the dancers were after the same manner. There were two others singing and knocking on a kettle for their music. They kept hopping up and down one after another, with a kettle of water in the midst standing warm upon some embers, to drink of when they were dry. They held on till it was almost night, throwing out wampum to the standers-by.

That night I asked them again if I should go home. They all as one said no, except my husband would come for me. When we were lain down, my master went out of the wigwam and by and by sent in an Indian called James the Printer, who told Mr. Hoar that my master would let me go home tomorrow if he would let him have one pint of liquor. Then Mr. Hoar called his own Indians, Tom and Peter, and bid them go and see whether he would promise it before all three; and if he would, he should have it; which he did, and he had it. Then Philip, smelling the business, called me to him and asked me what I would give him to tell me some good news and speak a good word for me. I told him I could not tell what to give him, I would anything I had, and asked him what he would have. He said, two coats and twenty shillings in money, and half a bushel of seed corn, and some tobacco. I thanked him for his love, but I knew the good news as well as the crafty fox.

My master after he had had his drink quickly came ranting into the wigwam again, and called for Mr. Hoar, drinking to him and saying he was a good man, and then again he would say, "Hang him rogue." Being almost drunk, he would drink to him, and yet presently say he should be hanged. Then he called for me. I trembled to hear him, yet I was fain to go to him, and he drank to me, showing no incivility. He was the first Indian I saw drunk all the while that I was amongst them. At last his squaw ran out, and he after her, round the wigwam, with his money jingling at his knees. But she escaped him. But having an old squaw, he ran to her, and so through the Lord's mercy we were no more troubled that night.

Yet I had not a comfortable night's rest, for I think I can say I did not sleep for three nights together. The night before the letter came from the Council I could not rest, I was so full of fears and troubles, God many times leaving us most in the dark when deliverance is nearest; yea, at this time I could not rest night or day. The next night I was overjoyed, Mr. Hoar being come, and that with such good tidings. The third night I was even swallowed up with the thoughts of things, viz., that ever I should go home again, and that I must go leaving my children behind me in the wilderness; so that sleep was now almost departed from mine eyes.

On Tuesday morning they called their General Court (as they call it) to consult and determine whether I should go home or no. And they all as one man did seemingly consent to it that I should go home, except Philip, who would not come among them.

But to return again to my going home, where we may see a remarkable change of providence. At first they were all against it, except my husband should come for me; but afterwards they assented to it, and seemed much to rejoice in it. Some asked me to send them some bread, others some tobacco; others shaking me by the hand offered me a hood and scarf to ride in; not one moving hand or tongue against it. Thus hath the Lord answered my poor desire, and the many earnest requests of others put up unto God for me.

In my travels an Indian came to me and told me if I were willing he and his squaw would run away and go home along with me. I told him no, I was not willing to run away but desired to wait God's time, that I might go home quietly and without fear. And now God hath granted me my desire. Oh, the wonderful power of God that I have seen, and the experience that I have had! I have been in the midst of those roaring lions and savage bears, that feared neither God nor man nor the Devil, by night and day, alone and in company, sleeping all sorts together, and yet not one of them ever offered the least abuse of unchastity to me, in word or action. Though some are ready to say I speak it for my own credit, I but speak it in the presence of God, and to his glory. God's power is as great now, and as sufficient to save, as when he preserved Daniel in the lions' den, or the three children in the fiery furnace. I may well say as his Psalm 107:1, *O give thanks unto the Lord, for he is good; for his mercy endureth for ever.* Let the redeemed of the Lord say so, whom he hath redeemed from the hand of the enemy, especially that I should come away in the midst of so many hundreds of enemies quietly and peaceably, and not a dog moving his tongue.

So I took my leave of them, and in coming along my heart melted into tears, more than all the while I was with them, and I was almost swallowed up with the thoughts that ever I should go home again. About the sundown, Mr. Hoar and myself and the two Indians came to Lancaster, and a solemn sight it was to me. There had I lived many comfortable years amongst my relations and neighbors, and now not one Christian to be seen, nor one house left standing. We went on to a farmhouse that was yet standing, where we lay all night, and a comfortable lodging we had, though nothing but straw to lie on. The Lord preserved us in safety that night, and raised us up again in the morning, and carried us along, that before noon we came to Concord. Now was I full of joy, and yet not without sorrow: joy to see such a lovely sight, so many Christians together, and some of them my neighbors. There I met with my brother and my brother-in-law, who asked me if I knew where his wife was. Poor heart! He had helped to bury her, and knew it not; she, being shot down by the house, was partly burnt, so that those who were at Boston at the desolation of the town and came back afterward and buried the dead did not know her. Yet I was not without sorrow, to think how many were looking and longing, and my own children amongst the rest, to enjoy that deliverance that I had now received, and I did not know whether ever I should see them again.

Being recruited with food and raiment, we went to Boston that day, where I met with my dear husband, but the thoughts of our dear children, one being dead and the other we could not tell where, abated our comfort to each other. I was not before so much hemmed in with the merciless and cruel heathen, but now as much with pitiful, tenderhearted, and compassionate Christians. In that poor and distressed and beggarly condition I was received in, I was kindly entertained in several houses; so much love I received from several (some of whom I knew, and others I knew not) that I am not capable to declare it. But the Lord knows them all by name: the Lord reward them sevenfold into their bosoms of his spirituals, for their temporals. The twenty pounds, the price of my redemption, was raised by some Boston gentlemen and Mrs. Usher, whose bounty and religious charity I would not forget to make mention of. Then Mr. Thomas Shepard of Charlestown received us into his house, where we continued eleven weeks; and a father and mother they were to us. And many more tenderhearted friends we met with in that place.

We were now in the midst of love, yet not without much and frequent heaviness of heart for our poor children, and other relations, who were still in affliction. The week following, after my coming in, the governor and Council sent forth to the Indians again, and that not without success, for they brought in my sister and Goodwife Kettle. Their not knowing where our children were was a sore trial to us still, and yet we were not without secret hopes that we should see them again. That which was dead lay heavier upon my spirit than those which were alive and amongst the heathen; thinking how it suffered with its wounds, and I was no way able to relieve it, and how it was buried by the heathen in the wilderness, from among all Christians. We were hurried up and down in our thoughts; sometimes we should hear a report that they were gone this way and sometimes that, and that they were come in, in this place or that. We kept inquiring and listening to hear concerning them, but no certain news as yet.

About this time the Council had ordered a day of public thanksgiving. Though I thought I had still cause of mourning, and being unsettled in our minds, we thought we would ride toward the eastward, to see if we could hear anything concerning our children. And as we were riding along (God is the wise disposer of all things) between Ipswich and Rowley, we met with Mr. William Hubbard, who told us that our son Joseph was come in to Major Waldron's, and another with him, which was my sister's son. I asked him how he knew it. He said the major himself told him so. So along we went till we came to Newbury, and their minister being absent, they desired my husband to preach the thanksgiving for them. He was not willing to stay there that night, but would go over to Salisbury, to hear further, and come again in the morning; which he did, and preached there that day. At night, when he had done, one came and told him that his daughter was come in at Providence. Here was mercy on both hands. Now hath God fulfilled that precious Scripture which was such a comfort to me in my distressed condition. When my heart was ready to sink into the earth (my children being gone I could not tell whither) and my knees trembled under me and I was walking through the valley of the shadow of death, then the Lord brought, and now had fulfilled, that reviving word unto me: *Thus saith the Lord, Refrain thy voice from weeping, and thine eyes from tears; for thy work shall be rewarded...and they shall come again from the land of the enemy.*

Now we were between them, the one on the east, and the other on the west. Our son being nearest, we went to him first, to

Portsmouth, where we met with him, and with the major also, who told us he had done what he could, but could not redeem him under seven pounds, which the good people thereabouts were pleased to pay. The Lord reward the major, and all thereat, though unknown to me, for their labor of love. My sister's son was redeemed for four pounds, which the Council gave order for the payment of. Having now received one of our children, we hastened toward the other. Going back through Newbury, my husband preached there on the Sabbath day, for which they rewarded him manyfold.

On Monday we came to Charlestown, where we heard that the Governor of Rhode Island had sent over for our daughter, to take care of her, being now within his jurisdiction: which should not pass without our acknowledgments. But she being nearer Rehoboth than Rhode Island, Mr. Newman went over and took care of her, and brought her to his own house. And the goodness of God was admirable to us in our low estate, in that he raised up compassionate friends on every side to us, when we had nothing to recompense any for their love. The Indians were now gone that way, that it was apprehended dangerous to go to her. But the carts which carried provision to the English Army, being guarded, brought her with them to Dorchester, where we received her safe. Blessed be the Lord for it, for great is his power, and he can do whatsoever seemeth him good.

Her coming in was after this manner. She was traveling one day with the Indians, with her basket at her back. The company of Indians were got before her, and gone out of sight, all except one squaw. She followed the squaw till night, and then both of them lay down, having nothing over them but the heavens and nothing under them but the earth. Thus she traveled three days together, not knowing whither she was going, having nothing to eat or drink but water and green whortleberries. At last they came into Providence, where she was kindly entertained by several of that town. The Indians often said that I should never have her under twenty pounds. But now the Lord hath brought her in upon free cost, and given her to me the second time. The Lord make us a blessing indeed, each to others. Now have I seen that Scripture also fulfilled, Deuteronomy

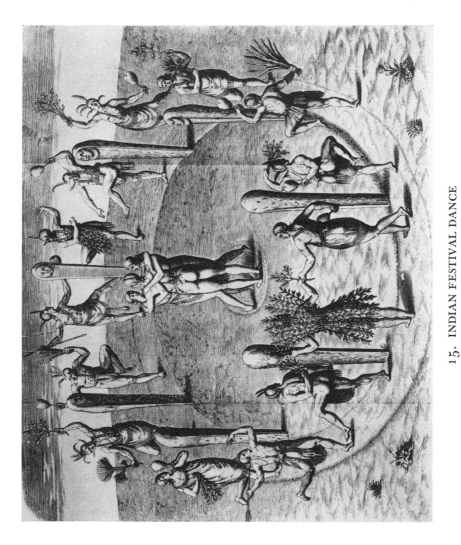

15. INDIAN FESTIVAL DANCE

De Bry, *The Great Voyages*, Part I; Frankfurt, 1590

30:4,7: *If any of thine be driven out to the outmost parts of heaven, from thence will the Lord thy God gather thee, and from thence will he fetch thee. And the Lord thy God will put all these curses upon thine enemies and on them that hate thee, which persecuted thee.*

Thus hath the Lord brought me and mine out of that horrible pit, and hath set us in the midst of tenderhearted and compassionate Christians. It is the desire of my soul that we may walk worthy of the mercies received, and which we are receiving.

5

INDIAN CONCEITS AND ANTICS

Perhaps because he became a popular myth, grimacing in front of cigar stores, the Indian has never seemed real to Americans. The eighteenth and nineteenth centuries regarded him as a frontier pest; the twentieth century looks on him as a charity case. Anthropologists have found him a superb laboratory specimen and studied him with might and main, after he died historically. The literature of the seventeenth century, when the race battle still hung in the balance, alone humanizes the red man. In the pages of the anthropologists we find Indians who behave very correctly as Indians, according to the forms of their classified subculture, but who seldom behave like human beings. Give me William Wood, who tells of a cuckolded Indian taken in by his wife's "whorish glozing and sirenlike tongue," till one night he catches her in sin and bastinadoes her lover so energetically that "his battered bones and bruised flesh made him a fitter object for some skillful surgeon than the lovely object of a lustful strumpet." Such a story gives us a sense of rapport with the exotic aliens.

These early descriptions tell us nearly as much about the English as about the Indians. Europeans had seen no primitive peoples in their own back yard, and found these the strangest phenomenon of a strange universe. The whites marveled at the red man's style of outdoor living. They laughed at the natives' bobbles when confronted with European culture, and at their occasional shrewd outwitting of the invaders. They wondered at the mythical traditions of the savages, which sometimes vaguely resembled the Scripture of Genesis. And they were amazed and alarmed at the wizards and sorcerers who trafficked with the Devil.

In a world swayed by witchcrafts and prodigies, the secret powers of the powaws (from which the present "powwow") had to command respect. The interplay between European and Indian beliefs in the occult, which we see only in these colonial writings, makes a dramatic moment in the history of the human mind. Cotton Mather believed in the magic of the powaws; he

267

even half suspected that they were behind the Salem witchcraft outbreak. After all, the Indians were heathen, they admitted to fearing and placating the Devil, and their high priests performed some diabolical deeds, thoroughly attested and vouched for by creditable witnesses.

Let no man scorn the sincerity of Indian belief. In northern Michigan I had occasion, in 1946, to talk with a number of Ojibwa and Sioux living on reservation plots in the midst of white civilization. They still live in the woods and still think in their traditions, although they speak fluent American and have had the white man's schooling. In fact, the better educated rationalize their concepts with the greatest skill. After I had listened to these dignified, pleasant-speaking elder statesmen explain about animal guardians and thunderbirds and bad Indians who turned into fire-breathing bears, and doctors who pulled pins and beads out of the bewitched—telling all this calmly, reasonably, with a plenitude of detail and corroboration—I had to grab hold of my senses to get back into the atomic age. A good Christian of the seventeenth century would accept all this at face value, realizing he spoke with heathen steeped in the black arts.

POWAW MAGIC

Cotton Mather

HAVING promised an account of the conversation of many Indians inhabiting these parts of America, it may be well expected I should say something of their religion while heathen.

They generally acknowledged and worshiped many gods, and therefore greatly esteemed and reverenced their priests, powaws, or wizards, as having immediate converse with the gods. To them therefore they addressed themselves in all difficult cases. Yet could not all that desire that dignity (as they esteemed it) obtain familiarity with the infernal spirits, nor were all powaws alike successful in their addresses; but they become such, either by immediate revelation or in the use of certain rites and ceremonies. Tradition had left a means conducing to that end, in so much that parents often out of zeal dedicated their children to the gods and educated them accordingly, observing certain diet, debarring sleep, et cetera. Yet of the many thus designed, but few obtained their desire.

Supposing that where the practice of witchcraft has been highly esteemed, there may be given the plainest demonstration of mortals having familiarity with infernal spirits, I am willing to let my reader know that not many years since died here one of the powaws, who never pretended to astrological knowledge, yet could precisely inform such who desire his assistance from whence goods stolen from them were taken, and whither carried, with many things of the like nature. Nor was he ever known to endeavor concealing that his knowledge was immediately from a god subservient to him that the English worshiped.

This powaw was desired by an Englishman worthy of credit (who lately informed me of the same) to advise him who had stolen certain goods which he had lost, having formerly been an eyewitness of his ability. The powaw, after a little pausing, demanded why he requested that from him, since the other served another God, that therefore he could not help him. But he added, "If you can believe that my God will help you, I will try what I can do." Which diverted the man from further inquiry.

I must a little digress, and tell my reader that this powaw's wife was accounted a godly woman and lived in the practice and profession of the Christian religion, not only by the approbation but encouragement of her husband. She constantly prayed in the family, and he could not blame her for that she served a God that was above him. But that as to himself, his god's continued kindness obliged him not to forsake his service.

That the powaws by the infernal spirits often killed persons, caused lameness and impotency, as well as showed their art in performing things beyond human, by diabolic skill—such who have conversed much among them have had no reason to question.

Their practice was either to desire the spirit appearing to them to perform what mischief they intended; or to form a piece of leather, like an arrowhead, tying an hair thereto, or using some bone, as of fish (that it might be known witchcraft to the bewitched), over which they performed certain ceremonies, and dismissed them to effect their desire.

Such enchanted things have most certainly either entered the bodies of those intended by them to be wounded, or the Devil hath formed the like within their flesh, without any outward breach of the skin. Such we have good reason to believe, the powaws acknowledging that practice, and such things having been taken out of the flesh of the ones supposed to be bewitched. Or they seize something of the spirit (as the Devil made them think) of those they intended to torment or kill, while it wandered in their sleep. This they kept, being in form of a fly, closely imprisoned; and accordingly as they dealt with this, so it fared with the body it belonged to.

Of the cures performed by them on the bewitched I could give many instances. I shall briefly hint at two.

The one is of an Indian on Martha's Vineyard, called afterward George. Having been some time greatly tormented, and now wholly impotent, his friends advised him to the powaws, concluding him to be bewitched. They met and danced round a great fire, the sick lying by, till some of the neighbors entered the house, being persuaded that a great powaw (now called to cure) had bewitched the sick. They threatened him that, as he had bewitched, unless he would cure the sick man they would burn him in the fire. After many excuses, too long here to relate, they took him up, resolving at least to a little singe him, who no sooner felt the heat of the fire near him but George immediately recovered. This was a thing publicly known to the English, as well as Indians, in the neighborhood. There can be no doubt of it.

The other I shall instance in was a relation from Captain Thomas Dagget, Esq., now deceased, and Richard Sarson, Esq., justices of the peace. They being on an island where a bewitched woman lay in great extremity and wholly impotent— the powaws there having without success endeavored the cure— the related sent to Martha's Vineyard for more famous powaws. The said gentlemen were admitted to be present on certain conditions.

The powaws went to dancing, and, with the spectators, used certain ceremonies usual in such cases. One of the powaws prayed to his god with such ardent desires and fervency that, Captain Dagget told me, had it been to the true God, it had been a prayer exceeding most that he had heard. The issue was, they in a deerskin caught the spirit (as they said) which entered the woman. This, they said, was the spirit of an Englishman drowned in the adjacent sound. (Yet it was then supposed the powaw was by who bewitched her.)

The issue was, she immediately recovered. The powaw told her that unless she removed to Martha's Vineyard she would again be sick, for being an English spirit he could not long confine it.

William Wood

Now of their worships. As it is natural to all mortals to worship something, so do these people, but exactly to describe to whom their worship is chiefly bent is very difficult. Ketan is their good god, to whom they sacrifice (as the ancient heathen did to Ceres) after their garners be full with a good crop. Upon this god likewise they invocate for fair weather, for rain in time of drought, and for the recovery of their sick; but if they do not hear them, then their powaws betake themselves to their exorcisms and necromantic charms, by which they bring to pass strange things, if we may believe the Indians.

They report of one Pissacannawa that he can make the water burn, the rocks move, the trees dance, metamorphize himself into a flaming man. But, it may be objected, this is but *deceptio visus.* He will therefore do more, for in winter, when there is no green leaves to be got, he will burn an old one to ashes, and putting those into the water, produce a new green leaf, which you shall not only see but substantially handle and carry away; and make of a dead snake's skin a living snake, both to be seen, felt, and heard. This I write but upon the report of the Indians, who confidently affirm stranger things.

But to make manifest that by God's permission, through the Devil's help, their charms are of force to produce effects of wonderment, an honest gentleman related this story to me, being an eyewitness of the same. A powaw having a patient with the stump of some small tree run through his foot, being past the cure of his ordinary surgery, betook himself to his charms, and being willing to show his miracle before the English stranger, he wrapped a piece of cloth about the foot of the lame man. Upon that wrapping a beaver skin, by his sucking charms he brought out the stump, which he spat into a tray of water, returning the foot as whole as its fellow in a short time.

The manner of their action in their conjuration is thus. The parties that are sick or lame being brought before them, the powaw sits down, the rest of the Indians give attentive audience to his imprecations and invocations, and after the violent expression of many a hideous bellowing and groaning, he makes a stop, and then all the auditors with one voice utter a short canto; which done, the powaw still proceeds in his invocations, sometimes roaring like a bear, other times groaning like a dying horse, foaming at the mouth like a chased boar, smiting on his naked breast and thighs with such violence as if he were mad. Thus will he continue sometimes half a day, spending his lungs, sweating out his fat, and tormenting his body in this diabolical worship. Sometimes the Devil for requital of their worship recovers the party, to nuzzle them up in their devilish religion.

In former time he was wont to carry away their wives and children, because he would drive them to these matins, to fetch them again to confirm their belief of this his much desired authority over them. But since the English frequented those parts, they daily fall from his colors, relinquishing former fopperies, and acknowledge our God to be supreme. They acknowledge the power of the Englishman's God, as they call him, because they could never yet have power by their conjurations to damnify the English either in body or goods. And besides, they say he is a good God that sends them so many things, so much good corn, so many cattle, temperate rains, fair seasons, which they likewise are the better for since the arrival of the English—the times and seasons being much altered in seven or eight years, freer from lightning and thunder, long droughts, sudden and tempestuous dashes of rain, and lamentable cold winters.

John Gyles

THE Indians are very often surprised with the appearance of ghosts and demons. Sometimes they are encouraged by the Devil, for they go to him for success in hunting, et cetera. I was once hunting with Indians who were not brought over to the Romish faith, and after several days' hunting they proposed to inquire, according to their custom, what success they should have.

They accordingly prepared many hot stones and laid them in a heap, and made a small hut covered with skins and mats. Then in the dark night two of the powaws went into this hot house with a large vessel of water, which at times they poured on those hot rocks, which raised a thick steam, so that a third Indian was obliged to stand without and lift up a mat to give it vent when they were almost suffocated.

There was an old squaw who was kind to captives, and never joined with them in their powawing, to whom I manifested an earnest desire to see their management. She told me that if they knew of my being there they would kill me, and that when she was a girl she had known young persons to be taken away by a hairy man, and therefore she would not advise me to go, lest the hairy man should carry me away. I told her I was not afraid of the hairy man, nor could he hurt me if she would not discover me to the powaws. At length she promised that she would not, but charged me to be careful of myself.

I went within three or four feet of the hot house, for it was very dark, and heard strange noises and yellings, such as I never heard before. At times the Indian who tended without would lift up the mat, and a steam rise up which looked like fire in the dark. I lay there two or three hours, but saw none of their hairy men or demons. And when I found that they had finished their ceremony, I went to the wigwam and told the squaw what had passed. She was glad I returned without hurt, and never discovered what I had done.

After some time inquiry was made what success we were likely to have in our hunting. The powaws said that they had very likely signs of success, but no real, visible appearance as at other times. A few days after, we moved up the river and had pretty good success.

One afternoon as I was in a canoe with one of the powaws, the dog barked, and presently a moose passed by within a few rods of us, so that the waves which he made by wading rolled our canoe. The Indian shot at him, but the moose took very little notice of it, and went into the woods to the southward. The fellow said, "I'll try if I can't fetch you back, for all your haste." The evening following we built our two wigwams on a sandy point on the upper end of an island in the river, northwest of the place where the moose went into the woods, and here the Indian powawed the greatest part of the night following. In the morning we had the fair track of a moose round our wigwams, though we did not see or taste of it. I am of opinion that the Devil was permitted to humor those unhappy wretches sometimes, in some things.

The Old Indian Chronicle

ON THE 28th day of August (1675) happened here at eleven o'clock at night a most violent storm of wind and rain. The like was never known before; it blew up many ships together that they bulged one another, some up towards Cambridge, some to Muddy River, doing much hurt to very many; also it broke down

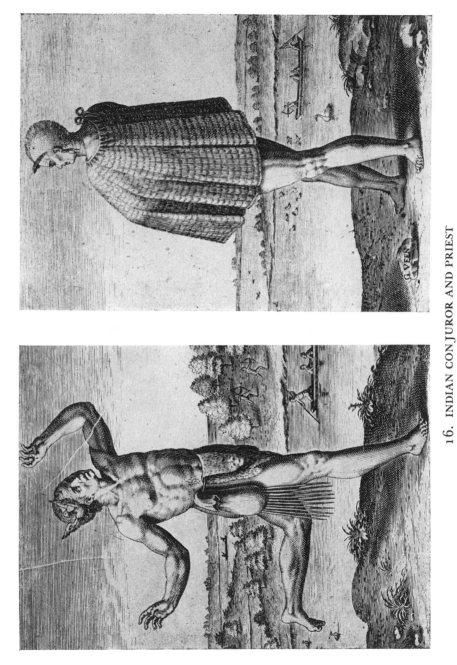

16. INDIAN CONJUROR AND PRIEST

De Bry, *The Great Voyages*, Part I; Frankfurt, 1590

many wharfs, and blew down some houses thereupon. The Indians afterwards reported that they had caused it by their powaw (i.e., worshiping the Devil). They further say that as many Englishmen shall die as the trees have by this wind been blown down in the woods. But these heathenish stories are consonant to their barbarous cruelty, and ought to be valued accordingly by all who own anything superior to it or them.

Robert Beverley

THE latest story of conjuration is this. Some few years ago there happened a very dry time towards the heads of the rivers, and especially on the upper parts of James River, where Colonel Byrd had several quarters of Negroes. This gentleman has for a long time been extremely respected and feared by all the Indians round about, who without knowing the name of any governor have ever been kept in order by him.

During this drought, an Indian well known to one of the colonel's overseers came to him and asked if his tobacco was not like to be spoiled. The overseer answered, Yes, if they had not rain very suddenly. The Indian, who pretended great kindness for his master, told the overseer that if he would promise to give him two bottles of rum he would bring him rain enough. The overseer did not believe anything of the matter, not seeing at that time the least appearance of rain, nor so much as a cloud in the sky; however, he promised to give him the rum when his master came thither, if he would be as good as his word.

Upon this the Indian went immediately a-powawing, as they call it; and in about half an hour there came up a black cloud into the sky that showered down rain enough upon this gentleman's corn and tobacco, but none at all upon any of the neighbors', except a few drops of the skirt of the shower.

The Indian for that time went away without returning to the overseer again, till he heard of his master's arrival at the falls, and then he came to him and demanded the two bottles of rum. The colonel at first seemed to know nothing of the matter, and asked the Indian for what reason he made that demand (although his overseer had been so overjoyed at what had happened that he could not rest till he had taken a horse and rid near forty miles to tell his master the story). The Indian answered with some concern that he hoped the overseer had let him know the service he had done him by bringing a shower of rain to save his crop. At this the colonel, not being apt to believe such stories, smiled and told him he was a cheat and had seen the cloud a-coming; otherwise he could neither have brought the rain nor so much as foretold it.

The Indian, at this seeming much troubled, replied, "Why, then, had not such a one and such a one (naming the next neighbors) had rain as well as your overseer, for they lost their crops? But I loved you, and therefore I saved yours."

The colonel made sport with him a little while, but in the end ordered him the two bottles of rum, letting him understand, however, that it was a free gift, and not the consequence of any bargain with his overseer.

John Lawson

THE cures I have seen performed by the Indians are too many to repeat here, so I shall only mention some few, and their method. They cure scald heads infallibly, and never miss. Their chief remedy, as I have seen them make use of, is the oil of acorns, but from which sort of oak I am not certain. They cure burns beyond credit. I have seen a man burned in such a manner (when drunk) by falling into a fire, that I did not think he could recover; yet they cured him in ten days so that he went about. I knew another blown up with powder, that was cured to admiration. I never saw an Indian have an ulcer or foul wound in my life; neither is there any such thing to be found amongst them. They cure the pox by a berry that salivates as mercury does; yet they use sweating and decoctions very much with it, as they do almost on every occasion, and when they are thoroughly heated they leap into the river.

We had a planter in Carolina who had got an ulcer in his leg, which had troubled him a great many years; at last he applied himself to one of these Indian conjurers, who was a Pamlico Indian, and was not to give the value of fifteen shillings for the cure. Now I am not positive whether he washed the ulcer with anything before he used what I am now going to speak of, which was nothing but the rotten, doted grains of Indian corn, beaten to a powder, and the soft down growing on a turkey's rump. This dried up the ulcer immediately, and no other fontanel was made to discharge the matter, he remaining a healthful man till the time he had the misfortune to be drowned, which was many years after.

Another instance (not of my own knowledge, but I had it confirmed by several dwellers in Maryland, where it was done) was of an honest planter that had been possessed with a strange lingering distemper, not usual amongst them, under which he emaciated and grew every month worse than another. It held him several years, in which time he had made trial of several doctors, as they call them, which I suppose were ship surgeons. In the beginning of this distemper the patient was very well to pass, and was possessed of several slaves, which the doctors purged all away, and the poor man was so far from mending that he grew worse and worse every day. But it happened that one day his wife and he were commiserating his miserable condition, and that he could not expect to recover but looked for death very speedily, and condoling the misery he should leave his wife and family in, since all his Negroes were gone. At that time, I say, it happened that an Indian was in the same room, who had frequented the house for many years and so was become as one of the family, and would sometimes be at this planter's house and at other times amongst the Indians.

This savage, hearing what they talked of, and having a great love for the sick man, made this reply to what he had heard. "Brother, you have been a long time sick, and I know you have given away your slaves to your English doctors. What made you do so, and now become poor? They do not know how to cure you; for it is an Indian distemper, which your people know not the nature of. If it had been an English disease, probably they could have cured you; and had you come to me at first I would have cured you for a small matter, without taking away your servants that made corn for you and your family to eat. And yet, if you will give me a blanket to keep me warm, and some powder and shot to kill deer withal, I will do my best to make you well still."

The man was low in courage and pocket too, and made the Indian this reply. "Jack, my distemper is past cure, and if our English doctors cannot cure it I am sure the Indians cannot."

But his wife accosted her husband in very mild terms, and told him he did not know but God might be pleased to give a blessing to that Indian's undertaking more than he had done to the English; and further added, "If you die I cannot be much more miserable by giving this small matter to the Indian; so I pray you, my dear, take my advice, and try him." To which, by her persuasions, he consented.

After the bargain was concluded, the Indian went into the woods and brought in both herbs and roots, of which he made a decoction and gave it the man to drink, and bade him go to bed, saying it should not be long before he came again. Which the patient performed as he had ordered; and the portion he had administered made him sweat after the most violent manner that could be, whereby he smelled very offensively both to himself and they that were about him.

But in the evening, towards night, Jack came, with a great rattlesnake in his hand alive, which frightened the people almost out of their senses, and he told his patient that he must take that to bed to him; at which the man was in a great consternation, and told the Indian he was resolved to let no snake come into his bed, for he might as well die of the distemper he had as be killed with the bite of that serpent.

To which the Indian replied, he could not bite him now nor do him any harm, for he had taken out his poison teeth; and he showed him that they were gone. At last with much persuasion he admitted the snake's company, which the Indian put about his middle, and ordered nobody to take him away upon any account. This was strictly observed, although the snake girded him as hard for a great while as if he had been drawn in by a belt which one pulled at with all his strength. At last the snake's twitches grew weaker and weaker, till by degrees he felt him not; and opening the bed he was found dead, and the man thought himself better. The Indian came in the morning and, seeing the snake dead, told the man that his distemper was dead along with that snake; which proved so as he said, for the man speedily recovered his health and became perfectly well.

DEVIL WORSHIP

Edward Johnson

As FOR any religious observation, they were the most destitute
of any people yet heard of, the Devil having them in very great
subjection, not using craft to delude them, as he ordinarily doth
in most parts of the world, but keeping them in a continual
slavish fear of him. Only the powaws, who are more conversant
with him than any other, sometimes recover their sick folk
with charms, which they use by the help of the Devil, and this
makes them to adore such.

One of them was seen, as is reported, to cure a squaw that was
dangerously sick by taking a snake's skin and winding it about
her arm, the which soon became a living snake crawling round
about her arms and body. Another caused the sick patient, for
healing, to pass barefooted through many burning coals. Those
that cannot cure them they call Squantam's powaws; but if the
patient live, he is had in great admiration, and then they cry,
"Much winnit Abbamocho," that is, "Very good devil" (for
Squantam is a bad devil and Abbamocho is their good devil).

It has been a thing very frequent, before the English came, for
the Devil to appear unto them in a bodily shape, sometimes very
ugly and terrible, and sometimes like a white boy, and chiefly in
the most hideous woods and swamps. They report that sometimes
he has come into their wigwams and carried away divers of them
alive; and since we came hither, they tell us of a very terrible
beast for shape and bigness that came into a wigwam toward the
northeast parts, remote from any English plantations, and took
away six men at a time, who were never seen afterward.

John Josselyn

THEY acknowledge a god whom they call Squantam but worship
him they do not, because (they say) he will do them no harm.

But Abbamocho or Cheepie many times smites them with incurable diseases, scares them with his apparitions and panic terrors, by reason whereof they live in a wretched consternation, worshiping the Devil for fear. One Black Robin, an Indian, sitting down in the cornfield belonging to the house where I resided, ran out of his wigwam frighted with the apparition of two infernal spirits in the shape of Mohawks. Another time two Indians and an Indess came running into our house crying out they should all die—Cheepie was gone over the field gliding in the air with a long rope hanging from one of his legs. We asked them what he was like. They said, all one Englishman, clothed with hat and coat, shoes and stockings, et cetera.

They have a remarkable observation of a flame that appears before the death of an Indian or English upon their wigwams in the dead of the night. The first time that I did see it, I was called out by some of them about twelve of the clock; it being a very dark night, I perceived it plainly mounting into the air over our church, which was built upon a plain little more than half a quarter of a mile from our dwelling house, on the north side of the church. Look on what side of a house it appears, from that coast respectively you shall hear of a corpse within two or three days.

William Wood

In the night they need not to be feared, for they will not budge from their own dwellings for fear of their Abbamocho (the Devil), whom they fear especially in evil enterprises. They will rather lie by an English fire than go a quarter of a mile in the dark to their own dwellings. But they are well freed from this scarecrow since the coming of the English, and less care for his delusions; and whereas it hath been reported that there are such horrible apparitions, fearful roarings, thundering and lightning raised by the Devil to discourage the English in their settling, I for mine own part never saw or heard of any of these things in the country.

Nor have I heard of any Indians that have lately been put in fear, saving two or three, and they worse scared than hurt. They, seeing a blackamoor in the top of a tree, looking out for his

way, which he had lost, surmised he was Abbamocho or the
Devil, deeming all devils that are blacker than themselves. And
being near to the plantation, they posted to the English and
entreated their aid to conjure this Devil to his own place; who,
finding him to be a poor wandering blackamoor, conducted him
to his master.

John Lawson

THEY are never fearful in the night, nor do the thoughts of
spirits ever trouble them, such as the many hobgoblins and bugbears that we suck in with our milk, and the foolery of our nurses
and servants suggests to us, who by their idle tales of fairies and
witches make such impressions on our tender years that at
maturity we carry pygmies' souls in giants' bodies and ever after
are thereby so much deprived of reason and unmanned as never
to be masters of half the bravery nature designed for us. Not
but that the Indians have as many lying stories of spirits and
conjurers as any people in the world, but they tell it with
no disadvantage to themselves. For the great esteem which the
old men bring themselves to is by making the others believe their
familiarity with devils and spirits, and whatever they after impose
upon the people is received as infallible.

They are so little startled at the thoughts of another world
that they not seldom murder themselves. As, for instance, a Bear
River Indian, a very likely young fellow, about twenty years of
age, whose mother was angry at his drinking of too much rum,
and chid him for it. He thereupon replied he would have her
satisfied, and he would do the like no more; upon which he made
his words good, for he went aside and shot himself dead. This
was a son of the politic King of the Machupunga I spoke of
before, who had the most cunning of any Indian I ever met
withal.

Louis Hennepin

THESE barbarians are one more superstitious than another, the
old men especially; and the women most obstinately retain the
traditions of their ancestors. When I told them it was a foolery

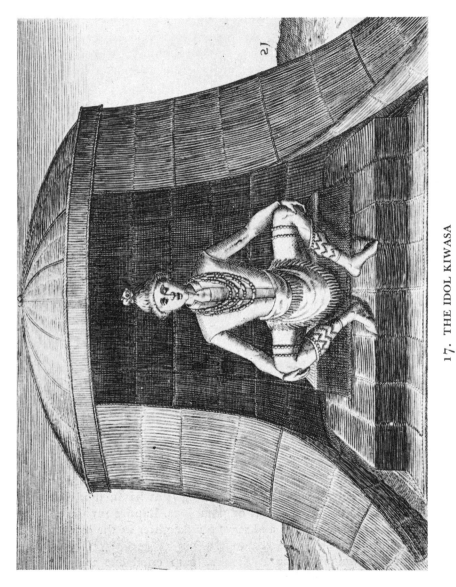

17. THE IDOL KIWASA

De Bry, *The Great Voyages*, Part I; Frankfurt, 1590

to believe so many dreams and fancies, they asked me how old I was. "You are not above thirty-five or forty years old, and do you pretend to know more than our ancient men? Go, go, you know not what you say. You may know what passes in your own country, because your ancestors have told you, but you cannot tell what has passed in ours, before the spirits, that is to say the Europeans, came hither."

I replied to these barbarians, that we knew all by the Scripture, which the great Master of Life has given us by his Son; that this Son died to deliver men from a place where burns an eternal fire, which would have been their lot, if he had not come into the world to save us from sin and from death; that all mankind were sinners in Adam, the first man of the world.

These savages, who have a large share of common sense, often asked me, "Did your spirits know of our being here before you came hither?"

I answered them, "No."

"You do not learn therefore all things by Scripture; it tells you not all things," replied they.

There are many of the savages that make the stories of their ancients the subject of their raillery, but others believe them. They have some sentiments of the immortality of the soul. They say there is a delicious country towards the west where there is good hunting, and where they kill as many beasts as they please. It is thither they say their souls go. They hope to see one another there. But they are yet more ridiculous in believing that the souls of caldrons, guns, and other arms, which they place near the sepulcher of the dead, go with them to be made use of in the Country of Souls.

A young savage maid dying after baptism, the mother seeing one of her slaves at the point of death said, "My daughter is all alone in the country of the dead, among the Europeans, without relations and without friends. The spring is at hand; it is time to sow Indian corn and citruls or pompions. Baptize my slave," says she, "that she may go and serve my daughter in the country of the Europeans."

A savage woman being at the last gasp cried out that she would not be baptized, for the savages that die Christians are burned in the Country of Souls by the Europeans. Some of them told me one day that we baptized them to make them our slaves in the other world. Others asked me if there was good hunting in the country whither their dying newly baptized infants were going. When I answered them that they lived there without eating and drinking, because they are there satisfied with the contemplation of the great Master of Life: "We will not go thither," say they, "because we must eat." If we reply that they will have no need of food, they clasp their hands upon their mouths in sign of admiration, and say, "You are a great liar. Can one live without eating?"

These people admit some sort of genius in everything; they all believe in one Master of Life, but they make divers applications of it. Some have a lean crow which they carry always about with them, and which they call their Master of Life. Others have an owl, others a bone, some the shell of a fish, and suchlike things. When they hear the owl hoot, they tremble and take it for an ill omen. They are great believers of dreams. They go unto their baths to procure good weather for hunting. They never give the bones of beavers or otters to their dogs. I asked them the reason; they answered me that there was an otkon or spirit in the wood which would tell the beaver and otters, and after that they would catch none. I asked them what that spirit was; they answered me that it was a woman that knew everything, who was the lady of hunting. But the greatest part of them do not believe these fables.

Whilst I was in the mission of Frontenac, a savage woman was poisoned in the wood by accident. The hunters brought her into her cabin; I went to see her after she was dead. I heard them discoursing near the body of the dead; they said they had seen upon the snow the winding tracks of a serpent which came out of her mouth. They related this very seriously. While they were discoursing thus, an old superstitious beldame said she had seen the spirit that had killed her.

A savage which we had decoyed into the fort, and who was the chief of his village, told me one day that Onontio, which is the name they give to the Governor-General of Canada (who at that time was the Count of Frontenac), would come such a day, when the sun was in such a place; which precisely came to pass as he had said. (This same old man, who was called The Bearded, was the only man of all the savages which I saw with a beard. The people of the northern America commonly pluck away the beard when it is but down, and for this reason they have no beards.) I must confess I knew not what to say when I saw the Count de Frontenac arrive. This man had heard no news from anybody. When I asked him how he came to know it, he said he had learned it of a juggler who pretended to foretell things. But I believed their predictions are rather the effect of hazard than of any commerce they have with the Devil.

Robert Beverley

THE Indians have their altars and places of sacrifice. Some say they now and then sacrifice young children, but they deny it, and assure us that when they withdraw these children it is not to sacrifice them but to consecrate them to the service of their God. Smith tells of one of these sacrifices in his time, from the testimony of some people who had been eyewitnesses. His words are these.

"Fifteen of the properest young boys between ten and fifteen years of age they painted white. Having brought them forth, the people spent the forenoon in dancing and singing about them with rattles. In the afternoon they put these children to the root of a tree. By them all the men stood in a guard, everyone having a bastinado in his hand, made of reeds bound together; they made a lane between them all along, through which there were appointed five young men to fetch these children. So every one of the five went through the guard, to fetch a child each after other by turns, the guard fiercely beating them with their bastinadoes, and they patiently enduring and receiving all, defending the children with their naked bodies from the unmerciful blows that pay them soundly, though the children escape. All this while the women weep and cry out very passionately, providing mats, skins, moss, and dry wood, as things fitting for their children's funeral. After the children were thus past the guard, the guards tore down the tree, branches and bows with such violence that they rent the body, made wreaths for their heads, and bedecked their hair with the leaves.

"What else was done with the children was not seen, but they were all cast on a heap in a valley as dead, where they made a great feast for all the company.

"The werowance, being demanded the meaning of this sacrifice, answered that the children were not dead, but that the Okee or Devil did suck the blood from the left breast of those who chanced to be his by lot, till they were dead, but the rest were kept in the wilderness by the young men till nine months were expired, during which time they must not converse with any; and of these were made their priests and conjurers."

How far Captain Smith might be misinformed in this account, I can't say, or whether their Okee's sucking the breast be only a delusion or pretense of the physician (or priest, who is always a physician) to prevent all reflection on his skill, when any happened to die under his discipline. This I choose rather to believe, than those religious romances concerning their Okee. For I take this story of Smith's to be only an example of huskanawing, which being a ceremony then altogether unknown to him, he might easily mistake some of the circumstances of it.

The solemnity of huskanawing is commonly practiced once every fourteen or sixteen years, or oftener as their young men happen to grow up. It is an institution or discipline which all young men must pass before they can be admitted to be of the number of the great men, or cockarouses, of the nation (whereas by Captain Smith's relation they were only set apart to supply the priesthood). The whole ceremony is performed after the following manner.

The choicest and briskest young men of the town, and such only as have acquired some treasure by their travels and hunting, are chosen out by the rulers to be huskanawed; and whoever refuses to undergo this process dare not remain among them. Several of those odd preparatory fopperies are premised in the beginning, which have been before related; but the principal part of the business is to carry them into the woods and there keep them under confinement and destitute of all society for several months. They are given no other sustenance but the infusion or decoction of some poisonous intoxicating roots, by virtue of which physic, and by the severity of the discipline which they undergo, they become stark staring mad, in which raving condition they are kept eighteen or twenty days.

During these extremities they are shut up, night and day, in a strong enclosure made on purpose. One of these I saw, belonging to the Pamunkey Indians, in the year 1694. It was in shape like a sugar loaf, and every way open like a lattice, for the air to pass through. In this cage thirteen young men had been huskanawed, and had not been a month set at liberty when I saw it.

Upon this occasion it is pretended that these poor creatures drink so much of that water of Lethe that they perfectly lose the remembrance of all former things, even of their parents, their treasure, and their language. When the doctors find that they have drank sufficiently of the wysoccan (so they call this mad potion) they gradually restore them to their senses again, by lessening the intoxication of their diet; but before they are perfectly well they bring them back into their towns, while they are still wild and crazy through the violence of the medicine. After this they are very fearful of discovering anything of their former remembrance; for if such a thing should happen to any of them, they must immediately be huskanawed again; and the second time the usage is so severe that seldom anyone escapes with life. Thus they must pretend to have forgot the very use of their tongues, so as not to be able to speak, nor understand anything that is spoken, till they learn it again.

Now whether this be real or counterfeit, I don't know; but certain it is that they will not for some time take notice of anybody nor anything with which they were before acquainted, being still under the guard of their keepers, who constantly wait upon them everywhere, till they have learned all things perfectly over again. Thus they unlive their former lives, and commence men, by forgetting that they ever have been boys. If under this exercise anyone should die, I suppose the story of Okee, mentioned by Smith, is the salvo for it; for (says he) Okee was to have such as were his by lot, and such were said to be sacrificed.

Now this conjecture is the more probable because we know that Okee has not a share in every huskanawing; for though there happened to come home short two young men in that of the Pamunkey Indians which was performed in the year 1694, yet the Appomattocs, formerly a great nation, though now an inconsiderate people, made an huskanaw in the year 1690 and brought home the same number they carried out.

I can account no other way for the great pains and secrecy of the keepers during the whole process of this discipline, but by assuring you that it is the most meritorious thing in the world to discharge that trust well in order to their preferment to the greatest posts in the nation, which they claim as their undoubted right in the next promotion. On the other hand, they are sure of a speedy passport into the other world if they should by their levity or neglect show themselves in the least unfaithful.

Those which I ever observed to have been huskanawed were lively, handsome, well-timbered young men, from fifteen to twenty years of age or upward, and such as were generally reputed rich.

I confess, I judged it at first sight to be only an invention of the seniors to engross the young men's riches to themselves; for after suffering this operation, they never pretended to call to mind anything of their former property. Their goods were either shared among the old men or brought to some public use, and so those younkers were obliged to begin the world again.

But the Indians detest this opinion, and pretend that this violent method of taking away the memory is to release the youth from all their childish impressions, and from that strong partiality to persons and things which is contracted before reason comes to take place. They hope by this proceeding to root out all the prepossessions and unreasonable prejudices which are fixed in the minds of children. So that, when the young men come to themselves again, their reason may act freely, without being biased by the cheats of custom and education. Thus also they become discharged from the remembrance of any ties by blood, and are established in a state of equality and perfect freedom, to order their actions and dispose of their persons as they think fit, without any other control than that of the law of nature. By this means also they become qualified, when they have any public office, equally and impartially to administer justice, without having respect either to friend or relation.

M Y T H S

Jasper Danckaerts

In the morning there came an Indian to our house, a man about eighty years of age, whom our people called Jasper, who lived at Ahakinsack or at Akinon. Concerning this Indian our old people related that when they lived on Long Island, it was once a very dear time; no provisions could be obtained, and they suffered great want, so that they were reduced to the last extremity. God the Lord then raised up this Indian, who went out a-fishing daily in order to bring fish to them when he caught a good mess, which he always did. If, when he came to the house, he found it alone and they were out working in the fields, he did not fail, but opened the door, laid the fish on the floor, and proceeded on his way. For this reason these people possess great affection for him and have given him the name of Jasper, and also "my *nitap*," that is, "my great friend." He never comes to the Manhattans without visiting them and eating with them, as he now did, as among his old friends.

We asked him why he had done so much kindness to these people. "I have always been inclined," he answered, "from my youth up to do good, especially to good people known to me. I took the fish to them because Maneto (the Devil) said to me, 'You must take fish to these people,' whispering ever in my ear, 'You must take fish to them.' I had to do it, or Maneto would have killed me."

Our old woman telling us he sometimes got drunk, we said to him he should not do so any more, that the great Sakemacker (the Lord), who is above, was offended at such conduct and would kill him.

"No," said he, laughing as if that were a mistake of ours, "it is Maneto who kills those who do evil, and leaves those who do good at peace."

"That is only," we replied, "because Maneto is the slave and executioner of the great Sakemacker above." And we then asked

290

him if he believed there was such a great and good Sakemacker
there.

"Undoubtedly," he said, "but he remains above, and does not
trouble himself with the earth or earthly things, because he does
nothing except what is good; but Maneto, who also is a Sakemacker, is here below, and governs all, and punishes and torments those men who do evil and drink themselves drunk."

Hereupon we inquired of him why he did so, then. "Yes," he
said, "I had rather not, but my heart is so inclined that it
causes me to do it, although I know it is wrong. The Christians
taught it to us, and give us or sell us the drink, and drink themselves drunk."

We said to him, "Listen! If we came to live near you, you
would never see us drunk, nor would we give or sell you or your
people any rum."

"That," he replied, "would be good."

We told him he must not make such a difference between himself and a Christian, because one was white and the other red,
and one wore clothes and the other went almost naked, or one
was called a Christian and the other an Indian; that this great
and good Sakemacker was the father of us all, and had made us
all, and that all who did not do good would be killed by Maneto
whether they were called Christians or Indians, but that all who
should do good would go to this good Sakemacker above.

"Yes," said he, "we do not know or speak to this Sakemacker,
but Maneto we know and speak to, but you people, who can
read and write, know and converse with this Sakemacker."

We asked him where he believed he came from. He answered,
from his father. "And where did your father come from," we
said, "and your grandfather and great-grandfather, and so on to
the first of the race?"

He was silent for a little while, either as if unable to climb up
at once so high with his thoughts or to express them without
help, and then took a piece of coal out of the fire where he sat
and began to write upon the floor. He first drew a circle, a little
oval, to which he made four paws or feet, a head, and a tail.
"This," said he, "is a tortoise, lying in the water around it," and
he moved his hand round the figure, continuing: "This was or
is all water, and so at first was the world or the earth, when the

tortoise gradually raised its round back up high, and the water ran off of it, and thus the earth became dry." Then he took a little straw and placed it on end in the middle of the figure, and proceeded: "The earth was now dry, and there grew a tree in the middle of the earth, and the root of this tree sent forth a sprout beside it and there grew upon it a man, who was the first male. This man was then alone, and would have remained alone, but the tree bent over until its top touched the earth, and there shot therein another root, from which came forth another sprout, and there grew upon it the woman; and from these two are all men produced."

Louis Hennepin

THE greatest part of the barbarians in North America have generally a notion of some sort of creation of the world. They say heaven, earth, and mankind were made by a woman, and she and her son govern the world. They say further that the son is the author of all good things, and the woman of all evil. The woman, they say, fell out of heaven big with child, and lighted upon the back of a tortoise, who saved her from drowning. When we object against the ridiculousness of their belief, they usually answer that such an objection is of force with them that make it but is of no weight against them, because they look upon themselves to be created after another manner than the Europeans are.

There are one sort of savages who dwell at the mouth of the river of St. Lawrence and Mississippi that tell us a very odd story. They say, much like the former, that a woman came down from heaven and hovered awhile in the air, because she could find no place to set her foot upon. The fish of the sea, compassionating her, held a council to determine who should receive her. The tortoise offered himself and presented his back above water. The woman placed herself upon it and stayed there. In time the filth of the sea, gathering and settling about the tortoise by little and little, formed a great extent of land, which at present is that we call America.

Now, say they, this same woman being uneasy at her living solitarily and troubled to have nobody to pass the time with more agreeably than she did, there descended from on high a spirit, who found her fallen asleep with melancholy. He approached her unperceived, and from that conjunction came forth two sons out of her side. These two children could never agree together after they were grown up. One was a better hunter than the other, and every day there was some scuffling between them. At length their animosities grew to that extremity that they could not endure one another. One of them especially was of a very violent humor and had a mortal hatred for his brother, who was better tempered. The last, unable any longer to submit to the rude behavior and ill-treatment which the other bestowed upon him perpetually, resolved to separate himself from him. So he flew up into heaven; whence, to denote his just resentment, he rattles his thunder from time to time over his unhappy brother's head.

Some time after the spirit came down again to the woman, and then she brought forth a daughter from whom, say the savages, is descended that numerous people who now take up one of the largest parts of the universe.

How fabulous soever this story be in itself, yet we may discern a run of truth in it. This woman's sleep and the birth of two sons has something in it akin to Adam's sleep, whilst God took one of his ribs to form Eve. The disagreement of the two brothers resembles the irreconcilable hatred of Cain and Abel. The retreat of one of them to heaven represents the death of Abel, and the thunder grumbling in the sky may be compared with the curse pronounced by God upon the wretched Cain, for inhumanly killing his brother.

One would be apt to suspect that these savages of America originally sprung from the Jews, some of whom might casually have been wrecked and cast upon that part of the world, for they have several customs not unlike theirs. They make their cabins in the form of tents, like as the Jews did. They anoint themselves with oil, and are superstitiously addicted to divination from dreams. They bewail over the dead with great lamentation. The women go into mourning for their near relations a whole year, during which time they abstain from dancing and feasting, and wear a sort of a hood upon their heads, and commonly the father or brother of the deceased take care of the widow.

Besides it seems as if God had laid a particular malediction upon them, as he did upon the Jews. They are brutish, and persist unalterably in their opinions. They have no certain fixed place of abode. They are very lascivious, and have such gross conceptions that, when we tell them souls are immortal and immaterial, they ask what they eat in the other world. Moreover, we may observe some conformity between Moses' relation of the creation of the world and the belief of these savages about it, as I observed above. But to speak frankly, these barbarians seem to have no kind of idea of the Deity, and yet they believe another life in which they hope to enjoy the same delights that they are pleased with here. They live without any subordination, without laws or any form of government or policy. They are stupid in matters of religion, subtle and crafty in their worldly concerns, but excessively superstitious.

Robert Beverley

THEY have likewise in other cases many fond and idle superstitions: as for the purpose, by the falls of James River upon Colonel Byrd's land, there lies a rock which I have seen, about a mile from the river, wherein is fairly impressed several marks like the footsteps of a gigantic man, each step being about five foot asunder. These they aver to be the track of their god.

This is not unlike what the fathers of the Romish Church tell us, that our Lord left the print of his feet on the stone whereon he stood while he talked with St. Peter; which stone was afterward preserved as a very sacred relic, and after several translations was at last fixed in the Church of St. Sebastian the Martyr, where it is kept, and visited with great expressions of devotion. So that the Indians, as well as these, are not without their pious frauds.

John Gyles

THAT it may appear how much they were deluded or under the influence of Satan, read two stories which were related and believed by the Indians.

18. THE MANNER OF PRAYING WITH RATTLES ABOUT A FIRE
De Bry, *The Great Voyages*, Part I; Frankfurt, 1590

The first is of a boy who was carried away by a large bird called a gulloua, who buildeth her nest on a high rock or mountain. A boy was hunting with his bow and arrow at the foot of a rocky mountain, when the gulloua came diving through the air, grasped the boy in her talons, and although he was eight or ten years of age, she soared aloft and laid him in her nest, a prey for her young. The boy lay still on his face, but would look sometimes under his arms and saw two young ones in the nest, with much fish and flesh, and the old bird constantly bringing more. The young ones not touching him, the old one clawed him up and set him where she found him, who returned and related the odd event to his friends.

As I have in a canoe passed near the mountain, the Indians have said to me, "There is the nest of the great bird that carried the boy away." And there seemed to be a great number of sticks put together in form of a nest on the top of the mountain. At another time they said, "There is the bird, but he is now as a boy to a giant to what he was in former days." The bird which they pointed to was a large speckled bird, like an eagle though somewhat larger.

The other notion is of a family who had a daughter that was accounted a finished beauty, and adorned with the precious jewel of an Indian education! She was so formed by nature and polished by art, they could not find her a suitable consort. At length, while they resided on the head of Penobscot River, under the White Hills, called the Teddon, this fine creature was missing, and her parents could have no account of her. After much time spent, pains, and tears showered in quest of her, they saw her diverting herself with a beautiful youth, whose hair like hers flowed down below his waist, swimming, washing, et cetera, in the water; but the youths vanished on their approach. This beautiful person, whom they imagined to be one of those kind spirits who inhabit the Teddon, they looked upon as their son-in-law, so that (according to custom) they called upon him for moose, bear, or whatever creature they desired, and if they did but go to the waterside and signify their desire, the creature which they would have came swimming to them!

I have heard an Indian say that he lived by the river, at the foot of the Teddon, and seeing the top of it through the hole left in the top of his wigwam for the passing of smoke, he was tempted to travel to it. Accordingly he set out early on a summer's morning, and labored hard in ascending the hill, all day, and the top seemed as distant from the place where he lodged at night as from the wigwam whence he began his journey. So he concluded the spirits were there, and never dared make a second attempt.

I have been credibly informed that several others have failed in the same attempt. Particularly, three young men toured the Teddon three days and a half, and then began to be strangely disordered and delirious. And when their imagination was clear, and they could recollect where they were and had been, they found themselves returned one day's journey. How they came down so far they can't guess, unless the genii of the place had conveyed them.

FOOLISH INDIANS

John Winthrop

AT Kennebec, the Indians wanting food and there being store in the Plymouth trading house, they conspired to kill the English there for their provisions. Some Indians coming into the house, Mr. Willett,* the master of the house, being reading in the Bible, his countenance was more solemn than at other times so as he did not look cheerfully upon them as he was wont to do. Whereupon they went out and told their fellows that their purpose was discovered. They asked them how it could be. The others told them that they knew it by Mr. Willett's countenance, and that he had discovered it by a book that he was reading. Thereupon they gave over their design.

Cotton Mather

THE Indians (as the captives inform us) being "hungry, and hardly bestead," passed through deserted Casco, where they spied several horses in Captain Brackett's orchard. Their famished squaws begged them shoot the horse, that they might be revived with a little roast meat; but the young men were for having a little sport before their supper.

Driving the horses into a pond, they took one of them and furnished him with a halter, suddenly made of the mane and the tail of the animal, which they cut off. A son of the famous Hegon was ambitious to mount this Pegasean steed, but being a pitiful horseman he ordered them, for fear of his falling, to tie his legs fast under the horse's belly. No sooner was this "beggar set on horseback," and the spark, in his own opinion, thoroughly equipped, but the mettlesome horse furiously and presently ran with him out of sight. Neither horse nor man were ever seen any more; the astonished tawnies howled after one of their nobility

* Thomas Willett, afterward the first English Mayor of New York.

298

disappearing by such an unexpected accident. A few days after, they found one of his legs (and that was all), which they buried in Captain Brackett's cellar, with abundance of lamentation.

John Smith

ARRIVING at Jamestown, complaint was made to the president that the Chickahominies, who all this while continued trade and seemed our friends, by color thereof were only thieves. And amongst other things a pistol being stolen and the thief fled, there was apprehended two proper young fellows that were brothers, known to be his confederates.

Now to regain this pistol, the one was imprisoned, the other was sent to return the pistol again within twelve hours, or his brother to be hanged. Yet the president, pitying the poor naked savage in the dungeon, sent him victual and some charcoal for a fire.

Ere midnight his brother returned with the pistol, but the poor savage in the dungeon was so smothered with the smoke he had made, and so piteously burned, that we found him dead. The other most lamentably bewailed his death, and broke forth into such bitter agonies that the president to quiet him told him that if hereafter they would not steal, he would make him alive again; but he little thought he could be recovered. Yet we doing our best with aqua vitae and vinegar, it pleased God to restore him again to life, but so drunk and affrighted that he seemed lunatic; the which as much tormented and grieved the other, as before to see him dead. Of which malady upon promise of their good behavior the president promised to recover him, and so caused him to be laid by a fire to sleep. In the morning, having well slept, he had recovered his perfect senses, and then being dressed of his burning, and each a piece of copper given them, they went away so well contented that this was spread among all the savages for a miracle, that Captain Smith could make a man alive that was dead.

Another ingenuous savage of Powhatan's, having gotten a great bag of powder, and the back of an armor, at Werowoco-moco amongst many of his companions, to show his extraordinary skill, he did dry it on the back as he had seen the soldiers at Jamestown. But he dried it so long, they peeping over it to see his skill, it took fire, and blew him to death, and one or two more; and the rest were so scorched, they had little pleasure to meddle any more with powder.

These and many other such pretty accidents so amazed and affrighted both Powhatan and all his people that from all parts with presents they desired peace, returning many stolen things which we never demanded nor thought of. And after that, those that were taken stealing, both Powhatan and his people have sent back to Jamestown to receive their punishment; and all the country became absolutely as free for us as for themselves.

The Old Indian Chronicle

ABOUT the 15th of August (1675), Captain Mosely with sixty men met with a company judged about three hundred Indians, in a plain place where few trees were, and on both sides preparations were making for a battle. All being ready on both sides to fight, Captain Mosely plucked off his periwig and put it into his breeches, because it should not hinder him in fighting

As soon as the Indians saw that they fell a-howling and yelling most hideously, and said, "Umh, umh, me no stay more fight Engismon, Engismon got two head, Engismon got two head, if me cut off un head he got noder a put on beder as dis"—with suchlike words in broken English, and away they all fled and could not be overtaken, nor seen any more afterwards.

Cotton Mather

SEVERAL persons remarkably escaped this bloody deluge, but none with more bravery than one Thomas Bickford, who had a house, a little pallisadoed, by the riverside, but no man in it besides himself. He dexterously put his wife and mother and children aboard a canoe, and sending them down the river, he alone betook himself to the defense of his house, against many Indians that made an assault upon him.

They first would have persuaded him with many fair promises, and then terrified him with as many fierce threatenings, to yield himself; but he flouted and fired at them, daring them to come if they durst. His main stratagem was to change his livery as frequently as he could, appearing sometimes in one coat, sometimes in another, sometimes in an hat, and sometimes in a cap; which caused his besiegers to mistake this one for many defendants. In fine, the pitiful wretches, despairing to beat him out of his house, even left him in it; whereas many that opened unto them, upon their solemn engagements of giving them life and good quarter, were barbarously butchered by them, and the wife of one Adams, then with child, was with horrible barbarity ripped up.

The Old Indian Chronicle

ON THE Lord's day an Indian came to Dorchester, to the house of Mr. Minor in sermon time, and there were then at home the maidservant and two young children, she keeping the door shut for safety. The Indian when he saw he could not come in at the door went about to come in at the window. She perceiving his resolution took two brass kettles under which she put the two children, ran upstairs, charged a musket, and fired at the Indian. (He had fired at her once or twice and missed her, but struck the top of one kettle under which a child was.) She shot him into his shoulder; then he let his gun fall, and was just coming in at the window when she made haste and got a fire shovel full of live coals and applied them to his face, which forced him to fly and escape. But one was found dead within five miles of that place afterwards, and was judged to be this by his scalded face.

Thomas Morton

THE sachem of the territories where the planters of New England are settled, not knowing what they were, or whether they would be friends or foes, and being desirous to purchase their friendship that he might have the better assurance of quiet trading with them, was desirous to prepare an ambassador with commission to treat on his behalf. And having one that had been in England, this savage he instructed how to behave himself in the treaty of peace. The more to give him encouragement to adventure his person amongst these new-come inhabitants, which was a thing the sachem durst not himself attempt without security or hostage, he promised that savage freedom who had been detained there as their captive.

This offer he accepted, and accordingly came to the planters, saluting them with welcome in the English phrase, which was of them admired, to hear a savage there speak in their own language, and the ꞌ used him with great courtesy. To them he declared the caι ᵴe of his coming, and contrived the business so that he broughᴛ the sachem and the English together, between whom was a fir١ ١ league concluded, which yet continueth.

After which ᵉague, the sachem being in company with the other whom hᴇ had freed and suffered to live with the English, espying a place where a hole had been made in the ground, where was their store of powder laid to be preserved from danger of fire, he demanded of the savage what the English had hid there underground. Who answered, "The plague," at which he startled, because of the great mortality lately happened by means of the plague; and the savage the more to increase his fear told the sachem if he should give offense to the English party, they would let out the plague to destroy them all, which kept him in great awe.

Not long after, being at variance with another sachem bordering upon his territories, he came in solemn manner and entreated the governor that he would let out the plague to destroy the sachem and his men who were his enemies, promising that he himself and all his posterity would be their everlasting friends. So great an opinion he had of the English.

John Lawson

THESE poor creatures have so many enemies to destroy them that it is a wonder one of them is alive near us. The smallpox I have acquainted you withal above, and so I have of rum, and shall only add that they have got away to carry it back to the westward Indians, who never knew what it was till within very few years. Now they have it brought them by the Tuscaroras, and other neighbor Indians, but the Tuscaroras chiefly, who carry it in rundlets several hundred miles amongst other Indians. Sometimes they cannot forbear breaking their cargo, but sit down in the woods and drink it all up, and then hollo and shout like so many bedlamites.

I accidentally once met with one of the drunken crews, and was amazed to see a parcel of drunken savages so far from any Englishman's house; but the Indians I had in company informed me that they were merchants, and had drunk all their stock, as is very common for them to do. But when they happen to carry it safe (which is seldom, without drinking some part of it and filling it up with water) and come to an Indian town, those that buy rum of them have so many mouthfuls for a buckskin, they never using any other measure. And for this purpose the buyer always makes choice of his man, which is one that has the greatest mouth, whom he brings to the market with a bowl to put it in. The seller looks narrowly to the man's mouth that measures it, and if he happens to swallow any down, either through willfulness or otherwise, the merchant or some of his party does not scruple to knock the fellow down, exclaiming against him for false measure. Thereupon the buyer finds another mouthpiece to measure the rum by, so that this trading is very agreeable to the spectators, to see such a deal of quarreling and controversy as often happens about it, and is very diverting.

SMART INDIANS

Robert Beverley

THEY have a remarkable way of entertaining all strangers of condition, which is performed after the following manner.

First, the King or Queen, with a guard and a great retinue, march out of the town a quarter or half a mile, and carry mats for their accommodation; when they meet the strangers, they invite them to sit down upon those mats. Then they pass the ceremony of the pipe, and afterwards, having spent about half an hour in grave discourse, they get up all together and march into the town. Here the first compliment is to wash the courteous traveler's feet. Then he is treated at a sumptuous entertainment, served up by a great number of attendants. After which he is diverted with antique Indian dances, performed both by men and women, and accompanied with great variety of wild music.

At this rate he is regaled till bedtime, when a brace of young beautiful virgins are chosen to wait upon him that night for his particular refreshment. These damsels are to undress this happy gentleman, and as soon as he is in bed, they gently lay themselves down by him, one on one side of him and the other on the other. They esteem it a breach of hospitality not to submit to everything he desires of them. This kind ceremony is used only to men of great distinction. And the young women are so far from suffering in their reputation for this civility that they are envied for it by all the other girls as having had the greatest honor done them in the world.

After this manner perhaps many of the heroes were begotten in old time, who boasted themselves to be the sons of some wayfaring god.

John Lawson

NEXT morning we set out early, breaking the ice we met withal in the stony runs, which were many. We passed by several cottages, and about eight of the clock came to a pretty big town, where we took up our quarters in one of their state houses, the men being all out hunting in the woods and none but women at home. Our fellow traveler of whom I spoke before, having a great mind for an Indian lass for his bedfellow that night, spoke to our guide, who soon got a couple, reserving one for himself.

That which fell to our companion's share was a pretty young girl. Though they could not understand one word of what each other spoke, yet the female Indian, being no novice at her game but understanding what she came thither for, acted her part dexterously enough with her cully to make him sensible of what she wanted, which was to pay the hire before he rode the hackney. He showed her all the treasure he was possessed of, as beads, red caddis, et cetera, which she liked very well, and permitted him to put them into his pocket again, endearing him with all the charms which one of a better education than Dame Nature had bestowed upon her could have made use of to render her consort a surer captive.

After they had used this sort of courtship a small time, the match was confirmed by both parties, with the approbation of as many Indian women as came to the house to celebrate our Winchester wedding. Every one of the bridesmaids were as great whores as Mrs. Bride, though not quite so handsome. Our happy couple went to bed together before us all, and with as little blushing as if they had been man and wife for seven years. The rest of the company, being weary with traveling, had more mind to take their rest than add more weddings to that hopeful one already consummated; so that, though the other virgins offered their service to us, we gave them their answer and went to sleep.

About an hour before day I awaked and saw somebody walking up and down the room, in a seemingly deep melancholy. I called out to know who it was, and it proved to be Mr. Bridegroom, who in less than twelve hours was bachelor, husband, and widower, his dear spouse having picked his pocket of the beads, caddis, and what else should have gratified the Indians for the victuals we received of them. However, that did not serve her turn, but she had also got his shoes away, which he had made the night before of a dressed buckskin. Thus early did our spark already repent his new bargain, walking barefoot in his penitentials, like some poor pilgrim to Loretto.

After the Indians had laughed their sides sore at the figure Mr. Bridegroom made, with much ado we mustered up another pair of shoes or moccasins and set forward on our intended voyage, the company (all the way) lifting up their prayers for the new-married couple, whose wedding had made away with that which should have purchased our food.

The Old Indian Chronicle

ON TUESDAY following, the barbarous infidels destroyed sixty and six houses, besides barns and building, in Seekonk, but we do not hear of any person there slain. On Wednesday they stormed Providence and consumed a greater part of the houses, but without taking away the life of any person, except one Wright, of whom it is reported that he was a man of a singular and sordid humor, of great knowledge in the Scriptures, but of no particular professed sect or persuasion; one that derided watches, fortifications, and all public endeavors and administrations for the common safety—in so much that, after all alarms round about, he refused to bring in any of his goods (which were of considerable value) or to shelter himself in any garrison, but presumed he should be safe in his own house, where the enemy found and butchered him. It is further credibly related concerning him that he had a strange confidence, or rather conceit, that whilst he held his Bible in his hand, he looked upon himself as secure from all kind of violence; and that the enemy, finding him in that posture, deriding his groundless apprehension or folly therein, ripped him open and put his Bible in his belly.

19. NORTHERN INDIAN WARRIOR

Du Creux, *Historiae Canadensis Libri Decem;* Paris, 1664

6

INDIAN TREATIES

*For ordinary reading purposes nothing might seem so dull as a
treaty document. But scholars poking in the archives of early
Americana have made a surprising discovery. In the series of
conferences and negotiations between the English and Indians
prior to American independence, a unique literature emerged,
incomparable, as Constance Rourke says, in the literal meaning
of the word. These detailed transcripts of daily conversations
preserve the oratory of two peoples, and indicate the presenta-
tions, ceremonies, and rituals which gave these conferences the
aspect of pageantry rather than tedious diplomacy. Miss Rourke
even contends that they represent the birth of American drama,
with their dialogue scenes, formal attitudes, and interspersed
dances and mimetic action.*

*About fifty of these treaties were printed, in small editions,
only five in the seventeenth century. They contain, if they do
not actually present, a stirring drama in all its human terms, the
race conflict between red man and white for the continent, with
its prefigured end already visible. The two full treaties and the
informal snatch of another here given are self-explanatory. They
deal with the customary problems of rum poisoning, military
alliance against the aggressive French, disputed landownership.
We must admire the dignified eloquence of Indian expression,
alongside which the white man's speeches seem pale and stiff.
The oration reported by Thomas Budd well represents the
Indian style, with its almost Biblical rhythms and simplicity.
In the two long treaties we can see the subtle pulls and tugs
beneath the surface of polite phrase-making, as the Mohawks
suggest the English improve their defenses against the French,
and the English suggest the Mohawks improve their scouting;
as the Maine tribes ask for their land back, and the Englishmen show them signed deeds, in the shadow of a man-of-
war. And we can appreciate the pathos of the Indian consternation and sudden lapse into bad manners, and the fitful consultation that must have gone on before they returned, necessarily, to
eat humble pie. You will notice how, in the last treaty, immedi-*

ately upon the signing of the document, the chiefs ask provisions for the winter. That was the fateful English trump.

The first and the best words about the Indian treaty as literature have been said by Lawrence C. Wroth.

"I am not, however, concerned here with the self-interest of both sides that the treaties reveal but with their importance as a neglected literary type that arose without conscious artistic design from the conflict of two civilizations on the same soil—a type in which one reads the passion, the greed, and the love of life of hard-living men brought into close relationship without parallel conditions in the history of either race to guide its conduct. In it are displayed certain raw human emotions; on the part of the Indians the fear of extinction, the desire to keep what the land holds, the love of life, of ease and security. Seething in the same pot with these were the white man's passion to acquire and till the land, to build, to fill the left hand with more and more of the stuff that the right hand has grasped. All this is in the Indian treaties, and in dramatic form. I wish that some teacher of history had poured for me this strong wine instead of the tea from the Boston harbor with which the genuine thirst of my youth was insufficiently slaked, or that some teacher of literature had given me to read these vivid, picturesque records instead of saying that the colonial period had nothing to show of literary production except dull sermons, political tracts, prosy essays, and poems of invincible mediocrity." *

* Lawrence C. Wroth, "The Indian Treaty as Literature," *The Yale Review*, Summer 1928 issue, copyright Yale University Press.

A CONFERENCE ON THE SALE OF RUM

Thomas Budd

THE INDIANS are but few in number, and have been very serviceable to us by selling us venison, Indian corn, peas and beans, fish and fowl, buckskins, beaver, otter, and other skins and furs. The men hunt, fish, and fowl, and the women plant the corn and carry burdens. They are many of them of a good understanding, considering their education; and in their public meetings of business they have excellent order, one speaking after another, and while one is speaking all the rest keep silent and do not so much as whisper one to the other.

We had several meetings with them. One was in order to put down the sale of rum, brandy, and other strong liquors to them, they being a people that have not government of themselves so as to drink it in moderation; at which there were eight Kings and many other Indians present.

The Indian Kings sat on a form, and we sat on another over against them. They had prepared four belts of wampum (so their current money is called, being black and white beads made of a fish shell) to give us as seals of the covenant they made with us. One of the Kings by the consent and appointment of the rest stood up and made this following speech.

"The strong liquors was first sold us by the Dutch, and they were blind, they had no eyes, they did not see that it was for our hurt. And the next people that came amongst us were the Swedes, who continued the sale of those strong liquors to us. They were also blind, they had no eyes, they did not see it to be hurtful to us to drink it, although we know it to be hurtful to us. But if people will sell it to us, we are so in love with it that we cannot forbear it. When we drink it, it makes us mad; we do not know what we do; we then abuse one another; we throw each other into the fire. Seven score of our people have been killed by reason of the drinking of it, since the time it was first sold us. Those people that sell it, they are blind, they have no eyes.

"But now there is a people come to live amongst us that have eyes, they see it to be for our hurt, and we know it to be for our hurt. They are willing to deny themselves of the profit of it if for our good; these people have eyes; we are glad such a people are come amongst us. We must put it down by mutual consent; the cask must be sealed up, it must be made fast, it must not leak by day nor by night, in the light nor in the dark.

"And we give you these four belts of wampum, which we would have you lay up safe and keep by you to be witness of this agreement that we make with you. And we would have you tell your children that these four belts of wampum are given you to be witness betwixt us and you of this agreement."

THE DESTRUCTION OF SCHENECTADY

(The first French and Indian War in America, known as King William's War, witnessed a series of savage border raids by both French and English with their Indian allies. In reprisal for attacks by the dreaded Iroquois of New York on his Canadian towns, Count de Frontenac in the winter of 1689-90 ordered three war parties to harry the English frontier. One of these, caught in a twenty-inch snowfall deep in the Mohawk Valley, contemplated surrendering to their sleeping enemy, but decided instead to try a surprise attack on Schenectady, thirteen miles west of Albany. On February 18, 1690, three hundred French and Indians fell on the unprepared settlement and laid it waste. A week later the English and their Mohawk allies met at Albany to discuss the tragedy, and indulge in some mutual recriminations.)

Propositions Made by the Sachems of the Three Maquas Castles, to the Mayor, Aldermen, and Commonalty of the City of Albany, and Military Officers of the Said City and County in the City Hall, February 25th, 1689/90.
Peter Schuyler Mayor, with Ten More Gentlemen, Then Present. Interpreted by Arnout and Hille.
The Names of the Sachems, Sinnonquiness, Speaker, Rode, Sagoddiockquisax, Oguedagoa, Tosoquatho, Odagurasse, Anharenda, Jagogthera.

Brethren:

1. We are sorry and extremely grieved for the murder lately committed by the French upon our brethren of Schenectady. We esteem this evil as if done to ourselves, being all in one covenant

chain. But what they have done is by way of stealth, by way of robbery unawares. Our brethren of New England will be sorry to hear of this sad disaster, but we must not be discouraged.

(They give a belt of wampum, according to their custom, to wipe off the tears.)

2. Brethren, we lament and condole the death of so many of our brethren so basely murdered at Schenectady; we cannot account it a great victory, for it is done by way of deceit. He [meaning the Governor of Canada] comes to our country by his messengers at Onondaga, and speaks of peace, with the whole house quite hither; but war is in his heart, as you find by woeful experience. But what shall we say? It is the same as he did at Cadarachqui, and the Senecas' country. This is the third time that he has done so; he has broken open the jewel of our house on both ends, the one end at Sinnondowanne, and the other here. But we hope to be revenged. There is one hundred of our young men out still, who will pursue them to their doors at Canada. Nay, the French shall not be able to cut a stick of wood, we will lay so close siege to them. We do now gather the dead together in order to their interment.

(They do give a belt of wampum.)

3. We are come here from our castles with tears in our eyes to bemoan the murder committed by the perfidious French at Schenectady. Our young Indians are gone out in pursuit of them, and while we are now busy in burying the dead that were murdered there, we may have bad news that our people that are gone out may be killed also; the same that is befallen you may befall us. We do therefore come and bury our brethren at Schenectady.

(They give a belt of wampum, according to their custom.)

4. Great is the mischief that is befallen us, it is come from the heavens upon us. We are taught by our forefathers, when any sad accident or disaster doth befall any of the covenant, to go with all convenient speed to bemoan their death.

(They give a belt of wampum, which they call a belt of vigilance, that is not to have too much thoughts on what is done that cannot be remedied, but to be watchful for the future; and they give eye-water to make the brethren sharp-sighted.)

5. We come to the house where we usually do renew the cov-

enant, which house we find defiled with blood. This is known to all the Five Nations, and we are now come to wipe off the blood and keep the house clean, and therefore pray that Corlaer and all they that are in office here at Albany may use all means and direct all affairs to be revenged of the enemy that hath done us this evil.

(They give a belt of wampum.)

6. Brethren, do not be discouraged, this is but a beginning of the war. We are strong enough, the whole house have their eyes fixed upon you, and they only stay your motion, and will be ready to do whatever shall be resolved upon by our brethren. Our covenant is a firm covenant, it is a silver chain and cannot be broke, it must not be broke. We are resolute and will continue the war, we will not leave off; if there were but thirty men of us left, we will proceed; therefore pray take good heart, do not pack up and go away; if the enemy should hear that, it would much encourage them. We are of the race of the bear, and a bear doth not yield as long as there is a drop of blood in its body; we must all be so.

(They give a belt of wampum.)

7. Brethren, be content, look up to the heavens; from thence the judgment is come now upon us. Be not discouraged, the same hand that hath chastised us can heal us. The sun which now hath been cloudy, and sent us this disaster, will shine again, and with its pleasant beams comfort us. Be encouraged.

(With many repetitions. And they give a bearskin.)

8. We were engaged in a bloody war with the French, about three years ago, and were encouraged to proceed, and no sooner were we well entered and got several prisoners, but a cessation came, and Corlaer hindered us to proceed, and demanded the prisoners from us. We were obedient and did deliver them, and laid down the hatchet, which if we might have gone forward, then the French would not have been in that capacity to do so much mischief as they do. But now we must die. Such obstructions will ruin us. If we might have had our wills, we would have prevented their planting, sowing, and reaping, and brought them low and mean. Nevertheless let us be steadfast, and not take such measures again, let us go on briskly with the war.

(They give a bearskin.)

9. We recommend the brethren to keep good watch, and if any enemies come, take care that messengers be more speedily sent to us than lately was done. We would not advise the brethren quite to desert Schenectady, but to make a fort there. The enemy would be too glorious to see it quite desolate, and the town here is not well fortified; the stockades are so short, the Indians can jump over them like a dog.

(They give a bearskin.)

10. This mischief is done at Schenectady, and it cannot be helped. But as soon as any enemy comes, let nothing hinder your speedy sending to us the news by posts, and firing great guns, that all may be alarmed. And our advice is that you get all the river Indians who are under your subjection to come and live near unto you, to be ready on all occasions. And send word to New England of all what's done here; undoubtedly they will awake and lend us their helping hand. Let us not be discouraged; the French are not so many as people talk of. If we but mind our business, they can be subdued, with the assistance of our neighbors of New England, whose interest it is to drive on this war as much as ours, that it may be speedily ended.

We desire that the brethren may recommend the smiths not to be too dear in repairing our arms, since money is so scarce, and we only go to warring and not to hunting. We shall take care to warn the Senecas and the Nations living above us to be in readiness, for we being one they hearken to us. And tell them of New England that we shall take care that the upper Nations be ready for our security and assistance, and let them be ready also with ships and great guns by water, and we will plague him by land. We are resolved not to go out a-hunting, but to mind the war, for the sooner the French be fallen upon the better, before they get men and provisions from France, as their usual custom is.

(They give a bearskin.)

ANSWER upon the Maquas Sachems' Propositions; by the Mayor, Aldermen, and Commonalty of the City of Albany, and Military Officers of the Said City and County: At the City Hall, February 26th, 1689/90.
Interpreted by Arnout, et cetera.

Brethren:

Your coming here according to the custom of your ancestors, to condole the death of your brethren murdered at Schenectady, is very acceptable, whereby your inclination toward us is demonstrated.

We must acknowledge that they did not keep so good watch as they ought, considering what a false and deceitful enemy they had to deal withal. But that which made them so secure, was the great trust which they reposed in the forty Maquas who came here and tendered their service to go and be the outwatch, and to spy the enemy. To which end powder and lead was given them as they desired. We were about hiring Christians to send thither, but were unhappily diverted by the said company of Maquas, who promised to have four posts ready, two to go to their own country, and two to come hither if any enemy should appear. For the brethren did assure us that no French could come here without being discovered, and then would all fall into our hands.

We are likewise mindful how that the Five Nations last fall, when the gentlemen of New England were here, did declare how they would encompass the French of Canada, that they could not break out this winter without being discovered and fallen upon. We did likewise propose by our messengers, Arnout and Robert Sanders, at the general meeting of Onondaga to have three or four hundred men sent hither to be ready on all occasions; but see none.

Now, brethren, this evil is done and cannot be called back again, and the only means to prevent the like for the future is to keep good watch, and to have good courage to oppose and resist the enemy. We are no ways discomfited for this misfortune. It is the fortune of war; we do not fear to be even with the French in a short time. We have already sent letters to all our neighbors of New England, Virginia, and Maryland, the subjects of the great King of England, and acquainted them of the evil done here by the French, and how requisite it is that ships be fitted out with all convenient speed to go to Quebec.

And to press the business the more, we do now send persons to New York and New England, apurpose to lay open the case before them, and to persuade them to rig out vessels, not only to hinder succor coming from France, but to take Quebec itself.

As also to send more men hither, that we may then send men along with you to annoy the enemy in their country.

In the meantime we recommend the brethren to send for two hundred men from the upper Nations to join with you, to keep the French in continual alarm, and do them what mischief imaginable. And Onondagas and Senecas must go down the river of Cadarachqui, and meet one another about Montreal, and annoy the enemy there. We shall in the meanwhile fortify the town and put ourselves in a good posture of defense, that we may not be surprised as they of Schenectady were, and make all preparations to oppose the enemy.

The brethren see that we are in war with France, now that there is no time to speak of peace. The French as you well observe have fallen on both ends of the chain, but not broke it. Let us keep the covenant so much the faster, which never has had the least crack since the very first the Christians came here. They strove to lull us all asleep, by their messengers at Onondaga speaking of peace, and then they were upon the way hither to commit this murder.

The brethren need not fear for a cessation to hinder us to pursue the enemy, for as we told you before, the KING that ordered that* was a Papist, and a great friend of the French, but our present great KING† will pursue the war to the utmost. Therefore we must all prepare for war. It will therefore be very requisite that the brethren for their better security come and plant this summer at Schenectady upon the land that cannot be cultivated this year, that we may be near to one another upon any occasion.

We must insist and recommend you to persuade them of Oneida to send the priest hither, for you have seen how dangerous it is to have such persons among you, who informs the enemy of all your doings and discovers all your designs. We shall secure him that he run not away, and when the owner demands him, and these troubles are over, shall be delivered, for he can do more harm in Oneida than an hundred men.

We think it convenient that one or two of the sachems stay here, and that a sachem of each Nation be here to assist in the management of the affairs of the war.

* James II.
† William of Orange.

(There was given them six belts of wampum, some duffles, tobacco, and some bags with provision.)

★

After the proposition was answered, they gave a shout according to their custom, which signified "Amen," that they would continue the war to the utmost.

After the said answer was made, the Maquas' sachems said, "We are glad to see you are not discouraged. A mistake can be made by the best and wisest of men, and we must see now to pursue the war with all vigor. We have an hundred men out in pursuit of the enemy still, who are good scouts. In the meantime, we expect all who will come to condole the death of our brethren murdered at Schenectady. You need not fear our being ready, we are soon fitted out, our ax is in our hand. But take care for yourselves to be in readiness. The ships that must do the principal work are long a-fitting out and rigging; we do not design to go out with a small troop as scouts, but as soon as the Nations come together we will go with a whole army to ruin the country. The business must be soon brought to a period; therefore send in all haste to New England, for we nor you cannot live long in this condition. We must order it so, that the French be in a continual fear and alarm. And that is the way to be in peace here."

A CONFERENCE OF HIS EXCELLENCY THE GOVERNOR
WITH THE SACHEMS AND CHIEF MEN OF THE EASTERN INDIANS

> *Georgetown on Arrowsick Island, August 9th, 1717, Annoque Regni Regis George II Magnae Britanniae et cetera*

HIS EXCELLENCY* being arrived here in His Majesty's ship the *Squirrel*, the Indians sent a message to him from Puddlestone's Island (where they were assembled) desiring to know when it would be His Excellency's pleasure that they should attend him.

His Excellency told them at three o'clock this afternoon, when

* Governor Samuel Shute.

20. NORTHERN INDIAN CHIEFTAIN

Du Creux, *Historiae Canadensis Libri Decem;* Paris, 1664

he would order the union flag to be displayed, at the tent erected
near Mr. Watts's house. And ordered a British flag to be delivered to the Indians for them to wear when they came, in token
of their subjection to His Majesty KING GEORGE.

At the time appointed, the flag being set up, the Indians forthwith came over, with the British flag in their headmost canoe.

His Excellency being seated under a large tent (erected for
the occasion), attended by several English gentlemen, eight
Indian sagamores and chief captains approached and made their
reverence to His Excellency, who was pleased to give them his
hand. And then directed that Captain John Gyles and Mr. Samuel Jordan, interpreters of the Indian language, should be sworn
to be faithful in that service, and Judge Sewall administered to
them an oath accordingly. And His Excellency was pleased to
make a speech to the sagamores, which was deliberately recited
and interpreted to them. And is as follows, viz.

INTERPRETER. Tell the sachems that notwithstanding the great
fatigue and danger of this expedition, yet to comply with my
own word and their desire I am now come to see them, and am
very glad to find so many of them in health.

Tell them that the English settlements that have lately been
made in these Eastern parts have been promoted partly on their
accounts, and that they will find the benefit of them in having
trade brought so near them, besides the advantage of the neighborhood and conversation of the English, to whom I have given
strict orders that they be very just and kind to the Indians upon
all accounts. And therefore if at any time they meet with any
oppression, fraud, or unfair dealing from the English in any of
their affairs, let them make their complaint to any of my officers
here, and then I shall soon hear of it, and take speedy and effectual care to do them right. Or if upon any great occasion they
choose to send any of their body to me directly they shall be very
welcome. I shall always be ready to protect and assist them, for I
would have them look upon the English Government in New
England as their great and safe shelter.

Tell them that if they have anything fit or reasonable to ask
of me at this time, they shall be very welcome to lay it before
me, and I shall give it all due consideration; and that I expect
an answer from them to what I have said.

Tell them, interpreter, that in token of my great sincerity and affection to them, and as an earnest of my future justice and kindness to them, I here give my hand to their sachems and chief captains.

Then His Excellency, taking an English and an Indian Bible in his hand, bid the interpreters tell them that he gave them those Bibles, and left them with Mr. Baxter their minister for their instruction, whenever they desire to be taught. "The minister will reside here, or hereabouts, and so will the schoolmaster, to instruct their children when they have a mind to send them."

Then His Excellency drank KING GEORGE's health to the chief sagamore Moxus, which he and all the rest pledged.

Wiwurna stood up, and said he was appointed to speak in the name of the rest.

GOVERNOR. Go on.

WIWURNA. We are very glad of this opportunity to see Your Excellency, when the sun shines so bright upon us, and hope the angels in heaven rejoice with us. We have been in expectation of this favor ever since we received Your Excellency's letter in the winter.

We are not now prepared to answer what Your Excellency has said to us, but shall wait on Your Excellency again tomorrow.

GOVERNOR. It is well. At what time?

WIWURNA. We desire His Excellency to appoint the time.

GOVERNOR. Let them come about nine o'clock, when they will see the flag set up. I will give them an ox for dinner, and let them send some to kill and dress it.

WIWURNA. We are very thankful to Your Excellency, for some of us have had little to eat for these two days.

Then the Indians took leave and withdrew.

August 10, 1717

The eight sachems and chief captains that attended yesterday appeared again with some other principal Indians accompanying them.

WIWURNA. It is a great favor of God we have this opportunity to wait on Your Excellency, and we have our answers ready.

GOVERNOR. Let them speak.

WIWURNA. We have done with the treaty at Piscataqua, and now proceed to a new one.

GOVERNOR. They ratify and confirm former treaties.

WIWURNA. Yes, we do.

His Excellency ordered the principal articles of their submission at Piscataqua to be read and interpreted to them, and then asked them whether they did remember and acknowledge them.

And the Indians answered, they did.

GOVERNOR. They must be obedient to KING GEORGE, and all just offers and usage shall be given them.

WIWURNA. We will be very obedient to the KING, if we are not molested in the improvement of our lands.

GOVERNOR. They must not call it their land, for the English have bought it of them and their ancestors.

WIWURNA. We pray leave to proceed in our answer, and to talk that matter afterward. We desire there may be no further settlements made. We shan't be able to hold them all in our bosoms, and to take care to shelter them, if it be like to be bad weather, and mischief be threatened.

As to the minister's instructing us:

All people have a love for their ministers, and it would be strange if we should not love them that come from God. And as to the Bibles Your Excellency mentioned, we desire to be excused on that point. God has given us teaching already, and if we should go from that, we should displease God. We are not capable to make any judgment about religion.

Your Excellency was not sensible how sick we were yesterday to see the man-of-war ashore. We were so faint we could not speak out with strength, and we are now very glad the ship is well.

We are very glad to wait on Your Excellency, and to tell you that we sent our young men early this morning to see if the ship was well, and were very glad to hear she was.

GOVERNOR. Tell them I accept their respects for His Majesty's Ship, and if the ship can help them at any time, it shall be ready to do it.

WIWURNA. We shall be very glad when we have concluded, that Your Excellency may have good winds and weather and get safe down this river and home.

GOVERNOR. Tell them they must be sensible and satisfied that the English own this land, and have deeds that show and set forth purchase from their ancestors. And they will not be molested in the improvement of the lands that belong to them.

Tell them also that complaints are made to me that some of them have violently taken things from some of the English, as the meat out of their pots, and other things, which is contrary to the law of God and man, and that they had forbid the English planting on their own lands, and that the night before last they had killed some of the young cattle belonging to the English (which indeed they had first informed of, and desired forgiveness), all which is contrary to their Articles.

WIWURNA. We desire time to consult.

GOVERNOR. They may have it, but tell them I expect to see them again at three o'clock, with a positive answer about the lands. And that they should always muzzle their dogs when they come upon the English lands where their cattle are.

WIWURNA. We are very thankful that Your Excellency gives us leave to consider, and shall attend Your Excellency at the time appointed with our answers, for it is not a jesting matter we are now upon.

Three o'clock in the afternoon

WIWURNA. We are willing to cut off our lands as far as the mills, and the coasts to Pemaquid.

GOVERNOR. Tell them we desire only what is our own, and that we will have. We will not wrong them, but what is our own we will be masters of.

WIWURNA. It was said at Casco Treaty that no more forts should be made.

GOVERNOR. Tell them the forts are not made for their hurt, and that I wonder they should speak against them, when they are for the security of both, we being all subjects of King George.

King George builds what forts he pleases in his own dominions, and has given me power to do it here, and they are for their security as well as ours, and the French do the like. They build what forts they please, and all Kings have that power, and the governors they appoint to do the same.

WIWURNA. We can't understand how our lands have been purchased; what has been alienated was by our gift.

(His Excellency hereupon ordered a deed of sale of lands on Kennebec River, made by six Indian sagamores to Richard Wharton, should be opened and exhibited to them, which was done and partly read and interpreted to them.)

WIWURNA. As for the west side of the Kennebec River, I have nothing to say but am sure nothing has been sold on the east side.

GOVERNOR. I expect their positive answer and compliance in this matter, that the English may be quiet in the possession of the lands they have purchased.

WIWURNA. We don't know what to think of new forts built.

GOVERNOR. I have spoke to that fully already, and told them they are for our mutual defense.

WIWURNA. We should be pleased with King George if there was never a fort in the Eastern parts.

GOVERNOR. Tell them that wherever there is a new settlement, I shall always order a fort, if I think it proper, and that it is for the security of them and us; and so do the French. Are any people under the same government afraid of being made too strong to keep out enemies?

WIWURNA. We are a little uneasy concerning these lands, but are willing the English shall possess all they have done, excepting forts.

GOVERNOR. Tell them we will not take an inch of their land, nor will we part with an inch of our own.

WIWURNA. We shall have fishing and fowling wherever we will?

GOVERNOR. It is freely consented to, and they are assured of it.

Then the Indians rose up at once and withdrew, in a hasty abrupt manner without taking leave, and left behind them their English colors, returning to their headquarters at Puddlestone's Island.

And in the evening brought to His Excellency a letter from Sebastian Rasle, their Jesuit, dated the 17th of August, 1717, wherein he says that Governor Vaudreville had written to them that when he was lately in France he inquired of the King of France whether he had in any treaty given away the Indians' lands to the English, and that the French King told him he had not but was ready to succor the Indians if their lands were encroached upon. Which His Excellency read and rejected as not worthy of his regard. And the Indians returned.

August 11, 1717

His Excellency went on board the *Squirrel* man-of-war, and ordered the fore-topsail to be loosed. Whereupon a canoe with two Indians hastened on board, and acknowledged the rudeness and ill manners they were guilty of yesterday, and prayed that they might see His Excellency again.

His Excellency told them they should if they quitted their unreasonable pretensions to the English lands and complied with what he had said, but not otherwise. Which, they promising to do, His Excellency appointed to meet them at six o'clock. And the Indians desired they might have the British colors again; which were given to them, and they returned.

And at the time appointed the sachems and principal men came over with the British colors, leaving behind them Wiwurna, because (as was said) he had behaved himself so improperly yesterday.

And they appointed Querebennit their speaker.

QUEREBENNIT. We are very sorry for our rude carriage yesterday, and pray it may be forgiven. As Your Excellency said, if anything should happen amiss, it should be rectified.

GOVERNOR. 'Tis well.

QUEREBENNIT. It was agreed in the Articles of Peace that the English should settle where their predecessors had done. And we agree to those Articles and confirm them. And desire the English may settle as far as ever they have done. (And then presented His Excellency a belt of wampum.) We desire to live in peace.

GOVERNOR. Tell them if they don't begin the quarrel they shall have no occasion from us.

QUEREBENNIT. We desire that by the favor of God we may always live in peace and unity.

GOVERNOR. We pray the same.

QUEREBENNIT. If any of our people should happen to be out

in cold and stormy weather, we desire the English to shelter them.

GOVERNOR. As long as they behave themselves well, kindness shall be shown them.

QUEREBENNIT. We shall always do the same for the English, and God Almighty hears us say it.

GOVERNOR. It is doing like Christians.

QUEREBENNIT. What I have said God Almighty hears (and presented another belt of wampum).

GOVERNOR. We say the same, what is done is done in the presence of God. Tell them I hear more complaints of some of them, that they have interrupted the English in their affairs, taken the meat out of their pots, et cetera. I expect that there be no more such miscarriages. If any of our people should do so to them they should be punished severely.

QUEREBENNIT. We pray supplies may be sent us.

GOVERNOR. Tell them that the traders here shall supply them. Ask them what they want most.

QUEREBENNIT. In the winter all necessaries are wanting, especially provisions and ammunition.

GOVERNOR. Tell them the traders shall have order to supply them with what they want, at reasonable rates.

QUEREBENNIT. We should be glad of one trading house that may serve us all.

GOVEROR. There shall be a place, or two or three, when I go home appointed, where they shall be supplied.

QUEREBENNIT. We desire that interpreter Jordan may be near us, to represent to Your Excellency anything that may happen.

GOVERNOR. I desire no better man.

QUEREBENNIT. We should be glad of a smith here, to mend our guns.

GOVERNOR. Here is one that has worked for you and complains he is not paid for it.

QUEREBENNIT. As to that, I don't know, but it is a long time before he will do our work, and then he won't do it well.

GOVERNOR. If you take care to pay for your work, I shall endeavor you shall have a good locksmith.

And tell them, that I thank them for their present.

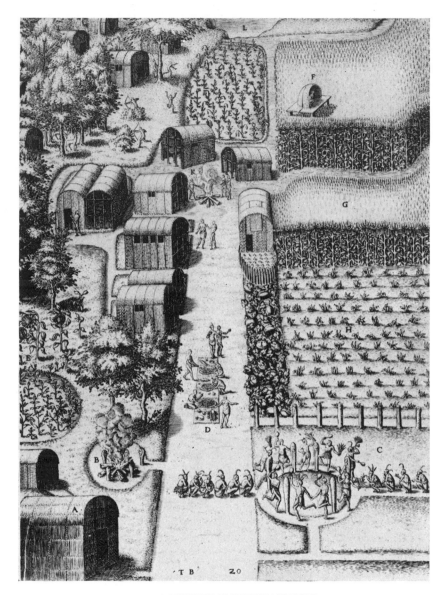

21. SOUTHERN INDIAN TOWN

De Bry, *The Great Voyages,* Part I; Frankfurt, 1590

His Excellency directed the following instrument to be drawn up and annexed to the Articles of their submission, made at Piscataqua, which was read and interpreted to them paragraph by paragraph by interpreter Jordan.

And they all readily and without any objection consented to the whole.

[The treaty document follows.]

August 12, 1717

This affair being finished, several sachems desired as it suited them that supplies might be sent to Winter Harbor, Casco, Macquoit, Rowsick, Small Point, and a sloop with supplies to Penobscot, which His Excellency told them he would gratify them in. As also that people should not hunt the fowl which floats.

Mug. complained he had left fifteen shillings with Captain Lane, and that he would not restore it to him.

And they desired that Captain Lane might be directed to use them better, or some other person sent in his room.

Sarumbamet complained that Mr. Nowel had employed him to procure for him an English young woman, a captive, promising him twenty pounds if he succeeded, and ten pounds if he attempted and did not succeed, and that he had endeavored it without success, and said Nowel refuses to comply with his bargain.

To all which His Excellency replied that he would take care that right should be done them.

Then all the sachems and chief men came with great respect and offered His Excellency their hands, one of them declaring that they desired the peace might continue as long as the sun and moon should endure.

And His Excellency ordered them a present of some provisions and ammunition, which they accepted very thankfully, and prayed that their young men might be allowed to come over and give His Excellency a dance, which His Excellency allowed of.

7

WITCHCRAFTS

In the seventeenth century the Devil with his minions was attempting, as indeed he had attempted through all creation, to infiltrate God's kingdom on earth, seduce the faithful, and corrupt humanity for his diabolical purposes. Sometimes he visited the shaky in person, offering them gold and favors, or fornicated with old crones desiring a bit of pleasure. His ranks recruited others, initiating them into the black art which mocked Christian ritual and subverted Christian believers.

All of this diabolism followed strict procedural rules, which Cotton Mather explicitly describes in his Wonders of the Invisible World. *When the reports of witchcrafts scattered throughout the century piled up into a flood toward its end, culminating in the series of trials at Salem, Mather desperately feared that the followers of Satan were about to take over New England. The diabolical plot was coming to a head. Only strong and prompt measures could save the land.*

But how could one tell a witch? Uncover her, and you could legally hang her for her practices, and stamp out the evil. The testimony of the bewitched must always be basic evidence. And yet this was "spectral" evidence, of witches in animal forms, of physical disturbances performed by invisible spirits, of witches in the shape of other people, perhaps innocent people.

There was the rub. How to distinguish the innocent from their impersonators? How to distinguish the genuinely bewitched from false libelers and rumormongers? Cotton Mather pondered these problems in sore perplexity.

One wanted to adjudge only the certainly guilty, yet one must act swiftly. The pious were being murdered with frightful witchcrafts, the country was in turmoil. So those accused were summoned before the courts and interrogated. What could they say when their accusers swooned in their faces? A few confessed, the hardiest denied, pleading skillfully, movingly, but perhaps with devilish dialectic. The more cunning their refutations, the more suspicion that they spoke with the Devil's tongue.

The Salem crisis died shortly after its crescendo, when too many prominent persons became accused. The judges recanted, the frenzy blew itself out, and the eighteenth century shuddered at the madness of its forebears.

NEW ENGLAND DISTRAUGHT

John Josselyn

THERE are none that beg in the country, but there be witches too many, bottle-bellied witches amongst the Quakers, and others that produce many strange apparitions if you will believe report. Of a shallop at sea manned with women. Of a ship and a great red horse standing by the mainmast; the ship being in a small cove to the eastward vanished of a sudden. Of a witch that appeared aboard of a ship twenty leagues to sea to a mariner, who took up the carpenter's broadax and cleft her head with it, the witch dying of the wound at home. With such-like bugbears and terriculamentae.

Jasper Danckaerts

1680, June 19th, Wednesday. We embarked at noon in the yacht of Mr. Padechal, supercargo and captain, residing in Boston. The woman who was going over with us was born at Rhode Island, in New England, and was the wife of the captain of the *Margaret,* one of Frederick Flipsen's ships. I have never in my whole life witnessed a worse, more foul, profane, or abandoned creature. She is the third individual we have met with from New England, and we remarked to each other, if the rest of the people there are to be judged by them, we might perhaps do them great injustice. For the first one from Boston whom we saw was a sailor, or he passed for one, on board the ship in which we sailed from the fatherland. They called him the doctor, and if he were not or had not been a charlatan, he resembled one. The second was our skipper, Padechal, who had told us so many lies; and now, this infamous woman. They all belong to this people who, it is said, pretend to special devoutness; but we found them, the sailor and the rest, like all other Englishmen, who, if they are not more detestable than the Hollanders, are at least no better.

I must here mention another word about Boston, which is, that I have never been in a place where more was said about witchcraft and witches. From time to time persons had been put in prison and executed; and a woman was in prison and condemned to die when we left there.* Very strange things were told of her, but I will not repeat them here.

* On May 20, 1680, Elizabeth Morse, the wife of William Morse, of Newbury, was indicted and tried in Boston, for practicing witchcraft upon her own husband.

THE ARCHENEMY

Increase Mather

ANOTHER providence happened at Portsmouth in New England, concerning which I have received the following account from a worthy hand.

"On June 11, 1682, being the Lord's day, at night showers of stones were thrown both against the sides and roof of the house of George Walton. Some of the people went abroad and found the gate at some distance from the house wrung off the hinges. Stones came thick about them, sometimes falling down by them, sometimes touching them without any hurt done to them. Though they seemed to come with great force, yet did no more but softly touch them; stones were flying about the room, the doors being shut; the glass windows were shattered to pieces by stones that seemed to come not from without but within, the lead of the glass casements, window bars, et cetera, being driven forcibly outwards, and so standing bent. While the secretary was walking in the room, a great hammer came brushing along against the chamber floor that was over his head and fell down by him. A candlestick beaten off the table. They took up nine of the stones and marked them, and laid them on the table, some of them being as hot as if they came out of the fire; but some of those marked stones were found flying about again. In this same manner, about four hours' space that night.

"The secretary then went to bed, but a stone came and broke up his chamber door, being put to (not locked); a brick was sent upon the like errand. The above-said stone the secretary locked up in his chamber, but it was fetched out and carried with great noise into the next chamber. The spit was carried up-chimney and came down with the point forward, and stuck in the backlog, and, being removed by one of the company to one side of the chimney, was by an unseen hand thrown out the window. This trade was driven on the next day, and so from day to day; now and then there would be some intermission, and then to it again. The stones were most frequent where the master of the house was, whether in the field or barn, et cetera. A black cat was seen once while the stones came, and was shot at, but she was too nimble for them. Some of the family say that they once saw the appearance of an hand put forth at the hall window, throwing stones towards the entry, though there was nobody in the hall the while. Sometimes a dismal hollow whistling would be heard; sometimes the noise of the trotting of an horse and snorting, but nothing seen.

"The man went up the great bay in his boat to a farm he had there, and while hauling wood or timber to the boat he was disturbed by the stones as before at home. He carried a stirrup iron from the house down to the boat, and there left it; but while he was going up to the house the iron came jingling after him through the woods, and returned to the house, and so again, and at last went away and was heard of no more. Their anchor leaped overboard several times as they were going home, and stopped the boat.

"A cheese hath been taken out of the press and crumbled all over the floor. A piece of iron with which they weighed up the cheese press stuck into the wall, and a kettle hung up thereon. Several cocks of English hay, mowed near the house, were taken and hung upon trees, and some made into small wisps, and put all up and down the kitchen, *cum multis aliis,* et cetera. After this manner have they been treated ever since at times; it were endless to particularize. Of late they thought the bitterness of death had been past, being quiet for sundry days and nights; but last week were some returnings again, and this week (August 2, 1682) as bad or worse than ever. The man is sorely hurt with some of the stones that came on him, and like to feel the effects of them for many days." Thus far is that relation.

I am moreover informed that the demon was quiet all the last winter, but in the spring he began to play some ludicrous tricks, carrying away some axes that were locked up safe. This last summer he has not made such disturbances as formerly; but of this no more at present.

There have been strange and true reports concerning a woman now living near the Salmon Falls in Berwick (formerly called Kittery), unto whom evil spirits have sometimes visibly appeared, and she has sometimes been sorely tormented by invisible hands; concerning all which an intelligent person has sent me the following narrative.

A brief narrative of sundry apparitions of Satan unto, and assaults at sundry times and places upon the person of Mary, the wife of Antonio Hortado, dwelling near the Salmon Falls. Taken from her own mouth, August 13, 1683.

"IN JUNE, 1682 (the day forgotten), at evening, the said Mary heard a voice at the door of her dwelling, saying, 'What do you here?' About an hour after, standing at the door of her house, she had a blow on her eye that settled her head near to the doorpost. Two or three days after, a stone, as she judged about half a pound or a pound weight, was thrown along the house within into the chimney, and going to take it up it was gone; all the family was in the house, and no hand appearing which might be instrumental in throwing the stone. About two hours after, a frying pan then hanging in the chimney was heard to ring so loud that not only those in the house heard it but others also that lived on the other side of the river near an hundred rods distant or more.

"Thereupon the said Mary and her husband going in a canoe over the river, they saw like the head of a man new-shorn, and the tail of a white cat, about two or three foot distance from each other, swimming over before the canoe, but nobody appeared to join head and tail together. And they returning over the river in less than an hour's time, the said apparition followed their canoe back again, but disappeared at landing. A day or two after, the said Mary was stricken on her head (as she judged) with a stone, which caused a swelling and much soreness on her head, being then in the yard by her house; and she, presently entering into her house, was bitten on both arms black and blue, and one of her breasts scratched. The impressions of the teeth, being like man's teeth, were plainly seen by many.

"Whereupon deserting their house to sojourn at a neighbor's on the other side of the river, there appeared to said Mary in the house of her sojourning a woman clothed with a green safeguard, a short blue cloak, and a white cap, making a proffer to strike her with a firebrand, but struck her not. The day following, the same shape appeared to her, but now arrayed with a gray gown, white apron, and white headclothes, in appearance laughing several times, but no voice heard. Since when, said Mary has been freed from those Satanical molestations.

"But the said Antonio being returned in March last with his family, to dwell again in his own house, and on his entrance there hearing the noise of a man walking in his chamber and seeing the boards buckle under his feet as he walked, though no man to be seen in the chamber (for they went on purpose to look), he returned with his family to dwell on the other side of the river. Yet planting his ground though he forsook his house, he hath had five rods of good log fence thrown down at once; the feeting of neat cattle plainly to be seen almost between every row of corn in the field, yet no cattle seen there, nor any damage done to his corn, not so much as any of the leaves of the corn cropped." Thus far is that narrative.

I am further informed that some (who should have been wiser) advised the poor woman to stick the house round with bays, as an effectual preservative against the power of evil spirits. This counsel was followed; and as long as the bays continued green, she had quiet; but when they began to wither, they were all by an unseen hand carried away, and the woman again tormented.

It is observable that at the same time three houses in three several towns should be molested by demons, as has now been related.

Lawrence Hammond

ANNO 1688. In New England, one J. Bradbent, an exciseman and a hectoring debauchee resident in Boston (where too many of the same stamp have lately multiplied), meeting an honest, ingenious countryman upon the road, inquired of him, "What news, countryman?" Who replied, "I know none."

The other then replied, "I'll tell you, son."

"What is it?" said the countryman.

Said the other, "The Devil is dead."

"How?" said the countryman. "I believe not that."

"Yes," said the other, "he is dead for certain."

"Well, then," said the countryman, "if he be dead, he hath left many fatherless children in Boston."

John Higginson

Salem, August 17, 1683

FOR THE Reverend Mr. Increase Mather, Teacher of the Church at the North End of Boston.

Reverend Sir: Being lately at Mr. Shepard's I understood from him that you do not confine yourself in giving instances of illustrious providences to things done in New England, which made me remember two instances which I now send you to consider of them and do as you see cause. The one is thus.

Godly Mr. Sharp, who was ruling elder of the church of Salem almost thirty years, often related it of himself, that being bred up to learning till he was eighteen years old, and then taken off and put to be an apprentice to a draper in London, he yet notwithstanding continued a strong inclination and eager affection to books, with a curiosity of hearkening after reading of the strangest and oddest books he could get—spending much of his time that way, to the neglecting of his business. At one time there came a man into the shop and brought a book with him, and said to him, "Here is a book for you; keep this till I call for it again." And so went away.

Mr. Sharp, after his wonted bookish manner, was eagerly affected to look into that book and to read in it, which he did. But as he read in it he was seized on by a strange kind of horror, both of body and mind, the hair of his head standing up, et cetera. Finding these effects several times, he acquainted his master with it, who observing the same effects, they concluded it was a conjuring book and resolved to burn it, which they did. He that brought it, in the shape of a man, never coming to call for it, they concluded it was the Devil. He, taking this as a solemn warning from God to take heed what books he did read, was much taken off from his former bookishness, confining himself to reading the Bible and other known good books of divinity which were profitable to his soul.

The other I heard at Guilford from a godly old man yet living. He came from Essex and hath been in New England about fifty years.

There was in Essex a man of considerable estate and of good esteem amongst his neighbors in the country where he lived, but was ambitiously affected to be counted a wise man. Being under the power and predominancy of that sinful distemper, God left him so far, that the Devil appeared to him and promised him that upon one condition he would make him famous for wisdom all the country over. The condition was that, when he was in reputation for wisdom, he should take all opportunities to instill it into the minds of people that came to him for counsel that there was neither God nor Devil, nor heaven nor hell. In the issue he made a covenant with the Devil, giving his soul to him after so many years, upon the former conditions.

He continued after in his former course without any change, of a civil conversation, doing no hurt unto any but good unto many, and by degrees grew in his reputation for a very wise man, insomuch as he was sought unto for his counsel far and near and he was all the country over called and counted a wise man, and his words were esteemed as oracles amongst the common sort of people. All the while for many years he took all occasions to disseminate those damned principles of atheism before mentioned, and yet was never suspected to be a witch till some few weeks before his covenant with the Devil was to expire.

Then he was dreadfully awakened and filled with horror, and would often with crying and roaring tell those that then came to him that now he knew there was a God and a Devil, and a heaven and a hell; and so he unsaid all that he had formerly said that way, telling them also what he had done, and of his fearful expectations of the Devil's fetching away his soul at the time appointed. So he died miserably, as a spectacle of the righteous judgments of God.

I commend you to the grace of God in Christ Jesus, and rest

Yours unfeignedly ever,

JOHN HIGGINSON

Rev. Andreas Sandel

1716, January 12. A dreadful thing happened in Philadelphia to the wife of a butcher who had quarreled with her husband. He asked her to make their bed, but she refused. Continuing to refuse, he told her he would turn her out of the house, but she told him if he did so she would break every window pane, and invoked the Devil to come for her if she did not do it.

The husband led her out of the house, she became highly excited, broke some of the panes, and through the kitchen made her way up to the attic with a candle and laid down on the bed greatly disturbed on account of her promise. Then she heard somebody coming up the stairs, but saw no one; this was repeated for half an hour. Becoming more and more agitated, fearing her awful invocation was about to be realized, she went down to her husband, telling him of her anguish and asking him to aid her. Lying down on a bench near the hearth, she perceived a dark human face, making horrid grimaces with mouth wide open and the teeth gnashing. Then she became thoroughly terrified, and asked her husband to read to her Psalm 21, which he did, and the face disappeared.

Soon afterwards she perceived at the window, one whose panes she had broken, that someone was standing there with both arms extended through the window, by which her fright was made greater. Then the figure approached and passed her, but she could not see where it disappeared. Her husband then clasped his arms around her, when the fumes of brimstone became so strong they could not remain indoors, and these fumes were apparent to all who came in later.

At one o'clock she sent for the minister, who also came and prayed with her the next day. Many persons visited her, but she had to fold her hands over her knees to keep from trembling. A few days later the same woman related to me and two other clergymen, Mr. Ross and Smith, this story.

THE GATHERING STORM

John Winthrop

AT THIS court one Margaret Jones of Charlestown was indicted and found guilty of witchcraft, and hanged for it [1648].

The evidence against her was: 1. That she was found to have such a malignant touch as many persons (men, women, and children) whom she stroked or touched with any affection or displeasure were taken with deafness, or vomiting, or other violent pains or sickness.

2. She practicing physic, and her medicines being such things as (by her own confession) were harmless, as aniseed, liquors, et cetera, yet had extraordinary violent effects.

3. She would use to tell such as would not make use of her physic that they would never be healed, and accordingly their diseases and hurts continued, with relapse against the ordinary course, and beyond the apprehension of all physicians and surgeons.

4. Some things which she foretold came to pass accordingly; other things she could tell of (as secret speeches, et cetera) which she had no ordinary means to come to the knowledge of.

5. She had (upon search) an apparent teat in her secret parts as fresh as if it had been newly sucked, and after it had been scanned, upon a forced search, that was withered and another began on the opposite side.

6. In the prison, in the clear daylight, there was seen in her arms, she sitting on the floor and her clothes up, a little child, which ran from her into another room, and the officer following it, it was vanished. The like child was seen in two other places, to which she had relation; and one maid that saw it fell sick upon it, and was cured by the said Margaret, who used means to be employed to that end.

Her behavior at her trial was very intemperate, lying notoriously and railing upon the jury and witnesses, and in the like distemper she died. The same day and hour she was executed, there was a very great tempest at Connecticut, which blew down many trees.

The *Welcome,* of Boston, about 300 tons, riding before Charlestown, having in her eighty horses and 120 tons of ballast, in calm weather fell a-rolling, and continued so about twelve hours, so as though they brought a great weight to the one side, yet she would heel to the other, and so deep as they feared her foundering. It was then the time of the county court at Boston, and the magistrates hearing of it, and withal that one Jones (the husband of the witch lately executed) had desired to have passage in her to Barbados, and could not have it without such payment, they sent the officer presently with a warrant to apprehend him, one of them saying that the ship would stand still as soon as he was in prison.

And as the officer went and was passing over the ferry, one said to him, "You can tame men sometimes, can't you tame this ship?"

The officer answered, "I have that here that (it may be) will tame her, and make her be quiet." And with that showed his warrant.

And at the same instant, the ship began to stop and presently stayed, and after Jones was put in prison moved no more.

A Jesuit Missionary

THIS year [1654] Father Francis Fitzherbert, destined for Maryland, at the first intimation of our Superior, without a single companion, with singular magnanimity and alacrity of mind entered upon an arduous expedition and a laborious and long journey among unknown men dissimilar in morals and religion. Nor during his whole journey was there wanting a harvest abundant according to his deserts, from his confidence in God and his patience. Four ships sailed together from England, which a fearful storm overtook, when carried beyond the Western Isles, and the ship in which the Father was carried the violent waves so shattered that, springing a leak by the continued violence of the sea, it almost filled its hold. But in carrying away and exhausting the water, the men, four at a time, not only of the ship's crew but of the passengers, every one in his turn sweated at the great pump in ceaseless labor, day and night.

Wherefore having changed their course, their intention was to make sail towards the island which the English call Barbados; but it could be accomplished by no art, by no labor. Then the design was, having abandoned the ship and its freight, to commit themselves to the long boat. But the sea, swelling with adverse winds and the huge mountainous waves, forbade. Many a form of death presenting itself to the minds of all, the habit of terror, now grown familiar, had almost excluded the fear of death. The tempest lasted two months in all, whence the opinion arose that it was not raised by the violence of the sea or atmosphere, but was occasioned by the malevolence of witches. Forthwith they seized a little old woman suspected of sorcery; and after examining her with the strictest scrutiny, guilty or not guilty, they slew her, suspected of this very heinous sin. The corpse, and whatever belonged to her, they cast into the sea.

But the winds did not thus remit their violence, or the raging sea its threatenings. To the troubles of the storm sickness was added, which, having spread to almost every person, carried off not a few. Nevertheless, the Father remained untouched by all the contagion, and unharmed, except that in working and exercising at the pump too laboriously he contracted a slight fever of a few days' continuance. Having passed through multiplied dangers, at length by the favor of God the ship contrary to the expectation of all reached the port of Maryland.

A Court Recorder
Complaint of Susannah Trimmings, of Little Harbor, Piscataqua, New Hampshire

ON LORD's day 30th of March, at night, going home with Goodwife Barton, she separated from her at the freshet next her house. On her return, between Goodman Evens's and Robert Davis's she heard a rustling in the woods, which she at first thought was occasioned by swine, and presently after there did appear to her a woman whom she apprehended to be old Goodwife Walford.

"She asked me where my consort was. I answered, I had none.

She said, Thy consort is at home by this time. Lend me a pound of cotton.

"I told her I had but two pounds in the house, and I would not spare any to my mother. She said I had better have done it; that my sorrow was great already, and it should be greater—for I was going a great journey, but should never come there. She then left me, and I was struck as with a clap of fire on the back, and she vanished toward the waterside, in my apprehension in the shape of a cat. She had on her head a white linen hood tied under her chin, and her waistcoat and petticoat were red, with an old green apron and a black hat upon her head."

Taken upon oath April 18, 1665, before

BRYAN PENDLETON,
HENRY SHERBURNE,
RENALD FERNALD.

Her husband Oliver says: "She came home in a sad condition. She passed by me with her child in her arms, laid the child on the bed, sat down on the chest, and leaned upon her elbow. Three times I asked her how she did. She could not speak. I took her in my arms and held her up, and repeated the question. She forced breath, and something stopped in her throat as if it would have stopped her breath. I unlaced her clothes, and soon she spake and said, Lord have mercy upon me, this wicked woman will kill me. I asked her what woman. She said, Goodwife Walford. I tried to persuade her it was only her weakness. She told me no, and related as above that her back was as a flame of fire, and her lower parts were as it were numb and without feeling. I pinched her and she felt not. She continued that night and the day and night following very ill, and is still bad of her limbs and complains still daily of it."

Sworn as above.

Rev. William Adams

ANNO 1672. Thomas Whitteridge's wife, being a woman of no commendable life, was by a fortuneteller told that she should meet with great trouble, if she escaped with her life. Afterward being in great horror, Mr. Richard Hubbard gave her several

Scriptures to consider of. When he was gone she turned the Bible the best part of an hour, saying there was another Scripture if she could find it, which what it was or whatever she found it being unknown to others she clapped the Bible to and said she would never look into it more; and by the just judgment of God she never did.

At night she told her son, a youth about twelve or thirteen years at the most, that it would be as the fortuneteller had said. The boy desired his mother that she would not mind what he had said, for he believed that he was a lying fellow, but that she would mind what was said in the word of God. At this word she flew up saying (as some report), "He is come!"

The door either by her or of itself being opened with great violence, she ran out. And being presently followed, no sight could be had of her, but a shrieking or groaning or both was heard. The next morning there was to be seen a path made through the thickest places of weeds and briars as if a great timber log had been drawn there, which being followed her coat was found therein, and she a little further with her face thrust into a little puddle of water not sufficient to cover all her face, lying dead. *Quam inscrutabilia judicie Dei!*

Cotton Mather

MR. PHILIP SMITH, aged about fifty years, a son of eminently virtuous parents, a deacon of a church in Hadley, a member of the General Court, a justice in the country court, a selectman for the affairs of the town, a lieutenant of the troop, and, which crowns all, a man for devotion, sanctity, gravity, and all that was honest, exceeding exemplary: such a man was, in the winter of the year 1684, murdered with an hideous witchcraft, that filled all those parts of New England with astonishment. He was by his office concerned about relieving the indigences of a wretched woman in the town who, being dissatisfied at some of his just cares about her, expressed herself unto him in such a manner that he declared himself thenceforward apprehensive of receiving mischief at her hands.

About the beginning of January he began to be very valetudinarious, laboring under pains that seemed sciatic. The standers-by could now see in him one ripening apace for another world, and filled with grace and joy to a high degree. He showed such weanedness from and weariness of the world that he knew not (he said) whether he might pray for his continuance here; and such assurance he had of the divine love unto him that in raptures he would cry out, "Lord, stay thy hand! It is enough, it is more than thy frail servant can bear!"

But in the midst of these things he still uttered a hard suspicion that the ill woman who had threatened him had made impressions with enchantments upon him. While he remained yet of a sound mind, he very sedately but very solemnly charged his brother to look well after him. Though, he said, he now understood himself, yet he knew not how he might be.

"But be sure," said he, "to have a care of me; for you shall see strange things. There shall be a wonder in Hadley! I shall not be dead, when 'tis thought I am!"

He pressed this charge over and over, and afterwards became delirious; upon which he had a speech incessant and voluble, and (as was judged) in various languages. He cried out not only of pains but also of pins tormenting him in several parts of his body, and the attendants found one of them.

In his distresses he exclaimed much upon the woman aforesaid, and others, as being seen by him in the room; and there was divers times, both in that room and over the whole house, a strong smell of something like musk, which once particularly so scented an apple roasting at the fire that it forced them to throw it away. Some of the young men in the town, being out of their wits at the strange calamities thus upon one of their most beloved neighbors, went three or four times to give disturbance unto the woman thus complained of, and all the while they were disturbing of her he was at ease and slept as a weary man; yea, these were the only times that they perceived him to take any sleep in all his illness.

Galley pots of medicine, provided for the sick man, were unaccountably emptied; audible scratchings were made about the bed when his hands and feet lay wholly still and were held by others. They beheld fire sometimes on the bed; and when the beholders began to discourse of it, it vanished away. Divers

22. COTTON MATHER

Peter Pelham, *ca.* 1727

people actually felt something often stir in the bed at a considerable distance from the man; it seemed as big as a cat, but they could never grasp it. Several trying to lean on the bed's head, though the sick man lay wholly still, the bed would shake so as to knock their heads uncomfortably. A very strong man could not lift the sick man to make him lie more easily, though he applied his utmost strength unto it; and yet he could go presently and lift a bedstead and a bed, and a man lying on it, without any strain to himself at all.

Mr. Smith dies. The jury that viewed his corpse found a swelling on one breast, his privates wounded or burned, his back full of bruises, and several holes that seemed made with awls. After the opinion of all had pronounced him dead, his countenance continued as lively as if he had been alive; his eyes closed as in a slumber, and his nether jaw not falling down.

Thus he remained from Saturday morning about sunrise till Sabbath day in the afternoon, when those who took him out of the bed found him still warm, though the season was as cold as had almost been known in any age—and a New England winter does not want for cold. On the night following his countenance was yet fresh as before, but on Monday morning they found the face extremely tumefied and discolored. It was black and blue, and fresh blood seemed running down his cheek upon the hairs. Divers noises were also heard in the room where the corpse lay, as the clattering of chairs and stools, whereof no account could be given. This was the end of so good a man.

And I could with unquestionable evidence relate the tragical deaths of several good men in this land, attended with such preternatural circumstances, which have loudly called upon us all to "work out our own salvation with fear and trembling."

THE AWFUL STRUGGLE

Cotton Mather

THAT the Devil is come down unto us with great wrath, we find, we feel, we now deplore. In many ways, for many years hath the Devil been assaying to extirpate the kingdom of our Lord Jesus here. New England may complain of the Devil, as in Psalm 129:1, 2. *Many a time have they afflicted me from my youth,* may New England now say. *Many a time have they afflicted me from my youth, yet they have not prevailed against me.*

But now there is a more than ordinary affliction with which the Devil is galling of us, and such an one as is indeed unparallelable. The things confessed by witches, and the things endured by others, laid together, amount unto this account of our affliction. The Devil, exhibiting himself ordinarily as a small black man, has decoyed a fearful knot of proud, froward, ignorant, envious, and malicious creatures to lift themselves in his horrid service, by entering their names in a book by him tendered unto them. These witches, whereof above a score have now confessed and shown their deeds, and some are now tormented by the devils for confessing, have met in hellish rendezvous wherein the confessors do say they have had their diabolical sacraments, imitating the baptism and the supper of our Lord.

In these hellish meetings, these monsters have associated themselves to do no less a thing than *to destroy the kingdom of our Lord Jesus Christ in these parts of the world.* And in order hereunto, first they each of them have their specters or devils, commissioned by them and representing of them, to be the engines of their malice. By these wicked specters they seize poor people about the country with various and bloody torments; and of those evidently preternatural torments there are some have died. They have bewitched some, even so far as to make self-destroyers; and others are in many towns here and there languishing under their evil hands.

The people thus afflicted are miserably scratched and bitten, so that the marks are most visible to all the world, but the causes utterly invisible; and the same invisible furies do most visibly stick pins into the bodies of the afflicted, and scale them, and hideously distort and disjoint all their members, besides a thousand other sorts of plagues beyond those of any natural diseases which they give unto them. Yea, they sometimes drag the poor people out of their chambers and carry them over trees and hills for divers miles together. A large part of the persons tortured by these diabolical specters are horribly tempted by them, sometimes with fair promises and sometimes with hard threatenings, but always with felt miseries, to sign the Devil's laws in a spectral book laid before them; which two or three of these poor sufferers, being by their tiresome sufferings overcome to do, they have immediately been released from all their miseries, and they appeared as specters then to torture those that were before their fellow sufferers.

The witches, which by their covenant with the Devil are become owners of specters, are oftentimes by their own specter required and compelled to give their consent for the molestation of some whom they had no mind otherwise to fall upon; and cruel depredations are then made upon the vicinage. In the prosecution of these witchcrafts, among a thousand other unaccountable things, the specters have an odd faculty of clothing the most substantial and corporeal instruments of torture with invisibility, while the wounds thereby given have been the most palpable things in the world.

Thus the sufferers, assaulted with instruments of iron wholly unseen to the standers-by (though, to their cost, seen by themselves), have upon snatching wrested the instruments out of the specters' hands, and everyone has then immediately not only beheld but handled an iron instrument taken by a devil from a neighbor. These wicked specters have proceeded so far as to steal several quantities of money from divers people, part of which money has, before sufficient spectators, been dropped out of the air into the hands of the sufferers, while the specters have been urging them to subscribe their covenant with death. In such extravagant ways have these wretches propounded the dragooning of as many as they can in their own combination, and the destroying of others with lingering, spreading, deadly diseases, till our country should at last become too hot for us.

Among the ghastly instances of the success which those bloody witches have had, we have seen even some of their own children so dedicated unto the Devil that in their infancy, it is found, the imps have sucked them, and rendered them venomous to a prodigy. We have also seen the Devil's first batteries upon the town, where the first church of our Lord in this colony was gathered, producing those distractions which have almost ruined the town. We have seen likewise the plague reaching afterwards into other towns far and near, where the houses of good men have the Devil's filling of them with terrible vexations!

This is the descent which, it seems, the Devil has now made upon us. But that which makes this descent the more formidable is the multitude and quality of persons accused of an interest in this witchcraft, by the efficacy of the specters which take their name and shape upon them. Very many good and wise men have cause to fear that many innocent, yea, and some virtuous, persons are by the devils in this matter imposed upon; that the devils have obtained the power to take on the likeness of harmless people, and in that likeness to afflict others. These then be so abused by prestigious demons that upon the look or touch of the true harmless one they shall be oddly affected.

Arguments from the providence of God, on the one side, and from our charity towards men on the other side, have made this now to become a most agitated controversy among us. There is an agony produced in the minds of men, lest the Devil should sham us with devices of perhaps a finer thread than was ever yet practiced upon the world.

The whole business is become hereupon so snarled, and the determination of the question one way or another so dismal, that our honorable judges have a room for Jehoshaphat's exclamation, *We know not what to do!* They have used, as judges have heretofore done, the spectral evidences to introduce their further inquiries into the lives of the persons accused; and they have thereupon, by the wonderful providence of God, been so strengthened with other evidences that some of the witch gang have been fairly executed. But what shall be done as to those against whom the evidence is chiefly founded in the dark world? Here they do solemnly demand our addresses to the Father of Lights, on their behalf. But in the meantime, the Devil improves the darkness of this affair to push us into a blind man's buffet, and we are even ready to be sinfully, yea, hotly and madly mauling one another in the dark.

The consequence of these things, every considerate man trembles at; and the more, because the frequent cheats of passion and rumor do precipitate so many that I wish I could say, the most were considerate.

A DREAD SECRET WEAPON

Cotton Mather

IN ALL the witchcraft which now grievously vexes us, I know not whether anything be more unaccountable than the trick which the witches have to render themselves and their tools invisible.

Witchcraft seems to be the skill of applying the plastic spirit of the world unto some unlawful purposes, by means of a confederacy with evil spirits. Yet one would wonder how the evil spirits themselves can do some things, especially at invisibilizing of the grossest bodies. I can tell the name of an ancient author who pretends to show the way how a man may come to walk about invisible, and I can tell the name of another ancient author who pretends to explode that way. But I will not speak too plainly lest I should unawares poison some of my readers, as the pious Hemingius did one of his pupils, when he only by way of diversion recited a spell which, they had said, would cure agues.

This much I will say: the notion of procuring invisibility by any natural expedient yet known is, I believe, a mere Plinyism. How far it may be obtained by a magical sacrament is best known to the dangerous knaves that have tried it. But our witches do seem to have got the knack; and this is one of the things that make me think witchcraft will not be fully understood until the day when there shall not be one witch in the world.

There are certain people very dogmatical about these matters: but I'll give them only these three bones to pick.

First, one of our bewitched people was cruelly assaulted by a specter that, she said, ran at her with a spindle, though nobody else in the room could see either the specter or the spindle. At last, in her miseries giving a snatch at the specter, she pulled the spindle away, and it was no sooner got into her hand but the other people then present beheld that it was indeed a real, proper, iron spindle, belonging they knew to whom; which when they locked up very safe, it was nevertheless by demons unaccountably stole away, to do further mischief.

Secondly, another of our bewitched people was haunted with a most abusive specter, which came to her, she said, with a sheet about her. After she had undergone a deal of tease from the annoyance of the specter, she gave a violent snatch at the sheet that was upon it, wherefrom she tore a corner, which in her hand immediately became visible to a roomful of spectators—a palpable corner of a sheet. Her father, who was now holding her, catched that he might keep what his daughter had so strangely seized, but the unseen specter had like to have pulled his hand off, by endeavoring to wrest it from him. However, he still held it, and I suppose has it still to show, it being but a few hours ago, namely, about the beginning of this October, that this accident happened, in the family of one Pitman, at Manchester.

Thirdly, a young man delaying to procure testimonials for his parents, who being under confinement on suspicion of witchcraft required him to do that service for them, was quickly pursued with odd inconveniences. An officer was going to put his brand on the horns of some cows belonging to these people, which though he had seized for some of their debts, yet he was willing to leave in their possession for the subsistence of the poor family; this young man helped in holding the cows to be thus branded. The three first cows he held well enough; but when the hot brand was clapped upon the fourth, he winced and shrunk at such a rate as that he could hold the cow no longer. Being afterwards examined about it, he confessed that at that very instant when the brand entered the cow's horn, exactly the like burning brand was clapped upon his own thigh; where he has exposed the lasting marks of it unto such as asked to see them.

Unriddle these things, *Et Eris mihi magnus Apollo.*

THE BATTLE AT SALEM

THE EXAMINATION
AND CONFESSION OF ANN FOSTER

Salem Village, July 15, 1692

After a while Ann Foster confessed that the Devil appeared to her in the shape of a bird at several times, such a bird as she never saw the like before; and that she had had this gift, viz., of striking the afflicted down with her eye, ever since. Being asked why she thought that bird was the Devil she answered, because he came white and vanished away black; and that the Devil told her that she should have this gift, and that she must believe him and she should have prosperity. She said that he had appeared to her three times and was always as a bird; that the last time was about half a year since; that it sat upon a table, had two legs and great eyes; that it was the second time of his appearance that he promised her prosperity; and that it was Carrier's wife about three weeks ago that came and persuaded her to hurt these people.

July 16. Ann Foster, examined, confessed that it was Goody Carrier that made her a witch. She came to her in person about six years ago and told her if she would not be a witch the Devil should tear her in pieces and carry her away, at which time she promised to serve the Devil. Since then she had bewitched a hog of John Loujoy's to death, and had hurt some persons in Salem Village. Goody Carrier came to her and would have her bewitch two children of Andrew Allin's, so she had then two poppets made and stuck pins in them to bewitch the said children, by which one of them died, and the other very sick. She was at the meeting of the witches at Salem Village, because Goody Carrier came and told her of the meeting and would have her go, so they got upon sticks and went said journey. Being there, she did see Mr. Burroughs the minister, who spake to them all. This was about two months ago. There were then twenty-five persons met together. She also said that she tied a knot in a rag and threw it into the fire to hurt Tim Swan, and that she did hurt the rest that complained of her by squeezing poppets like them and so almost choked them.

July 21. Ann Foster, examined, owned her former confession, being read to her, and further confessed that the discourse amongst the witches at the meeting at Salem Village was that they would afflict there to set up the Devil's kingdom.

This confession is true as witness my hand.

Ann Foster signed and owned the above examination and confession before me

JOHN HIGGINSON, *Justice of the Peace*
Salem, September 10, 1692

TRIAL OF GEORGE JACOBS

Warrant

To the constables in Salem

You are in Their Majesties' names hereby required to apprehend and forthwith bring before us George Jacobs, Senior, of Salem and Margaret Jacobs, the daughter of George Jacobs, Junior, of Salem, singlewoman, who stand accused of high suspicion of sundry acts of witchcraft by them both committed on sundry persons in Salem to their great wrong and injury, and hereof fail not. (Dated Salem, May 1, 1692.)

JOHN HATHORNE, ⎱ *Assists.*
JONATHAN CORWIN, ⎰

Indictment

The jurors for our sovereign Lord and Lady the King and Queen present, that George Jacobs, Senior, of Salem in the county of Essex, the 11th day of May in the fourth year of the reign of our sovereign Lord and Lady William and Mary by the grace of God of England, Scotland, France, and Ireland King and Queen, Defenders of the Faith et cetera, and divers other days and times as well before as after, certain detestable arts called witchcrafts and sorceries wickedly and feloniously hath used, practiced, and exercised at and within the township of Salem in the county of Essex aforesaid, in, upon, and against one Mercy Lewis of Salem Village, singlewoman, by which said wicked arts the said Mercy Lewis the 11th day of May in the fourth year above-said and divers other days and times as well before as after was and is tortured, afflicted, pined, consumed, wasted, and tormented, and also for sundry other acts of witchcraft by said George Jacobs committed and done before and since that time against the peace of our sovereign Lord and Lady the King and Queen, their crown and dignity, and against the form of the statutes in that case made and provided.

Witnesses { MERCY LEWIS, ELIZ. HUBBARD, MARY WALCOTT, SARAH CHURCHILL.

Examination, May 10, 1692

MAGISTRATE. Here are them that accuse you of acts of witchcraft.

JACOBS. Well, let us hear who are they and what are they.

MAGISTRATE. Abigail Williams. (*Jacobs laughed.*)
Why do you laugh?

JACOBS. Because I am falsely accused. Your Worships, all of you, do you think this is true?

MAGISTRATE. Nay, what do you think?

JACOBS. I never did it.

MAGISTRATE. Who did it?

JACOBS. Don't ask me.

MAGISTRATE. Why should we not ask you? Sarah Churchill accuseth you, there she is.

JACOBS. I am as innocent as the child born tonight. I have lived thirty-three years here in Salem.

MAGISTRATE. What then?

JACOBS. If you can prove that I am guilty I will lie under it.

MAGISTRATE. Sarah Churchill said last night, "I was afflicted at Deacon Ingersoll's"; and Mary Walcott said, "It was a man with two staves, it was my master."

JACOBS.	Pray do not accuse me. I am as clear as Your Worships—you must do right judgments.
MAGISTRATE.	What book did he bring you, Sarah?
CHURCHILL.	The same that the other woman brought.
JACOBS.	The Devil can go in any shape.
MAGISTRATE.	Did he not appear on the other side of the river and hurt you—did not you see him?
CHURCHILL.	Yes, he did.
MAGISTRATE.	Look there, she accuseth you to your face, she chargeth you that you hurt her twice. Is it not true?
JACOBS.	What would you have me say? I never wronged no man in word nor deed.
MAGISTRATE.	Here are three evidences.
JACOBS.	You tax me for a wizard, you may as well tax me for a buzzard. I have done no harm.
MAGISTRATE.	Is it no harm to afflict these?
JACOBS.	I never did it.
MAGISTRATE.	But how comes it to be in your appearance?
JACOBS.	The Devil can take any likeness.
MAGISTRATE.	Not without their consent.
JACOBS.	Please Your Worship it is untrue. I never showed the book. I am silly about these things as the child born last night.
MAGISTRATE.	That is your saying; you argue you have lived so long; but what then? Cain might live long before he killed Abel, and you might live long before the Devil had so prevailed on you.
JACOBS.	Christ hath suffered three times for me.
MAGISTRATE.	What three times?
JACOBS.	He suffered the Cross and Gall.
CHURCHILL.	You had as good confess if you are guilty.
JACOBS.	Have you heard that I have any witchcraft?
CHURCHILL.	I know you live a wicked life.
JACOBS.	Let her make it out.
MAGISTRATE.	Doth he ever pray in his family?
CHURCHILL.	Not unless by himself.
MAGISTRATE.	Why do you not pray in your family?
JACOBS.	I cannot read.

MAGISTRATE.	Well, but you may pray for all that. Can you say the Lord's Prayer? Let us hear you.
	(*He might in several parts of it and could not repeat it right after Mary Mialls.*)
MAGISTRATE.	Sarah Churchill, when you wrote in the book you was showed your master's name, you said.
CHURCHILL.	Yes, sir.
JACOBS.	If she say so, if you do not know it what will you say?
MAGISTRATE.	But she saw you or your likeness tempt her to write.
JACOBS.	One in my likeness! The Devil may present my likeness.
MAGISTRATE.	Were you not frighted, Sarah Churchill, when the representation of your master came to you?
CHURCHILL.	Yes.
JACOBS.	Well! Burn me, or hang me, I will stand in the truth of Christ. I know nothing of it.

The Second Examination, May 11, 1692

	(*The bewitched fell into most grievous fits and shriekings when he came in.*)
MAGISTRATE.	Is this the man that hurts you?
	(*Abigail Williams cried out,* "This is the man," *and fell into a violent fit.*
	Ann Putnam said, "This is the man, and he hurts and brings the book to her and would have her write in the book and she should be as well as his granddaughter.")
MAGISTRATE.	Mercy Lewis, is this the man?
LEWIS.	"This is the man" (*after much interruption by fits*), "he almost kills me."
MAGISTRATE.	Mary Walcott, is this the man?
	(*After much interruptions by fits she said,* "This is the man; he used to come with two staves and beat me with one of them.")
MAGISTRATE.	What do you say, are you not a witch?
JACOBS.	No, I know it not, if I were to die presently.

(*Mercy Lewis went to come near him but fell into great fits. Mercy Lewis's testimony read.*)

MAGISTRATE. What do you say to this?

JACOBS. Why, it is false. I know not of it any more than the child that was born tonight.

(*Ann Putnam said,* "Yes, you told me so, that you had been so this forty years."

Ann Putnam and Abigail Williams had each of them a pin stuck in their hands and they said it was this old Jacobs.)

MAGISTRATE. Are not you the man that made disturbance at a lecture in Salem?

JACOBS. No great disturbance. Do you think I use witchcraft?

MAGISTRATE. Yes, indeed.

JACOBS. No, I use none of them.

THE TRIAL OF SUSANNA MARTIN
AT THE COURT OF OYER AND TERMINER, HELD BY ADJOURNMENT AT SALEM, JUNE 29, 1692

Cotton Mather

I. Susanna Martin, pleading not guilty to the indictment of witchcraft brought in against her, there were produced the evidences of many persons very sensibly and grievously bewitched, who all complained of the prisoner at the bar as the person whom they believed the cause of their miseries. And now, as well as in the other trials, there was an extraordinary endeavor by witchcrafts, with cruel and frequent fits, to hinder the poor sufferers from giving in their complaints, which the court was forced with much patience to obtain, by much waiting and watching for it.

II. There was now also an account given of what passed at her first examination before the magistrates, the cast of her eye then striking the afflicted people to the ground, whether they saw that cast or no. There were these among other passages between the magistrates and the examinate.

MAGISTRATE.	Pray, what ails these people?
MARTIN.	I don't know.
MAGISTRATE.	But what do you think ails them?
MARTIN.	I don't desire to spend my judgment upon it.
MAGISTRATE.	Don't you think they are bewitched?
MARTIN.	No, I do not think they are.
MAGISTRATE.	Tell us your thoughts about them, then.
MARTIN.	No, my thoughts are my own, when they are in, but when they are out they are another's. Their master . . .
MAGISTRATE.	Their master? Who do you think is their master?
MARTIN.	If they be dealing in the black art, you may know as well as I.
MAGISTRATE.	Well, what have you done towards this?
MARTIN.	Nothing at all.
MAGISTRATE.	Why, 'tis you or your appearance.
MARTIN.	I cannot help it.
MAGISTRATE.	Is it not your master? How comes your appearance to hurt these?
MARTIN.	How do I know? He that appeared in the shape of Samuel, a glorified saint, may appear in anyone's shape.

It was then also noted in her, as in others like her, that if the afflicted went to approach her, they were flung down to the ground. And when she was asked the reason of it, she said, "I cannot tell; it may be the Devil bears me more malice than another."

III. The court accounted themselves alarmed by these things, to inquire further into the conversation of the prisoner and see what there might occur to render these accusations further credible. Whereupon John Allen of Salisbury testified that he refusing, because of the weakness of his oxen, to cart some staves at the request of this Martin, she was displeased at it and said, *It had been as good that he had, for his oxen should never do him much more service.*

Whereupon this deponent said, "Dost thou threaten me, thou old witch? I'll throw thee into the brook."

Which to avoid, she flew over the bridge and escaped. But as

he was going home one of his oxen tired, so that he was forced
to unyoke him, that he might get him home. He then put his
oxen, with many more, upon Salisbury Beach, where cattle did
use to get flesh. In a few days, all the oxen upon the beach were
found by their tracks to have run into the mouth of Merrimack
River and not returned; but the next day they were found come
ashore upon Plum Island. They that sought them used all imaginable gentleness, but they would still run away with a violence
that seemed wholly diabolical, till they came near the mouth of
Merrimack River, when they ran right into the sea, swimming
as far as they could be seen. One of them then swam back again,
with a swiftness amazing to the beholders, who stood ready to
receive him and help up his tired carcass. But the beast ran furiously up into the island, and from thence through the marshes
up into Newbury Town, and so up into the woods; and there
after a while was found near Amesbury. So that, of fourteen good
oxen, there was only this saved. The rest were all cast up, some
in one place, and some in another, drowned.

IV. John Atkinson testified that he exchanged a cow with a son
of Susanna Martin's, whereat she muttered, and was unwilling
he should have it. Going to receive this cow, though he ham-
stringed her and haltered her, she from a tame creature grew so
mad that they could scarce get her along. She broke all the ropes
that were fastened unto her, and though she were tied fast unto
a tree, yet she made her escape, and gave them such further
trouble as they could ascribe to no cause but witchcraft.

V. Bernard Peache testified that being in bed on the Lord's day
night, he heard a scrabbling at the window, whereat he then saw
Susanna Martin come in and jump down upon the floor. She
took hold of this deponent's feet, and drawing his body up into
a heap, she lay upon him near two hours; in all which time he
could neither speak nor stir. At length, when he could begin to
move, he laid hold on her hand and pulling it up to his mouth
he bit three of her fingers, as he judged, unto the bone. Whereupon she went from the chamber, down the stairs, out at the
door. This deponent thereupon called unto the people of the
house, to advise them of what passed; and he himself did follow
her. The people saw her not; but there being a bucket at the left

hand of the door, there was a drop of blood found upon it, and several more drops of blood upon the snow newly fallen abroad. There was likewise the print of her two feet just without the threshold, but no more sign of any footing further off.

At another time this deponent was desired by the prisoner to come unto an husking of corn at her house, and she said, *If he did not come, it were better that he did!* He went not; but the night following, Susanna Martin, as he judged, and another came towards him. One of them said, "Here he is!" But he, having a quarterstaff, made a blow at them. The roof of the barn broke his blow, but following them to the window he made another blow at them and struck them down; yet they got up and got out, and he saw no more of them.

About this time there was a rumor about the town that Martin had a broken head, but the deponent could say nothing to that.

The said Peache also testified the bewitching the cattle to death, upon Martin's discontents.

VI. Robert Downer testified that this prisoner being some years ago prosecuted at court for a witch, he then said unto her he believed she was a witch. Whereat she being dissatisfied said, *That some she-devil would shortly fetch him away!* Which words were heard by others, as well as himself. The night following, as he lay in his bed, there came in at the window the likeness of a cat, which flew upon him, took fast hold of his throat, lay on him a considerable while, and almost killed him. At length he remembered what Susanna Martin had threatened the day before, and with much striving he cried out, "Avoid, thou she-devil! In the name of God the Father, the Son, and the Holy Ghost, avoid!" Whereupon it left him, leaped on the floor, and flew out at the window.

And there also came in several testimonies that before ever Downer spoke a word of this accident, Susanna Martin and her family had related how this Downer had been handled!

VII. John Kembal testified that Susanna Martin, upon a causeless disgust, had threatened him about a certain cow of his, *That she should never do him any more good;* and it came to pass accordingly. For soon after the cow was found stark dead on the dry ground, without any distemper to be discerned upon her. Upon which he was followed with a strange death upon more of his cattle, whereof he lost in one spring to the value of thirty pounds.

But the said John Kembal had a further testimony to give in against the prisoner which was truly admirable.

Being desirous to furnish himself with a dog, he applied himself to buy one of this Martin, who had a bitch with whelps in her house. But she not letting him have his choice, he said he would supply himself then at one Blezdel's. Having marked a puppy which he liked at Blezdel's, he met George Martin, the husband of the prisoner, going by, who asked him whether he would not have one of his wife's puppies, and he answered no. The same day one Edmond Eliot, being at Martin's house, heard George Martin relate where this Kembal had been and what he had said. Whereupon Susanna Martin replied, "If I live, I'll give him puppies enough!"

Within a few days after, this Kembal coming out of the woods, there arose a little black cloud in the northwest, and Kembal immediately felt a force upon him which made him not able to avoid running upon the stumps of trees that were before him, albeit he had a broad plain cartway before him; but though he had his ax also on his shoulder to endanger him in his falls, he could not forbear going out of his way to tumble over them. When he came below the meetinghouse, there appeared unto him a little thing like a puppy, of a darkish color, and it shot backwards and forwards between his legs. He had courage to use all possible endeavors of cutting it with his ax, but he could not hit it. The puppy gave a jump from him and went, as to him it seemed, into the ground. Going a little further, there appeared unto him a black puppy, somewhat bigger than the first, but as black as a coal. Its motions were quicker than those of his ax; it flew at his belly and away; then at his throat; so, over his shoulder one way, and then over his shoulder another way. His heart now began to fail him, and he thought the dog would have tore his throat out. But he recovered himself, and called upon God in his distress; and naming the name of JESUS CHRIST, it vanished away at once.

The deponent spoke not one word of these accidents for fear

of affrighting his wife. But the next morning Edmond Eliot going into Martin's house, this woman asked him where Kembal was. He replied, At home abed, for ought he knew. She returned, "They say he was frighted last night." Eliot asked, "With what?" She answered, "With puppies." Eliot asked where she heard of it, for he had heard nothing of it. She rejoined, "About the town." Although Kembal had mentioned the matter to no creature living.

VIII. William Brown testified that heaven having blessed him with a most pious and prudent wife, this wife of his one day met with Susanna Martin; but when she approached just unto her, Martin vanished out of sight, and left her extremely affrighted. After which time the said Martin often appeared unto her, giving her no little trouble; and when she did come, she was visited with birds that sorely pecked and pricked her. And sometimes a bunch like a pullet's egg would rise in her throat ready to choke her, till she cried out, "Witch, you shan't choke me!"

While this good woman was in this extremity, the church appointed a day of prayer on her behalf, whereupon her trouble ceased; she saw not Martin as formerly, and the church instead of their fast gave thanks for her deliverance. But a considerable while after, she being summoned to give in some evidence at the court against this Martin, quickly thereupon this Martin came behind her, while she was milking her cow, and said unto her, "For thy defaming me at court, I'll make thee the miserablest creature in the world." Soon after which, she fell into a strange kind of distemper, and became horribly frantic and incapable of any reasonable action—the physicians declaring that her distemper was preternatural, and that some devil had certainly bewitched her. And in that condition she now remained.

IX. Sarah Atkinson testified that Susanna Martin came from Amesbury to their house at Newbury in an extraordinary season, when it was not fit for any to travel. She came (as she said unto Atkinson) all that long way on foot. She bragged and showed how dry she was; nor could it be perceived that so much as the soles of her shoes were wet. Atkinson was amazed at it, and professed that she should herself have been wet up to the knees, if she had then came so far. But Martin replied, *She scorned to be drabbled!* It was noted that this testimony upon her trial cast her in a very singular confusion.

X. John Pressy testified that being one evening very unaccountably bewildered near a field of Martin's, and several times as one under an enchantment returning to the place he had left, at length he saw a marvelous light, about the bigness of a half bushel, near two rod out of the way. He went and struck at it with a stick, and laid it on with all his might. He gave it near forty blows, and felt it a palpable substance. But going from it, his heels were struck up, and he was laid with his back on the ground, sliding, as he thought, into a pit; from whence he recovered by taking hold on the bush (although afterwards he could find no such pit in the place). Having, after his recovery, gone five or six rod, he saw Susanna Martin standing on his left hand, as the light had done before; but they changed no words with one another. He could scarce find his house on his return, but at length he got home extremely affrighted. The next day it was upon inquiry understood that Martin was in a miserable condition by pains and hurts that were upon her.

It was further testified by this deponent that after he had given in some evidence against Susanna Martin many years ago, she gave him foul words about it and said, *He should never prosper more;* particularly, *That he should never have more than two cows; that though he was never so likely to have more, yet he should never have them.* And that from that very day to this, namely, for twenty years together, he could never exceed that number, but some strange thing or other still prevented his having any more.

XI. Jervis Ring testified that about seven years ago he was oftentimes and grievously oppressed in the night, but saw not who troubled him until at last, he lying perfectly awake, plainly saw Susanna Martin approach him. She came to him and forcibly bit him by the finger, so that the print of the bite is now, so long after, to be seen upon him.

XII. But besides all of these evidences, there was a most wonderful account of one Joseph Ring produced on this occasion.

This man had been strangely carried about by demons from

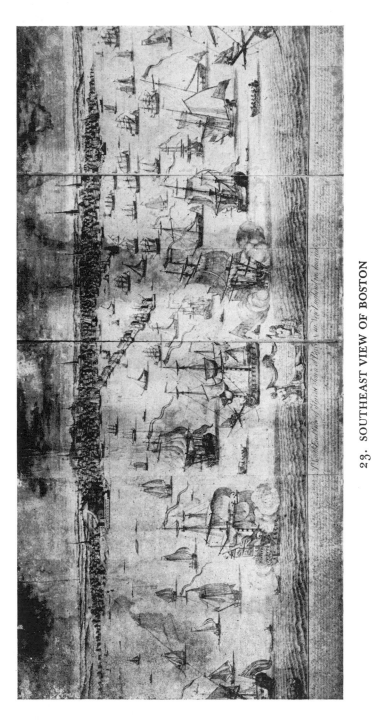

23. SOUTHEAST VIEW OF BOSTON

Line engraving by I. Harris, *ca.* 1722

one witch-meeting to another for near two years together; and for one-quarter of this time they have made him and keep him dumb, though he is now again able to speak. There was one T. H. who having, as 'tis judged, a design of engaging this Joseph Ring in a snare of devilism, contrived awhile to bring this Ring two shillings in debt unto him.

Afterwards, this poor man would be visited with unknown shapes, and this T. H. sometimes among them, who would force him away with them unto unknown places, where he saw meetings, feastings, dancings; and after his return, wherein they hurried him along through the air, he gave demonstrations to the neighbors that he had indeed been so transported. When he was brought unto these hellish meetings, one of the first things they still did unto him was to give him a knock on the back, whereupon he was ever as if bound with chains, incapable of stirring out of the place, till they should release him. He related that there often came to him a man who presented him a book whereto he should have him set his hand, promising to him that he should have then even what he would, and presenting him with all the delectable things, persons, and places that he could imagine. But he refusing to subscribe, the business would end with dreadful shapes, noises, and screeches, which almost scared him out of his wits. Once with the book there was a pen offered him, and an inkhorn with liquor in it that seemed like blood; but he never touched it.

This man did now affirm that he saw the prisoner at several of those hellish rendezvous.

Note. This woman was one of the most impudent, scurrilous, wicked creatures in the world; and she did now throughout her whole trial discover herself to be such an one. Yet when she was asked what she had to say for herself, her chief plea was, *That she had led a most virtuous and holy life.*

8

FOREST WARS

On Marston Moor rival armies battled each other across the open heath. Heavy ordnance cannonaded massed troops; charging cavalry scattered pikesmen and musketeers with brandished steel; serried rows of foot soldiers shot their muskets in unison at the onrushing foe; brilliantly dressed officers rode up and down the ranks directing strategy. Thus England fought her Civil War, in the spectacular manner of European military traditions.

At about the same time another mortal conflict was being waged across the sea, as New England settlers and Indian tribes grappled for race mastery. But, save that men were killing each other, the two scenes offered no points of resemblance. In place of the open field and the massed army, little bands of stealthy men sneaked through thicket and swamp and gully. The farmers called to arms against the savages found scant use for cavalry, armor, swords, pikes, uniforms, standards, or baggage trains. They discarded the cumbersome matchlock musket for the quicker-firing flintlock, carried pistols instead of swords, and so traveled light with heavy fire power. From the Indian they rapidly copied the techniques of ambush, torture, and total war on mothers and babes, homes and goods; overnight they learned to fight behind wooden stockades and blockhouses instead of stone castles and manor houses, and to prize the dripping scalp rather than gleaming silver as trophies of the slaughter. Warriors in the New World might well sigh for the safer glories of the old, as did this veteran of Indian combat:

> And now I am old, I would fain die a natural death or like a soldier in the field, with honor, and not to have a sharp stake set in the ground and thrust into my fundament, and to have my skin flayed off by piecemeal, and cut in pieces and bits, and my flesh roasted and thrust down my throat, as these people have done, and I know will be done to the chiefest people in the country by hundreds, if God should deliver us into their hands, as justly he may for our sins.

To the Puritans, the red men were literally scourges of the Devil, who could contaminate their souls as well as maim their

*bodies. God's chosen saints would never traffic with these hea-
then sinners, hence the New Englanders failed to achieve the
relative amity enjoyed by the Quakers, Dutch, and French. The
bloodiest Indian battles of the seventeenth century occurred on
New England soil.*

*The Puritans fought their forest neighbors on two levels,
the spiritual and the military, and the combination served them
well. Each church congregation resolved itself easily into a town
assembly to vote or a training company to drill, for the Puritan
village acted as a solid social unit. Pastors exhorted their flock
to the battle, and interpreted the providences that signaled God's
favor or wrath. Only when their chaplain prayed to the Lord
for guidance, and received his answer, would Captain Mason's
men consent to attack the Pequots by land and not by sea.*

*Rugged, out-of-doors farmers and fishermen, the New England
civilians took readily to forest fighting and produced some
doughty Indian slayers. Heroes of the Pequot War and King
Philip's War like John Underhill and Benjamin Church knew
perfectly the woodland haunts and tactics of their foes, and
tracked them through the swamps like bloodhounds. The red
men too could point to valiant leaders. Canonchet, a Narragansett sachem, spurned to keep his life on his captor's terms, for "he
liked it well that he should die before his heart was soft or had
spoken anything unworthy of himself."*

*In the end personal valor counted for less than the stodgy
factor of food reserves; the Indians could not fight and hunt at
the same time. After a winter of King Philip's War they were
living off groundnuts and plundered cattle, which only upset
their stomachs. The historian Hubbard tells how one Indian,
"having eaten much horseflesh, complained that he had before
eaten horse, and now horse began to eat him, meaning some
deadly disease growing upon his eating such rank flesh, unwhole-
some for their bodies, especially without salt, as their usual
manner is."*

*By our standards these were toy wars. Massachusetts assigned
twenty men to help Connecticut against the Pequots. But in fact
they were life-and-death struggles. The Pequots were completely
liquidated as a tribe, the survivors being forced to join the Narragansetts or Mohegans. Before King Philip's league was crushed,*

one out of every sixteen New England men had died, twenty Massachusetts and Rhode Island towns had been destroyed or abandoned, and ninety thousand pounds had been spent. Weakened New England lost its charter and independence to the Crown shortly after. We find, too, the customary social consequences, as in mammoth wars. After the Pequot struggle, veterans get land grants, defenses are expanded, allies enter hot debate as to who won the war (Connecticut with her ninety or Massachusetts with her twenty soldiers), and the leading actors publish conflicting memoirs. With the personal narratives of these Indian tamers begins the literature of American military autobiography, and the tradition that can boast of Grant and Eisenhower commences worthily enough with the homespun chronicles of selectman John Underhill and carpenter Ben Church.

The quotations are from "Leift Lion Gardener his relation of the Pequot Warres," in the *Collections of the Massachusetts Historical Society,* 3rd series, III (1833), 152; William Hubbard, *A Narrative of the Troubles with the Indians in New England, from the first planting thereof in the year 1607 to this present year 1677* (Boston, 1677), 81-82, and "A Postscript," 8.

THE PEQUOT WAR

Captain John Underhill

(Recognizing that events had gone beyond conventional hostilities, the General Court at Hartford ordered a war against the Pequot Indians on May 1, 1637. The Pequots were a formidable tribe which had invaded the lush Connecticut Valley before the whites did, forced tribute from the Narragansetts to their east and the Mohegans to their west, and sparred with Dutch traders. When English settlers from Massachusetts moved into Connecticut in 1635, an explosive situation developed immediately, which resulted in an uneasy alliance between the English and the Mohegans against their common enemy. Provoked by a wanton murder, Massachusetts sent an expedition against Block Island, an Indian stronghold, in 1636, and another the next year into Connecticut under Captain John Underhill, who helped the Connecticut forces annihilate a large body of Pequots at Mystic Fort. The Pequots surrendered July 13, 1637, ending the first war in American history.

John Underhill, author of the following crude but classic account of the Massachusetts part in the war, had a checkered career in the colonies. In the main he was a professional soldier, serving as a cadet in the guard of the Prince of Orange, coming to Boston in 1630 to organize the militia, and, after the Pequot trouble, fighting Indians in New York for the Dutch, and then fighting the Dutch for the English. But he also mixed in the Puritans' antimonian controversy, for which he was disfranchised, tried to start an independence movement in New Hampshire, for which he was chastised, and confessed to adultery, for which he was excommunicated.)

I shall not spend time (for my other occasions will not permit) to write largely of every particular but shall, as briefly as I may, perform these two things: first, give a true narration of the warlike proceedings that hath been in New England these two years last past; secondly, I shall discover to the reader divers places in New England that would afford special accommodations to such persons as will plant upon them.* I had not time to do either of these as they deserved; but wanting time to do it as the nature of

* The passages on the second topic have been omitted.

the thing required, I shall, according to my ability, begin with a relation of our warlike proceedings, and will interweave the special places fit for new plantations, with their descriptions, as I shall find occasion in the following discourse. But I shall, according to my promise, begin with a true relation of the New England wars against the Block Islanders, and that insolent and barbarous nation called the Pequots, whom, by the sword of the Lord and a few feeble instruments, soldiers not accustomed to war, were drove out of their country and slain by the sword to the number of fifteen hundred souls, in the space of two months and less; so as their country is fully subdued and fallen into the hands of the English. And to the end that God's name might have the glory, and his people see his power and magnify his honor for his great goodness, I have endeavored according to my weak ability to set forth the full relation of the war, from the first rise to the end of the victory.

The cause of our war against the Block Islanders was for taking away the life of one Master John Oldham, who made it his common course to trade amongst the Indians. He coming to Block Island to drive trade with them, the islanders came into his boat and, having got a full view of commodities which gave them good content, consulted how they might destroy him and his company, to the end they might clothe their bloody flesh with his lawful garments. The Indians having laid the plot, into the boat they came to trade, as they pretended; watching their opportunities, knocked him in the head, and martyred him most barbarously, to the great grief of his poor distressed servants, which by the providence of God were saved. This island lying in the roadway to Lord Saye and the Lord Brooke's plantation, a certain seaman called to John Gallop, master of the small navigation standing along to the Massachusetts Bay, and seeing a boat under sail close aboard the island, and perceiving the sails to be unskillfully managed, bred in him a jealousy whether that the island Indians had not bloodily taken the life of our countrymen, and made themselves master of their goods. Suspecting this, he bore up to them, and approaching near them was confirmed that his jealousy was just. Seeing Indians in the boat, and knowing her to be the vessel of Master Oldham, and not seeing him there, he gave fire upon them and slew some; others leaped overboard, besides two of the number which he preserved alive and brought to the Bay.

The blood of the innocent called for vengeance. God stirred up the heart of the honored governor, Master Henry Vane, and the rest of the worthy magistrates, to send forth a hundred well-appointed soldiers, under the conduct of Captain John Endicott, and in company with him that had command, Captain John Underhill, Captain Nathan Turner, Captain William Jenningson, besides other inferior officers. I would not have the world wonder at the great number of commanders to so few men, but know that the Indians' fight far differs from the Christian practice. For they most commonly divide themselves into small bodies, so that we are forced to neglect our usual way and to subdivide our divisions to answer theirs, not thinking it any disparagement to any captain to go forth against an enemy with a squadron of men, taking the ground from the old and ancient practice when they chose captains of hundreds and captains of thousands, captains of fifties and captains of tens. We conceive a captain signifieth the chief in way of command of anybody committed to his charge for the time being, whether of more or less, it makes no matter in power, though in honor it does.

Coming to an anchor before the island, we espied an Indian walking by the shore in a desolate manner, as though he had received intelligence of our coming. Which Indian gave just ground to some to conclude that the body of the people had deserted the island.

But others knowing them for the generality to be a warlike nation, a people that spend most of their time in the study of warlike policy, were not persuaded that they would upon so slender terms forsake the island, but rather suspected they might lie behind a bank, much like the form of a barricade. Myself with others rode with a shallop and made towards the shore, having in the boat a dozen armed soldiers. We drawing near to the place of landing, a number rose from behind the barricade, between fifty or sixty able fighting men, men as straight as arrows, very tall and of active bodies, having their arrows notched. They drew near to the waterside and let fly at the soldiers, as though they had meant to have made an end of us all in a moment. They shot a young gentleman in the neck through a collar, for stiffness as if it had been an oaken board, and entered his flesh a good depth. Myself received an arrow through my coat sleeve, a second against my helmet on the forehead; so as if God in his providence had not moved the heart of my wife to persuade me to carry it along with me (which I was unwilling to do), I had been slain.

Give me leave to observe two things from hence. First, when the hour of death is not yet come, you see God useth weak means to keep his purpose unviolated. Secondly, let no man despise advice and counsel of his wife, though she be a woman. It were strange to nature to think a man should be bound to fulfill the humor of a woman, as to what arms he should carry; but you see God will have it so, that a woman should overcome a man. What with Delilah's flattery and with her mournful tears, they must and will have their desire, when the hand of God goes along in the matter; and this is to accomplish his own will. Therefore let the clamor be quenched I daily hear in my ears, that New England usurp over their wives, and keep them in servile subjection. The country is wronged in this matter, as in many things else. Let this precedent satisfy the doubtful, for that comes from the example of a rude soldier. If they be so courteous to their wives as to take their advice in warlike matters, how much more kind is the tender, affectionate husband to honor his wife as the weaker vessel? Yet mistake not. I say not that they are bound to call their wives in council, though they are bound to take their private advice (so far as they see it make for their advantage and their good); instance Abraham.

But to the matter. The arrows flying thick about us, we made haste to the shore; but the surf of the sea being great hindered us, so as we could scarce discharge a musket but were forced to make haste to land. Drawing near the shore, through the strength of wind and the hollowness of the sea we durst not adventure to run ashore, but were forced to wade up to the middle; but once having got up off our legs, we gave fire upon them. They finding our bullets to outreach their arrows, fled before us. In the meanwhile Colonel Endicott made to the shore, and some of this number also repulsed him at his landing, but hurt none. We thought they would stand it out with us, but they perceiving we were in earnest, fled and left their wigwams (or houses) and provisions to the use of our soldiers. Having set forth our sentinels and laid out our pardues, we betook ourselves to the guard, expecting hourly they would fall upon us; but they observed the old rule, " 'Tis good sleeping in a whole skin," and left us free from an alarm.

The next day we set upon our march, the Indians being retired into swamps, so as we could not find them. We burnt and spoiled both houses and corn in great abundance, but they kept themselves in obscurity. Captain Turner stepping aside to a swamp met with some few Indians and charged upon them, changing some few bullets for arrows. Himself received a shot upon the breast of his corselet, as if it had been pushed with a pike, and if he had not had it on he had lost his life.

A pretty passage worthy observation. We had an Indian with us that was an interpreter. Being in English clothes, and a gun in his hand, he was spied by the islanders, who called out to him, "What are you, an Indian or an Englishman?" "Come hither," said he, "and I will tell you." He pulls up his cock and let fly at one of them, and without question was the death of him.

Having spent that day in burning and spoiling the island, we took up the quarter for that night. About midnight myself went out with ten men about two miles from our quarter, and discovered the most eminent plantation they had in the island, where was much corn, many wigwams, and great heaps of mats; but fearing lest we should make an alarm by setting fire on them, we left them as we found them, and peaceably departed to our quarter; and the next morning with forty men marched up to the same plantation, burnt their houses, cut down their corn, and destroyed some of their dogs instead of men, which they left in their wigwams.

Passing on towards the waterside to embark our soldiers, we met with several famous wigwams, with great heaps of pleasant corn ready shelled; but not able to bring it away, we did throw their mats upon it, and set fire and burnt it. Many well-wrought mats our soldiers brought from thence, and several delightful baskets. The Indians playing least in sight, we spent our time and could no more advantage ourselves than we had already done, and having slain some fourteen and maimed others, we embarked ourselves, and set sail for Saybrook Fort, where we lay through distress of weather four days. Then we departed.

The Pequots having slain one Captain Norton and Captain Stone with seven more of their company, order was given us to visit them, sailing along the Nahanticot shore with five vessels. The Indians spying of us came running in multitudes along the waterside, crying, "What cheer, Englishmen, what cheer, what do you come for?" They not thinking we intended war, went on cheerfully until they come to Pequot River. We, thinking it the best way, did forbear to answer them: first that we might the better be able to run through the work; secondly, that by delaying of them, we might drive them in security, to the end we might have the more advantage of them. But they seeing we would make no answer, kept on their course, and cried, "What, Englishmen, what cheer, what cheer, are you hoggery, will you cram us?" (That is, Are you angry, will you kill us, and do you come to fight?) That night the Nahanticot Indians and the Pequots made fire on both sides of the river, fearing we would land in the night. They made most doleful and woeful cries all the night, so that we could scarce rest, hallooing one to another, and giving the word from place to place to gather their forces together, fearing the English were come to war against them.

The next morning they sent early aboard an ambassador, a grave senior, a man of good understanding, portly carriage, grave and majestical in his expressions. He demanded of us what the end of our coming was. To which we answered that the governors of the Bay sent us to demand the heads of those persons that had slain Captain Norton and Captain Stone, and the rest of their company, and that it was not the custom of the English to suffer murderers to live; and therefore, if they desired their own peace and welfare, they will peaceably answer our expectation, and give us the heads of the murderers.

They being a witty and ingenious nation, their ambassador labored to excuse the matter, and answered, "We know not that any of ours have slain any English. True it is," saith he, "we have slain a number of men; but consider the ground of it. Not long before the coming of these English into the river, there was a certain [Dutch] vessel that came to us in way of trade. We used them well, and traded with them, and took them to be such as would not wrong us in the least matter. But our sachem or prince coming aboard, they laid a plot how they might destroy him; which plot discovereth itself by the event, as followeth. They keeping their boat aboard, and not desirous of our company, gave us leave to stand hallooing ashore, that they might work their mischievous plot. But as we stood they called to us, and demanded of us a bushel of wampumpeke (which is our money). This they demanded for his ransom. This peal did ring terribly in our ears, to demand so much for the life of our prince, whom we thought was in the hands of honest men, and we had never wronged them. But we saw there was no remedy; their expectation must be granted, or else they would not send him ashore, which they promised they would do if we would answer their desires. We sent them so much aboard, according to demand, and they, according to their promise, sent him ashore, but first slew him. This much exasperated our spirits and made us vow a revenge.

"Suddenly after came these [English] captains with a vessel into the river, and pretended to trade with us, as the former did. We did not discountenance them for the present, but took our opportunity and came aboard. The sachem's son succeeding his father was the man that came into the cabin of Captain Stone, and Captain Stone having drunk more than did him good fell backwards on the bed asleep. The sagamore took his opportunity and, having a little hatchet under his garment, therewith knocked him in the head. Some being upon the deck and others under, suspected some such thing; for the other Indians aboard had orders to proceed against the rest at one time. But the English, spying treachery, run immediately into the cookroom and, with a firebrand, had thought to have blown up the Indians by setting fire to the powder. These Devil's instruments,* spying this plot of the English, leaped overboard as the powder was a-firing and saved themselves; but all the English were blown up. This was the manner of their bloody action."

Saith the ambassador to us, "Could ye blame us for revenging

---

* Underhill keeps mixing up the ambassador's and his own points of view.

so cruel a murder? For we distinguish not between the Dutch and English, but took them to be one nation, and therefore we do not conceive that we wronged you, for they slew our King; and thinking these captains to be of the same nation and people as those that slew him made us set upon this course of revenge."

Our answer was, "You are able to distinguish between Dutch and English, having had sufficient experience of both nations; and therefore, seeing you have slain the King of England's subjects, we come to demand an account of their blood, for we ourselves are liable to account for them."

The answer of the ambassador was, "We know no difference between the Dutch and the English; they are both stranger to us, we took them to be all one; therefore we crave pardon; we have not willfully wronged the English."

"This excuse will not serve our turns, for we have sufficient testimony that you know the English from the Dutch. We must have the heads of those persons that have slain ours, or else we will fight with you."

He answered, "Understanding the ground of your coming, I will entreat you to give me liberty to go ashore, and I shall inform the body of the people what your intent and resolution is; and if you will stay aboard, I will bring you a sudden answer."

We did grant him liberty to get ashore, and ourselves followed suddenly after before the war was proclaimed. He, seeing us land our forces, came with a message to entreat us to come no nearer but stand in a valley, which had between us and them an ascent that took our sight from them; but they might see us to hurt us, to our prejudice. Thus from the first beginning to the end of the action they carried themselves very subtilely; but we, not willing to be at their direction, marched up to the ascent, having set our men in battalia. He came and told us he had inquired for the sachem, that we might come to a parley, but neither of the two princes were at home; they were gone to Long Island.

Our reply was, "We must not be put off thus, we know the sachem is in the plantation, and therefore bring him to us that we may speak with him, or else we will beat up the drums and march through the country and spoil your corn."

His answer: "If you will but stay a little while, I will step to the plantation and seek for them."

We gave them leave to take their own course, and used as much patience as ever men might, considering the gross abuse they offered us, holding us above an hour in vain hopes. They sent an Indian to tell us that Mommenoteck was found and would appear before us suddenly. This brought us to a new stand the space of an hour more. There came a third Indian persuading us to have a little further patience, and he would not tarry, for he had assembled the body of the Pequots together, to know who the parties were that had slain these Englishmen. But seeing that they did in this interim convey away their wives and children, and bury their chiefest goods, we perceived at length they would fly from us; but we were patient and bore with them, in expectation to have the greater blow upon them. The last messenger brought us this intelligence from the sachem, that if we would but lay down our arms, and approach about thirty paces from them, and meet the heathen prince, he would cause his men to do the like, and then we shall come to a parley.

But we seeing their drift was to get our arms, we rather chose to beat up the drum and bid them battle. Marching into a champaign field, we displayed our colors; but none would come near us, but standing remotely off did laugh at us for our patience. We suddenly set upon our march, and gave fire to as many as we could come near, firing their wigwams, spoiling their corn, and many other necessaries that they had buried in the ground we raked up, which the soldiers had for booty. Thus we spent the day burning and spoiling the country. Towards night embarked ourselves. The next morning we landed on the Nahanticot shore, where we were served in like nature; no Indians would come near us, but run from us as the deer from the dogs. But having burnt and spoiled what we could light on, we embarked our men and set sail for the Bay, having ended this exploit. We came off with one man wounded in the leg, but certain numbers of theirs slain and many wounded.

This was the substance of the first year's service. Now followeth the service performed in the second year.

This insolent nation, seeing we had used much lenity towards them, and themselves not able to make good use of our patience, set upon a course of greater insolence than before, and slew all they found in their way. They came near Saybrook Fort and made many proud challenges and dared them out to fight.*

The lieutenant went out with ten armed men, and starting three Indians they changed some few shot for arrows. Pursuing them, a hundred more started out of the ambushments, and almost surrounded him and his company; and some they slew, others they maimed, and forced them to retreat to their fort, so that it was a special providence of God that they were not all slain. Some of their arms they got from them, others put on the English clothes and came to the fort jeering of them and calling, "Come and fetch your Englishmen's clothes again; come out and fight, if you dare; you dare not fight; you are all like women. We have one amongst us that if he could kill but one of you more, he would be equal with God, and as the Englishman's God is, so would he be." This blasphemous speech troubled the hearts of the soldiers, but they knew not how to remedy it, in respect of their weakness.

The Connecticut plantation, understanding the insolence of the enemy to be so great, sent down a certain number of soldiers, under the conduct of Captain John Mason, for to strengthen the fort. The enemy, lying hovering about the fort, continually took notice of the supplies that were come, and forbore drawing near it as before; and letters were immediately sent to the Bay, to that right worshipful gentleman, Master Henry Vane, for a speedy supply to strengthen the fort. For assuredly unless supply suddenly came, in reason all would be lost and fall into the hands of the enemy. This was the trouble and perplexity that lay upon the spirits of the poor garrison. Upon serious consideration, the governor and Council sent forth myself, with twenty armed soldiers, to supply the necessity of those distressed persons, and to take the government of that place for the space of three months. Relief being come, Captain John Mason with the rest of his company returned to the plantation again.

We sometimes fell out, with a matter of twenty soldiers, to see whether we could discover the enemy or no. They seeing us (lying in ambush) gave us leave to pass by them, considering we were too hot for them to meddle with us. Our men being com-

* As the commander of the Saybrook fort, Captain Gardiner, pointed out, the Massachusetts men pillaged and departed, leaving the Connecticut people to suffer the Pequots' reprisals.

pletely armed, with corselets, muskets, bandoleers, rests, and swords (as they themselves related afterward), did much daunt them. Thus we spent a matter of six weeks before we could have anything to do with them, persuading ourselves that all things had been well.

But they, seeing there was no advantage more to be had against the fort, enterprised a new action and fell upon Watertown, now called Wethersfield, with two hundred Indians. Before they came to attempt the place they put in to a certain river, an obscure small river running into the main, where they encamped and refreshed themselves, and fitted themselves for their service, and by break of day attempted their enterprise, and slew nine men, women, and children. Having finished their action they suddenly returned again, bringing with them two maids captives. They put poles in their canoes, as we put masts in our boats, and upon them hung our English men's and women's shirts and smocks, instead of sails, and in way of bravado came along in sight of us as we stood upon Saybrook Fort. And seeing them pass along in such a triumphant manner, we much feared they had enterprised some desperate action upon the English. We gave fire with a piece of ordnance, and shot among their canoes. And though they were a mile from us, yet the bullet grazed not above twenty yards over the canoe where the poor maids were. It was a special providence of God it did not hit them, for then should we have been deprived of the sweet observation of God's providence in their deliverance. We were not able to make out after them, being destitute of means, boats and the like.

★

I told you before that when the Pequots heard and saw Saybrook Fort was supplied, they forbore to visit us. But the old serpent, according to his first malice, stirred them up against the Church of Christ, and in such a furious manner as our people were so far disturbed and affrighted with their boldness that they scarce durst rest in their beds, for fear of their persons and cattle. So insolent were these wicked imps grown that like the Devil, their commander, they run up and down as roaring lions, compassing all corners of the country for a prey, seeking whom they might devour. It being death to them for to rest without some wicked employment or other, they still plotted how they might wickedly attempt some bloody enterprise upon our poor native countrymen.

One Master Tilly, master of a vessel, being brought to an anchor in Connecticut River, went ashore, not suspecting the bloody-mindedness of those persons, who fell upon him and a man with him, whom they wickedly and barbarously slew; and (by relation) brought him home, tied him to a stake, flayed his skin off, put hot embers between the flesh and the skin, cut off his fingers and toes, and made hatbands of them. Thus barbarous was their cruelty! Would not this have moved the hearts of men to hazard blood, and life, and all they had, to overcome such a wicked insolent nation?

But letters coming into the Bay that this attempt was made upon Wethersfield in Connecticut River, and that they had slain nine men, women, and children and taken two maids captives, the Council gave order to send supply. In the meanwhile the Connecticut plantations sent down one hundred armed soldiers, under the conduct of Captain John Mason and Lieutenant Seily, with other inferior officers, who by commission were bound to rendezvous at Saybrook Fort, and to consult with those that had command there, to enterprise some stratagem upon these bloody Indians. The Connecticut company having with them threescore Mohegans, whom the Pequots had drove out of their lawful possessions, these Indians were earnest to join with the English, or at least to be under their conduct, that they might revenge themselves of those bloody enemies of theirs. The English, perceiving their earnest desire that way, gave them liberty to follow the company, but not to join in confederation with them. The Indians promised to be faithful and to do them what service lay in their power. But now there arose great jealousy in the hearts of those that had chief oversight of the company, fearing that the Indians in time of greatest trial might revolt and turn their backs against those they professed to be their friends, and join with the Pequots. This perplexed the hearts of many very much, because they had had no experience of their fidelity. But Captain Mason having sent down a shallop to Saybrook Fort, and sent the Mohegans overland to meet and rendezvous at Saybrook Fort, himself came down in a great massy vessel, which was slow in coming and very long detained by cross winds. The Indians coming to Saybrook were desirous to fall out on the Lord's day to see whether they could find any Pequots near the fort, persuading themselves that the place was not destitute of some of their enemies. But it being the Lord's day, order was given to them to forbear until the next day. Given liberty, they fell out early in the morning and brought home five Pequots' heads, one prisoner, and mortally wounded a seventh. This mightily encouraged the hearts of all, and we took this as a pledge of their further fidelity.*

Taking a boat, I rowed up to meet the rest of the forces. The minister, one Master Stone, that was sent to instruct the company, was then in prayer solemnly before God in the midst of the soldiers; and this passage worthy observation I set down, because the providence of God might be taken notice of, and his name glorified, that is so ready for to honor his own ordinance. The hearts of all in general being much perplexed, fearing the infidelity of these Mohegans, having not heard what an exploit they had wrought, it pleased God to put into the heart of Master Stone this passage in prayer, while I lay under the vessel and heard it (he not knowing that God had sent him a messenger to tell him his prayer was granted). "O Lord God, if it be thy blessed will, vouchsafe so much favor to thy poor distressed servants as to manifest one pledge of thy love, that may confirm us of the fidelity of these Indians towards us, that now pretend friendship and service to us, that our hearts may be encouraged the more in this work of thine." Immediately stepping up, I told him that God had answered his desire, and that I had brought this news, that those Indians had brought in five Pequots' heads, one prisoner, and wounded one mortally; which did much encourage the hearts of all, and replenished them exceedingly, and gave them all occasion to rejoice and be thankful to God.

* Underhill neglects to mention the treatment given this Pequot prisoner. "They tied one of his legs to a post, and twenty men, with a rope tied to the other, pulled him in pieces: Captain Underhill shooting a pistol through him to dispatch him." (Philip Vincent, "A True Relation of the late Battell fought in New-England, between the English and the Pequot Salvages," London, 1638.)

A little before we set forth, came a certain ship from the Dutch plantation and cast an anchor under the command of our ordnance. We desired the master to come ashore. The master and merchant, willing to answer our expectation, came forth, and sitting with us awhile unexpectedly revealed their intent, that they were bound for Pequot River to trade. Knowing the custom of war that it was not the practice, in a case of this nature, to suffer others to go and trade with them our enemies, with such commodities as might be prejudicial unto us and advantageous to them, as kettles or the like, which make them arrowheads, we gave command to them not to stir, alleging that our forces were intended daily to fall upon them. This being unkindly taken, it bred some agitations between their several commanders; but God was pleased, out of his love, to carry things in such a sweet, moderate way as all turned to his glory and his people's good.

These men, seeing they could not have liberty to go upon their design, gave us a note under their hands that if we would give them liberty to depart, they would endeavor to the utmost of their ability to release those two captive maids, and this would be the chief scope and drift of their design. Having these promises, depending upon their faithfulness, we gave them liberty. They set sail and went to Pequot River, and sent to shore the master of the vessel to Sassacus, their prince, to crave liberty to trade. And what would they trade for but the English maids? Which Sassacus much disliked. Suddenly withdrawing himself, the master returned back to the vessel, and by way of policy allured seven Indians into the bark, some of them being their prime men. Having them aboard, he acquainted them with his intent, and told them without the Dutch might have the two captives delivered safely aboard, they must keep them as prisoners and pledges, until such time they had treated with the sagamore. One of the Dutch called to them on the shore, and told them they must bring the two captive maids, if they would have the seven Indians.

"And therefore, briefly, if you will bring them, tell us; if not, we set sail, and will turn all your Indians overboard in the main ocean, so soon as ever we come out."

They taking this to be a jest, slighted what was said unto them.

The Dutch weighing anchor set sail and drew near the mouth of the river. Then the Pequots discerned they were in earnest, and desired them to return and come to an anchor, and they would answer their expectation. So they brought the two maids, and delivered them safely aboard, and the Dutch returned to them the seven Indians. Then they set sail and came to Saybrook Fort.

Now for the examination of the two maids after they arrived at Saybrook Fort. The eldest of them was about sixteen years of age. Demanding of her how they had used her, she told us they did solicit her to uncleanness*; but her heart being much broken and afflicted under that bondage she was cast in, had brought to her consideration these thoughts: "How shall I commit this great evil and sin against my God?" Their hearts were much taken up with the consideration of God's just displeasure to them, that had lived under so prudent means of grace as they did, and had been so ungrateful toward God, and slighted that means, so that God's hand was justly upon them for their remissness in all their ways.

The Indians carried them from place to place, and showed them their forts and curious wigwams and houses, and encouraged them to be merry. But the poor souls, as Israel, could not frame themselves to any delight or mirth under so strange a King. Hanging their harps upon the willow trees, they gave their minds to sorrow; hope was their chiefest food, and tears their constant drink. Behind the rocks and under the trees, the eldest spent her breath in supplication to her God; and though the eldest was but young, yet must I confess the sweet affection to God for his great kindness and fatherly love she daily received from the Lord, which sweetened all her sorrows and gave her constant hope that God would not nor could not forget her poor distressed soul and body. "Because," saith she, "his loving-kindness appeareth to me in an unspeakable manner, though sometimes I cried out, David-like, I shall one day perish by the hands of Saul, I shall one day die by the hands of these barbarous Indians; and specially if our people should come forth to war against them. Then is there no hope of deliverance. Then must I perish. Then will they cut me off in malice." But suddenly the

* This is contrary to all evidence on Indian treatment of white women.

24. DEFEAT OF THE PEQUOTS

John Underhill, *Newes from America;* London, 1638

poor soul was ready to quarrel with itself. "Why should I distrust God? Do not I daily see the love of God unspeakably to my
poor distressed soul? And he hath said he will never leave me nor
forsake me. Therefore I will not fear what man can do unto me,
knowing God to be above man, and man can do nothing without God's permission."

These were the words that fell from her mouth when she was
examined in Saybrook Fort. I having command of Saybrook
Fort, she spake these things upon examination, in my hearing.

★

Having embarked our soldiers, we weighed anchor at Saybrook Fort and set sail for the Narragansett Bay, deluding the
Pequots thereby, for they expected us to fall into the Pequot
River; our crossing their expectation bred in them a security.
We landed our men in the Narragansett Bay and marched overland above two days' journey before we came to Pequot. Quartering the last night's march within two miles of the place, we
set forth about one of the clock in the morning, having sufficient
intelligence that they knew nothing of our coming. Drawing near
to the fort, we yielded up ourselves to God, and entreated his
assistance in so weighty an enterprise. We set on our march to
surround the fort: Captain John Mason approaching to the west
end, where it had an entrance to pass into it; myself marching
to the south side, surrounding the fort; the Indians, for we had
about three hundred of them, placed outside of our soldiers in
a ring battalia, giving a volley of shot upon the fort.

So remarkable it appeared to us as we could not but admire at
the providence of God in it that soldiers so unexpert in the use
of their arms should give so complete a volley, as though the finger of God had touched both match and flint. Which volley
being given at break of day, and the Pequots fast asleep for the
most part, bred in them such a terror that they brake forth into
a most doleful cry; so as if God had not fitted the hearts of men
for the service, it would have bred in us a commiseration towards
them. But every man, being bereaved of pity, fell upon the work
without compassion, considering the blood they had shed of our
native countrymen and how barbarously they had dealt with
them and slain, first and last, about thirty persons.

Having given fire, we approached near to the entrance, which they had stopped full with arms of trees, or brakes. Myself approaching to the entrance found the work too heavy for me to draw out all those which were strongly forced in. We gave order to one Master Hedge, and some other soldiers, to pull out those brakes. Having this done, and laid them between me and the entrance, and without order themselves, they proceeded first on the south end of the fort. But remarkable this was to many of us. Men that run before they are sent most commonly have an ill reward.

Worthy reader, let me entreat you to have a more charitable opinion of me (though unworthy to be better thought of) than is reported in the other book. You may remember there is a passage unjustly laid upon me, that when we should come to the entrance I should put forth this question, "Shall we enter?" Others should answer again, "What came we hither for else?" It is well known to many, it was never my practice in time of my command, when we are in garrison, much to consult with a private soldier or to ask his advice in point of war—much less in a matter of so great a moment as that was, which experience had often taught me was not a time to put forth such a question; and therefore pardon him that hath given the wrong information.*

Having our swords in our right hand, our carbines or muskets

---

* Underhill refers to the following passage in P. Vincent's "A True Relation of the late Battell fought in New-England, between the English and the Pequet Salvages" (London, 1638), which makes Master Hedge, here criticized for advancing without orders, the hero of the assault.

"The English went resolutely up to the door of the fort. What! shall we enter? said Captain Underhill. What come we for else? answered one Hedge, a young Northamptonshire gentleman; who, advancing before the rest, plucked away some bushes and entered. A stout Pequot encounters him, shoots his arrow, drawn to the head, into his right arm, where it stuck. He slashed the savage betwixt the arm and shoulder, who, pressing towards the door, was killed by the English. Immediately Master Hedge encountered another, who perceiving him upon him before he could deliver his arrow, gave back; but he struck up his heels and run him through; after him he killed two or three more. Then about half the English entered, fell on with courage, and slew many."— (Collections of the Massachusetts Historical Society, 3rd series, VI, 1837, p. 37.)

in our left hand, we approached the fort. Master Hedge was shot through both arms, and more wounded. Though it be not commendable for a man to make mention of anything that might tend to his own honor, yet because I would have the providence of God observed, and his name magnified, as well for myself as others, I dare not omit but let the world know that deliverance was given to us that command, as well as to private soldiers. Captain Mason and myself entering into the wigwams, he was shot, and received many arrows against his headpiece. God preserved him from many wounds. Myself received a shot in the left hip, through a sufficient buff coat, that if I had not been supplied with such a garment the arrow would have pierced through me. Another I received between neck and shoulders, hanging in the linen of my headpiece. Others of our soldiers were shot, some through the shoulders, some in the face, some in the head, some in the legs. Captain Mason and myself lost each of us a man, and had near twenty wounded. Most courageously these Pequots behaved themselves.

But seeing the fort was too hot for us, we devised a way how we might save ourselves and prejudice them. Captain Mason entering a wigwam brought out a firebrand, after he had wounded many in the house. Then he set fire on the west side, where he entered; myself set fire on the south end with a train of powder. The fires of both, meeting in the center of the fort, blazed most terribly and burnt all in the space of half an hour. Many courageous fellows were unwilling to come out, and fought most desperately through the palisadoes, so as they were scorched and burnt with the very flame, and were deprived of their arms —the fire burnt their bowstrings—and so perished valiantly. Mercy they did deserve for their valor, could we have had opportunity to have bestowed it. Many were burnt in the fort, men, women, and children. Others were forced out and came in troops to the Indians, twenty and thirty at a time, which our soldiers received and entertained with the point of the sword. Those that escaped us fell into the hands of the Indians that were in the rear of us. It is reported by themselves that there were about four hundred souls in this fort, and not above five of them escaped out of our hands. Great and doleful was the bloody sight to the view of young soldiers that never had been in war, to see so many souls lie gasping on the ground, so thick in some places that you could hardly pass along. It may be demanded, Why should you be so furious? (as some have said). Should not Christians have more mercy and compassion? But I would refer you to David's war. When a people is grown to such a height of blood and sin against God and man, and all are confederates in the action, there he hath no respect to persons, but harrows them and saws them and puts them to the sword and the most terrible death that may be. Sometimes the Scripture declareth women and children must perish with their parents. Sometimes the case alters; but we will not dispute it now. We had sufficient light from the word of God for our proceedings.

Having ended this service, we drew our forces together to battalia. Being ordered, the Pequots came upon us with their prime men, and let fly at us. I had twelve or fourteen men to encounter with them, but they finding our bullets to outreach their arrows, forced themselves often to retreat. When we saw we could have no advantage against them in the open field, we requested our Indians for to entertain fight with them. Our end was that we might see the nature of the Indian war; which they granted us, and fell out, the Pequots, Narragansetts, and Mohegans changing a few arrows together after such a manner as I dare boldly affirm they might fight seven years and not kill seven men. They came not near one another, but shot remote and not point-blank, as we often do with our bullets but at rovers; and then they gaze up in the sky to see where the arrow falls, and not until it is fallen do they shoot again. This fight is more for pastime than to conquer and subdue enemies.

But spending a little time this way, we were forced to cast our eyes upon our poor maimed soldiers, many of them lying upon the ground, wanting food and such nourishable things as might refresh them in this faint state. But we were not supplied with any such things whereby we might relieve them, but only were constrained to look up to God, and to entreat him for mercy towards them. Most were thirsty, but could find no water. The provision we had for food was very little. Many distractions seized upon us at the present. A chirurgeon we wanted; our chirurgeon, not accustomed to war, durst not hazard himself where we ventured our lives but, like a fresh-water soldier, kept aboard, and by this means our poor maimed soldiers were brought to a great strait and faintness, some of them swooning away for want of speedy help. But yet God was pleased to preserve the lives of them, though not without great misery and pain to themselves for the present.

Distractions multiplying, strength and courage began to fail with many. Our Indians, that had stood close to us hitherto, were fallen into consultation, and were resolved for to leave us in a land we knew not which way to get out. Suddenly after their resolution, fifty of the Narragansett Indians fell off from the rest, returning home. The Pequots, spying them, pursued after them. Then came the Narragansetts to Captain Mason and myself, crying, "Oh, help us now, or our men will be all slain."

We answered, "How dare you crave aid of us, when you are leaving us in this distressed condition, not knowing which way to march out of the country? But yet you shall see it is not the nature of Englishmen to deal like heathens, to requite evil for evil, but we will succor you."

Myself falling on with thirty men, in the space of an hour rescued their men and in our retreat to the body, slew and wounded above a hundred Pequots, all fighting men, that charged us both in rear and flanks.

Having overtaken the body, we were resolved to march to a certain neck of land that lay by the seaside, where we intended to quarter that night, because we knew not how to get our maimed men to Pequot River. As yet we saw not our pinnaces sail along, but feared the Lord had crossed them, which also the master of the bark much feared. We gave them order to set sail on the Narragansett Bay, about midnight, as we were to fall upon the fort in the morning, so that they might meet us in Pequot River in the afternoon; but the wind, being cross, bred in them a great perplexity what would become of us, knowing that we were but slenderly provided, both with munition and provision. They, being in a distracted condition, lifted up their hearts to God for help. About twelve of the clock the wind turned about and became fair; it brought them along in sight of us, and about ten o'clock in the morning carried them into Pequot River. Coming to an anchor at the place appointed, the wind turned as full against them as ever it could blow. How remarkable this providence of God was, I leave to a Christian eye to judge.

Our Indians came to us and much rejoiced at our victories, and greatly admired the manner of Englishmen's fight, but cried, "Mach it, mach it"; that is, "It is nought, it is nought, because it is too furious, and slays too many men." Having received their desires, they freely promised and gave up themselves to march along with us, wherever we would go. God having eased us from that oppression that lay upon us, thinking we should have been left in great misery for want of our vessels, we diverted our thoughts from going to that neck of land, and faced about, marching to the river where our vessels lay at anchor.

One remarkable passage. The Pequots playing upon our flanks, one Sergeant Davis, a pretty courageous soldier, spying something black upon the top of a rock, stepped forth from the body with a carbine of three feet long and, at a venture, gave fire, supposing it to be an Indian's head, turning him over with his heels upward. Our Indians observed this, and greatly admired that a man should shoot so directly. The Pequots were much daunted at the shot, and forbore approaching so near upon us.

Being come to the Pequot River we met with Captain Patrick, who under his command had forty able soldiers and was ready to begin a second attempt. But many of our men being maimed and much wearied, we forbore that night, and embarked ourselves, myself setting sail for Saybrook Fort. Captain Mason and Captain Patrick marching overland burned and spoiled the country between the Pequot and Connecticut River, where we received them.

The Pequots, having received so terrible a blow and being much affrighted with the destruction of so many, the next day fell into consultation. Assembling their most able men together, they propounded these three things: whether they would act upon a sudden revenge upon the Narragansetts, or attempt an enterprise upon the English, or fly. They were in great dispute one amongst another. Sassacus, the chief commander, was all for blood, the rest for flight, alleging these arguments. "We are a people bereaved of courage; our hearts are saddened with the death of so many of our dear friends; we see upon what advantage the English lie, what sudden and deadly blows they strike, what advantage they have of their pieces to us, who are not able to reach them with our arrows at a distance. They are supplied with everything necessary; they are fleet, and heartened in their victory. To what end shall we stand it out with them? We are not able; therefore let us rather save some than lose all."

This prevailed. Suddenly after, they spoiled all those goods they could not carry with them, broke up their tents and wigwams, and betook themselves to flight.

KING PHILIP'S WAR

(The struggle with the Indians in southern New England begun in the Pequot War ended with King Philip's War. From June 18, 1675, to August 11, 1676, destructive raids on isolated villages and counterexpeditions into the swamps and woods decimated both sides, until the white victory removed forever the Indian challenge from the interior to the frontier. Philip, chief of the Wampanoags and leader of a loose tribal league, was a son of the Pilgrims' old friend Massasoit. But times had changed; the whites no longer needed Indian help in a strange land, and they did need their hunting preserves. When the Wampanoags chafed, and collected arms, the people of Plymouth demanded them, and a fine to boot. A Christian Indian, John Sassamon, informed the whites of a planned attack; his murdered body was soon after found in an icy pond; three Wampanoags were executed for the deed; Indian warriors devastated a village in reprisal, and the war was on. An agricultural and a hunting society were fighting for the American soil.

Two rival Puritan ministers, William Hubbard and Increase Mather, rushed into print with annals of the war upon its terminus. Hubbard gives the meatier narrative, and remains our chief source of information for such high points as the disastrous ambush of Captain Lathrop's supply train at Muddy Brooks, and for the homely details of day-by-day skirmishing.)

AN OMEN

William Hubbard

ON THE 26th of June a foot company under Captain Daniel Henchman, with a troop under Captain Thomas Prentice, were sent out of Boston toward Mount Hope [Philip's stronghold]. It being late in the afternoon before they began to march, the central eclipse of the moon in Capricorn happened the evening before they came up to Neponset River, about twenty miles from Boston, which occasioned them to make an halt for a little repast, till the moon recovered her light again. Some melancholy fancies would not be persuaded but that the eclipse falling out at that instant of time was ominous, conceiving also that in the center of the moon they discerned an unusual black spot, not a little resembling the scalp of an Indian. As some others, not long before, imagined they saw the form of an Indian bow, accounting that likewise ominous—although the mischief following was done by guns, not by bows.

Both the one and the other might rather have thought of what Marcus Crassus the Roman general, going forth with an army against the Parthians, once wisely replied to a private soldier that would have dissuaded him from marching that time because of an eclipse of the moon in Capricorn: *That he was more afraid of Sagittarius than of Capricornus.* Meaning the arrows of the Parthians (accounted very good archers), from whom, as things then fell out, was his greatest danger.

But after the moon had waded through the dark shadow of the earth, and borrowed her light again, by the help thereof the two companies marched on.

THE BRAVERY OF CAPTAIN CHURCH

William Hubbard

UPON Thursday, July 7th [1675], Captain Fuller with Captain Church went into Pocasset to seek after the enemy or else, as occasion might serve, to treat with those Indians at Pocasset with whom Mr. Church was very well acquainted, always holding good correspondence with them. After they had spent that day and most of the night in traversing the said Pocasset Neck, and watching all night in a house which they found there, yet could hear no tidings of any Indians, Captain Fuller began to be weary of his design. Mr. Church in the meanwhile assured him that they should find Indians before long; yet for greater expedition they divided their company, Captain Fuller taking down toward the seaside. Where it seems after some little skirmishing with them, wherein one man only received a small wound, he either saw or heard too many Indians for himself

25. KINGS CASTLE AND SOUTHAMPTON FORT

Captain John Smith, *The Generall Historie of Virginia, New-England, and the Summer Isles*; London, 1624

and his company to deal with, which made him and them betake themselves to a house near the waterside, from whence they were fetched off by a sloop before night to Rhode Island.

Captain Church (for so may he well be styled after this time) marched further into the Neck, imagining that if there were Indians in the Neck, they should find them about a pease-field not far off. As soon as ever they came near the said field he espied two Indians in the pease, who also had at the same time espied him. And presently making some kind of shout, a great number of Indians came about the field, pursuing the said Captain Church and his men in great numbers to the seaside—there being not above fifteen with Church, yet seven or eight score of the Indians pursuing after them. Now was a fit time for this young captain and his small company to handsel their valor upon this great rout of Indians, just ready to devour them.

But victory stands no more in the number of soldiers than verity in the plurality of voices. And although some of these fifteen had scarce courage enough for themselves, yet their captain had enough for himself, and some to spare for his friends, which he there had an opportunity of improving to the full. When he saw the hearts of any of his followers to fail, he would bid them be of good courage and fight stoutly, and (possibly by some divine impression upon his heart) assured them not a bullet of the enemy should hurt any one of them. Which one of the company, more dismayed than the rest, could hardly believe, till he saw the proof of it in his own person; for the captain, perceiving the man was not able to fight, made him gather rocks together for a kind of shelter and barricade for the rest, that must either of necessity fight or fall by the enemy's hand. It chanced as this fainthearted soldier had a flat stone in his arms, and was carrying it to the shelter that he was making upon the bank, a bullet of the enemy was thus warded from his body, by which he must else have perished—which experience put new life into him, so as he followed his business very manfully afterward. Thus they defended themselves under small defense hastily made up, all that afternoon not one being either slain or wounded. Yet it was certainly known that they killed at least fifteen of their enemies. And at the last, when they had spent all their ammunition, and made their guns unserviceable by often firing, they were fetched off by Captain Golding's sloop and carried safe to Rhode Island in default of all their enemies.

Yea, such was the bold and undaunted courage of this champion Captain Church that he was not willing to leave any token behind of their flying for want of courage. In the face of his enemies he went back to fetch his hat, which he had left at a spring, whither the extreme heat of the weather and his labor in fighting had caused him to repair for the quenching of his thirst an hour or two before.

Thomas Church

MR. CHURCH was moved, with other wounded men, over to Rhode Island, where in about three months' time he was in some good measure recovered of his wounds and the fever that attended them. And then went over to the General [Josiah Winslow] to take his leave of him, with a design to return home.

But the general's great importunity again persuaded him to accompany him in a long march into the Nipmuc country, though he had then tents in his wounds, and so lame as not able to mount his horse without two men's assistance.

In this march the first thing remarkable was, they came to an Indian town where there were many wigwams in sight, but an icy swamp lying between them and the wigwams prevented their running at once upon it as they intended. There was much firing upon each side before they passed the swamp. But at length the enemy all fled, and a certain Mohegan that was a friend Indian pursued and seized one of the enemy that had a small wound in his leg, and brought him before the general, where he was examined. Some were for torturing him to bring him to a more ample confession of what he knew concerning his countrymen. Mr. Church, verily believing he had been ingenuous in his confession, interceded and prevailed for his escaping torture. But the army being bound forward in their march, and the Indian's wound somewhat disenabling him for traveling, it was concluded he should be knocked on the head. Accordingly he was brought before a great fire and the Mohegan that took him was allowed, as he desired, to be his executioner.

Mr. Church, taking no delight in the sport, framed an errand at some distance among the baggage horses. When he had got ten rods or thereabouts from the fire, the executioner fetched a blow with a hatchet at the head of the prisoner, who, being aware of the blow, dodged his head aside, and the executioner missing his stroke, the hatchet flew out of his hand and had like to have done execution where it was not designed. The prisoner upon his narrow escape broke from them that held him, and notwithstanding his wound made use of his legs, and happened to run right upon Mr. Church. He laid hold on him, and a close scuffle they had. But the Indian having no clothes on slipped from him and ran again, and Mr. Church pursued the Indian, although being lame there was no great odds in the race, until the Indian stumbled and fell, and they closed again, scuffled and fought pretty smartly, until the Indian by the advantage of his nakedness slipped from his hold again, and set out on his third race, with Mr. Church close at his heels endeavoring to lay hold on the hair of his head, which was all the hold could be taken of him. And running through a swamp that was covered with hollow ice, it made so loud a noise that Mr. Church expected (but in vain) that some of his English friends would follow the noise, and come to his assistance. But the Indian happened to run athwart a large tree, that lay fallen near breast-high, where he stopped and cried out aloud for help. But Mr. Church being soon upon him again, the Indian seized him fast by the hair of his head, and endeavored by twisting to break his neck. But though Mr. Church's wounds had somewhat weakened him, and the Indian was a stout fellow, yet he held him in play, and twisted the Indian's neck as well, and took the advantage of many opportunities, while they hung by each other's hair, to give him notorious bunts in the face with his head.

In the heat of this scuffle they heard the ice break with somebody's coming apace to them, which when they heard, Church concluded there was help for one or other of them, but was doubtful which of them must now receive the fatal stroke. Anon somebody comes up to them, who proved to be the Indian that had first taken the prisoner. Without speaking a word he felt them out (for it was so dark he could not distinguish them by sight), the one being clothed and the other naked. Feeling where Mr. Church's hands were fastened in the netop's * hair, he with one blow settled his hatchet in between them, and ended the strife. He then spoke to Mr. Church, and hugged him in his arms, and thanked him abundantly for catching his prisoner; and cut off the head of his victim, and carried it to the camp; and giving an account to the rest of the friend Indians in the camp how Mr. Church had seized his prisoner, they all joined in a mighty shout.

STRATAGEMS OF THE INDIAN ALLIES

William Hubbard

IT IS worth the noting what faithfulness and courage some of the Christian Indians with the said Captain Pierce showed in the fight. One of them, Amos by name, after the captain was shot in his leg or thigh, so as he was not able to stand any longer, would not leave him but, charging his gun several times, fired stoutly upon the enemy, till he saw that there was no possibility for him to do any further good to Captain Pierce, nor yet to save himself, if he stayed any longer. Therefore he used this policy. Perceiving the enemy had all blacked their faces, he also stooping down pulled out some blacking out of a pouch he carried with him, discolored his face therewith, and so making himself look as like Hobamocko † as any of his enemies, he ran amongst them a little while and was taken for one of themselves, as if he had been searching for the English, until he had an opportunity to escape away among the bushes. Therein imitating the cuttlefish, which, when it is pursued or in danger, casteth out of its body a thick humor, as black as ink, through which it passes away unseen by the pursuer.

It is reported of another of these Cape Indians (friends to the English of Plymouth) that, being pursued by one of the enemies, he betook himself to a great rock, where he sheltered himself for

* An English corruption of a Narragansett word used, often sarcastically, to signify "Indian friend."
† The Indian Devil.

a while. At last perceiving that his enemy lay ready with his gun on the other side, to discharge upon him as soon as he stirred never so little away from the place where he stood, he thought of this politic stratagem to save himself and destroy his enemy (for as Solomon said of old, wisdom is better than weapons of war). He took a stick and hung his hat upon it, and then by degrees gently lifted it up, till he thought it would be seen, and so became a fit mark for the other that watched to take aim at him. The other, taking it to be his head, fired a gun and shot through the hat; which our Christian Indian perceiving, boldly held up his head and discharged his own gun upon the real head, not the hat, of his adversary, whereby he shot him dead upon the place, and so had liberty to march away with the spoils of his enemy.

The like subtle device was used by another of the Cape Indians at the same time, being one of them that went out with Captain Pierce. For being in like manner pursued by one of Philip's Indians, as the former was, he nimbly got behind the butt end of a tree newly turned up by the roots, which carried a considerable breadth of the surface of the earth along with it (as is very usual in these parts, where the roots of the trees lie very flat in the ground) which stood up above the Indian's height, in form of a large shield, only it was somewhat too heavy to be easily wielded or removed. The enemy Indian lay with his gun ready to shoot him down, upon his first deserting his station; but a subtle wit taught our Christian netop a better device. For boring a hole through this his broad shield, he discerned his enemy, who could not so easily discern him; a good musketeer need never desire a fairer mark to shoot at. Whereupon discharging his gun, he shot him down. What can be more just than that he should himself be killed who lay in wait to kill another man?

Instances of this nature show the subtlety and dexterousness of these natives. If they were improved in feats of arms, and possibly if some of the English had not been too shy in making use of such of them as were well affected to their interest, they need never have suffered so much from their enemies. It has been found upon late experience that many of them have proved not only faithful but very serviceable and helpful to the English, they usually proving good seconds, though they have not ordinarily confidence enough to make the first onset.

TORTURE OF AN INDIAN PRISONER

William Hubbard

AMONGST the rest of the prisoners then taken was a young sprightly fellow, seized by the Mohegans, who desired of the English commanders that he might be delivered into their hands, that they might put him to death, *more majorum:* sacrifice him to their cruel genius of revenge, in which brutish and devilish passion they are most of all delighted. The English, though not delighted in blood, yet at this time were not unwilling to gratify their humor, lest by a denial they might disoblige their Indian friends, of whom they lately made so much use; partly also that they might have an ocular demonstration of the savage, barbarous cruelty of these heathen. And indeed, of all the enemies that have been the subjects of the precedent discourse, this villain did most deserve to become an object of justice and severity. For he boldly told them that he had with his gun dispatched nineteen English, and that he had charged it for the twentieth; but not meeting with any of ours, and unwilling to lose a fair shot, he had let fly at a Mohegan, and killed him, with which, having made up his number, he told them he was fully satisfied.

But as is usually said, Justice Vindictive hath iron hands, though leaden feet. This cruel monster is fallen into their power, that will repay him sevenfold. In the first place therefore, making a great circle, they placed him in the middle, that all their eyes might at the same time be pleased with utmost revenge upon him. They first cut one of his fingers round in the joint, at the trunk of his hand, with a sharp knife, and then broke it off, as men do with a slaughtered beast before they uncase him. Then they cut off another and another, till they had dismembered one hand of all its digits, the blood sometimes spurting out in streams a yard from his hand—which barbarous and unheard-of cruelty the English were not able to bear, it forcing tears from their eyes. Yet did not the sufferer ever relent, or show any sign of anguish. For being asked by some of his tormentors how he liked the war, he might have replied as the Scotch gentleman did after the loss of a battle, when asked how he liked the match with our Prince of Wales (which then was the occasion of the quarrel), who made answer, he liked the match well enough, but no whit liked the manner of the wooing written by such lines of blood. But this unsensible and hardhearted monster answered, he liked it very well, and found it as sweet as Englishmen did their sugar.

In this frame he continued, till his executioners had dealt with the toes of his feet as they had done with the fingers of his hands, all the while making him dance round the circle and sing, till he had wearied both himself and them. At last they broke the bones of his legs, after which he was forced to sit down, which 'tis said he silently did, till they had knocked out his brains.

THE AMBUSH OF CAPTAIN LATHROP

William Hubbard

BUT THE sufferings of the English were not as yet come to their height. For after they were come to Hadley, the commander in chief, taking counsel with the officers of the soldiers, ordered them that were then present to garrison the towns about: some to be at Northampton, Hatfield, Deerfield, and some to remain at Hadley, where were the headquarters of the English. But perceiving that little good was to be done upon the enemy in those parts, it was agreed that what corn was left at Deerfield, being threshed out as well as they could in those tumults (about three thousand bushels was supposed to be there standing in stacks), should be brought to Hadley, and wait further time to fight the enemy. It came to Captain Lathrop's turn, or rather it was his choice with about eighty men to guard several carts laden with corn and other goods. (The company under Captain Mosely then quartering at Deerfield intended that day to pursue after the enemy.)

But upon September 18th, that most fatal day, the saddest that ever befell New England, as the company were marching along with the carts (it may be too securely), never apprehending danger so near, were suddenly set upon and almost all cut off, not above seven or eight escaping. Which great defeat came to pass by the unadvised proceeding of the captain (who was himself slain in the first assault), although he wanted neither courage nor skill to lead his soldiers; but he had taken up a wrong notion about the best way and manner of fighting with the Indians (which he was always wont to argue for) viz., that it were best to deal with the Indians in their own way, by skulking behind trees, and taking their aim at single persons, which is the usual manner of the Indians fighting one with another. But herein was his great mistake, in not considering the great disadvantage a smaller company would have in dealing that way with a greater multitude; for if five have to deal with one, they may surround him, and everyone take his aim at him, while he can level but at one of his enemies at a time. Which gross mistake of his was the ruin of a choice company of young men, the very flower of the county of Essex, all culled out of the towns belonging to that county, none of which were ashamed to speak with the enemy in the gate: their dear relations at home mourning for them, like Rachel for her children, and would not be comforted, not only because they were not, but because they were so miserably lost.

For had he ordered his men to march in a body, as some of his fellow commanders advised, either backward or forward, in reason, they had not lost a quarter of the number of them that fell that day by the edge of the sword. For the Indians, notwithstanding their subtlety and cruelty, durst not look an Englishman in the face, in the open field, nor ever yet were known to kill any man with their guns, unless when they could lie in wait for him in an ambush or behind some shelter, taking aim undiscovered. So that although it was judged by those that escaped that there were seven or eight hundred Indians at least that encountered that company of eighty of English, yet if they had kept together in a body, and fought marching, they might have escaped the numbers of the enemy with little loss in comparison of what they sustained.

For the valiant and successful Captain Mosely and his lieutenant, coming (though too late) to their rescue, marched through and through that great body of Indians, and yet came off with little or no loss in comparison of the other. And having fought all those Indians for five or six hours upon a march, lost not above two men all that while, nor received other damage besides eight or nine that were wounded, which yet were carried to their quarters at night at Hatfield. Whereas if these had proceeded in the same way of fighting as Captain Lathrop did in the morning they might have been surrounded, and so have been served as the former were. But God had otherwise determined in his secret counsel, and therefore that was hid from the one which was a means to preserve the other company.

THE DEATH OF KING PHILIP

Cotton Mather

ONE thing which emboldened King Philip in all his outrages was an assurance which his magicians (consulting their oracles) gave him, that no Englishman should ever kill him. And indeed, if any Englishman might have had the honor of killing him, he must have had a good measure of grace to have repressed the vanity of mind whereto he would have had some temptations.

But this will not extend the life of that bloody and crafty wretch above "half his days"! A man belonging to Philip himself, being disgusted at him for killing an Indian who had propounded an expedient of peace with the English, ran away from him to Rhode Island, where Captain Church was then recruiting of his weary forces; and upon the intelligence hereof, Captain Church, with a few hands of both English and Indians, immediately set forth upon a new expedition.

That very night Philip (like the man in the army of Midian) had been dreaming that he was "fallen into the hands of the English." And now, just as he was telling his dream, with advice unto his friends to fly for their lives, lest the knave who had newly gone from them should show the English how to come at them, Captain Church, with his company, fell in upon them. Philip

26. ATTACK ON AN INDIAN VILLAGE

Sieur de Champlain, *Voyages et Descouvertes faites en la Nouvelle France;*
Paris, 1619

attempted a flight out of the swamp, at which instant, both an Englishman and an Indian endeavoring to fire at him, the Englishman's piece would not go off, but the Indian's presently shot him through his venomous and murderous heart. And in that very place where he first contrived and commenced his mischief, this Agag was now cut in quarters, which were then hanged up, while his head was carried in triumph to Plymouth, where it arrived on the very day that the church there was keeping a solemn thanksgiving to God. God sent 'em in the head of a leviathan for a thanksgiving feast!

KING WILLIAM'S WAR

(With the tribes of southern New England eliminated from the scene, the danger zone shifted to the northern frontier, where the Indian problem was aggravated by the competition between the French and English settlers for furs and land. The great French and Indian Wars belong to the eighteenth century, but the first one, setting the pattern of border raids and Indian incitement, began with the accession of William and Mary to the English throne in 1689, and lasted till the Peace of Ryswick in 1697. The rancor between England's Protestant monarchs and the embittered Catholic sovereigns of France soon made itself felt in the New World, adding religious to economic rivalry. Jesuit missionaries incited the Abnaki to attack the English trading post of Pemaquid, in reprisal for an English spoliation, and thereafter the Maine and New Hampshire villages suffered disastrous pillagings. The overseas reinforcements and the major invasions planned by both sides proved abortive and less consequential than the Indian and colonist forays. The final peace settled nothing.

Cotton Mather wrote up the war shortly after its conclusion in a work entitled "Decennium Luctuosum"—the Sorrowful Decade—in the regular Puritan didactic manner and his own inimitable style. He later included it in the *Magnalia Christi Americana*. The portion which follows, the successful repulse of a French and Indian attack on the town of Wells, Maine, June 20 and 21, 1692, describes one of the few bright spots on the English record.)

THE MEMORABLE ACTION AT WELLS

Cotton Mather

BUT NOW, reader, the longest day of the year is to come on, and if I mistake not, the bravest act in the war fell out upon it. Modockawando is now come, according to his promise a twelve-month ago. Captain Converse was lodged in Storer's garrison at Wells with but fifteen men; and there came into Wells two sloops, with a shallop, which had aboard supplies of ammunition for the soldiers and contribution for the needy. The cattle this day came frighted and bleeding out of the woods, which was a more certain omen of Indians a-coming than all the prodigies that Livy reports of the sacrificed oxen. Converse immediately issued out his commands unto all quarters, but especially to the sloops just then arrived. The sloops were commanded by Samuel Storer and James Gouge, and Gouge being two miles up the river, he wisely brought her down undiscovered unto Storer's, by the advantage of a mist then prevailing. A careful night they had on't! The next morning before daylight one John Diamond, a stranger that came in the shallop on a visit, came to Captain Converse's garrison, where the watch invited him in; but he chose rather to go aboard the sloops, which were little more than a gunshot off. And, alas, the enemy, issuing out from their lurking places, immediately seized him and hauled him away by the hair of the head (in spite of all the attempts used by the garrison to recover him) for an horrible story to be told by and concerning him.

The general of the enemy's army was Monsieur Burniff, and one Monsieur Labrocree was a principal commander (the enemy said he was lieutenant-general). There were also divers other Frenchmen of quality, accompanied with Modockawando, and Moxus, and Egeremet, and Warumbo, and several more Indian sagamores. The army made up in all about five hundred men, or fierce things in the shape of men, all to encounter fifteen men in one little garrison, and about fifteen more men (worthily called such!) in a couple of open sloops. Diamond having informed 'em how 'twas in all points (only that for fifteen, by a mistake he said thirty), they fell to dividing the persons and plunder, and agreeing that such an English captain should be slave to such a one, and such a gentleman in the town should serve such a one, and his wife be a maid of honor to such or such a squaw proposed, and Mr. Wheelwright (instead of being a worthy counselor of the province, which he now is!) was to be the servant of such a netop; and the sloops, with their stores, to be so and so parted among them. There wanted but one thing to consummate the whole matter, even the chief thing of all, which I suppose they had not thought of; that was, for heaven to deliver all this prize into their hands. But, *Aliter statutum est in caelo!* [It was decreed otherwise in heaven.]

A man habited like a gentleman made a speech to them in English, exhorting 'em to courage, and assuring them that if they would courageously fall upon the English, all was their own. The speech being ended, they fell to the work and with a horrid shout and shot made their assault upon the feeble garrison. But the English answered with a brisk volley and sent such a leaden shower among them that they retired from the garrison to spend the storm of their fury upon the sloops.

You must know that Wells Harbor is rather a creek than a river, for 'tis very narrow, and at low water in many places dry. Nevertheless, where the vessels ride it is deep enough, and so far off from the bank that there is from thence no leaping aboard. But our sloops were sorely incommoded by a turn of the creek, where the enemy could lie out of danger so near 'em as to throw mud aboard with their hands. The enemy was also privileged with a great heap of plank lying on the bank, and with a haystack, which they strengthened with posts and rails; and from all these places they poured in their vengeance upon the poor sloops, while they so placed smaller parties of their savages as to make it impossible for any of the garrisons to afford 'em any relief. Lying thus within a dozen yards of the sloops, they did with their fire arrows divers times desperately set the sloops on fire. But the brave defendants, with a swab at the end of a rope tied unto a pole and so dipped into the water, happily put the fire out. In brief, the sloops gave the enemy so brave a repulse that at night they retreated.

When they renewed their assault, finding that their fortitude would not assure the success of the assault unto them, they had recourse unto their policy. First, an Indian comes on with a slab for a shield before him, when a shot from one of the sloops pierced the slab, which fell down instead of a tombstone with the dead Indian under it; on which, as little a fellow as he was, I know not whether some will not reckon it proper to inscribe the epitaph which the Italians use to bestow upon their dead Popes: When the dog is dead, all his malice is dead with him.

Their next stratagem was this. They brought out of the woods a kind of a cart, which they trimmed and rigged and fitted up into a thing that might be called a chariot, whereupon they built a platform, shotproof in the front, and placed many men upon that platform. Such an engine they understood how to shape without having read (I suppose) the description of the *Pluteus* in Vegetius! * This chariot they pushed on towards the sloops till they were got, it may be, within fifteen yards of them; when, lo, one of their wheels, to their admiration, sunk into the ground. A Frenchman stepping to heave the wheel with a helpful shoulder, Storer shot him down. Another stepping to the wheel, Storer with a well-placed shot sent him after his mate; so the rest thought it was best to let it stand as it was. The enemy kept galling the sloops from their several batteries, and calling 'em to surrender, with many fine promises to make them happy, which ours answered with a just laughter, that had now and then a mortiferous bullet at the end of it. The tide rising, the chariot overset, so that the men behind it lay open to the sloops, which immediately dispensed a horrible slaughter among them; and they that could get away, got as fast and as far off as they could.

In the night the enemy had much discourse with the sloops. They inquired who were their commanders. And the English gave an answer, which in some other cases and places would have been too true, that they had a great many commanders. But the Indians replied, "You lie, you have none but Converse, and we will have him too before morning!" They also knowing that the magazine was in the garrison, lay under a hillside pelting at that by times; but Captain Converse once in the night sent out three or four of his men into a field of wheat for a shot, if they could get one. There seeing a black heap lying together, ours all at once let fly upon them a shot that slew several of them that were thus caught in the corn, and made the rest glad that they found themselves able to run for it.

Captain Converse was this while in much distress about a scout of six men which he had sent forth to Newichawanoc the morning before the arrival of the enemy, ordering them to return the day following. The scout returned into the very mouth of the enemy that lay before the garrison. But the corporal, having his wits about him, called out aloud (as if he had seen Captain Converse making a sally forth upon 'em) "Captain, wheel about

* Vegetius was the chief Roman writer on the military art; the *pluteus* was a shed or penthouse to protect soldiers while attacking a fortification.—Charles H. Lincoln.

your men round the hill and we shall catch 'em; there are but a few rogues of 'em!" Upon which the Indians, imagining that Captain Converse had been at their heels, betook themselves to their heels; and our folks got safe into another garrison.

On the Lord's-day morning, there was for a while a deep silence among the assailants; but at length getting into a body, they marched with great formality towards the garrison, where the captain ordered his handful of men to lie snug and not to make a shot until every shot might be likely to do some execution. While they thus beheld a formidable crew of dragons coming with open mouth upon them to swallow them up at a mouthful, one of the soldiers began to speak of surrendering; upon which the captain vehemently protested that he would lay the man dead who should so much as mutter that base word any more! And so they heard no more on't. But the valiant Storer was put upon the like protestation to keep 'em in good fighting trim aboard the sloops also. The enemy, now approaching very near, gave three shouts that made the earth ring again; and crying out in English, "Fire," and "Fall on, brave boys!" the whole body, drawn into three ranks, fired at once. Captain Converse immediately ran into the several flankers, and made their best guns fire at such a rate that several of the enemy fell, and the rest of 'em disappeared almost as nimbly as if they had been so many specters. Particularly, a parcel of them got into a small deserted house, which having but a board wall to it, the captain sent in after them those bullets of twelve to the pound, that made the house too hot for them that could get out of it. The women in the garrison on this occasion took up the Amazonian stroke, and not only brought ammunition to the men but also with a manly resolution fired several times upon the enemy.

The enemy, finding that things would not yet go to their minds at the garrison, drew off to try their skill upon the sloops, which lay still abreast in the creek, lashed fast one to another. They built a great firework, about eighteen or twenty feet square, and filled it up with combustible matter, which they fired; and then they set it in the way for the tide now to float it up unto the sloops, which had now nothing but an horrible death before them. Nevertheless, their demands of both the garrison and the sloops to yield themselves were answered no otherwise than with death upon many of them, spit from the guns of the besieged. Having towed their firework as far as they durst, they committed it unto the tide; but the distressed Christians that had this deadly fire swimming along upon the water towards 'em, committed it unto God, and God looked from heaven upon them, in this prodigious article of their distress. *These poor men cried, and the Lord heard them, and saved them out of their troubles.* The wind, unto their astonishment, immediately turned about, and with a fresh gale drove the machine ashore on the other side, and split it so that the water being let in upon it, the fire went out. So, the godly men that saw God from heaven thus fighting for them cried out with an astonishing joy, *If it had not been the Lord who was on our side, they had swallowed us up quick; blessed be the Lord, who hath not given us a prey to their teeth; our soul is escaped, as a bird out of the snare of the fowlers!*

The enemy were now in a pitiful pickle, with toiling and moiling in the mud, and blackened with it, if mud could add blackness to such miscreants. And their ammunition was pretty well exhausted, so that now they began to draw off in all parts, and with rafts get over the river, some whereof breaking, there did not a few cool their late heat by falling into it. But first they made all the spoil they could upon the cattle about the town; and giving one shot more at the sloops, they killed the only man of ours that was killed aboard 'em. Then, after about half an hour's consultation, they sent a flag of truce to the garrison, advising 'em with much flattery to surrender. But the captain sent 'em word that he wanted for nothing but for men to come and fight him.

The Indian replied unto Captain Converse, "Being you are so stout, why don't you come and fight in the open field, like a man, and not fight in a garrison, like a squaw?"

The captain rejoined, "What a fool are you? Do you think thirty men a match for five hundred? No," says the captain (counting, as well he might, each of his fifteen men to be as good as two), "come with your thirty men upon the plain, and I'll meet you with my thirty, as soon as you will."

Upon this the Indian answered, "Nay, mee own, English fashion is all one fool; you kill mee, mee kill you! No, better lie somewhere, and shoot a man, and hee no see! That the best soldier!"

Then they fell to coaxing the captain, with as many fine words as the fox in the fable had for the allurement of his prey unto him, and urged mightily that Ensign Hill, who stood with the flag of truce, might stand a little nearer their army. The captain for a good reason, to be presently discerned, would not allow that; whereupon they fell to threatening and raging, like so many defeated devils, using these words, "Damn ye, we'll cut you as small as tobacco, before tomorrow morning." The captain bid 'em to make haste, for he wanted work. So the Indian throwing his flag on the ground ran away, and Ensign Hill nimbly stripping his flag ran into the valley, but the savages presently fired from an ambushment behind a hill, near the place where they had urged for a parley.

And now for poor John Diamond! The enemy retreating (which opportunity the sloops took to burn down the dangerous haystack) into the plain, out of gunshot, they fell to torturing their captive John Diamond, after a manner very diabolical. They stripped him, they scalped him alive, and after a castration, they finished that article in the punishment of traitors upon him; they slit him with knives between his fingers and his toes; they made cruel gashes in the most fleshy parts of his body, and stuck the gashes with firebrands, which were afterwards found sticking in the wounds. Thus they butchered one poor Englishman with all the fury that they would have spent upon them all, and performed an exploit for five hundred furies to brag of at their coming home. Ghastly to express! What was it then to suffer?

They returned then unto the garrison and kept firing at it now and then till near ten o'clock at night, when they all marched off, leaving behind 'em some of their dead. Whereof one was Monsieur Labocree, who had about his neck a pouch with about a dozen relics ingeniously made up, and a printed paper of indulgences, and several other implements; but it seems none of the amulets about his neck would save him from a mortal shot in the head. Thus in forty-eight hours was finished an action as worthy to be related as perhaps any that occurs in our story.

SOURCES

THIS BOOK has been designed for the nonspecialist reading audience, and the texts have been edited with that end in mind. This editing involves the elimination of excessive capital letters and italics, the clarification of serpentine sentences, the modernizing of spelling, and the excision of long-winded passages. The aim has been to choose seventeenth-century selections, but some of the best reading for the period, like the *Magnalia*, the histories of Beverley and Lawson, and the captivity of John Gyles, spills over into the 1700's.

Some few references to the seminal scholarship on early American writings should be acknowledged here. The great pioneer work was done by Moses Coit Tyler, whose *History of American Literature, 1607 to 1765* (1878) opened up the field. Howard Mumford Jones has done a series of brilliant studies from the point of view of the history of ideas: "Origins of the Colonial Idea," in his volume, *Ideas in America* (Cambridge, 1944), 45-69; "The Image of the New World," in *Elizabethan Studies and Other Essays in Honor of George F. Reynolds* (Boulder, Colorado, 1945), 62-84; "The Colonial Impulse, an Analysis of the 'Promotion' Literature of Colonization," *Proceedings of the American Philosophical Society*, XC (1946), 131-161; "The Literature of Virginia in the Seventeenth Century," *Memoirs of the American Academy of Arts and Sciences*, XIX, Pt. 2 (1946), 3-47.

Valuable articles on the literature of Indian captivities are Phillips D. Carleton, "The Indian Captivity," *American Literature*, XV (1943-44), 169-180; and Roy Harvey Pearce, "The Significances of the Captivity Narrative," *American Literature*, XIX (1947-48), 1-20, which takes issue with Carleton's block treatment of the captivities as a single genre.

For meaty comments on the colonial Indian treaties see Lawrence C. Wroth, "The Indian Treaty as Literature," *Yale Review*, n. s., XVII (1927-1928), 749-766; Constance Rourke, *The Roots of American Culture* (Harcourt, Brace and Co., New York, c. 1942), 60 ff.; and the indispensable bibliography by Henry F. De Puy, *A Bibliography of the English Colonial Treaties with the American Indians, including a synopsis of each treaty* (New York, printed for the Lenox Club, 1917).

Information about the Indian tribes encountered by the settlers can be found in Frederick W. Hodge, *Handbook of American Indians North of Mexico,* Bureau of American Ethnology Bulletin 30, Smithsonian Institution (2 parts, Washington, Government Printing Office, 1907-1910). Hodge regularizes the spellings of Indian tribal and place names, and supplies bibliographical references from the early writers.

Attention was called to the exaggerative qualities of travelers' tales (chiefly eighteenth century) by James R. Masterson, in "Travelers' Tales of Colonial Natural History," *Journal of American Folklore,* LIX (Jan.-March and April-June, 1946), 51-71, 174-188.

The most exciting account of witchcraft and its folklore elements remains George Lyman Kittredge's *Witchcraft in Old and New England* (Harvard University Press, Cambridge, 1929), with its exhaustive bibliographies of the English and German collections.* The Salem trials are retold by Marion L. Starkey, *The Devil in Massachusetts* (Alfred A. Knopf, New York, 1949).

Little has been done on the military tactics of the seventeenth-century race conflict. See, however, Morrison Sharp, "Leadership and Democracy in the Early New England System of Defense," *American Historical Review,* L. (1944-1945), 244-260.

A helpful guide to colonial journals and diaries has been compiled by William Mathews, with the assistance of Roy Harvey Pearce, *American Diaries, An Annotated Bibliography of American Diaries Written Prior to the Year 1861* (University of California Press, Berkeley and Los Angeles, 1945).

The great storehouse of early American writings is of course the series edited by J. Franklin Jameson under the title Original Narratives of Early American History (Charles Scribner's Sons, New York, 1906-1924). These are expertly edited and prefaced. Individual volumes deal with most of the colonies, with major themes such as Voyages, Insurrections, Witchcraft Cases, and with separate works, as the journals of Winthrop, Johnson, and Danckaerts.

* But note the reservations of R. Trevor Davies in *Four Centuries of Witch-Beliefs* (London, c. 1947), 16.

THE following list contains all the sources from which the present texts are taken, with their complete page references. The short title list that follows this gives page references to the portions of the material reprinted and edited.

Adams, Rev. William, of Dedham, Massachusetts, Diary 1666-1682, *Collections of the Massachusetts Historical Society*, 4th series, I (1852), 8-22.

Ashe, Thomas, "Carolina, or a Description of the Present State of that Country" (1682), in B. R. Carroll, *Historical Collections of South Carolina*, II (1836), 59-84.

"The Beginning, Progress, and Conclusion of Bacon's Rebellion in Virginia, in the years 1675 and 1676" (26 pp.), in Force, I, No. 8.

Beverley, Robert, *The History and Present State of Virginia* (1705). Edited with an Introduction by Louis B. Wright. Published for The Institute of Early American History and Culture at Williamsburg, Virginia, by The University of North Carolina Press (Chapel Hill, 1947).

Budd, Thomas, *Good Order Established in Pennsylvania and New Jersey*. Reprinted from the original edition of 1685. With Introduction and Notes by Frederick J. Shepard (Cleveland, 1902).

Church, Thomas, *The Entertaining History of King Philip's War, which began in the month of June, 1675. As also of expeditions more lately made against the common enemy, and Indian rebels, in the eastern parts of New-England: with some account of the Divine Providence towards Col. Benjamin Church* (Boston, printed, 1716. Newport, Rhode Island: reprinted and sold by Solomon Southwick, in Queen-Street, 1772).

Clayton, John, Rector of Crofton at Wakefield in Yorkshire, "A Letter to the Royal Society, May 12, 1688. Giving an Account of several Observables in Virginia, and in his Voyage thither, more particularly concerning the Air" (48 pp.), in Force, III, No. 12.

"Complaint of Susannah Trimmings, of Little-Harbor, Pascataqua, Court of Associates, June, 1656," *Collections of the New Hampshire Historical Society*, I (1824), 255-257.

Council for Virginia, "A True Declaration of the estate of the Colonie in Virginia, with a confutation of such scandalous reports as have tended to the disgrace of so worthy an enterprise." Published by advise and direction of the Councell of Virginia, 1610 (28 pp.), in Force, III, No. 1.

Danforth, Rev. Samuel, Records of the First Church in Roxbury, Mass., 1664-1667, *New England Historical and Genealogical Register*, XXXIV (1880), 162-166.

Danckaerts, Jasper, and Sluyter, Peter, *Journal of a Voyage to New York and a Tour in Several of the American Colonies in 1679-80*. Translated from the original manuscript in Dutch for the Long Island Historical Society, and edited by Henry C. Murphy, *Memoirs of the Long Island Historical Society*, I (Brooklyn, 1867). (The name "Dankers" given in this edition is corrected to "Danckaerts" in the Original Narratives Series edition.)

The Destruction of Schenectady: "Propositions Made by the Sachems of the Three Maquas Castles to the Mayor, Aldermen and Commonalty at Albany, 25th February 1689/90" (Boston, 1690), *Collections of the New York Historical Society for 1869*, 165-172.

Eliot, Rev. John, "Record of Church Members, Roxbury, Mass.," transcribed by William B. Trask, *New England Historical and Genealogical Register*, XXXV (1881), 241-247.

(Foster, Ann). "The Prosecution of Philip English and his wife for Witchcraft, *Historical Collections of the Essex Institute*, III (1861), 67-79. (The examination and confession of Ann Foster at Salem Village 15 July 1692, from Vol. *Salem Witchcraft*, pp. 427-428.)

"Georgetown on Arrowsick Island 9th August 1717. A Conference of the Governor with the Sachems of the Eastern Indians" (Boston, 1717), *Collections of the Maine Historical Society*, 1st series, III (1853), 361-375.

Green, Rev. Joseph, of Salem Village, Diary of, 1706-1713, *Historical Collections of the Essex Institute*, X, Pt. 1 (1869), 73-104.

Gyles, John, *Memoirs of Odd Adventures, Strange Deliverances, &c. In the Captivity of John Gyles, Esq., Commander of the Garrison on St. George's River* (Boston, 1736). Photostat

Americana, 2d series, 1936 (photostated at the Massachusetts Historical Society, Boston).

Hammond, Lawrence, Diary 1677-1694, *Proceedings of the Massachusetts Historical Society*, 2d series, VII (1891, 1892), 144-161.

Hennepin, Louis, *A New Discovery of a Vast Country in America*. Reprinted from the second London issue of 1698, ed. Reuben Gold Thwaites (2 vols., Chicago, 1903).

Higginson, Francis, "New-Englands plantation, or a Short and True Description of the Commodities and Discommodities of that Countrey" (1630), *Proceedings of the Massachusetts Historical Society*, LXII (Oct., 1928-June, 1929), 305-321.

Higginson, John, Letter to Increase Mather from Salem, 17 August 1683, *Collections of the Massachusetts Historical Society*, 4th series, VIII (1868), 285-287.

Hubbard, William, *A Narrative of the Troubles with the Indians in New-England, from the first planting thereof in the year 1607 to this present year 1677. But chiefly of the late Troubles in the two last years, 1675 and 1676. To which is added a Discourse about the Warre with the Pequods in the year 1637* (Boston; printed by John Foster, in the year 1677).

(Jacobs, George). Stone, Lincoln R., "An Account of the Trial of George Jacobs, for Witchcraft," (1692), *Historical Collections of the Essex Institute*, II (1860), 49-57.
"In connexion with the above, it may not be inappropriate to insert the certified copy of all the proceedings of this trial from the records in the office of the clerk of the courts for this county—which has been copied and presented to the archives of the Institute by Ira J. Patch of this city" (p. 52).

Jesuit Missionaries, "Extracts from the Annual Letters of the English Province of the Society of Jesus," in Hall, *Narratives of Early Maryland*, 118-144.

Johnson, Edward, "Wonder-Working Providence of Sions Saviour in New England," *Collections of the Massachusetts Historical Society*, 2d series, VII (2d ed., 1826), 1-58 (Bk. 2,

Chs. 7-25, 1637-1644); and VIII (2d ed., 1826), 1-39 (Bk. 3, Chs. 1-12, 1645-1651).

Jogues, Father Isaac, of the Society of Jesus, Captivity of, among the Mohawks (1643), in *Perils of the Ocean and Wilderness: or, Narratives of Shipwreck and Indian Captivity*, Gleaned from early missionary annals by John Gilmary Shea (Boston, 1857), Ch. 2, pp. 16-62.

In "The Jogues Papers," tr. and arr. John G. Shea, *Collections of the New York Historical Society*, 2d series, III, Pt. 1 (1857), 121-229, the captivity is supplemented by other documents describing the escape of Jogues, his return to France, his coming back to Canada, and his recapture by the Iroquois and death at their hands.

Josselyn, John, "An Account of Two Voyages to New-England" (1675), *Collections of the Massachusetts Historical Society*, 3d series, III (1833), 211-354.

Josselyn, John, "New England's Rarities Discovered" (1672), ed. Edward Tuckerman, *Transactions and Collections of the American Antiquarian Society: Archaeologia Americana*, IV (1860), 138-238.

Knott, Father Edward, Provincial of the English Province, Annual Letter of 1638, in Hall, *Narratives of Early Maryland*, 119-124.

Lawson, John, *Lawson's History of North Carolina containing the exact description and natural history of that country, together with the present state thereof and a journal of a thousand miles traveled through several nations of Indians, giving it a particular account of their customs, manners, etc., etc.* (1714), ed. Frances Latham Harriss, sponsored by the North Carolina Society of the Colonial Dames of America (Garrett and Massie, Publishers, Richmond, Va., 1937).

Levett, Christopher, "A Voyage into New England, begun in 1623 and ended in 1624" (1628), *Collections of the Massachusetts Historical Society*, 3d series, VIII (1843), 159-190.

Mather, Cotton, *Decennium Luctuosum: An History of Remarkable Occurrences in the Long War, which New-England hath had with the Indian Salvages, from the year 1688, to the year 1698, faithfully Composed and Improved* (1699). Reprinted in *Narratives of the Indian Wars, 1675-1699*, ed.

Charles H. Lincoln, Original Narratives of Early American History (Charles Scribner's Sons, New York, c. 1913), pp. 179-300.

Mather, Cotton, *Magnalia Christi Americana; or, The Ecclesiastical History of New-England; from its first planting, in the year 1620, unto the year of our Lord 1698* (1702). With an Introduction and Occasional Notes by the Rev. Thomas Robbins, and Translations of the Hebrew, Greek, and Latin Quotations by Lucius F. Robinson (2 vols., Hartford, 1853-1855).

Mather, Cotton, *The Wonders of the Invisible World. Being an Account of the Tryals of Several Witches Lately Executed in New-England* (1692). Library of Old Authors (London, 1862).

Mather, Increase, Diary, March 1675-December 1676, Together with extracts from another diary by him, 1674-1687, ed. Samuel A. Green (Cambridge, 1900).

Mather, Increase, *Remarkable Providences illustrative of the earlier days of American Colonisation* (1684, originally titled "An Essay for the Recording of Illustrious Providences"). With introductory preface by George Offor (London, 1890).

Montanus, Arnoldus, "Description of New Netherland" (translated from the Dutch printing, 1671), in E. B. O'Callaghan, *The Documentary History of the State of New York,* IV (Albany, 1851), 75-84.

Morton, Thomas, "New English Canaan; Or, New Canaan, containing an abstract of New England," 1632 (128 pp.), in Force, II, No. 4.

"A New and Further Narrative of the state of New-England" (1676), in Drake, *The Old Indian Chronicle,* 207-246.

Norwood, Colonel Henry, "A Voyage to Virginia," n.d. (52 pp.), in Force, III, No. 10.

Pory, John, *Lost Description of Plymouth Colony in the Earliest Days of the Pilgrim Fathers. Together with contemporary accounts of English Colonization elsewhere in New England and in the Bermudas* (c. 1622). Edited with an Introduction and Notes by Champlin Burrage (Houghton Mifflin Company, Boston and New York, 1918).

"The Present State of New-England with respect to the Indian War" (1675), in Drake, *The Old Indian Chronicle*, 119-169.

Rowlandson, Mary, *The Soveraignty and Goodness of GOD, Together With the Faithfulness of His Promises Displayed; Being a Narrative of the Captivity and Restauration of Mrs. Mary Rowlandson. Commended by her, to all that desires to know the Lords doings to, and dealings with Her. Especially to her dear Children and Relations. The second Addition Corrected and amended* (Cambridge, Printed by Samuel Green, 1682). Reprinted in *Narratives of the Indian Wars, 1675-1699*, ed. Charles H. Lincoln, Original Narratives of Early American History (Charles Scribner's Sons, New York, c. 1913), 112-167.

Russell, Noahdiah, Tutor at Harvard College, Diary of, 1682-1684, *New England Historical and Genealogical Register*, VII (1853), 53-59.

Sandel, Rev. Andreas, Pastor of "Gloria Dei" Swedish Lutheran Church, Philadelphia, Extracts from the Journal of, 1710-1718 (translated from the Swedish by B. Elfoing), *Pennsylvania Magazine of History and Biography*, XXX (1906), 445-452.

Sewall, Samuel, Diary 1674-1714, *Collections of the Massachusetts Historical Society*, 5th series, V (1878) and VI (1879).

Smith, John, President of Virginia and Admiral of New England, *Travels and Works* (1608-1631). Edited by Edward Arber. A New Edition, with a Biographical and Critical Introduction by A. G. Bradley (2 vols., John Grant, Edinburgh, 1910).
It should be noted that Smith is an editor and compiler as well as an author, which explains why in his works he may be referred to in the third person. The authors he incorporates are named in the above edition.

Underhill, John, "Newes From America; or, a new and experimentall discoverie of New England; containing, a true relation of their war-like proceedings these two yeares last past, with a figure of the Indian fort or palizado" (1638), *Collections of the Massachusetts Historical Society*, 3d series, VI (1837), 3-28.

Winthrop, John, *Journal "History of New England" 1630-1649*, ed. James Kendall Hosmer, *Original Narratives of Early American History* (2 vols., Charles Scribner's Sons, New York, 1908).

Wood, William, *New England's Prospect. A true, lively, and experimentall description of that part of America, commonly called New England: discovering the state of that Countrie, both as it stands to our new-come English planters; and to the old Native Inhabitants. Laying downe that which may both enrich the knowledge of the mind-travelling Reader, or benefit the future Voyager* (1634). (Reprinted with introduction by Eben Moody Boynton, of West Newbury, 1898, n.d., n.p.)

COLLECTIONS REFERRED TO ABOVE

Drake, Samuel G., *The Old Indian Chronicle; being a collection of exceeding rare tracts, written and published in the time of King Philip's War (1675-1676), by persons residing in the country.* To which are now added an Introduction and Notes, by Samuel G. Drake (Boston, 1867).

Force, Peter, *Tracts and Other Papers Relating Principally to the Origin, Settlement, and Progress of the Colonies in North America, from the Discovery of the Country to the Year 1776.* (Washington, printed by P. Force, 1836-1846. 4 vols.) Reprinted under the auspices of the Out-of-Print Books Committee of the American Library Association (Peter Smith, New York, 1947).

Hall, Clayton Colman, *Narratives of Early Maryland, 1633-1684*, Original Narratives of Early American History (Charles Scribner's Sons, New York, c. 1910). "Extracts from the Annual Letters of the English Province of the Society of Jesus, 1634-1681," 118-144.

1. VOYAGES

Josselyn, "A Voyage to New England," Two Voyages 213-233.

Norwood, "A Voyage to Virginia," Force III No. 10 pp. 3-30.

2. NATURAL WONDERS

FERTILITY

Higginson, "New England's Plantation," MHSP 307-315.

Pory, "Seafish," Lost Description 37-41.

Clayton, "Doves Hide the Sun," Force III No. 12 p. 30.

FLORA AND FAUNA

I. Mather, "Wonderful Antipathies," Remarkable Providences 70-72.

Josselyn, "Strange Creatures," Two Voyages 252-253.

Wood, "Bears," Prospect 21-22.

Josselyn, "Wolves," Two Voyages 267-268.

Josselyn, "The Skunk," Two Voyages 267-268.

Josselyn, "The Porcupine," Rarities 152.

Ashe, "Turtles," SCHC II 75-78.

Lawson, "The Alligator," North Carolina 131-132.

Clayton, "The Rattlesnake," Force III No. 12 pp. 38-39.

Lawson, "The Horn Snake," North Carolina 134-135.

Lawson, "The Bat," North Carolina 129.

Montanus, "Eagles," DHSNY IV 78-79.

Josselyn, "Tobacco," Two Voyages 261-262.

Beverley, "The Jamestown Weed," Virginia 139.

Beverley, "Love Flowers," Virginia 140.

Lawson, "The Tulip Tree," North Carolina 95.

Lawson, "The Cypress," North Carolina 98-99.

Josselyn, "The Ancient New England Standing Dish," Rarities 224-225.

Josselyn, "The Power of Rum," Rarities 227.

UGLY RUMORS

Levett, MHSC 3d series VIII 182-183.

Council for Virginia, Force III No. 1 pp. 15-16.

Beverley, Virginia 297-302.

Hennepin, New Discovery I 160-161.

3. REMARKABLE PROVIDENCES

JUDGMENTS

Smith, "A Rat Plague," Works II 658-659.

Danckaerts, "A Plague of Weevils," Journal 218-220.

C. Mather, "A Whoredom Unmasked," Magnalia II 404-405.
C. Mather, "Of Buggery," Magnalia II 405-406.
Winthrop, "A Heretic Bears a Monster," Journal I 266-268.
I. Mather, "Of Railing Quakers," Remarkable Providences 241-243.
I. Mather, "Blasphemers, Drunkards and Heathen," Remarkable Providences 252-255.
A Jesuit Missionary, "God Strikes the Foulmouthed," Narr. of Early Md. (Letter of 1640) 133-134.
Winthrop, "God Strikes the Foulmouthed," Journal I 82.
Eliot, "Ungodly Servants," NEGHR XXXV 242.
Johnson, "A Talky Barber," MHSC 2d series VII 19-20.
Green, "Trouble with Jades," EIHC 2d series II 87-89.
Winthrop, "Of New England's Enemies," Journal II 9-12, 82-83.

DELIVERANCES
Smith (and) The Council for Virginia, "The Starving Time in Virginia and the Preservation through Sir Thomas Gates," Works II 498-499 (and) Force III No. 1 pp. 10-11.
C. Mather, "Mortal Wounds that do not Kill," Magnalia II 605-607.
A Jesuit Missionary, "Mortal Wounds that do not Kill," Narr. of Early Md. (Letter of 1642) 137-139.
John Smith, "Escapes from the Deep," Works II 650-652.
Knott, "Escapes from the Deep," Narr. of Early Md. (Letter of 1638) 122.

PRODIGIES
C. Mather, "Heralds of War," Magnalia II 559.
Bacon's Rebellion in Virginia, "Heralds of War," Force I No. 8 pp. 7-8.
Sewall, "Omens and Signs in Diaries," MHSC 5th series V 402.
I. Mather, "Omens and Signs in Diaries," Diary 45-46, 62.
C. Mather, "Before and After Death," Magnalia II 468-470.
Smith, "Actions of a Dunghill Cock," Works II 683.
Winthrop, "Necromancy with a Pinnace," Journal II 153, 155-156.
Russell, "Specter Ships," NEHGR VII 53-54.
Lawson, "Specter Ships," North Carolina, 62.

Winthrop, "Specter Ships," Journal II 346.
C. Mather, "Specter Ships," Magnalia I 83-84.

ACCIDENTS
I. Mather, "An Injury," Remarkable Providences 23-24.
I. Mather, "Lightning," Remarkable Providences 86-87 (and) preface.
Danforth, "Lightning," NEHGR XXXIV 165.
Sewall, "Falling into Things," MHSC 5th series VI 51-52, 238.

4. INDIAN CAPTIVITIES

Smith, "The Capture of John Smith," Works II 395-401.
C. Mather, "The Condition of the Captives," Magnalia II 597-600.
C. Mather, "A Notable Exploit Performed by a Woman," Magnalia II 634-636.
Jogues, "The Captivity of Father Isaac Jogues among the Mohawks," Perils 16-62.
Gyles, "Memoirs of Odd Adventures and Signal Deliverances in the Captivity of John Gyles, Esq.," 1-21, 32-34, 37-40.
Rowlandson, "A Narrative of the Captivity and Restoration of Mrs. Mary Rowlandson," Narratives of the Indian Wars 118-136, 147-158, 161-165.

5. INDIAN CONCEITS AND ANTICS

POWAW MAGIC
C. Mather, Magnalia II 425-427.
Wood, Prospect 86-88.
Gyles, Memoirs 21-22.
The Old Indian Chronicle 158 (The Present State of New-England with respect to the Indian War).
Beverley, Virginia 204-205.
Lawson, North Carolina 231-233.

DEVIL WORSHIP
Johnson, MHSC 2d series VIII 28-29.
Josselyn, Two Voyages 300.
Wood, Prospect 80-81.
Lawson, North Carolina 213-214,

Hennepin, New Discovery II 535-540.
Beverley, Virginia 205-209.

MYTHS
Danckaerts, Journal 149-151.
Hennepin, New Discovery II 450-456.
Beverley, Virginia 211-212.
Gyles, Memoirs 23, 29-30.

FOOLISH INDIANS
Winthrop, Journal I 322-323.
C. Mather, Magnalia II 628-629.
Smith, Works II 469-470.
Old Indian Chronicle 149 (The Present State of New-England
     with respect to the Indian War).
Morton, New English Canaan, Force II No. 5 pp. 70-71.
Lawson, North Carolina 238.

SMART INDIANS
Beverley, Virginia 188-189.
Lawson, North Carolina 37-39.
Old Indian Chronicle 223-224 (A New and Further Narrative
     of the state of New-England).
Smith, Works II 534.

6. INDIAN TREATIES

Budd, Good Order Established 64-66.
"The Destruction of Schenectady," NYHSC 1869 pp. 165-172.
"George Town on Arrowsick Island," MeHSC III 36-375.

7. WITCHCRAFTS

NEW ENGLAND DISTRAUGHT
Josselyn, Two Voyages 332.
Danckaerts, Journal 369-370, 419.
I. Mather, Remarkable Providences 114-118.

THE ARCHENEMY
Hammond, MHSP 2d series VII 147.
Higginson, MHSC 4th series VIII 285-286.
Sandel, Pa. Mag. Hist. Biog. XXX 450.

THE GATHERING STORM
Winthrop, Journal II 344-346.
A Jesuit Missionary, Narr. of Early Md. (Letter of 1654) 140-141.
"Complaint of Susannah Trimmings," NHHSC I 255-256.
Adams, MHSC 4th series I 17-18.
C. Mather, Magnalia II 454-456.

THE AWFUL STRUGGLE
C. Mather, Wonders 80-84.
A DREAD SECRET WEAPON
C. Mather, Wonders 161-163.

THE BATTLE AT SALEM
"The Examination and Confession of Ann Foster," EIHC III
     68-69.
"Examination of George Jacobs," EIHC II 53-55.
"The Trial of Susanna Martin," in C. Mather, Wonders 138-148.

8. FOREST WARS

THE PEQUOT WAR
Underhill, MHSC 3d series VI 3-13, 15-19, 23-28.

KING PHILIP'S WAR
Hubbard, "An Omen," Narrative 17-18.
Hubbard, "The Bravery of Captain Church," Narrative 23-25.
Church, "The Bravery of Captain Church," Entertaining History
     30-32.
Hubbard, "Stratagems of the Indian Allies," Narrative 64-66.
Hubbard, "Torture of an Indian Prisoner," Narrative Pt. 2 pp.
     9-10.
Hubbard, "The Ambush of Captain Lathrop," Narrative 38-39.
C. Mather, "The Death of King Philip," Magnalia II 576.

KING WILLIAM'S WAR
C. Mather, "The Memorable Action at Wells," Decennium
     Luctuosum 233-239.

INDEX OF AUTHORS